PENGUIN  CLASSICS

EARLY SOCRATIC DIALOGUES

PLATO (c. 427–347 BC) stands with Socrates and Aristotle as one of the shapers of the whole intellectual tradition of the West. He came from a family that had long played a prominent part in Athenian politics, and it would have been natural for him to follow the same course. He declined to do so, however, disgusted by the violence and corruption of Athenian political life, and sickened especially by the execution in 399 of his friend and teacher, Socrates. Inspired by Socrates' inquiries into the nature of ethical standards, Plato sought a cure for the ills of society not in politics but in philosophy, and arrived at his fundamental and lasting conviction that those ills would never cease until philosophers became rulers or rulers philosophers. At an uncertain date in the early fourth century BC he founded in Athens the Academy, the first permanent institution devoted to philosophical research and teaching, and the prototype of all Western universities. He travelled extensively, notably to Sicily as political adviser to Dionysius II, ruler of Syracuse.

Plato wrote over twenty philosophical dialogues, and there are also extant under his name thirteen letters, whose genuineness is keenly disputed. His literary activity extended over perhaps half a century: few other writers have exploited so effectively the grace and precision, the flexibility and power, of Greek prose.

TREVOR SAUNDERS was born in Wiltshire in 1934, and was educated at Chippenham Grammar School, University College London and at Emmanuel College, Cambridge. He taught at the universities of London and Hull, and at the time of his death in 1999 was Professor of Greek at the University of Newcastle upon Tyne, where he had taught since 1965. He was also a Visiting Member of the Institute for Advanced Study, Princeton, and Visiting Fellow of the Humanities Research Centre, Canberra. His main interest was in Greek philosophy, especially political, social and legal theory, on which he published numerous works, including two Penguin Classics: a translation of Plato's *Laws* and a revision and re-representation of T. A. Sinclair's translation of Aristotle's *Politics*. In 1991 he published *Plato's Penal Code*, a study of the penology of the *Laws* in its historical context, and in 1995 he published a translation of *Politics: Books I and II* for Clarendon Press. His recreations included railway history and the cinema.

ROBIN WATERFIELD was born in 1952. He graduated from Manchester University in 1974 and went on to research ancient Greek philosophy at King's College, Cambridge. He has been a university lecturer, and both copy editor and commissioning editor for Penguin. He is now a self-employed writer with publications ranging from academic articles to children's fiction. He has translated various Greek philosophical texts, including several for Penguin Classics: Xenophon's *Conversations of Socrates* and *Hiero the Tyrant and Other Treatises*, Plutarch's *Essays*, Plato's *Philebus* and *Theaetetus* and (in Plato's *Early Socratic Dialogues*) *Hippias Major*, *Hippias Minor* and *Euthydemus*. His biography of Kahlil Gibran, *Prophet: The Life and Times of Kahlil Gibran*, is published by Penguin. He has also edited *The Voice of Kahlil Gibran* for Penguin Arkana.

DONALD WATT was born in Argyll in 1955, and was educated at Oban High School, the University of Edinburgh and Balliol College, Oxford. His main academic interests are Greek drama and philosophy. He now lives in London, where he works in publishing.

IAIN LANE was born in Essex in 1961, but has spent most of his life in Yorkshire. He was educated at Bradford Grammar School and Corpus Christi College, Oxford. His main academic interest is moral philosophy, especially the ethical theories of Plato and Aristotle. He is married, and serves in the Anglican Priesthood.

PLATO
Early Socratic Dialogues

Edited with a General Introduction by TREVOR J. SAUNDERS

ION
Translated and introduced by TREVOR J. SAUNDERS

LACHES
Translated and introduced by IAIN LANE

LYSIS, CHARMIDES
Translated and introduced by DONALD WATT

HIPPIAS MAJOR, HIPPIAS MINOR, EUTHYDEMUS
Translated and introduced by ROBIN WATERFIELD

With some fragments of Aeschines of Sphettus,
translated and introduced by TREVOR J. SAUNDERS

PENGUIN BOOKS

TO THE MEMORY OF
BETTY RADICE

PENGUIN BOOKS

Published by the Penguin Group
Penguin Books Ltd, 80 Strand, London WC2R ORL, England
Penguin Group (USA) Inc., 375 Hudson Street, New York, New York 10014, USA
Penguin Group (Canada), 10 Alcorn Avenue, Toronto, Ontario, Canada M4V 3B2
(a division of Pearson Penguin Canada Inc.)
Penguin Ireland, 25 St Stephen's Green, Dublin 2, Ireland (a division of Penguin Books Ltd)
Penguin Group (Australia), 250 Camberwell Road, Camberwell, Victoria 3124,
Australia (a division of Pearson Australia Group Pty Ltd)
Penguin Books India Pvt Ltd, 11 Community Centre,
Panchsheel Park, New Delhi – 110 017, India
Penguin Group (NZ), cnr Airborne and Rosedale Roads, Albany,
Auckland 1310, New Zealand (a division of Pearson New Zealand Ltd)
Penguin Books (South Africa) (Pty) Ltd, 24 Sturdee Avenue, Rosebank 2196, South Africa

Penguin Books Ltd, Registered Offices: 80 Strand, London WC2R ORL, England

www.penguin.com

These translations first published 1987
Reprinted with a new Preface and revised Bibliography 2005

3

General introduction copyright © Trevor J. Saunders, 1987
ION: introduction, translation, commentary and notes copyright © Trevor J. Saunders, 1987
LACHES: introduction, translation, commentary and notes copyright © Iain Lane, 1987
LYSIS, CHARMIDES: introduction, translation, commentary and notes copyright © Donald Watt, 1987
HIPPIAS MAJOR, HIPPIAS MINOR, EUTHYDEMUS: introduction, translation,
commentary and notes copyright © Robin Waterfield, 1987
FRAGMENTS OF AESCHINES OF SPHETTUS: translation and commentary
copyright © Trevor J. Saunders, 1987
Preface copyright © Chris Emlyn-Jones, 2005
All rights reserved

Printed in England by Clays Ltd, St Ives plc
Typeset in Linotron 202 Plantin

ISBN-13: 978–0–140–45503–8
ISBN-10: 0–140–45503–5

CONTENTS

CONTENTS

CHARMIDES

HIPPIAS MAJOR AND HIPPIAS MINOR

EUTHYDEMUS

APPENDIX

BIBLIOGRAPHIES 381

SELECTIVE INDEX
OF GREEK PERSONAL NAMES 397

PREFACE TO 2005 EDITION

The publication in 1987 of an edition of these seven short dialogues of Plato was hailed by reviewers as a landmark in the history of Penguin Classics. The team of editors, under the distinguished leadership of the late Professor Trevor Saunders, produced translations and commentaries that were clear, informative and, at the same time, scholarly. At the time their work was 'state of the art' and in most respects it remains so; this volume, not least Saunders' own contribution to it, is one of the most stimulating and reliable guides for anyone studying these dialogues in translation.

For this reason revision of the original text is unnecessary. In the intervening period, however, scholarship on Plato has moved on, and it is appropriate that early twenty-first-century readers should have the opportunity of a bibliographical update. Since the late 1980s the general emphasis of Socratic/Platonic scholarship has changed in some respects: for example, the existence and nature of a clearly defined 'Socratic period' in the history of Plato's *oeuvre*, assumed rather than argued for in this volume, has been the subject of discussion and controversy. Much attention has also been given to the basic nature and purpose of Platonic composition, and in particular the balance between dramatic and philosophical elements in individual dialogues – already, as the reader will learn, a live issue in the various discussions to be found in this volume. On a practical note, for readers who wish for more biographical information about the numerous individuals other than Socrates who pass through the pages of these dialogues, J. K. Davies' *Athenian Propertied Families* can now be replaced with the invaluable purpose-designed reference work by Debra Nails, *The People of Plato: A Prosopography of Plato and Other Socratics* (Indianapolis and Cambridge 2002).

The flood of publications since 1987 on these seven dialogues alone has been enormous; to attempt an update on the scale of the original volume would have doubled the length of the bibliography. I have therefore confined myself to adding the more significant and approachable publications in English.

Chris Emlyn-Jones

EDITOR'S PREFACE

Each contributor to this volume has attempted to translate Plato's subtle
and elusive Greek into clear and idiomatic English; beyond this minimum
requirement I have not sought to impose any uniformity of style. Nor
have I required any particular philosophical stance, or any particular
interpretation of any of the dialogues: each contributor has been free to
expound, argue and assess as he thought fit. However, we have all written
the various aids to the reader in accordance with the following triple
guideline: that the *introduction* to each dialogue should be synoptic and
discursive, offering guidance and suggestions on its problems and overall
significance; that the italicized '*signposts*' in the texts should elucidate and
comment on the successive stages of the argument; and that the *footnotes*
should provide succinct information on points of historical, literary and
philosophical detail.

Since the primary purpose of the enterprise is a philosophical one, each
translator has paid particular attention to the rendering of the key terms,
and to their elucidation (with frequent transliteration) in the introductions, signposts and footnotes. Though we have aimed at a high degree of
consistency within each dialogue, and between them, no guarantee is
offered of a wholly invariable one-for-one translation of any term in the
volume as a whole: the subject-matter is far too complex for that.

The 'Introduction to Socrates' is strictly for beginners: it does not
assume knowledge of ancient Greece in general or of Socrates in particular.
Its purpose is to set out in palatable form Socrates' main characteristics
as a man and a philosopher, as a basis for understanding the more detailed
and specialized introductions to the individual dialogues. Further reading
may be found in the bibliographies; each section of the volume, at the
cost of some repetition, has its own, self-contained bibliography where
full details are given of those works which are referred to by the names of
their authors alone.

In sum, the reader is invited to make use of any or all of five forms of
aid to his or her understanding of these dialogues: (i) general introduction,
(ii) the introduction to each dialogue, (iii) signposts at intervals in the text,
(iv) footnotes, (v) bibliographies. The variety and richness of Plato's text
deserve no less.

9

Each dialogue has been translated from volume III of the Oxford Classical Text of Plato (ed. J. Burnet, 5 vols., 1901–6); departures from it are pointed out in footnotes.

The traditional mode of detailed reference to Plato's text is by the numbers of the pages in the edition of Stephanus (1578), which are printed in the margin, together with the subsections a, b, c, d, e.

References to works of Plato are made by their names alone. His version of Socrates' speech at his trial, the *Apology of Socrates*, is abbreviated to *Apology*; the Greek word *apologia* means simply 'speech in defence'.

Detailed information about some of Socrates' interlocutors, and about some of the persons mentioned in the course of the conversations, may be found in J. K. Davies, *Athenian Propertied Families, 600–300 B.C.* (Oxford 1971). An illustrated booklet by M. L. Lang, *Socrates in the Agora* (Princeton 1978), seeks to find Socrates 'in the material world and physical surroundings of his favorite stamping-grounds, the Athenian Agora' (market-place).

From time to time, in reprinting, bibliographies are brought up to date and other minor adjustments made.

T.J.S.

ACKNOWLEDGEMENTS

I express my most cordial thanks to all those who have in various ways given me the benefit of their knowledge and advice in the preparation of this volume: Dr P. V. Jones, Professor G. B. Kerferd, Mr J. F. Lazenby, Mrs M. Midgley, Dr P. Murray, Mr D. B. Robinson, Dr R. W. Sharples, Professor M. C. Stokes and Professor M. M. Willcock. The proofs benefited greatly from the vigilant scrutiny they received from my wife, Teresa.

Betty Radice, the editor of the series, suggested this collection of Socratic dialogues and gave me invaluable help and encouragement in its early stages. She died, however, before it was completed. Her long editorship of the Penguin Classics was fruitful and distinguished. This volume is gratefully dedicated to her memory. (TJS)

I am most grateful to Professor T. J. Saunders, Professor I. G. Kidd and Professor A. J. Woodman for their help. (RAHW)

I should like to thank Professor Trevor Saunders for his patience, advice and support. A particular debt of gratitude is owed to Mr David Robinson of the University of Edinburgh who read through drafts of both dialogues and provided invaluable help and encouragement. (DMW)

In particular I would like to thank Mr R. E. F. Green, who introduced me to the *Laches*, and Professor Trevor Saunders, who has been a consistently patient and helpful editor. A more general, though no less heavy, debt of gratitude is owed to all those from whose scholarship and enthusiasm I have learned so much. I am especially grateful to Professor M. C. Stokes for an invaluable set of comments on an early draft of the introduction to the *Laches*. Thanks are due also to my wife and my parents for their tolerance and encouragement. (IRL)

INTRODUCTION TO SOCRATES

1. *Childish Questions*

'Mummy, why can't we have yesterday again?'
'Mummy, would I be me if Daddy had married somebody else?'
'Daddy, will you go and fetch the moon for me?'[1]

Parental answers to such questions are apt to be brisk and short: 'What nonsense!' or 'Don't be silly!' Yet the puzzlement felt by the child is neither unnatural nor unintelligent. Teddy Bear has 'gone', into the toy-cupboard. Yesterday has 'gone'. Teddy Bear can come back (and will in the morning). So why cannot yesterday too come back? Daddy can fetch a cup of milk, or a ball; so why can he not fetch the moon? Faced with discouraging answers, most of us learn to discriminate the various uses of words and to distinguish acts which are practically possible from those which are not. We learn, that is, to stop asking naïve questions. In a sense, to grow up is to give up.

But there are disconcertingly direct questions of another kind, which are not so easily outgrown. The child who wonders protestingly, 'Why must I eat up my rice pudding?', grows into the adult who asks, 'Why ought I to care for my elderly parents?', or 'Why must I not steal?' Commonly, of course, we simply learn to acquiesce in the accepted standards of our society, or of some group within it, and refuse to allow the hard questions of principle to bother us except intermittently. Our natural childish wonder is eroded, and we in turn become the irritated parents who give testy answers. But there is one person who never grows out of the childhood habit of asking for answers to awkward questions: the philosopher. For it is his business to be a child who never grows up.[2]

But he does not ask *all* types of difficult question. The development of science and technology has solved empirically, or made empirically solvable, many problems which used to be regarded as the province of philosophy. When we want to know how a thing works or what it is made of, we can use tested and agreed methods of chemical or other analysis which will, at least within certain limits, give us precise answers. With these problems, in so far as they are merely factual or technological, the

1. I owe the first two of these questions to Mary Midgley.

2. cf. J. L. Ackrill, *Aristotle the Philosopher* (Oxford 1981), pp. 5–7. On wonder as the mainspring of philosophy, see Aristotle, *Metaphysics* 982b12 ff.

philosopher has no concern. What engages him is any unsolved *conceptual* problem, for instance the relationship between hypothesis and induction in scientific inquiry and experiment, the moral responsibilities of the scientist or doctor, the rights of individuals against the claims of society, and in general a vast range of moral, social, legal, political, religious, logical and linguistic ideas. His job (it is a surprisingly arduous one) is to analyse and clarify the assumptions, methods and criteria employed by those who are working 'in the field' on a practical level – scientists, doctors, lawyers, politicians, priests and so forth. If such conceptual matters were ever elucidated with the same degree of demonstrable precision as is attainable in problems of science and technology, the philosopher would simply lose interest in them. In that case, the profession of philosophy would presumably wither away; for the world would have no need of it.

2. *Socrates and His Predecessors*

In Socrates' heyday[1] Greek philosophy had been a going concern for about a century and a half. The questions his predecessors had asked were diverse, wide-ranging and breathtakingly comprehensive; and for the reasons I have given many of them would not now be regarded as belonging to philosophy at all, but to the various special sciences:[2]

What was the origin of the physical world, and what
  is the nature of physical change?
What is the constitution of the heavenly bodies, and why do they
  move as they do?
What are the origins of the human race?
How did civilization develop to its present state?
How does the human body function?
What are the mechanics and validity of sense-perception?
What is the relationship between reality and thought?
How are law and nature related?
Ought moral standards to vary from time to time and
  from place to place, or ought they to be in some sense
  absolute or universal?

1. The late fifth century: he lived from 469 till 399 B.C.
2. I have of course inferred these questions from the surviving remains of very large numbers of thinkers in the early period of Greek philosophy, and 'pemmicanized' them into a tidy list. A good selection of the sources and up-to-date accounts may be found in G. S. Kirk, J. E. Raven and M. Schofield, *The Presocratic Philosophers* (2nd ed., Cambridge 1983); see also Guthrie, I and II.

What sort of answers were given? Some of the assertions of Socrates' predecessors and contemporaries are naïve, even crude; some are of the utmost subtlety and sophistication; all are fragmentary and difficult to interpret; and we often have to rely not on the actual words of these thinkers but on reports and summaries of their views in later writers. In general their beliefs were formulated not by controlled experimental method, but by informal observation, homely analogy and shrewd reasoning.

Socrates' own influence on Greek philosophy is often represented as having been so highly decisive as to have turned it into quite new channels. Cicero, for instance, in a celebrated judgement,[1] said that 'Socrates . . . was the first to call philosophy down from the sky and put her in cities, and bring her even into homes and compel her to inquire about life and ethics, and good and evil.' But in the first place, the sorts of question about the physical world which I have indicated continued to be asked during Socrates' lifetime and for many centuries afterwards, and at an infinitely higher level of technological sophistication they are still asked today: Socrates does not represent a clean break, at which one style of inquiry stopped and another began. In the second place, even before him, and certainly during his own lifetime, there was plenty of other speculation about 'the lives and affairs of men': Socrates did not invent moral philosophy as such. True, he liked to mark himself off from other thinkers in certain well-defined respects. For instance, he appears to have been, at least after a certain stage in his career, intolerant of speculation about the nature and workings of the physical world. But he did not put an end to it; and his own contribution is only one step, though a particularly influential and far-reaching one, in the progress of Greek philosophy.

Socrates made two crucial assumptions: (i) that the precision of knowledge attainable in practical skills like pottery or carpentry or ship-building is in principle possible in moral conduct; (ii) that this precise knowledge is to be won by analysing moral language. Let us examine this approach: how does it work?

3. The Sources for Socrates

But no. We are already on slippery ground. Do we *know* that Socrates thought what I have suggested? He himself wrote nothing, and (as in the

---

1. *Tusculan Disputations*, V. 4. 10; cf. Aristotle, *Metaphysics* 987b1 ff. and *Parts of Animals* 642a24 ff. See Xenophon, *Memorabilia* I. 1 and IV. 7, and Plato, *Phaedo* 96a ff. and *Apology* 19b–d, for Socrates' views on the various sciences.

case of Jesus) we are wholly dependent on the writings of others for our knowledge of his activities and opinions. These authors differ sharply in their portrait of Socrates, and their comparative historical reliability is a matter of controversy.[1] They are chiefly four:

1. *Xenophon* (c. 430–c. 354) was a military man turned country gentleman who had a strong interest in practical education. He had a fervent admiration for Socrates and had heard some of his conversations. He wrote a great deal about him, mainly but not exclusively in the form of purported reminiscences, and often with the professed intent of defending his memory against misunderstanding and misrepresentation.[2] He portrays him as a sort of crackerbarrel sage, much inclined to giving avuncular advice to young men. Here is a specimen:

I shall now describe how Socrates used to help people with honourable ambitions by making them apply themselves to the objects of those ambitions.

One day he heard that Dionysodorus had come to Athens and was offering to teach the art of generalship. So he said to one of his companions who he knew was eager to attain the rank of general in the state, 'You know, my boy, it's a poor thing for one who wants to be a general in the state to neglect the opportunity of instruction when it's available. Such a person would be more justly liable to public prosecution than one who undertook to make statues without having learned how to do it; because in the perils of war the whole state is entrusted to the care of the general, and the good effects of his success and the bad effects of his failures are likely to be equally far-reaching. So a man who did his best to get himself elected to this office without troubling to learn how to discharge it would surely deserve to be penalized.'

By using arguments like these Socrates persuaded his friend to go and take lessons. (*Memorabilia* III. 1.1–3, trans. H. Tredennick; for Dionysodorus, see *Euthydemus*)

There is nothing here to make the blood race. One may note the moral earnestness and the emphasis on knowledge; these and other features of Xenophon's portrait of Socrates may be found, in subtler and stronger forms, in Plato's accounts; but if Socrates had been merely the genially edifying person Xenophon describes, then clearly he would never have become such a celebrated figure. Xenophon's Socrates is indeed a considerable conversationalist, who holds certain views and makes certain assumptions about the world that deserve to be taken seriously;[3] but hi. strong point is massive horse-sense, not philosophical acumen.

1. Good general discussions of this problem are: W. D. Ross, 'The Problem of Socrates', *Proceedings of the Classical Association*, 30 (1933), pp. 7–24, Guthrie, III, pp. 349–55, and Lacey, 'Our Knowledge of Socrates', in Vlastos, *Socrates* (1971).

2. See e.g. *Memorabilia init.*

3. See for instance *Memorabilia* I. 4 and IV. 3, and pp. 25 ff. below, for his teleology.

2. *Aristophanes* (c. 450–c. 385), the comic dramatist, portrays Socrates in his *Clouds* as running a *phrontistērion*, a 'thinking-shop', in which all manner of new-fangled intellectual fantasticalities are taught to the young. Strepsiades wishes to enter his son for instruction, and when inspecting the establishment is scandalized by a conversation he has with the proprietor:

SOCRATES: These, these [the Clouds] then alone, for true Deities own, the rest are all God-ships of straw.

STREPSIADES: Let Zeus be left out: He's a God beyond doubt: come, that you can scarcely deny.

SOCRATES: Zeus, indeed! There's no Zeus: don't you be so obtuse. STREPSIADES: No Zeus up aloft in the sky!

Then, you first must explain, who it is sends the rain; or I really must think you are wrong.

SOCRATES: Well then, be it known, these send it alone: I can prove it by arguments strong.

Was there ever a shower seen to fall in an hour when the sky was all cloudless and blue?

Yet on a fine day, when the Clouds are away, he might send one, according to you.

STREPSIADES: Well, it must be confessed, that chimes in with the rest: your words I am forced to believe.

Yet before, I had dreamed that the rain-water streamed from Zeus and his chamber-pot sieve.

But whence then, my friend, does the thunder descend? that does make me quake with affright!

SOCRATES: Why 'tis they, I declare, as they roll through the air. STREPSIADES: What, the Clouds? did I hear you aright?

SOCRATES: Ay: for when to the brim filled with water they swim, by Necessity carried along,

They are hung up on high on the vault of the sky, and so by Necessity strong

In the midst of their course, they clash with great force, and thunder away without end.

STREPSIADES: But is it not He who compels this to be? does not Zeus this Necessity send?

SOCRATES: No Zeus have we there, but a Vortex of air. STREPSIADES: What! Vortex? that's something, I own,

I knew not before, that Zeus was no more, but Vortex was placed on his throne!

(Aristophanes, *Clouds* 365–81, trans. B. B. Rogers)

Necessity and Vortex were current cosmological concepts, notably of the atomists Leucippus and Democritus. That Socrates was at one period of his life interested in such topics is perfectly possible;[1] but the point is

1. See *Phaedo* 96a ff.; but cf. *Apology* 19b–d and Aristotle, *Metaphysics* 987b1–2.

that he is treated by Aristophanes throughout the play – not, I think, without a certain affection[1] – as a sort of composite 'intellectual' embodying a great many of the fashionable philosophical speculations of the time, and as something of a subversive influence (witness the shock to Strepsiades' religious belief administered by Socrates' 'naturalistic' or 'scientific' explanation of thunder). A comedian must no doubt put *some* recognizably true characteristics into his representation of known persons; but he is not on oath, and will distort freely in order to raise a laugh. Aristophanes' account of Socrates probably tells us more about the intellectual climate of fifth-century Athens and the popular reaction to philosophers in general than about Socrates in particular.[2]

3. By far the most striking, persuasive and influential account of Socrates comes from the pen of *Plato* (c. 427–347). If we are to believe what we find in the dialogues, Socrates was a man of immense charm, but with a turn of deadly irony; a man of simple religious faith,[3] yet possessing logical prowess of a high order; and above all a formidable conversationalist, whose razor-sharp dialectic maddened his interlocutors to the amusement of the audience. Whether this portrait of Socrates is entirely historical may be doubted: it seems just too good, and somewhat larger than life. It probably owes much to the literary genius of Plato, who observed certain traits in Socrates' character and conversations, and wrote them up into the irresistibly brilliant portrait which has fascinated the world ever since.[4] Hence we are not to suppose that the dialogues written by Plato actually took place in the form in which he has written them. Obviously they must be based on something historical:[5] but their literary elegance suggests an extensive degree of Platonic manipulation. In the end, however, what matters is not their historical accuracy but their philosophy.

4. This is our cue to bring on our last witness, *Aristotle* (384–322), who tells us in his *Metaphysics:* 'There are two things which you may fairly

1. At any rate, the two men are represented in Plato's *Symposium* (e.g. 212c, 223c) as having been on convivial terms in the year 416.

2. For an excellent account of Aristophanes' portrayal of Socrates, see Dover.

3. For discussions of the religious side of Socrates, in particular his 'divine sign' (*daimonion*), his attitude to the Delphic oracle's statement that no man was wiser than he, and his views on life after death, see Guthrie, III, pp. 402–9, 473–84.

4. Controversy about Socrates continued after his execution in 399, and 'Socratic' literature (some of it favourable to him, some critical) became a minor industry. For a few fragments of such literature, see the appendix to this volume.

5. Memories of conversations with Socrates were at least sometimes verified by reference to notes taken on the occasion, which could themselves be referred to Socrates for correction and supplementation (*Theaetetus* 142d, cf. *Symposium* 173b).

attribute to Socrates: inductive arguments and general definition' (1078b27–9). Aristotle was born too late to have known Socrates; but he spent twenty years in Plato's Academy, and presumably read his dialogues as well as other sources; he probably absorbed a good deal of anecdotal evidence also. The word 'fairly' suggests that there was some controversy about Socrates' contribution to philosophy, and that Aristotle is trying to settle it.[1] Certainly, what he attributes to Socrates, 'inductive arguments and general definition', are central to Plato's early Socratic dialogues.

4. *Induction*

An inductive argument is one which reasons from a *frequent* connection of A with B to an *invariable* connection of A with B:

A	B
I went swimming last month	and caught a cold.
I went swimming last week	and caught a cold.
I went swimming yesterday	and caught a cold.

Therefore 1. Whenever I go swimming I catch a cold.
Therefore 2. If I go swimming next week, I shall catch a cold.

The inferences 1 and 2 are plausible and perhaps very likely, but they are not cast-iron: I may swim next week and *not* catch a cold. However many cases (i.e. combinations of A and B, of swimming and cold-catching) are collected, inferences (1 above) from them and their predictive power (2 above) are always less then certain.[2]

Induction is closely related to analogy.[3] In Plato,[4] Socrates frequently reasons analogically along these lines:

1. Probably Aristotle does not mean to imply that inductive arguments (*epaktikoi logoi*) and general definition (*to horizesthai katholou*) were *original* to Socrates, but that whereas earlier thinkers had displayed only instinctive adumbrations of them, Socrates had made them his central concern and had sought systematically to bring them into an explicit relationship; see further Guthrie, II, pp. 483–4, and III, p. 425 ff. For a comprehensive review of Aristotle's account of Socrates, see T. Deman, *Le Témoignage d'Aristote sur Socrate* (Paris 1942).

2. For the character of induction in Plato's early Socratic dialogues, see Robinson, pp. 33–8. Since it usually consists of only a small handful of items, it is 'intuitive' rather than 'enumerative' (Robinson's terms). It is 'not the same as modern induction, but more like a generalization from one or more convincing examples' (J. Annas, *Aristotle's Metaphysics, Books M and N* (Oxford 1976), p. 154, citing *Protagoras* 350, *Laches* 193, *Gorgias* 514 and *Euthydemus* 288–9).

3. Aristotle, *Rhetoric* 1393a26–b8, and Robinson, Chapters 4 and 12.

4. See, for example, *Apology* 19d ff., and compare the parallel between statue-making and generalship in the passage of Xenophon on p. 16.

In carpentry, there is an expert (the carpenter) in a defined body of knowledge, which has its own precise rules, procedures, techniques, and criteria of excellence.

In ship-building, the same is true.

In house-building, the same is true.

Therefore in moral action, the same is true.

In other words, morality is a skill or ability which like any skill or ability rests on a set body of knowledge. However, we do not, at least as yet, possess this body of knowledge,[1] nor do we have the precise rules, procedures, techniques, and criteria of excellence; nor do we know who the moral expert is. Socrates seems to have supposed that such knowledge and rules could be acquired by a careful inspection of moral terms and of the way they are applied in reporting and assessing conduct.

Now, what is striking about moral terms is that the same word is applied to a wide variety of cases. For instance:

I pay my debts, and that is a just act.

I support my elderly parents, and that is a just act.

I punish a criminal, and that is a just act.

What feature (or set of features) is present to and common to all these and all other just acts, and entitles them to the description 'just', without which they would not *be* just? Will not that common feature be precisely the general term 'justice'? Let us suppose we could acquire precise knowledge of that concept, just as a carpenter has precise knowledge of the criteria of good carpentry. We should then need, when assessing whether a given act is just or not (and there are many such difficult moments in human life), only to examine it to see whether it exhibits justice, the essential feature of all just acts.[2] This feature would be cast in the form of the second of the two innovations Aristotle ascribes to Socrates: a definition.

5. *Definition*

What is a Socratic definition? It is a *logos*, a form of words, an account.[3] Take several things with the same name: my table, your table, his table.

1. cf. *Euthyphro* 7b ff.

2. See, for example, *Euthyphro* 6e and 15d on the application of the knowledge of piety, and compare Xenophon, *Memorabilia* IV. 4. 7–8.

3. On Socratic definition, see Vlastos (1981), 'What Did Socrates Mean by His "What is F?" Question?', as against Penner, who holds that Socrates is searching not for meanings (of

Each of them has one or more properties (a flat top, say) which are essential to it, without which it would not *be* a table. A Socratic definition is a description of the constitution or structure of a bundle of those essential properties which, being present in certain particular objects, justify their being called tables. If one of these properties is not essential to the table's being a table – if, that is, the table could be a table without it – then that property does not form part of the definition of table. For instance, a table may or may not be large, or black, or three-legged; but these qualities are not essential to it *qua* table; they are not part of its *ousia*, its essence.[1] The bundle of *essential* properties Socrates often calls an *eidos* or an *idea*,[2] the 'appearance' or 'look' of a particular class of things, which is present in and common to all the members of that class, and which serves to mark that class off from every other class of thing. In the case of tables it is tableness; in the case of just acts, justice; in that of pious acts, piety.

If the *eidos* were not present to the object, the object would not be what it is; add the *eidos*, and the object is what it is. It is the presence or absence of the *eidos* that makes the crucial difference. Hence it is easy to think of the *eidos* as a cause, something which by coming makes the object what it essentially is, and by departing deprives it of that status. To conceive of an *eidos* as a cause, as a thing in its own right, is however probably a development introduced by Plato (see pp. 32–3). Socrates himself seems to have concentrated on the *eidos* only as that which is simply *there* in all objects of a given class, and which needs to be described in terms of a definition.

There is a problem in the logic of Socratic definition. The procedure relies on an induction which is based on the assumption that the objects or acts which are the subject of the induction are correctly named, i.e. correctly identified as instances of the general term we are seeking. For instance, we collect several 'just' acts, and attempt to define 'justice'. But we may be mistaken in having supposed those acts to be 'just' in the first place. In that case, one or more non-just acts will have vitiated our definition. The definition, which is supposed to enable us to discriminate just action from unjust, seems to depend on the prior availability of the knowledge it is itself intended to supply. For how can we know that the

---

piety etc.) but for psychological *explanations*, i.e. psychic states and causes that make men pious in their actions. cf. Burnyeat, 'Virtues in Action', in Vlastos, *Socrates* (1971).

1. cf. *Euthyphro* 11 a–b.

2. e.g. *Meno* 72c. The two words are used by Socrates without apparent distinction. Each may be rendered into English by 'idea' or 'form'; the latter term is now the more common.

acts listed in the induction, which is intended to tell us what 'justice' is, *are* just, if we do not know what 'justice' is in the first place?[1]

Throughout the dialogues we find Socrates asking apparently simple questions such as 'What is piety?', 'What is courage?' and 'What is justice?' These questions, like the questions asked by children with which we started, have a startling directness; but they are in some ways rather sophisticated, in that they presuppose some reflection on the relationship between particulars and general terms, and to assume that such concepts as justice, piety, etc., somehow exist and can be formulated in words (cf. Section 11). They have also the important implication that moral values are in some sense fixed and absolute. On this point, Socrates collides head on with the intellectual orthodoxy of his day. Many people, including some (but not all) of the thinkers known generally as the 'Greek sophists',[2] observing that moral ideas and actions vary from time to time and from state to state in practice, concluded that the same applies in principle: that is, they *ought* to be essentially variable and freely adaptable to the needs and desires of individuals and communities. In the starkest contrast, Socrates argued, implicitly rather than explicitly, that moral concepts such as piety etc. are unchanging standards against which individual actions must be judged. The attack by Socrates on moral relativism is at the heart of Greek philosophical debate of the time.

6. *Practical Implications*

It is clear that Socrates embarks on his inquiries not merely out of philosophical curiosity, but for pressing reasons of practical prudence: they are intended to yield results, a body of knowledge which can be applied with precision in the pursuit of the most moral life, which Socrates (see pp. 25–7) assumes is the most happy one. And since every moral virtue, each in its own particular sphere of conduct, seems to be a matter of knowing what is good and what is evil, Socrates was inclined to think that they must all be fundamentally 'one'.[3] Moreover, as virtue consists in knowing something, it must presumably be teachable: it must be a skill or craft

1. cf. P. T. Geach, *Logic Matters* (Oxford 1972), p. 33 ff. (reprinted from *The Monist*, 50 (1966)), and W. D. Ross, *Plato's Theory of Ideas* (Oxford 1953), p. 16. Some discussions: Santas (1972), Beversluis, Irwin pp. 40–41, 294, and P. Woodruff, *Plato, Hippias Major* (Oxford 1982), pp. 138–41. Vlastos (1985), esp. pp. 20–26, argues that the difficulty is illusory. See also p. 19 n. 2 above.

2. The best brief account of the sophists is Kerferd's; see also pp. 26, 33–4 below.

3. See *Laches* 199d–e, *Protagoras* 361a–c, Aristotle, *Nicomachean Ethics* 1144b30 ff., Gulley p. 151 ff., Penner.

(*technē*), which like any other skill or craft produces precise practical results from exact calculation. In brief, to discover what virtue is is the means to become virtuous – and therefore happy – oneself. Philosophy thus becomes, or should become, crucial to the pursuit of the good life.

It is precisely because moral inquiry has practical implications that Plato takes care, by means of the dramatic framework that surrounds and permeates the philosophical content of the dialogues, to locate the inquiries in the context of the confusion and puzzlement about moral terms experienced by representative Athenians in their everyday life. So far as philosophy itself was concerned, he had no need to imitate or report Socrates' inquiries in the form of dramatic dialogue: he could have simply set out their philosophical substance, and the steps in the argumentation, in plain and frugal form. But life generates puzzles of conduct; philosophy is intended to solve them; and in his Socratic dialogues Plato's literary skill combined philosophy and life to superb effect.

A second and connected reason for the dramatic setting was, of course, Plato's desire to demonstrate and popularize the practice of philosophy by writing material that would be found attractive to read or listen to (see pp. 35–6). Indeed, to some readers the dialogues' literary polish has always been their chief appeal. 'Macaulay's diary for the month of July 1853 is full of Plato. "I read the *Protagoras* at dinner. The childish quibbling of Socrates provokes me. It is odd that such trumpery fallacies should have imposed on such powerful minds. Surely Protagoras reasoned in a better and more manly strain. I am more and more convinced that the merit of Plato lies in his talent for narrative and description, in his rhetoric, in his humour, and in his exquisite Greek." '[1]

7. *Socrates' Paradoxes*

Socrates' intellectualist approach to morality and to problems of conduct becomes particularly clear in the two celebrated paradoxes attributed to him by Plato. The first is, 'Virtue is knowledge.' 'Virtue' is the commonly accepted but somewhat misleading translation of *aretē*, 'excellence', 'efficiency', 'goodness'. The point of the aphorism is that if we are to act morally and thus live happily, it is not enough simply to have virtuous intentions or even virtuous habits: there is a certain body of *knowledge* that must be acquired – knowledge, presumably, of the meaning of moral

1. G. O. Trevelyan, *The Life and Letters of Lord Macaulay* (popular edition, London 1889), p. 602. On the relation between drama and philosophy in a Socratic dialogue, see the introduction to the *Laches*.

terms such as justice, piety, etc.[1] Only if we know what these are can we be excellent and efficient in moral conduct.

The purport of the second paradox is fundamentally the same: 'No one does wrong willingly.' The ambiguity of the Greek word *hamartanei* ('he goes/does wrong') is crucial. If we *do* wrong it is because we have *gone* wrong. That is to say, we have acted in ignorance of, or in error about, justice or piety or some other moral term. If we really knew them, then naturally we would *never*[2] do wrong (unless, of course, we were forced, or lacked non-moral technical resources or opportunity). Since to do right is to be happy (see further Section 8), no one can ever *really want* to do wrong;[3] if a man does so want, it must be because he is misinformed about moral terms. The ambiguity of *hamartanei* tends to preclude the possibility of arguing that morally wrong conduct is consistent with happiness. For while the proposition 'He who *goes* wrong/makes a mistake (*hamartanei*) about moral questions cannot be happy' seems plausible enough (mistakes usually lead to suffering or disaster), it seems to bring with it the proposition 'He who *does* wrong (*hamartanei*) cannot be happy.' This latter proposition, which is wholly contrary to the intuition of the ordinary man, was indeed one of Socrates' most firmly held beliefs.

The claim that no one does wrong willingly would, if true, have startling consequences for penology; for how could it ever be reasonable to *punish* a criminal, who *ex hypothesi* did not 'really intend' to do wrong? In brief, Socrates' answer was that punishment is not, or ought not to be, the infliction of suffering in return for past misdeeds, but the 'cure' of the criminal's involuntarily wicked psychic state for the future: it helps his soul to acquire, if not moral knowledge, then at least correct moral opinions. The wrongdoer who persists in doing wrong is less happy than the wrongdoer who is cured of his vice (see Section 8). Hence a criminal ought to seek punishment just as a sick man seeks medical treatment.[4] That punishment is essentially cure is maintained, with some vehemence, in Plato's last work, the *Laws*, and has some influence, at least theoretically, on the model penal code Plato draws up for use in the ideal state depicted in that dialogue.[5]

---

1. See also pp. 27–8.
2. See also p. 27.
3. *Meno* 78a, *Protagoras* 358c–d.
4. *Gorgias* 477e ff.
5. For a discussion of the penology of the *Laws*, see my Penguin translation, pp. 367–9.

INTRODUCTION

8. *Socratic Eudaemonism*

'Happiness' is the conventional but somewhat misleading translation of
eudaimonia. It is not primarily a *feeling*, a warm glow of serenity and
contentment; it is rather an objective state of affairs, something like
'achievement and success in living'. Now according to Socrates, 'To do
right is to be happy', and 'To do wrong is to be unhappy.' These propositions are very hard to swallow. Yet they are fundamental to his ethics.
The courageous man,[1] for instance, knows what actions to fear and avoid
(for these are painful and lead to misery), and what actions need not be
feared and avoided (for these are not painful and lead to happiness). Given
this knowledge, and given all men's desire for 'good', it is inconceivable
that the courageous man, in the sphere of conduct to which the particular
virtue of courage is relevant, should make mistakes in his choice of action.
Knowledge is both a necessary and a sufficient condition of a choice which
brings 'happiness'.[2]

Of course, the virtuous/knowledgeable man may be frustrated by things
and events external to himself from actually doing the morally correct
actions which he has chosen. More importantly, it is notorious that the
wicked often flourish, while the virtuous often do not. In ancient Greece
this observation led, at least in certain thinkers, to a belief that in spite of
appearances the wicked always suffer eventually for their crimes, either
later in this life or in the next. But Socrates seems to have resolutely
maintained the stronger thesis that if a wicked man appears here and now
to be happier than a virtuous one, it is mere illusion. For already, here
and now, in *this* world, the just man creates his own heaven, the unjust
his own hell. No harm can come to the just man; whatever tribulations
befall him he is always happier than the unjust. To persuade people of
this is very difficult.[3] What did Socrates mean by it?

Socrates' view of the world was fundamentally teleological. He saw it
as a rationally ordered structure, in which men, like many other things,[4]
have a function. That function is to fit in with the whole; that is what man
is, in some sense, *for*. To fit in, to fulfil one's function, is presumably
advantageous and leads to happiness. Moral knowledge is, therefore,
knowledge of that function, that is to say knowledge of what will bring
good and what will bring evil. If that knowledge is virtue, then ignorance

1. *Laches* 194d ff.
2. *Apology* 30b, 41d, *Protagoras* 347c–e.
3. *Laws* 660e ff., 733d ff.
4. Xenophon, *Memorabilia* I. 4, IV. 3; cf. *Apology* 41d, *Republic* 352d ff., 601d.

25

will be vice; the ignorant man does not know how to fulfil his function, which is the means to his own happiness.

Hence the word *aretē*, commonly translated 'virtue', is better thought of as 'excellence': since 'virtue' is knowledge, the man who has *aretē* is the man who has knowledge, and who is therefore *excellently equipped* to fulfil his function and be happy. In this respect Socrates stands firmly within ordinary Greek usage: *aretē* is excellence *in* or *for* something; but according to him that something was none of the goals which men commonly set themselves, such as power or wealth or luxury, but the achievement of *eudaimonia*, happiness, by fulfilment of function.

Although Socrates never quite puts the point in explicit terms, he is one of a long line of thinkers who have sought to find moral rules and standards in 'nature', as being somehow 'given' and fixed by the very structure of the world and man's place in it. These standards, whatever they may turn out to be on inquiry, are objectively 'there', as matters of fact, whether we like it or not, and we ignore them to our cost; hence the importance of discovering them. The so-called immoralists of the fifth century (notably Thrasymachus in *Republic* I and Callicles in the *Gorgias*) appealed to the 'facts of nature' to support what broadly amounted to a doctrine of 'might is right'. However much Socrates' moral philosophy and 'immoralist' moral philosophy differ, they are fundamentally alike in assuming that moral norms exist as fixed and discoverable facts.[1]

This still does not meet the objection that the virtuous man, for all his knowledge, cannot possibly be happy if he is prevented from applying it and achieving advantageous action, and that if put on the rack he must be actually unhappy. But Socrates seems to have held that in the end moral knowledge is unshakeably satisfying to its possessor, in that it renders him indifferent to bodily discomfort or even death; in fine, no real (i.e. psychical) harm can come to the good man.[2] In Plato, this issue is the central problem of the *Republic*. What Socrates there undertakes to prove is that justice is, as we would say, its own reward. He is challenged to show that justice, when stripped bare of all external consequences, whether good or ill, is for its possessor more valuable than anything else. 'Platonic justice' is an internal, psychological state, the condition of functional harmony between the rational, spirited and appetitive 'parts' of the

---

1. *Both*, therefore, oppose the moral relativism described at the end of Section 5.

2. *Apology* 23b, 28b–d, 30c–d, 31b, 41d; cf. Xenophon, *Memorabilia* II.1. For a discussion of the difficulties entailed by this position, see Vlastos (1984). Note also the intriguing question posed by Bernard Williams in M. I. Finley (ed.), *The Legacy of Greece* (Oxford 1981), p. 249: 'Why, if bodily hurt is not real harm, is bodily hurt what virtue so strongly requires one not to inflict on others?' Cf. Brickhouse and Smith (1987) and Vlastos (1991), 200–232.

soul, a harmony crucially characterized by the domination exercised by reason and knowledge. A man with such a harmony may live in squalor and deprivation; but he is many times happier than the unjust man in his palace, whose soul is dominated by appetite and passion. Whether Plato succeeds in demonstrating anything of the kind is highly disputable; some hold that in the last resort psychic justice is valued in the *Republic* for the social justice to which it leads in the state – that is to say, for its external consequences.[1]

9. *Other Paradoxes*

The Socratic paradoxes entail some further paradoxes.

1. The virtuous man, he held, prefers being wronged to doing wrong, and never willingly does wrong *even in return for wrong*.[2] Consequently, he will never disobey a law, even one that bears on him unjustly; for to break a law is itself to act contrary to justice.[3] Such action is the action of an unjust man's soul; and the unjust man is by definition ignorant of moral values and hence of the means to his own happiness. The just man not only will not, but cannot, do wrong, in any circumstances, because he knows that it would harm his own soul and militate against his own happiness: unjust action prevents him from 'fitting in' with the ordered structure of the world by fulfilling his function. He is therefore incapable of performing actions which he knows will make him as unhappy as the unjust man.[4] To cultivate the *locus* of his moral knowledge should therefore, on prudential grounds, be a man's first care: in Socratic terms this is to 'cultivate his soul', which is much more valuable than his bodily wellbeing or his material possessions.[5]

2. What the Greeks called *akrasia* (moral weakness, failure to control and check one's desires and emotions) seems effectively abolished. For Socrates' key assumption is that no man does voluntarily anything except that which he judges best. The virtuous man really knows that what is

---

1. See (i) D. Sachs, 'A Fallacy in Plato's *Republic*', *Philosophical Review*, 72 (1963), pp. 141–58; (ii) R. Demos, 'A Fallacy in Plato's Republic?', ibid., 73 (1964), pp. 395–8; (iii) G. Vlastos, 'Justice and Happiness in the *Republic*', in his *Plato* II (1971), pp. 66–95, esp. 91–2. This collection includes reprints of (i) and (ii); Vlastos (1981) contains a reprint of (iii).

2. *Crito* 49a ff., *Republic* 335a–e.

3. *Crito* 49e ff.

4. *Crito* 49b, *Republic* 442c–e ff., 589c–e; 470e; cf. *Gorgias* 470e.

5. Xenophon, *Memorabilia* I.2.2 ff., IV.3.14; *Apology* 29d ff. A classic account of Socrates' 'care of the soul' is J. Burnet, 'The Socratic Doctrine of the Soul', in his *Essays and Addresses* (London 1929), pp. 126–62 (reprinted from *Proceedings of the British Academy*, 1915–16, pp. 235–59); see also Gulley, p. 192 ff.

morally right is more advantageous than anything else; hence he is never torn between what he knows to be morally right and an apparently pleasurable alternative.[1] If one objects, 'That is contrary to experience: often I know what I ought to do, but do some other act instead, because it is more pleasurable', then Socrates would claim that such a person's lack of virtue does not consist in acting contrary to his knowledge, but in not possessing *knowledge* at all: he has only a vacillating *correct opinion*, vulnerable to the pressures of desires and emotion, which somehow displace that opinion in favour of another opinion, a false one, namely that to indulge pleasure and emotion is best. But real knowledge of piety, justice, etc., is knowledge not only *of* piety and justice, but also knowledge *that* piety and justice, not impiety and injustice, bring the greatest advantage. Such knowledge is immovable and invariably leads to correct action: for no man chooses to do what he knows will bring him less advantage in preference to what he knows will bring him more.

3. For the same reasons, a virtuous act performed by a man without moral knowledge may be in practice identical to a virtuous act performed by a man who does possess such knowledge.[2] But the former person will be acting only in a state of 'right opinion', formed by mere habituation or on advice and instruction. Moral opinion is feeble and tottering; moral knowledge is strong and stable.

10. *The Supreme Socratic Paradox*

Today we should be inclined to say that, morally, man cannot but live in the dark: he is often unsure, in particular situations, that what he is doing is right. After a certain point, after all moral deliberation, he has personally to commit himself to some course of action, while still unsure that it is morally correct. The real test of his moral character is the size of the moral 'risk' he is prepared to take, the personal commitment he feels (rather than knows) he has to make to certain moral standards and actions. Now Socrates devoted his life to a search for definitions, norms which were intended to give precise answers to particular moral questions which arise in particular situations of moral difficulty.[3] The supreme Socratic paradox

1. See Walsh, 'The Socratic Denial of Akrasia', in Vlastos (*Socrates* 1971), and Vlastos (1981), pp. 416–17. Aristotle, *Nicomachean Ethics* VII, 2–3, contains criticism of Socrates' position.

2. cf. *Meno* 97a ff., *Timaeus* 51e.

3. That this aim is in principle misguided is one of Aristotle's central criticisms of Socratic moral philosophy: see Gulley, pp. 1 ff., 126 ff.

is, therefore, that he died[1] in defence of a quest which, had it been success-ful, would have told him infallibly whether or not to die was in fact the right thing to do. In the circumstances in which he found himself, he could not, on his own grounds, have known it to be right when he did it.[2] He made the supreme commitment in defence of a method that was designed to abolish moral risk-taking, and to make personal commitments unnecessary.

11. *Socratic* Elenchus

Before embarking on an investigation of a term, Socrates insists on certain conditions. First, for reasons which will emerge shortly, the interlocutor must himself believe in the answers he gives to Socrates' questions. Second, his answer must take the form of a *general definition*, e.g. of piety. To advance a specific example of piety, i.e. a particular pious action, will not do:[3] all a single action can do is to show the application of the general concept in a single context, and then only to someone who knows the general concept in the first place; a single instance of piety, considered in isolation, cannot reveal what *all* pious acts have in common. Answers in the form of a particular action are also vulnerable to the negative example, i.e. an act which satisfies the definition as offered but demonstrates its inadequacy. Here is a simple case: 'Justice is the returning of what we have borrowed.' 'But not, surely, if the borrowed object is a weapon, and the lender has now gone mad?'[4] The third condition is that the interlocutor should not give a mere description rather than a definition: Socrates insists that we cannot say *what sort of thing* the concept in question is until we know *what* it is. For example, we cannot know whether virtue is *teachable* before we know what virtue *is*.[5]

After one or more false starts which breach one or more of these con-ditions, the typical pattern of a conversation with Socrates is as follows. Socrates again asks 'What is *x*?', where *x* is what is meant by the general term in question, e.g. justice or piety. The interlocutor then states at some

1. For the charges against him, which led to his execution in 399, see p. 33.
2. The one point of superiority over other men which Socrates claims is that he 'knows he does not know': *Apology* 21b-d, 29a-b. Vlastos ('Elenchus' 1983, and 1985), however, argues that Socrates believed he did have some knowledge, in the sense of 'elenctically justified true belief' (1985, p. 9 n. 25). See further p. 30 n. 2 below, and Mackenzie ('Virtues' 1988).
3. e.g. *Euthyphro* 6d.
4. *Republic* 331c.
5. e.g. *Meno* 86d–e, *Protagoras* 360e–361d; cf. *Republic* 354b, *Euthyphro* 15d.

level of generality acceptable to Socrates[1] what he thinks x is (let us call his statement proposition A). Socrates, after a certain amount of bowing and scraping in deference to the interlocutor's surpassing wisdom, and lamentation of his own ignorance, wonders whether the answer can be right. Will he consent to answer a few questions to clear up Socrates' puzzlement? By all means. Socrates, starting from a second proposition, or set of propositions, which sounds obvious (let us call it/them B), and to which the interlocutor readily agrees, then asks a series of simple questions. Step by step the interlocutor is led on, till he finds himself assenting to some apparently unavoidable conclusion from B, which is nevertheless at odds with A. After some bewilderment, he tries again. He offers either a new A, or the first A modified in the light of the results of Socrates' interrogation. This sequence, which is called *elenchus* ('testing', 'refutation'), can then be repeated several times: new questions and objections from Socrates elicit modified or new answers. In theory, presumably, the progressive refinement of A could be carried to the point where it becomes irrefutable; but to judge from the dialogues this desirable result is never achieved in practice.

Sooner or later, as the *elenchus* proceeds, the interlocutor is disconcerted to find that he cannot have both A and B. In theory he could jettison B at any moment; but since B sounds so obviously true that no reasonable man could deny it, in practice it is A that has to be abandoned. The only truth established is not-A, and even that only so long as the interlocutor sticks by B, or so long as it is assumed that B is true. In that sense the progress made seems entirely negative: we discover several things that x is not; and invariably the conversation ends inconclusively, in what is called *aporia*, a state of helplessness or 'flap'. But in another sense the progress is positive: the interlocutor becomes convinced of the falsity of A and hence of his own ignorance of the moral value which he had thought he could define.[2]

1. See Santas, pp. 98–100, for 'a list of all the definitions in the Socratic dialogues, which are accepted by Socrates as syntactically or formally correct though not necessarily as true or adequate'.

2. This condensed and generalized account of *elenchus*, which is often a long and complex process, takes its inspiration from the important reconstruction of it by Vlastos, *Elenchus* (1983). See also (i) R. Kraut's reply, 'Comments on Gregory Vlastos, "The Socratic Elenchus" ', ibid., pp. 59–70; (ii) Vlastos' reply to the reply, 'Afterthoughts on the Socratic Elenchus', *ibid.*, pp. 71–4; (iii) T. C. Brickhouse and N. D. Smith, 'Vlastos on the Elenchus', ibid., 2 (1984), pp. 185–95; (iv) R. M. Polansky, 'Professor Vlastos' Analysis of the Socratic Elenchus', ibid., 3 (1985), pp. 247–59. In the latter part of his article Vlastos develops the challenging thesis that Socrates believes *elenchus* demonstrates the *truth of his own beliefs*, as being the only ones that do not crumble under elenctic assault. For other analyses of *elenchus* see Robinson, Chapters 2 and 3, and Gulley, p. 37ff. Socrates himself describes it in informal

This conviction of ignorance is, according to Socrates, a good thing, as it clears the ground for the beginning of wisdom. *Elenchus* does not of itself tell the interlocutor what the truth is, or which proposition to abandon; it is intended to stimulate him to pursue his inquiries and reach the truth.[1] That is why Socrates insists that the interlocutor must himself believe in his answer.[2] It is not enough that he should answer in a spirit of disinterested intellectual experiment, to see if an idea 'stands up'. He must be unreservedly committed to his answer, so that if it is refuted the educational effect may be as salutary as possible to him.[3]

Interlocutors, however, so far from feeling gratitude for being relieved of their misconceptions, would often become decidedly irritated, not only at being refuted, but by the frequent protestations of ignorance from Socrates himself; for they suspected him of knowing but concealing the right answer. They termed it 'irony', *eirōneia*, by which they meant not just 'irony' in the modern sense, but something like 'slipperiness' or 'tricksiness'. Socrates, they understandably felt, was 'real sneaky', and more concerned to trip up and humiliate than to enlighten them.[4]

The conviction of ignorance forced on the interlocutor by the demonstration of the falsity of his opinion was not intended to produce in him what on many occasions it no doubt did produce: the conclusion that if the moral opinions which he had been accustomed to hold are wrong, then he was free to adopt others at whim. That is why the parents of the young men who were attracted to Socrates' conversations thought of him as a negative and destructive influence.[5] On the contrary: Socrates' fundamental assumption was that moral standards have some sort of objective existence, and can be isolated and defined, given patient inquiry. Socratic dialectic is a strict discipline; it is not an invitation to smash conventional standards and 'do your own thing'.

The essentially educational purpose of *elenchus* distinguishes it from:[6]

---

terms in *Meno* 84a–c, *Apology* 21b–24b and *Sophist* 229c–230e.

1. *Apology* 29d ff., *Meno* 84a–c; cf. Xenophon, *Memorabilia* IV.2.39–40.

2. e.g. *Gorgias* 495a ff., 500b, *Crito* 49d, *Laches* 193c, *Hippias Minor* 365c. Hence if Socrates himself commits a fallacy, it is presumably not deliberate (cf. pp. 307–9). But see G. Klosko, 'Criteria of Fallacy and Sophistry for Use in the Analysis of Platonic Dialogues', *Classical Quarterly*, 33 (1983), pp. 363–74, and *American Journal of Philology*, 108 (1987), 612–26.

3. The effects of engaging in conversation with Socrates are described in *Laches* 187e ff., *Symposium* 215a ff. See further Vlastos (1987), pp. 94–5.

4. e.g. *Republic* 337a–e. Dr Johnson would no doubt have regarded dialectic as mere impertinence: 'Questioning is not the mode of conversation among gentlemen' (Boswell, *Life*, March 1776). The subtle purposes of Socrates' irony are elucidated by Vlastos (1987).

5. *Apology* 23c ff., cf. *Republic* 537c ff.

6. The following summary of terms draws on the excellent account in Kerferd, pp. 28–9 and Chapter 6; see also pp. 299–303 below.

(a) *epideixis*, lecture/exposition/display, designed to impress and persuade discursively rather than by tight argument;[1] (b) *eristic*, aggressive conversation using any and every verbal manoeuvre simply in order to win arguments, without regard for the truth;[2] (c) *antilogic*, 'disputation by contradiction', systematic derivation of contradictory entailments from an opponent's position, often but not always with eristic intent.[3]

Epideixis is fairly distinct. *Eristic* and *antilogic* are methodologically related, and because of their combative disregard for truth, they are often terms of abuse. *Elenchus*, though formally a variety of *antilogic*, is in Socrates' hands never used eristically; it is a prized tool in *dialectic*, advanced and procedurally correct philosophical discussion.[4]

12. *Socrates and Plato*

All Plato's Socratic dialogues are amalgams of Socrates and Plato: they contain genuine historical reportage of at least Socrates' general style of argument, worked up by Plato into more or less systematic treatments of particular philosophical difficulties, in the light of his own reflections and researches. The precise line of division between the two philosophers is impossible to draw with certainty.[5] There is, however, general agreement that Aristotle was right to attribute to Plato two crucial developments.[6]

First, he extended Socrates' notion of 'universals' (i.e. essential qualities common to all things of the same name, which entitle them to that name) from moral acts to all things whatever. For instance, just as all pious acts have piety in common, so do all beds have bedness in common. Plato thus developed Socrates' attempt to define moral terms into a comprehensive theory of the relationship between particulars and general terms.

Second, whereas Socrates thought of these essential qualities as somehow present *within* all the members of a given class of act or thing, Plato attributes a real independent existence to them: piety and bedness are in some sense real things, existing somewhere and somehow. These 'ideas' or 'forms'[7] are unchanging and unique, perfect of their kind, and stand

1. *Protagoras* 320c ff., *Hippias Major* 282b–d, *Hippias Minor* 363a–d.

2. *Euthydemus* 271c–272c.

3. e.g. *Euthydemus* 276 ff., and its introduction. Note that *antilogic* does not mean 'opposition to logic'.

4. *Meno* 75c–d, *Republic* 534 b–c.

5. As C. H. Kahn puts it (*Classical Quarterly*, 31 (1981), p. 305), 'The Socrates of the dialogues is an ambiguous figure, at once Plato's historical master and his literary puppet.'

6. *Metaphysics* 987b2, 1078b30–32, 1086a32–b5.

7. On the terminology, see p. 21 n. 2.

apart from particulars, which 'share in' or 'participate in' them more or less imperfectly. The nature of this participation is never made clear. Apparently a red object is red because it 'shares in' redness, which is somehow present or available to it. The assumption seems to be that redness is itself red, and indeed perfectly so. But in that case shall we not require some third entity, say REDNESS, to account for the redness both of redness and red objects – and so on *ad infinitum?*[1]

13. *Socrates and Greek Democracy*

Accounts of Socrates commonly start by inquiring what can be said for sure about his life and personality (not much, in view of our sources), and by telling in detail the endlessly fascinating and controversial story of his trial and execution in 399, when he was brought to court on the triple charge of not recognizing the gods recognized by the state, of importing other, new divinities, and of corrupting the young. I do not propose to rehearse these matters, partly because there are excellent descriptions readily available elsewhere,[2] partly because the nature of this volume demands an elementary introduction to Socrates' *philosophy*, and partly also because it is only after one has learned something of the implications of his philosophical methods and assumptions that one can begin to see why he was executed. For Socrates did not die just because he was an irritating conversationalist, or because he had certain private beliefs and personal practices that could be represented at his trial as religiously suspect and educationally corrupting, or even because he had consorted with persons who after the restoration of democracy to Athens in 403 were odious to democrats. He died at least partly because of his philosophy. Many ancient Greeks, like many people today, believed (i) that in technical matters there are indeed fixed rules and standards, which depend on a body of exact knowledge, possessed by the various practitioners; (ii) that this is *not* the case in moral, social and political questions, in which one man's opinions and standards are in principle as valid as another's, so that individuals and states may legitimately adopt whatever moral principles

1. See *Parmenides* 131e–132b. The problem of the self-predication of the forms, commonly called the 'third man' problem (man, manness, MANNESS), is one of a series of apparently devastating arguments brought against the theory of forms in the *Parmenides*; their effects on Plato's later thought are keenly debated. (The modern controversy on the subject started with G. Vlastos, 'The Third Man Argument in the *Parmenides*', *Philosophical Review*, 63 (1954), pp. 319–49. Bibliography down to 1972 may be found in id. (1981), pp. 361–2, and Chapters 13, 14 and 18; post-1972 publications are too numerous for listing here.)

2. e.g. Dover, and Guthrie, III.

and practices convenience or exigence dictates. As we have seen, Socrates agreed with (i), but used it to undermine (ii). If he is right, and correct moral conduct does depend on exact knowledge of general moral terms, then presumably one had better defer to the moral expert, to the one who 'knows' – whoever that is (Socrates seems never to have claimed the title for himself). In thus making the discovery of true moral values into an intellectual and élitist activity,[1] and by implying that once the expert establishes moral knowledge his prescriptions will become binding on the rest of us,[2] Socrates was bound to look askance at the principles and practices of democracy; and indeed his mocking hostility to that type of regime was well known.[3]

Plato, better than anyone, saw the political implications, and in his *Republic* he pursued them to the uttermost. In this celebrated (or notorious) dialogue he represents Socrates as advocating a utopia in which all moral and aesthetic standards, and all social and political power, depend entirely on an intellectual élite which had spent an arduous lifetime in the pursuit of absolute moral truth. His utopia is as far removed from democracy as could possibly be imagined.

The crucial point for the reader of the dialogues in this volume is that when Plato explores, through Socrates, the difficulties and implications of Socrates' own assumptions and arguments, he is not exploring matters of purely theoretical interest. For to Plato and Socrates philosophy is morals, philosophy is politics, philosophy is *life*.[4] If the difficulties in Socratic philosophy could be demonstrably resolved, so that it was left holding the field against its rivals, then the political and social consequences would be immense. That is ultimately why Plato, and a long line of philosophers down to the present day, have devoted their efforts to the analysis and criticism of Socrates' arguments.

1. In practice, that is. No doubt in principle Socrates' assumptions licence any man to investigate morality. 'But while the Socratic method makes moral inquiry open to everyone, it makes it easy for no one' (Vlastos, *Socrates* (1971), p. 20; cf. Gulley, p. 62 ff.

2. Or will they? Is not the moral expert too to be exposed to *elenchus*? Presumably he is; but he will never be refuted. Ought one therefore to *rely* on him, without bothering to think the issues through, so as to arrive at moral knowledge for oneself? If so, what becomes of Socrates' dictum, 'the unexamined life is not worth living for a man' (*Apology* 38a)? Does it apply only *before* the emergence of a moral expert?

3. e.g. Xenophon, *Memorabilia* III.7.6 and III.9.10; cf. *Meno* 94e ff., *Gorgias* 481d ff., 517a ff., *Protagoras* 319b, *Apology* 31e ff. There is a good brief discussion of the point in Guthrie, III, p. 409 ff., and a valuable analysis of the evidence in Vlastos, 'Historical Socrates' (1983).

4. *Laches* 187e–188a.

14. *The Purpose of the Dialogues*

If that is indeed the aim of the dialogues, for what recipients were they written? Were they intended only for a private readership? Or to be read aloud to audiences? Or even performed, perhaps to philosophical clubs of some kind, or for 'fringe' competitions at the Olympic games?[1] So far as their immediate use and destination are concerned, it is one of the curiosities of literature that no one quite knows what the Platonic dialogues were for. Nor is it known, except within rather broad limits, when they were composed, nor in what order, nor how many antedate the foundation of Plato's Academy, nor indeed when that foundation took place. If any do antedate it, they were perhaps intended for a relatively wide readership and/or large audiences, rather than small and specialized ones. That would account in part for the characteristics of the earliest of the three groups into which the dialogues are customarily divided. Most of these are fairly brief, and moderately dramatic and humorous; but philosophically they are tougher than they seem at first reading. Most of them reflect the historical Socratic *elenchus*, in that they end inconclusively in *aporia*; and their immediate purpose would have been, at least in part, to commemorate and defend Socrates' memory. The 'middle' dialogues are much longer, dramatically brilliant, and sometimes very funny indeed; they develop doctrine along lines which are indeed Socratic, but which probably go, in a Platonic direction, well beyond anything Socrates ever thought of. In the 'late' dialogues the dialogue form wears thin, and there are only touches of life and humour here and there; virtual lectures are frequent, the Greek is both technical and mannered, and the philosophy is exceedingly difficult and sophisticated. One supposes that these works were rarely studied except by dedicated philosophers, and their use may well have been confined to advanced students of the Academy, perhaps in seminars.

But whatever the dialogues' immediate use, their strictly philosophical purpose is intimately related to Plato's conception of philosophy as a human activity. Books, he makes Socrates say,[2] cannot be argued with; they always say the same thing to you, however often you read them. Plato knew that if he had reduced his philosophical tenets at any stage of his career to a set of propositions, his companions would have simply repeated them parrot-fashion. He believed that the only way to philosophize was

1. For these and other perhaps tongue-in-cheek suggestions, see Gilbert Ryle, *Plato's Progress* (Cambridge 1966).
2. *Phaedrus* 275d, cf. *Letter VII*, 341c–e.

to engage in the give and take, the argument and counter-argument, of rational conversation, in which the interlocutors care passionately for the truth and not at all for winning a dispute. Hence he never wholly abandoned the dialogue form. The dialogues always promote Platonic doctrines, but they never *order* one what to think: every opinion expressed in them is the refutable opinion of a particular person. They stimulate the reader, or ought to stimulate him, to respond to the argumentation; they challenge him to do philosophy on his own account. Whenever two or more people fall to arguing about a passage in a Platonic dialogue, they are doing exactly what Plato intended. And no one would be more pleased than he if they were to correct and improve his own work, gain deeper insight into the issues, and perhaps even solve the problems. For it is largely owing to Socrates' conversations, and to Plato's dialogues, that philosophy is not a jealous discipline.

It is in this spirit that the reader of this volume should approach the seven dialogues it contains. They are all from the early period,[1] and they make a good collection. The *Ion*, the slightest but the most amusing piece, assails the pretentious claims to knowledge made by a fatuously self-confident Homeric rhapsode, and floats some suggestive ideas on the nature of poetic inspiration. The *Laches* is an attempt to define courage, the *Lysis* to define friendship, *Charmides* self-control, and the *Hippias Major* fineness. All four are rich in suggestion, but all end in *aporia*. The *Hippias Minor* explores paradoxes thrown up by Socrates' favourite analogy, between morality and technical skills. In the *Euthydemus* Socrates tangles entertainingly with a couple of 'antilogical'[2] sophists. If any or all of these dialogues provoke the reader into exclaiming, 'But that can't be right!', or 'I can think of an answer to that one', then Socrates' formula for philosophy will be doing its magic. The magic worked in the ancient world, and it still works today.

---

1. The date of each of them is discussed in their individual introductions. On the question of dating in general, see C. H. Kahn, 'Did Plato Write Socratic Dialogues?', *Classical Quarterly*, 31 (1981), pp. 305-20.

2. See p. 32.

ION

INTRODUCTION TO *ION*

The *Ion* of Plato is among the shortest of his dialogues; but it has provoked controversy out of all proportion to its length. It is light and amusing, with vivid characterization, a clearly defined structure and a limited theme. Yet it is not easy to interpret, and its wider implications are baffling.[1] The question it poses is: 'Do poets know what they are talking about?' Socrates, clearly, thinks the answer is 'no'; indeed, he believes that poets are ignorant fellows who can write poetry only when in a state of madness. What exactly does he mean by these apparently outrageous judgements? And does he intend them to apply to writers of prose, and to painters and sculptors and all artists of any kind whatever? And even if he is right, we are surely entitled to ask (for Socrates does not volunteer the information) why we should bother our heads about it for one moment. In asking, we are responding to Socrates' dialectic in a way in which he himself would have wished. The purpose of this introduction is to attempt to give an intelligible answer.

Ion was a rhapsode. What did rhapsodes do? Gorgeously attired, they recited the works of Homer and other poets, apparently in some sort of chant, and usually without the musical accompaniment employed by earlier Homeric singers. Their performances were dramatic: they threw themselves into the part of whatever character Homer was depicting, and acted his scenes. Their audiences could be private or public; in the latter case, large crowds could be attracted, especially at civic festivities. They were professionals, and expected to be paid.[2]

Some rhapsodes, Ion among them, did more: they lectured. For the

1. The *Ion* is a mystery in other ways too. We cannot tell the date at which the conversation is supposed to have taken place; but such slender indications as there are point to a time before 412 (see p. 64 n. 2). Nor do we know its date of composition, nor its place in the sequence of Plato's writings and the development of his thought. Presumably it comes early in his literary career (see p. 35), not many years after Socrates' death in 399. Ion himself is probably historical, but as he is known only from this dialogue, we cannot be quite sure. Moore's article on the dating contains also a brief review of the difficulties raised by the dialogue's form and content.

2. For further discussion of rhapsodes, see M. L. West, *Journal of Hellenic Studies*, 101 (1981), pp. 113–15, and G. S. Kirk, *The Songs of Homer* (Cambridge 1962), pp. 91, 312–15. The word 'rhapsode' meant 'stitcher of songs', though the implications of the expression are not quite clear. Few performances (except at festivals) could have been of the *Iliad* or *Odyssey* entire; so perhaps they usually consisted of extracts 'stitched together' in some coherent manner. More probably, the term referred to the detailed composition or assembling of Homeric

Greeks regarded Homer not only as an authoritative teacher of human relationships and conduct,[1] but also as a repository of worthwhile information on technical matters of many kinds, ranging from purely technological processes to social and intellectual skills such as oratory, teaching and generalship.[2] The rhapsodes undertook to elucidate Homer's lines and to expatiate, apparently in eulogistic terms,[3] on their practical and moral relevance.[4] This side of their activities was in effect an early form of literary criticism.

We may now approach the dialogue itself. It has three well-defined episodes:

A. Socrates raises a problem: why is Ion, a devotee of Homer, able to expound descriptions of technical matters, for instance divination or arithmetic, in poets other than Homer only when their descriptions coincide with those given by Homer himself? For normally a skill is possessed 'as a whole', in the sense that it confers the ability to assess the comparative quality of descriptions by different observers of the same technical matters. Ion professes not to have this ability; so if it is true that he is able to assess technical passages in Homer only, it cannot be in virtue of a *skill* that he does so. There must be some other explanation.

B. Socrates advances the hypothesis that Ion, as a rhapsode, is at the end of a long chain of 'inspiration' or 'possession'. A particular Muse inspires particular poets to particular kinds of poetry; these poets, by their works, in turn inspire particular rhapsodes; finally, the rhapsodes communicate by their performance their own inspiration and excitement to their

---

poetry from phrases, formulae, lines, etc., and to its continuous performance, which would by its nature and sheer length be different from the performance of other kinds of poetry. A third explanation connects 'rhapsode' with *rhabdos*, the staff wielded by the rhapsode to heighten the dramatic effectiveness of his performance, and perhaps to help mark the rhythm.

1. *Protagoras* 325e–326a, *Republic* 606e, *Laws* 858c–e; Aristophanes, *Frogs* 1006–12, 1030–36; Xenophon, *Symposium* III. 5; Isocrates, *Panegyricus* 159.

2. *Republic* 598d–e, and the evidence of the *Ion* in general. The statements in Xenophon, *Symposium* IV. 6–7, where several skills are said to be imparted by Homer, are perhaps derived from the *Ion* and so are not independent evidence; yet evidently they seemed plausible to Xenophon. Greek workmen, of course, learned their trade from each other, and had no need of Homer as a technical handbook. Presumably Greek laymen admired Homer's technical descriptions (of ship-building or chariot-driving, for instance) because they found in them specialized information in a simplified and palatable form, with a sufficient sprinkling of jargon and patina of technicality to make them feel at least a little wiser – much as we today might enjoy a description of an atom-smasher or a rocket or the techniques of spies or racing-car drivers in a novel or magazine. See further Guthrie, IV, p. 208 n. 2.

3. *Ion* 533d, 536d, 541e, 542b. For *epideixis*, 'lecture', see pp. 32 and 50.

4. Verdenius (1943), pp. 251–2.

audiences. Thus Ion's limited ability, to recite and expound Homer alone, is a mad, non-rational thing, the result of some divine dispensation. It is not a matter of knowledge; it is not a *skill*.

C. Ion stoutly resists the suggestion that he is 'mad' and 'possessed'. Socrates, however, adduces a series of technical passages of Homer, and in each case shows that it is the relevant technical expert who can judge them best. If a rhapsode does have a skill, it is the skill of rhapsody, not of carpentry or medicine. But Ion claims to be able to judge all technical passages in Homer, in any field, and wildly asserts that by virtue of his competence to judge matters of generalship described by Homer, he himself is a good general. Socrates teases him appropriately, and closes the conversation.

To a modern reader, such a conversation may well seem eccentric or even pointless. However, if we remember Socrates' basic assumptions, we shall not find it difficult to understand why he should have wished to deny that rhapsodes and poets possessed skill (*technē*: see pp. 20, 22–3, 171, 267 ff.).[1] For he believed *morality* to be a skill, acquired by dialectic; and if that skill could ever be discovered, it would lead to conduct far different from the models of human behaviour offered by the poets – or at any rate, to the same conduct, but based on sharply different calculations (see p. 28). In general terms, therefore, what the *Ion* attempts is a demolition job on the claims of poets and rhapsodes to be teachers of morality; their pretensions to skill having been swept away, the moral skill to be imparted by Socratic dialectic is left holding the field.

But if this is indeed Socrates' intention, the way he sets about it is exceedingly strange. Let us divide the whole process of composition and presentation of poetry into six activities or stages:

1. The creative and imaginative element in his work which the *poet* may feel originates from outside and beyond himself; that part of his ability to compose which just 'comes' to him by inspiration without being reducible to rules, and in a way which he himself may well be at a loss to account for.

2. The technical part of the *poet's* work: the observance of certain rules of diction and metre, the choice of words and rhythms which he knows will convey his meaning and achieve the effect he wishes to have on his audience; the construction of episodes and speeches of the right length, tone, etc.

(Stage 2 is not wholly reducible to rules, and in any case is in practice intimately dependent on stage 1 and difficult to separate from it. Neverthe-

1. On *technē* in the *Ion*, see Sprague.

less, there is some more or less strict technique in the process of composition; and in that ancient poetry (particularly epic) is tightly constrained by observance of, and variations on, verbal formulae and metrical conventions, this technical aspect perhaps bulks larger in an ancient poet's work than in that of a modern.)

3. The quality of the *poet's* description of the world, of men and artefacts, and of technical and social skills.

4. The *rhapsode's* mastery of delivery: his adoption of gestures, postures and tones of voice calculated to achieve an effect appropriate to the passage he is reciting; in brief, his total performance.

5. The *rhapsode's* ability to explain and assess the poet's description of technical and social skills. This explanation, which is part of a more general elucidation or eulogy of the text, presumably need not take the form of a complete exposition of the technical process or social skill in question: it could consist simply of showing how the poet adapts or abridges such a process or skill by selection of some elements in it and omission of others, for his own purpose. Nevertheless, the rhapsode will need *some* technical knowledge to give an adequate account, even for these limited ends.

6. The interest and excitement which stages 4 and 5 generate in the *audience*.

The oddities in the argument of the *Ion* may now emerge:

(a) *Inspiration (stage 1)*. Socrates' description of the 'inspired' state is loaded. Greek poets certainly thought of themselves as 'inspired', that is to say assisted, by divinities, notably the Muses; that is why they commonly invoked them at the beginning of their poems. This assistance, they hoped, would take two forms:[1] (i) the providing of factual information about the story or theme of the proposed poem; (ii) the conferring of the more or less permanent ability to compose and perform.[2] However, they never supposed that such aid dispensed them from effort: they expected to have to work hard at composition, and within the conventions of style and metre to exercise their inventiveness and powers of imagination.[3] 'Possession', on the other hand, is, as Socrates says (534a), a frenzied state characteristic of the devotees of certain ecstatic religions. In this state the

1. For a good account of this matter, see the article by Murray.

2. In an oral poet, to compose and to perform are to a large extent the same activity: he 'thinks on his feet'. See Murray, pp. 94–6.

3. It is characteristic of early Greek thought to 'overdetermine' causation: 'Zeus made me do it' and 'I did it myself' are not exclusive. Homer, *Odyssey* XXII, 347–8 demonstrates the point neatly: Phemius (see p. 53 n. 3) says, 'I am self-taught, and a god has planted in my mind all manner of songs.'

poet is not simply assisted by the god, but is his passive mouthpiece: the god speaks *through* him (534d–e). There is just enough obvious similarity between 'inspiration' and 'possession' for Plato (or Socrates) to assimilate them; and the assimilation is tendentious in the extreme, for whereas inspiration allows scope for human skill, possession does not.[1]

(b) *Technical Knowledge (stages 3 and 5)*. The rhapsode, in stage 5, may well have less technical knowledge than the technical expert. So what? His elucidation of technical passages is a perfectly rational and calculated activity, and will be sufficient for his purpose, that is for commenting on poetry. Similarly, in stage 3, the poet himself knows enough for *his* purposes, that is the composition of a passage of poetry with sufficient technical elaboration plausibly to conjure up a scene or episode. So even though the poet and the rhapsode commonly do have much less technical knowledge than the expert, it seems an exaggeration to say they have none.

(c) *Artistic Skill (stages 2 and 4)*. In stage 4, admittedly, the rhapsode has to throw himself into the scenes and characters portrayed in the text, and to that extent his performance may be frenzied or irrational; at any rate, he does imagine himself to be present at places where he is not present (535b–c). Yet to deny calculation and control in his choice of gestures and so forth with which to manipulate his audience (535e) is to deny an important element of skill in his performance. Similar considerations apply to the poet's choice of rhythms etc. in stage 2.

(d) *Possession*. Though there is some obvious plausibility in seeing possession in stage 1, it is less plausible to find it in stages 2 and 4, less still in stage 3, and wholly unconvincing to find it in stage 5 (as Ion says, 536d, and we believe him).

In short, Socrates uses the agreed comparative lack of technical knowledge in stages 3 and 5 to divert attention[2] from the extent to which artistic skill is present in stages 2 and 4. He then fills all the stages 2–5, thus evacuated of expertise, with 'possession'.[3]

The *Ion*, then, makes a single point in a clever and provocative manner:

1. On poetic inspiration and Plato's ascription of 'possession' to poets, see Tigerstedt's two works. If (as seems likely) it was an innovation on Plato's part, he has a bit of a nerve to describe it (*Laws* 719c) as 'an ancient story'.

2. Certainly the attention of Ion: he never makes the obvious answer to Socrates, that a poet's skill lies in stage 2, and a rhapsode's in stage 4. This is the more surprising in that Socrates himself mentions a 'rhapsodic' *technē* at 538b–d and 539e ff. – but perhaps only for the sake of argument. For a review of the answers Ion could have made to Socrates' questions, see Delcourt's article.

3. Plato's view of stage 5 is well put by LaDrière (p. 31): 'The image of the magnet is plain in its significance. There is no new *afflatus* for the critic, distinct from the poet's; the critic's inspiration is the poet's, communicated to him by the poetry.'

poets and rhapsodes are irrationally possessed, not knowledgeable and skilled. But we ought not let that provocation blind us to the deeper considerations that animate the argument. It is clear that Plato objected to the poets' claim to be moral experts, in rivalry to the moral expert hopefully to be produced by dialectic. But that rivalry arises ultimately from two radically different ways of looking at the world. To Plato, particular things in this world are mere *reflections* of the world of forms; to rise above these reflections and to discover the forms themselves, by reason and dialectic, is to penetrate to knowledge of truth, to absolute moral standards, and hence to the secret of a happy life (see pp. 25–7). Poets, by contrast, appeal not to reason but to reason's enemies, the emotions. They never even try to rise above particulars: they simply adopt (and then in turn influence) the accepted standards of society, and relate their moral lessons to no objective norm at all.

However, the poets were taken to be not only moral guides but knowledgeable on technical matters too. If Plato had merely attacked them as moral guides, he would have been open to the poets' riposte, 'But how do *you*, Plato, know what moral action is? Are *you* (or this fellow Socrates, whom you admire so much) a moral expert?' Plato therefore concentrated his attack on the poets at the point at which they (and rhapsodes) are demonstrably most vulnerable: technical expertise. For here acknowledged experts do exist, who invariably know more than the poets, and are able to judge technical matters better than they can. The poets are seen to be merely skating over the surface of the subject-matter in a manner which is impressive only to the layman.[1] But why should that matter? What on earth has the poets' superficial knowledge of *technical* subjects to do with their status as *moral* teachers?

Plato might put the point to the poets somewhat as follows: 'If you do not treat thoroughly and accurately such humdrum things as technical processes, how can you hope to be authoritative on an intensely difficult subject like morality? To take a simple example, how can you hope to describe accurately the life of the gods? Your audience is only too ready to use your accounts of immorality among the gods to justify their own wicked conduct.[2] You affect to offer moral guidance; but you rely on descriptions of human affairs and human relationships which are just as superficial as your description of technical matters.[3] Superficiality is dictated by the very nature of your activity; if you were less superficial, you would be less attractive; you would not be poets, and no one would

1. cf. *Republic* 601a–b.
2. *Laws* 941b.
3. cf. *Republic* 600e–601a.

listen to you. Try giving a full and accurate description of anything, whether of technical matters or of moral concepts; it would destroy you as artists.'[1]

It would not avail a poet to abandon his role as an explicit teacher, and claim only to enlarge our sensibility and moral awareness by moving us to pity, tears, sympathy or indeed hilarity at the human condition and at the moral dilemmas experienced in human life.[2] Even that kind of moral discourse, Plato would say, is not based on knowledge and skill in the relevant field, the dialectic of moral concepts. Of the superficiality of the poets' treatment of matters moral their superficiality in matters technical is a sufficient paradigm. In neither area can they 'give an account' of what they do; and the ability to 'give an account' is evidence of the systematic rational knowledge of a possessor of a skill. Irrational possession by a god prevents poets from intelligibly communicating the nature of their activity.[3]

One defence is left to the poet: 'My poetic *process* is indeed inexplicable; but my poetic *product*, my poem, may nevertheless state the truth.' Plato would reply: 'No doubt it sometimes does (as indeed I admitted in my *Laws*, 682a); but that is only because you have stumbled across it accidentally, not because of a skill.'

In this introduction I have made an attempt to draw out the Platonic implications of the single and limited point made by Socrates in the *Ion*. But it is a major obstacle in interpreting the dialogue that such attempts may be quite anachronistic. In form, the *Ion* is an attack on rhapsodes, not on poets. If criticism of poets is present, it is by virtue of the strong implication of the image of the magnet: that *mutatis mutandis* poets are to be given the same satirically unfavourable assessments as rhapsodes, and for fundamentally the same reasons (cf. p. 43 n. 3). Nor does Socrates say anything about poets (or rhapsodes) as moral teachers; he says nothing about forms; it is not even quite clear that he intends to go beyond the ostensible tone of light amusement, and to condemn poetry (and perhaps the products of the other arts too) as quite valueless; for all he claims about poets is that they are not skilled but possessed by a god, which not everyone would interpret as a criticism.[4] Plato's more systematic treat-

1. cf. *Republic* 601b.

2. This, I take it, would be the line likely to be adopted by a modern poet, who (unlike an ancient) would not claim authority to teach, except perhaps in some remote sense.

3. On 'giving an account', see e.g. *Republic* 534b–c, *Gorgias* 465a, and cf. *Apology* 22a ff.

4. Indeed, it is a difficulty for Socrates' position that if a god speaks 'through' the poet, and gods tell no lies (*Republic* 381e ff), we ought to treat the poet's utterance as true, and worth the most serious attention. The difficulty is compounded by Plato's occasional description of other categories of persons also as 'inspired' and 'possessed', for example statesmen (*Meno*

ment of poetry comes in dialogues that are presumably later than the *Ion*;[1] and in them, though elaborately and bitterly critical of its truth-value and its moral influence, he seems on occasion prepared to accord it some limited usefulness (entirely ignored in the *Ion*), chiefly on a fairly low social, political and educational level.[2]

To go into these larger considerations would call for an introduction many times longer; here I can only point out that they may or may not have been present to Plato's mind when he wrote the *Ion*. I believe, but cannot prove, that they were.[3] Yet it must be admitted that the *Ion* has a disconcertingly casual air, as though it were no more than a preliminary skirmish in the 'ancient quarrel between poetry and philosophy' (*Republic* 607b). It reads like a somewhat arrogant work of Plato's youth, when intoxicated by the prospect of discovering an exact science of morals he briefly dismissed poetry by attacking it at what he thought was its weakest point, its lack of *technē*, and supposed he had thereby demolished its claim to serious attention. His argument has a touch of crudity, and few readers will think that he does justice either to poetry or to philosophy. Does he not do something like what it is fashionable nowadays to do in some educational circles, namely to reproach the arts for not employing the 'scientific method', and for not producing precisely quantifiable results?[4] The *Ion*, for all its slightness, raises this and other important issues that are still with us today.[5]

99d). Presumably the human medium introduces distortion – yet how, if he is entirely passive, as Plato seems to claim? Cf. pp. 42–3, and n. 2 on 534e below.

1. Notably *Republic* 376–403, 595–608.

2. e.g. *Phaedrus* 245a, 248e, *Symposium* 209a, *Republic* 398a–b, 607a, *Laws* 817b–d.

3. Flashar's book examines in detail the possible connections of the *Ion* with other dialogues.

4. cf. LaDrière, p. 33, and D. Daiches, *Critical Approaches to Literature* (Englewood Cliffs, N.J., 1956), p. 9: 'Socrates begs the fundamental question concerning the difference between *Dichtung* and *Wahrheit*, between poetry and science . . .' Contrast Aristotle, *Poetics* XXV, 1–10.

5. See in particular Schaper for a good demonstration of how the problems posed by the *Ion* are fundamental to aesthetics.

SUMMARY OF *ION*

A. Ion's Skill: Is It Genuine?

B. The Nature of Poetic Inspiration

C. Ion's Choice: To be Skilled or Inspired

ION

Speakers

SOCRATES
ION: A rhapsode, not known except in this dialogue

ION

A. *Ion's Skill: Is It Genuine?*

*Socrates points up the paradox of Ion's claim to be able to expound technical
passages of Homer, but of no other poet (unless they say the same as Homer).
In other fields, technical knowledge entails an ability to judge the comparative
merits of differing technical accounts. If, therefore, Ion really is able to judge
technical passages in Homer, and in Homer alone, it can hardly be by virtue
of a skill. Socrates thus fastens on the weakest point in Ion's activities; he
completely ignores all other aspects of the relationship between poet, rhapsode
and audience, notably Ion's undoubted success in performances. Ion appears
conceited and naive to a degree, and Socrates' ostensibly polite questions have
a slightly cutting tone.*

SOCRATES: Good day to you, Ion. Where have you come from on this 530a
visit to us? From your home in Ephesus?[1]

ION: Oh no, Socrates, from Epidaurus, from the festival of Asclepius.

SOCRATES: You mean to say the Epidaurians honour the god by a
competition of rhapsodes too?[2]

ION: They certainly do, and of the arts in general.

SOCRATES: I see. Well then, did you take any part in the competition?
And how did you fare in it?

ION: We carried off the first prize, Socrates. b

SOCRATES: That's splendid news. Now make sure we win at the Pan-
athenaic festival too![3]

ION: That we shall, God willing.

SOCRATES: I must confess, Ion, I've often envied you rhapsodes your
art, which makes it right and proper for you to dress up and look as grand
as you can. And how enviable also to have to immerse yourself in a great
many good poets, especially Homer, the best and most inspired of them,
and to have to get up his thought and not just his lines! For if one didn't c
understand what the poet says, one would never become a good rhapsode,

1. Ephesus was a city founded under Athenian leadership on the west coast of Asia Minor.

2. Epidaurus, in the north-east of the Peloponnese, held a festival every four years in honour
of Asclepius, the Greek god of healing. 'Too' perhaps expresses acidulously polite surprise that
rhapsodes were taken so seriously.

3. The Panathenaea was an Athenian festival celebrated annually on the birthday of the
goddess Athena. Every fourth year the festivities were held on a more elaborate scale, and
included a contest of rhapsodes.

because a rhapsode has to be an interpreter of the poet's thought[1] to the audience, and that's impossible to do properly if one does not understand what he is saying. So all this is worth envying.

ION: True, Socrates, true. At any rate, I find this side of my art has given me a lot of work, and I reckon I talk on Homer better than anybody.
d Neither Metrodorus of Lampsacus nor Stesimbrotus of Thasos, nor Glaucon,[2] nor anyone else who has ever lived has had so many fine thoughts to deliver about Homer as I.

SOCRATES: I'm glad to hear it, Ion – since obviously you're not going to grudge me an exhibition[3] of them.

ION: Yes indeed, Socrates, it's well worth hearing how splendidly I have embellished Homer. I think I've got to the point where I deserve to have the Homeridae[4] crown me with a golden crown.

SOCRATES: Yes *indeed*,[5] and one day I'll find myself time to listen to
531a you. For the moment, however, answer me just this: does your expertise extend to Homer alone, or to Hesiod and Archilochus too?[6]

ION: By no means – only to Homer. That strikes me as enough.

SOCRATES: But is there any topic on which Homer and Hesiod say the same?

ION: Oh, I expect there are plenty.

SOCRATES: So on these topics would you give a better explanation of what Homer says, or of what Hesiod says?

ION: On these topics, on which they say the same things, Socrates, I'd
b be equally good in either case.

SOCRATES: What about topics on which they do *not* say the same? For instance, both Homer and Hesiod say something about divination.[7]

1. In this paragraph 'thought' renders *dianoia*, Homer's 'meaning' or 'intention', i.e. the use or purpose to which he puts his subject-matter. In the next paragraph Ion picks up the word and employs it in the plural to refer to his own edifying exposition (*epideixis*) of him (see pp. 32 and 40).

2. The identification of Glaucon is uncertain. Metrodorus (and possibly Stesimbrotus too) was an allegorical interpreter of Homer. But there is no implication that Ion's own expositions were of this type; he produced not *huponoiai* ('allegories'), but *dianoiai* ('thoughts', 'reflections'): see *Republic* 378d, Xenophon, *Symposium* III.6, Diogenes Laertius, II.11, and Tigerstedt, p. 23.

3. i.e. a 'performance' (*epideixis*); cf. n.1 and Socrates' last long speech of the dialogue.

4. 'Sons of Homer', i.e. members of a society of rhapsodes, originally claiming descent from him.

5. This echo of Ion's own words is perhaps mild mockery of his eagerness to show off.

6. Hesiod, commonly thought to have composed *c.* 700 B.C., a little later than Homer, was the author of the *Theogony* (*Birth of the Gods*) and of a didactic poem entitled *Works and Days*. Archilochus (mid seventh century) wrote 'personal' poetry on a wide variety of topics.

7. Prediction of the future by inspection of 'signs', e.g. the condition of animal entrails, or (as at 539b–c) the flight of birds.

ION: That's right.

SOCRATES: Now then, in their descriptions of divination these two poets sometimes agree and sometimes differ. In either case, who would give a better explanation of their words, you or one of the good prophets?

ION: One of the good prophets.

SOCRATES: And if you were a prophet, then since you'd be capable of explaining the points on which the poets' statements agree, you'd also know how to expound those on which their statements differ, wouldn't you?

ION: Obviously.

SOCRATES: Then why on earth does your prowess extend to Homer, c but not to Hesiod or the other poets? Or does Homer have themes which are *different* from themes which all the other poets have? Hasn't he mostly described warfare, and how men associate with one another – good men and rogues, laymen and professionals? And about how gods behave when they associate with one another and with mankind? And about what goes on in the heavens and in Hades, and the origins of gods and heroes? Isn't d this the subect-matter on which Homer has composed his poetry?

ION: That's right, Socrates.

SOCRATES: What of the other poets? Don't they talk about these same topics?

ION: Yes – but Socrates, they haven't composed like Homer has.

SOCRATES: Oh, really? Worse?

ION: Much worse.

SOCRATES: Homer has done it better?

ION: Yes, yes, better, by Zeus.

SOCRATES: So then, Ion, my dear chap, when several people are discussing number, and one of them speaks best of them all, someone, I imagine, will know which of them this good speaker is?

ION: I agree.   e

SOCRATES: Will that be exactly the same person who also knows which speakers are bad, or someone different?

ION: The same, I suppose.

SOCRATES: And that's the possessor of skill in numbers, isn't it?

ION: Yes.

SOCRATES: Well then, when several people are discussing what sorts of food are healthy, and one of them speaks best of them all, will the person who recognizes the excellence of what the excellent speaker says be different from the person who recognizes the lower quality of what the second-rate speaker says? Or will it be the same person?

ION: I reckon the answer's obvious: the same.

SOCRATES: And who is he? What do we call him?

ION: A doctor.

SOCRATES: So to put it in a nutshell, we're saying that when several people are discussing the same topics, in every case the same person will know both who is speaking well and who is speaking badly. Otherwise, if he's not going to recognize the bad speaker, clearly he's not going to recognize the good one either, at least when the subject-matter is the same.

ION: Quite so.

SOCRATES: So the same person turns out to be expert on both kinds of speaker?

ION: Yes.

SOCRATES: And you assert that Homer and the other poets, among them Hesiod and Archilochus, do talk about the same topics, but with unequal success – Homer being good at it, the rest inferior?

ION: I do assert that, and it's true.

SOCRATES: So, given that you recognize the good speaker, you'll also recognize the poorer quality of what the second-rate speakers say.

ION: Apparently.

SOCRATES: So, my excellent fellow, we shan't go wrong if we say Ion is an expert equally in Homer and in the other poets,[1] seeing that you yourself admit that the same person will be an adequate judge of all who speak on the same themes, and that almost all poets do take the same themes to compose on.

ION: Then what on earth is the reason, Socrates, why when someone converses about any other poet I don't pay attention and can't make any worthwhile contribution at all, but just doze off – whereas when anyone mentions Homer, I'm awake in a flash, I'm all attention, and have a lot to say?

SOCRATES: Guessing that's not difficult, my friend. It's obvious to everyone that you are unable to speak about Homer with skill and knowledge – because if you *were* able to do it by virtue of a skill, you would be able to speak about all the other poets too. You see, I suppose there exists an art of poetry as a whole, doesn't there?

ION: Yes, there does.

SOCRATES: So whatever other skill you take as a whole, the same method of inquiry will apply to every one of them? Do you want to hear me explain the point I'm making, Ion?

1. This apparent compliment is doubly double-edged. Ion claims to be an expert on Homer, and must therefore be 'equally' an expert on other poets too – a conclusion he is reluctant to accept. Conversely, if he is *not* an expert in the other poets, he must be 'equally' (i.e. non-) expert in Homer – a conclusion he would of course resist even more strenuously.

ION: Yes, by Zeus, Socrates, I do. I love listening to you clever fellows.

SOCRATES: How I wish that were right, Ion! But I suspect it's you rhapsodes and actors who are clever, and the authors whose compositions you sing, whereas I just speak the truth and nothing but, as is natural in a layman. Now, as to that question I asked you a moment ago: look how e trivial and commonplace it is. Anyone can see the point I made, namely that whenever one takes a skill as a whole, the same inquiry applies. Let's get the point by reasoning like this: an art of painting exists as a whole, doesn't it?

ION: Yes.

SOCRATES: And there exist, and have existed, many painters good and bad?

ION: Surely.

SOCRATES: So have you yet seen anyone who is an expert at demonstrating which paintings of Polygnotus,[1] son of Aglaophon, are good and which are bad, but can't do the same for the other painters? And who, 533a when someone expounds the works of the other painters, nods off and gets confused and has nothing to contribute – but when he has to give his opinion about Polygnotus or any other painter you like, in isolation, he's awake and alert and has plenty to say?

ION: No, by Zeus, I certainly haven't.

SOCRATES: Then again, in sculpture, have you yet seen anyone who is an expert at explaining which of the creations of Daedalus son of Metron are good ones, or of Epeius son of Panopeus, or of Theodorus the Samian,[2] b or of any other one sculptor, but when among the works of the other sculptors becomes confused and nods off, having nothing to say?

ION: No, by Zeus, I've not noticed anyone like that either.

SOCRATES: I go further, and reckon that in pipe-playing too, and in playing the lyre and in singing to its accompaniment, and in rhapsody, you have never seen a man who is an expert at giving an explanation in the case of Olympus or Thamyras or Orpheus, or Phemius the rhapsode c of Ithaca,[3] but who on Ion of Ephesus falls into confusion and cannot

1. One of the most famous painters of the mid fifth century. He came from the island of Thasos, and gained Athenian citizenship.

2. Daedalus was a legendary craftsman of exceptional versatility; he was noted especially for his lifelike sculptures. Epeius, with Athena's help, made the wooden horse which the Greeks sent into Troy (*Iliad* VIII, 493). Theodorus was a celebrated artist of the middle of the sixth century.

3. According to legend, Olympus invented pipe-playing. Thamyras, a mythical Thracian player of the lyre, boasted he would win a contest even against the Muses (*Iliad* II, 594 ff.). Orpheus, a mythical Thracian, sang so sweetly as to charm even trees and animals. Phemius was the rhapsode whom the suitors of Penelope compelled to perform for them (*Odyssey* I,

contribute an opinion as to which of his rhapsodic performances are good and which are not.

ION: On that point, how can I contradict you, Socrates? But I'm as sure as sure can be about this, that on Homer I am the finest speaker of mankind, and I'm full of things to say, and everybody else agrees what a good speaker I am – but not on the other poets. Now then, see what that amounts to!

B. *The Nature of Poetic Inspiration*

Part A seemed to indicate that if Ion is able to expound technical passages of Homer, it is not by virtue of a skill. How then does such an ability arise? Socrates now suggests an explanation in terms of the whole poetic process. There is a magnet-like chain of irrational divine inspiration, from Muse to poet, from poet to rhapsode, and from rhapsode to audience. The reason why Ion cannot expound poets other than Homer is that he is caught in one particular chain – Homer's – and not in any other. Again, Socrates ignores large parts of the activities of poet and rhapsode, notably the technical skills of rhythm, gesture, etc., that rhapsodes and poets must have.

The tone of this part is elusive. The dialogue as a whole shows Ion to be a feather-brain (evidently the common opinion of rhapsodes: see Xenophon, Symposium, III.6 and Memorabilia, IV.2.10), and Socrates' two long and ostensibly admiring speeches contain obvious irony and satire (see especially 534b, on the poet as a 'flighty' thing). Yet with the satire there may be mingled some cautious respect: Ion is after all, in some distant and muddled way, in touch with something divine.

SOCRATES: I do see, Ion, and now I'm going to show you what I make
d   of it. This fine speaking of yours about Homer, as I was saying a moment ago,[1] is not a skill at all. What moves you is a divine power, like the power in the stone which Euripides dubbed the 'Magnesian', but which most people call the 'Heraclean'.[2] This stone, you see, not only attracts iron rings on their own, but also confers on them a power by which they can in turn reproduce exactly the effect which the stone has, so as to attract

---

154, and XXII, 330) during the absence of her husband Odysseus from his home on Ithaca.

1. 532c.

2. Euripides, fr. 567 in A. Nauck, *Tragicorum Graecorum Fragmenta* (2nd ed., Leipzig 1889). The references are probably to Magnesia on the Maeander, in Caria in Asia Minor, and to the place called Heraclea to the south; but we cannot be sure, as there existed several Magnesias and many Heracleas.

other rings. The result is sometimes quite a long chain of rings and scraps   e
of iron suspended from one another, all of them depending on that stone
for their power. Similarly, the Muse herself makes some men inspired,
from whom a chain of other men is strung out who catch their own inspiration from theirs. For all good epic poets recite all that splendid poetry
not by virtue of a skill, but in a state of inspiration and possession. The
same is true of good lyric poets as well: just as Corybantic worshippers
dance without being in control of their senses,[1] so too it's when they are   534a
not in control of *their* senses that the lyric poets compose those fine lyric
poems. But once launched into their rhythm and musical mode, they
catch a Bacchic frenzy: they are possessed, just like Bacchic women, who
when possessed and out of their senses draw milk and honey from rivers[2] –
exactly what the souls of the lyric poets do, as they say themselves. You
see, I understand the poets inform us that they bring their lyric poetry to
us from certain gardens and glades of the Muses, by gathering it from   b
honey-springs, like bees, and flying through the air like they do. And they
are right. A poet, you see, is a light thing, and winged and holy, and
cannot compose before he gets inspiration and loses control of his senses
and his reason has deserted him. No man, so long as he keeps that, can
prophesy or compose. Since, therefore, it is by divine dispensation and
not in virtue of a skill that they compose and make all those fine observations about the affairs of men, as you do about Homer, the only thing   c
they can compose properly is what the Muse impels them to – dithyrambs[3]
in one case, poems of praise in another, or dancing-songs, or epic, or
iambics.[4] Each of them is hopeless at anything else. The reason is that
they utter these words of theirs not by virtue of a skill, but by a divine
power – otherwise, if they knew how to speak well on one topic thanks to
a *skill*, they would know how to speak about every other topic too. That's
why the god relieves them of their reason, and uses them as his ministers,
just as he uses soothsayers and divine prophets – so that we who listen to   d
them may realize that it is not they who say such supremely valuable
things as they do, who have not reason in them, but that it is the god
himself who speaks, and addresses us through them. A most weighty

1. Corybants were mythical quasi-divine attendants on Cybele, a Phrygian goddess of nature
and fertility; like them, her human worshippers engaged in frenzied dancing.

2. See Euripides, *Bacchae* 708 ff. As at *Laws* 790d–e, Plato treats the ecstasy and dancing
of Corybantic and Bacchic ritual as essentially similar. Bacchus (Dionysus) was the god of raw
natural vitality.

3. Choral songs in honour of Dionysus.

4. Iambic rhythm ($\cup -\cup -$) was used not only for the passages of conversation (as distinct from
choral lyric) in drama, but also for satirical poetry; presumably it is the latter use which Socrates
has in mind.

proof of this is Tynnichus the Chalcidian, who never composed any other
poem one would think worth mentioning, but did compose the paean[1]
which everyone sings, and which is pretty well the finest of all lyrics –
e   literally, to use his own language, 'an invention of the Muses'. In him
especially, I think, the god indicated to us, lest we doubt it, that these
fine poems are not on the human level nor the work of humankind, but
divine, and the work of gods, whereas the poets are nothing but the
gods' interpreters,[2] each possessed by his own possessing god. By way of
showing us this, the god deliberately sang the finest lyric through the most
535a hopeless poet. Or don't you think I've got it right, Ion?

ION: By Zeus, I think you have. Somehow or other your words touch
my soul, Socrates, and I do believe good poets interpret these messages
from the gods for us by divine dispensation.

SOCRATES: So you rhapsodes in turn interpret[3] the words of the poets,
don't you?

ION: You're right in that, too.

SOCRATES: So your role is to be interpreters of interpreters?

ION: Surely.

b   SOCRATES: Hold on a minute, Ion, and tell me this – and do be frank
about answering whatever I may ask you. When you give a performance
of epic and stun your audience, and you sing of Odysseus leaping on to
the threshold and revealing himself to the suitors and pouring forth his
arrows before his feet,[4] or of Achilles rushing at Hector,[5] or one of those
piteous episodes about Andromache or Hecuba or Priam,[6] are you, at that
moment, in control of your senses? Or are you taken out of yourself, and
c   does your soul, inspired as it is, imagine itself present at the events you

1. Hardly anything is known of Tynnichus. Paeans were choral hymns sung in honour of a
god, especially Apollo as Healer.

2. *Hermēneus*: 'mouthpiece' (Guthrie, III, p. 203, with n. 1); cf. 530c. Only in Plato (see,
for instance, *Meno* 99c–e, *Laws* 719c–d) is the poet as passive as this implies. On the ordinary
Greek view, the god is *not* a ventriloquist: he consigns (the substance of) his 'message' or
'information' *to* the poet for casting *by* the poet into words, rhythms, etc. This the poet may
indeed achieve 'lacking his reason' in the sense that he does it instinctively, by non-ecstatic
inspiration or help from the god himself, and without knowing or being able to describe how.
But that is not to say that the poet is entirely passive: by whatever means, it is he himself who
is the composer of his poetry, not the god. Cf. pp. 42–3 and 45 n. 4.

3. By intonation, gestures, etc.

4. *Odyssey* XXII *init*. At the end of his wanderings after the Trojan war Odysseus, disguised
as a beggar, finally arrives at his home on the island of Ithaca. The house is full of fellow-
Ithacans, who, supposing him to be long since dead, are paying court to his wife Penelope

5. *Iliad* XXII, 312 ff. Achilles killed Hector in order to avenge the death of his fri υ
Patroclus, whom Hector had slain.

6. e.g. *Iliad* VI, 369 ff., XXII, 405 ff. Priam was king of Troy; Hecuba was his wife;
Andromache was the wife of Hector.

describe – either at Ithaca or Troy or wherever else the scene of the epic is set?

ION: How vividly you've proved your point, Socrates! I'll tell you in all frankness. When I say something piteous, my eyes fill with tears. When it's something frightening or terrible, my hair stands on end with fear, and my heart thumps.

SOCRATES: Well then, Ion, take a man dressed up at a feast or festival   d
in elaborate clothing and golden crowns. If he has lost none of these things, but nevertheless breaks out in tears, or if he gets into a panic in spite of standing among more than twenty thousand friends, when no one is denuding him or doing him any harm, are we to say he's in his senses at that moment?

ION: No, by Zeus, not at all, Socrates, if the truth be told.

SOCRATES: And do you realize that you people have exactly these effects on most of your spectators?

ION: Yes, I'm very well aware of it. At each performance, I look down   e
on them from up there on the platform as they weep and look at me with dire emotion in their eyes, in amazement at my story. You see, I have to pay a lot of attention to them – since if I make them cry I shall laugh all the way to the bank, whereas if I provoke their laughter, it's I who'll do the crying, for loss of my money.

SOCRATES: Well then, do you realize that your spectator is the last of those rings which I said received their power from one another, under the influence of the Heraclean stone? The intermediate one is you, the rhapsode and actor; the first is the poet himself. Through the agency of all   536a
these the god draws the souls of men wherever he wishes, by hitching one man to the power of another. An immense chain of dancers and teachers and assistant teachers dangles down, as if from that stone – all dangling sideways from the rings in the series suspended from the Muse. One poet depends on one Muse, another on another. Our description of this is 'he is possessed' – and that's pretty close, because 'held' is just what he is.[1]   b
Starting from these first rings, the poets, one man dangles from another and catches the inspiration – from Orpheus in one case, Musaeus in another;[2] but most are possessed by Homer. You're one of them, Ion: you are possessed by Homer, and when someone recites the lines of some other

1. Translation unavoidably blunts Socrates' point, which is (whimsically?) over-sharp. In 'Greek 'he is held' is *echetai*, while 'he is possessed' is *katechetai*, a compound form of the same verb. Socrates exploits the similarity in order to use the (alleged) truth of *echetai* of a poet as a justification for the (alleged) common use of *katechetai* to describe him.

2. For Orpheus, see p. 53 n. 3. Musaeus was a legendary singer and priest, often connected with him (e.g. *Republic* 364e, where they are attacked for their teaching).

poet, you drop off to sleep and you're stumped for something to say. But when someone voices a melody of this poet Homer, you're wide awake at once, and your soul goes a-dancing and you've plenty of observations on

c him. This is because you say what you say about Homer not in virtue of skill or knowledge, but through a divine dispensation and possession, just as Corybantic revellers are acutely sensitive to one melody alone, that of the god by whom they are possessed: they've a great store of gestures and phrases to suit *that* melody, but to others they do not respond at all. It's just like that in your case, Ion: someone only has to mention Homer and you're full of things to say; but on the others you're stumped. So in reply

d to your question – the reason for this fluency of yours about Homer, but not about the others – the answer is that your tremendous eulogies of Homer come by divine dispensation, not skill.

C. *Ion's Choice: To be Skilled or Inspired*

Socrates now once again concentrates on Ion's claim to technical knowledge. He allows Ion to show his paces by reciting several technical passages in Homer, and has no difficulty in showing that in each case the person best able to judge them is a technical expert, not a rhapsode. The technical skills described by Homer are different both from one another and from the skill of a rhapsode (note that the existence of such a skill is now acknowledged). The mere fact that Ion has the ability to recount in performance the functions of a doctor, for example, does not make him a doctor. Ion, however, fails to see the difference: he believes that the skill of a general and the skill of a rhapsode are the same – yet he will not allow that a good general is a good rhapsode, only that a good rhapsode is a good general (541a–b).

After some elegantly ironic mockery by Socrates of this absurd position, the conversation comes to an end, without any explicit renunciation by Ion of his claim to technical knowledge. Are we to suppose that he has been in the least improved by Socratic dialectic (cf. p. 31)?

In the closing words Socrates pronounces Ion to be 'divine', not 'skilled'. The conclusion of the dialogue is thus in a sense 'aporetic' (see p. 30): it has done no more than establish something poetry is not, namely a vehicle of knowledge of fact. Of what, then, being 'divine', is it a vehicle? Of fiction, presumably. But does that entirely condemn it? Formally, at least, Socrates leaves the door ajar for the possibility that poetry may describe for us something with a truth-value other than the literally factual. By implication, he raises, but does not even attempt to solve, the whole problem of the nature and status of poetry and of the arts in general (cf. Schaper, pp. 51–2).

ION: That's well put, Socrates. None the less, I'd be surprised if you could put it so well as to persuade me that it is in a state of madness and possession that I praise Homer. And I reckon *you* wouldn't think so either, if you were to listen to me talking about him.

SOCRATES: I'm very ready to listen to you – but not before you answer me this: which of the things which Homer mentions do you speak well   e
about? Not about them all, I suppose.

ION: Rest assured, Socrates, on every single one of them.

SOCRATES: But surely not on those which Homer mentions, but which you, in fact, don't know about?

ION: And what sort of things does Homer mention, but I don't know about?

SOCRATES: Well, doesn't Homer, in many passages, have a lot to say   537a
about *skills*? For instance, about driving chariots – if I recall the lines, I'll give you them.

ION: No, no, I'll do it – I have them by heart.

SOCRATES: So tell me what Nestor says to his son Antilochus, when he advises him to take good care at the turning-post, in the horse-race in honour of Patroclus.

ION: 'Lean over,' he says, 'yourself, in your well-polished chariot,
    A fraction to their left; then to the horse on the right   b
    Shout out and urge him on, and slacken his reins in your hands.
    And at the post let the horse on your left hug it close,
    So that the nave of your well-wrought wheel
    May seem to touch the edge; but avoid grazing the stone.'[1]

SOCRATES: That's enough. Now, in these lines, Ion, which will know   c
better whether Homer's description is correct or not – a doctor or a charioteer?

ION: A charioteer, of course.

SOCRATES: Because he possesses this particular skill, or in virtue of something else?

ION: No, because he has the skill.

SOCRATES: So the god has incorporated into[2] each skill an ability to understand some particular function? You see, I reckon that what we understand by virtue of the skill of a pilot, we shall not understand by the skill of a doctor too.

1. *Iliad* XXIII, 335–40. Nestor was an old man, respected for his counsel, in the Greek army at Troy. The 'post' marks the turning-point at the other end of the stadium from the starting-point. Nestor describes how to avoid a spillage in the dangerous manoeuvre of doubling back as fast as possible in a left-hand U-turn round the post.

2. Literally, 'has conferred on'; in modern terms, 'every skill implies an ability to understand . . .'

ION: Indeed not.

SOCRATES: Nor shall we understand by means of a carpenter's skill that which we understand by means of a doctor's.

ION: Indeed not.

d   SOCRATES: So isn't it like that in the case of *all* skills – what we understand by means of one, we shall not understand by means of a second? But answer me this first: do you agree that one skill is distinct from another?

ION: Yes.

SOCRATES: My criterion for calling two skills 'distinct' is that the objects of knowledge in the one field should be different from those in the other. Is that your criterion too?

e   ION: Yes.

SOCRATES: For, presumably, if we were to find some field of knowledge that covered the same things, in what respect would we say the one skill is different from the other, when we would be able to know the same things from both of them? For instance, I know that these fingers of mine are five, and you know the same about them as I do. And if I were to ask you whether you and I know the same by virtue of the same skill, that of numbers, or by a different one, you, no doubt, would say, 'by the same'.

ION: Yes.

538a   SOCRATES: So give the answer to the question I was going to ask you just now. Is it your view that, in the case of all skills, we necessarily know the same things by the same skill, but different things by a different skill? But if the skill *is* different, so too must be the things we know.

ION: Yes, that's my view, Socrates.

SOCRATES: Then anyone who does not possess a given skill will not be able to have a good knowledge of the words or deeds that lie within its province?

ION: True.

b   SOCRATES: So in the case of the lines you quoted, will it be you or a charioteer who knows better whether Homer puts the matter well or not?

ION: A charioteer.

SOCRATES: Presumably because you are a rhapsode, not a charioteer.

ION: Yes.

SOCRATES: And the skill of a rhapsode is different from that of a charioteer?

ION: Yes.

SOCRATES: So then, if it is different, it is also a knowledge of different objects.

ION: Yes.

SOCRATES: So what about Homer's description of how Hecamede, Nestor's mistress, gives a potion to the wounded Machaon to drink? He puts it more or less like this:

c

'. . . of Pramneian wine,' he says, 'and over it
He grated the cheese of a goat, with a grater of bronze,
And then an onion as relish for the drink.'[1]

Is it the business of a doctor's skill to decide whether Homer describes this scene correctly, or of a rhapsode's?

ION: A doctor's.

SOCRATES: And what about when Homer says,

'She went down deep like a plummet,
which on the horn of an ox of the field
speeds to bring pain to the ravenous fishes.'?[2]

d

Are we to assert that it is more the business of a fisherman's skill, or of that of a rhapsode, to assess what he says, and whether he says it well or not?

ION: Obviously, Socrates, it's the business of the fisherman's.

SOCRATES: Look – if you were the questioner, and if you were to ask me this: 'So then, Socrates, now that you are finding in Homer, in the case of each of these skills, passages appropriate for it to judge – come on now, find me some for the prophet and *his* skill: what sort of passages are appropriate for *him* to distinguish as well or ill composed?' Look, what a true and simple answer I'm going to give you! In the *Odyssey*, Homer relates such matters often enough, as for instance when the prophet of Melampus' house, Theoclymenus, says to the suitors:

e

'You blessed fellows, what affliction is this you suffer?
Your heads and faces and limbs below are shrouded in night,
There's a blaze of lamentation, and your cheeks are streaked
with tears;
The porch is full, the hall is full, of spirits
Hastening to Erebus beneath the gloom. The sun has been
Annihilated from the heavens, and an evil mist has come
billowing abroad.'[3]

539a

b

1. *Iliad* XI, 639–40, the second part of the second line being replaced largely by the second part of 630. For Nestor see p. 59, n. 1. Machaon was a doctor in the Greek army. 'Pramneian' wine had a reputation for being salutiferous, but we do not know its place of production; *Republic* 405e–406a.
2. *Iliad* XXIV, 80–82. The passage is a brief simile describing the swift plunge of Iris, goddess of the rainbow, into the sea on an errand from Zeus. The details of the fishing-tackle are obscure; the horn may serve to protect the line.
3. *Odyssey* XX, 351–7 (minus 354), and with *daimonioi* ('blessed', ironically) instead of

And not only there, but in the *Iliad* too, for example in the battle before the walls. The passage runs:

> 'For as they pressed to pass across, there came a bird upon them,
> An eagle that flies on high, constraining the host on the left,
c> Carrying in its claws a monstrous blood-red snake,
> Alive and writhing in resistance still, not yet relinquishing its lust to fight.
> For back it bent and struck its captor on the breast
> Beside the neck, who racked with pain let it drop away
> Towards the ground, and cast it to the middle of the crowd,
d> And shrieking loudly flew away upon the rushing wind.'[1]

My claim will be that it's these and similar sequences which are the proper business of the prophet to scrutinize and judge.

ION: And you're quite right, Socrates.

SOCRATES: And you're quite right too, Ion. Now, I picked out for you, both from the *Odyssey* and from the *Iliad*, the sort of thing that concerns
e the prophet, the doctor and the fisherman. So you do the same: you have a closer acquaintance with Homer's works than I have, so you, Ion, pick out for me the sort of thing which concerns the rhapsode and the rhapsode's skill, and which the rhapsode properly examines and judges better than the rest of us.

ION: I maintain he judges *everything*, Socrates.

SOCRATES: Oh no, you don't maintain it's *everything*, Ion. Or are you as forgetful as that? Yet it would hardly do for someone who's a rhapsode to be forgetful!

540a ION: What on earth am I forgetting?

SOCRATES: Don't you remember you asserted that the skill of a rhapsode is different from that of a charioteer?

ION: I remember.

SOCRATES: So you agree that, by virtue of being different, it'll know different things?

ION: Yes.

SOCRATES: So on your argument the skill of a rhapsode will not know everything, nor will the rhapsode either.

ION: *That* sort of thing being the exception, Socrates.

'wretches' (*deiloi*) in 351. Erebus was a dark region between earth and the place of departed spirits, Hades. Theoclymenus claimed descent from Melampus, a mythical prophet; here he rebukes the suitors of Penelope, Odysseus' wife, for mocking Telemachus, Odysseus' son.

1. *Iliad* XII, 200–207: a portent appears to the Trojans as they ponder their next move.

SOCRATES: By 'that sort of thing' you mean more or less the things b
that belong to the other skills. But if not 'everything', exactly what sort
of thing *will* he know?

ION: What may suitably be said by a man, I reckon, and the sort of
thing suitably said by a woman; the sort suitable for a slave to say, and
the sort suitable for a freeman; and the sort of thing suitable in the mouth
of a ruler, and the sort suitable in that of a subject.

SOCRATES: You mean that a rhapsode will know better than a steersman what sort of thing is appropriately said by someone in charge of a
ship tossed around in a storm at sea?

ION: Oh no. That, the steersman knows better.

SOCRATES: Then again, will a rhapsode know better than a doctor what c
sort of thing is appropriately said by someone in charge of a sick person?

ION: No, not that, either.

SOCRATES: Do you mean he'll know what is appropriate for a slave?

ION: Yes.

SOCRATES: Take a slave who is a cowherd, for example, and is calming
down his cows when they are provoked. Will a rhapsode, and not a cowherd, know what it is appropriate for him to say?

ION: Certainly not.

SOCRATES: Then will he know what it is appropriate for a spinning-
woman to say about working wool?

ION: No. d

SOCRATES: Then will he know what is appropriate in the mouth of
someone who's a general, when he is exhorting his troops?

ION: Oh yes, a rhapsode would know that sort of thing.

SOCRATES: So, the skill of a rhapsode is that of a general, is it?

ION: Well, at all events, *I* would know what it is appropriate for a
general to say.

SOCRATES: Perhaps that's because you're into generalship too, Ion.
And if you were into horsemanship as well as playing the lyre, you would
recognize when a horse was handled well and when badly. But suppose e
my question to you were, 'By which skill do you recognize a well-handled
horse, Ion? By the one which makes you a horseman, or by the one which
makes you a player of the lyre?' How would you answer me?

ION: I'd answer, by the one that makes me a horseman.

SOCRATES: So, if you were picking out the good lyre-player too, you'd
admit that you did so by virtue of the skill that makes you a lyre-player,
not by the one that makes you a horseman.

ION: Yes.

SOCRATES: And when you make a judgement about military matters, do you judge in virtue of your skill in generalship, or in virtue of the skill that makes you a good rhapsode?

ION: There's no difference, so far as I can see.

541a   SOCRATES: No difference? How on earth can you say that? Are you saying that the skill of a rhapsode and the skill of a general are one skill, or two?

ION: One, I think.

SOCRATES: So, anyone who's a good rhapsode is in fact a good general too?

ION: Certainly, Socrates.

SOCRATES: So too, then, anyone who is in fact a good general is also a good rhapsode?

ION: No, that's not my view.

SOCRATES: Yet it *is* your view that anyone who's a good rhapsode is b also a good general?

ION: Oh, indeed.

SOCRATES: Now then, are you, as a rhapsode, the best among the Greeks?

ION: By a long chalk, Socrates.

SOCRATES: So, as a general too, are you the best among the Greeks?

ION: Have no doubt of it, Socrates; that too I learnt from the works of Homer.

SOCRATES: Well then, in the name of the gods, Ion, since you are the best among the Greeks at both activities, at being a general and at being a rhapsode, why do you traipse round[1] them as a rhapsode, but not as a c general? Or is it your view that the Greeks are in sore need of a rhapsode crowned with a golden crown, but have no need of a general at all?

ION: That's because our city, Socrates, is ruled by you Athenians,[2] and is under your generals, and a general of our own is not needed; and apart from that, your city and Sparta would hardly elect me as one, since you reckon you are good enough at it yourselves.

SOCRATES: My splendid Ion, you know Apollodorus of Cyzicus,[3] don't you?

ION: And what sort of person might *he* be?

SOCRATES: He's someone whom the Athenians have often elected as d their general, foreigner though he is; and Athens also appoints to general-

---

1. 'Traipse round': in Greek, *periiōn*.

2. This remark may entail that the dramatic date of the *Ion* falls before 412, the year in which Ephesus revolted from Athenian control. The references to Phanosthenes and Heraclides a little below may therefore be anachronisms: see p. 65 n. 1.

3. Apollodorus is not otherwise known.

ships and the other posts Phanosthenes of Andros and Heraclides of Clazo-
menae,[1] even though they are foreigners, because they have demonstrated
their merit. So, won't Ion of Ephesus, if he is thought to have merit, be
elected and honoured? Come on now, weren't you Ephesians originally
Athenians,[2] and isn't the city of Ephesus second to none? But really, Ion, e
if there is truth in your claim that it is thanks to skill and knowledge that
you have the ability to praise Homer, you're not playing fair with me.
You assure me that you know a great many fine things about him, and
you undertake to give an exhibition[3] of them. But you're deceiving me,
and you're nowhere near giving an exhibition. You're not even willing to
tell me what these objects of your expertise are, despite my repeated
requests. You're a proper Proteus:[4] you go twisting high and low and take
every shape under the sun, until at last you've escaped my clutches and
popped up as a general, so as to avoid displaying your terrific wisdom   542a
about Homer. So, if you do have skill, and as I remarked just now, your
promise of an exhibition is just a trick on me, you're not playing fair.
However, if you do not possess skill, but it is because of divine dispensation and because you are possessed by Homer that you say a lot of fine
things about that poet, in a state of ignorance, as I said was your condition,
then you are *not* unfair. So, choose which alternative you prefer: to have
us think of you as an unfair fellow, or as a divine one?

ION: There's a lot of difference, Socrates: it's a much finer thing to be   b
thought divine.

SOCRATES: Well then, let's grant you this finer status in our eyes, Ion:
as a eulogist of Homer you are not skilled, but divine.

1. Both these persons were probably granted Athenian citizenship in the last few years of
the fifth century; for details, see Moore's article, pp. 427–8.

2. Ephesus was founded by Androclus, son of Codrus, an early Athenian king.

3. Cf. p. 50, with notes.

4. A minor god of the sea, reputed to have knowledge of the future, which he was reluctant
to divulge; would-be questioners had to catch him first, whereupon he would assume many
different shapes (e.g. of animals) in order to escape and avoid the necessity of answering; but
if held firmly and forced to resume his true shape, he would prophesy the truth: see *Odyssey*
IV, 382 ff, and cf. *Euthydemus* 288b–c.

LACHES

INTRODUCTION TO *LACHES*

The *Laches* is an entertaining and thought-provoking piece of philosophical drama.[1] It combines lively depiction of character, which occasionally comes close to caricature, with serious discussion of philosophical issues. However, this very combination poses a fundamental problem of interpretation: what is the *relation* between the philosophical and the dramatic elements?

First, a summary of the plot:

Two elderly Athenians, Lysimachus and Melesias, have invited their friends, the distinguished generals Nicias and Laches, to join them in watching a display of military training given by a reputed expert, Stesilaus. Feeling that their own education was neglected, Lysimachus and Melesias are anxious to provide their sons with the opportunities and advantages they themselves missed,[2] and they would like to know whether the generals think the course offered by Stesilaus is worthwhile. They would also be grateful for any advice on education which Nicias and Laches are able to give. Laches is surprised that he and Nicias have been preferred to Socrates, who is something of an authority on educational matters and happens to have been standing near them watching the display. It appears, moreover, that Socrates is the son of an old friend of Lysimachus and so can be relied upon to be sympathetic to his problem. Socrates is indeed happy to join in the discussion, but characteristically suggests that the older and more experienced men should give their view first. Nicias is strongly in favour of professional instruction, but his colleague has serious doubts and is inclined to think that it does more harm than good.

Lysimachus now turns to Socrates, who refuses to be drawn into giving a casting vote: he feels that the real need is for an *expert* opinion, and that

1. No firm date of composition can be established, and there is no consensus on its philosophical relationship to other dialogues. There is, however, general agreement that it is among Plato's earlier works. The dramatic date is *c.* 420. It must fall between 424, the battle of Delium (181b), and 418, the death of Laches at Mantinea. There is no immediate reference to a state of war, hence it is probable that the *Laches* is set in the uneasy peace of 421–418, which Nicias had negotiated on the Athenian side, and which formed an armistice in the Peloponnesian War (431–404). A useful summary of scholarly opinion on the dramatic date will be found in Hoerber, pp. 95–6.

2. According to *Meno* 94a, c, both Lysimachus and Melesias received an excellent education: perhaps what was missing was the active support and interest of their parents; cf. 179c.

the two generals must each prove their qualification to the title before offering any further advice. Military training is a kind of education, so it is in the latter that they must demonstrate their expertise. The aim of education, Socrates argues, is to instil goodness (*aretē*), and it follows that the mark of an educational expert will be his ability to give an account of goodness and 'say what it is'. He therefore suggests that they prove their fitness to offer advice by giving such an account, if not of goodness itself, at least of bravery (*andreia*), the part of goodness which is most relevant to military training.

Laches takes up the challenge with a confidence that betrays his philosophical inexperience. He is a military man and naturally thinks in military terms: for him it is the mark of a brave man to stand his ground and fight. Socrates agrees, but gently explains that this is not the kind of answer he had expected. Bravery is not confined to the battlefield, and there are many other examples which one could choose to illustrate what it means to call someone brave. To give an *account*, however, is a matter of examining all these different examples and uncovering in them the common element that makes them all examples of bravery.

Laches takes the point and now suggests that bravery is endurance (*karteria*). This is the kind of answer for which Socrates has been looking, but it seems to be inadequate. There must be some distinction, Socrates argues, between the mere stubbornness of the fool and the wise man's rationally determined endurance. However, as the discussion proceeds, both Socrates and Laches find themselves forced to admit that a man who is foolish can act more bravely than a man who is wise. This is a serious difficulty, as it contradicts their basic conviction that ignorance is always bad, whereas bravery and wisdom are always good. They see no way to reconcile the conflict and are in a state of confusion (*aporia*),[1] totally at a loss how to proceed. Can Nicias help?

Nicias believes he can. He is an intellectual. Unlike Laches, he is familiar with philosophical discussions, and his approach is altogether more sophisticated. This does nothing to endear him to his colleague, who is scornful of what he regards as academic pretensions, and it takes all Socrates' tact to avoid a premature end to the debate. What so irritates Laches is Nicias' view that bravery is a special kind of knowledge. If true, as Socrates points out, this would mean that it is a mistake to say, as we often do, that animals and children are brave, because they cannot in the strictest sense *know* anything. Without pressing the point, however, he turns the discussion to inquire more deeply into the kind of knowledge that bravery might be, and another difficulty emerges. Nicias says that

1. See p. 30.

bravery is 'the knowledge of what is fearful or encouraging', and in the
final argument (197e–199e) Socrates takes him through the stages of a
proof that this knowledge is equivalent to the knowledge of good and evil.
He then points out that the knowledge of good and evil is too wide a
definition for bravery alone. If virtue is knowledge, Nicias has defined not
bravery but goodness itself, of which bravery was said to be only a part.

Nicias remains convinced that his account is not far from the truth, but
as neither he nor his companions can suggest how to proceed, the discussion draws to a close leaving the issue unresolved. In the circumstances,
Socrates feels unable to accept an invitation to act as teacher to the sons
of Lysimachus and Melesias and suggests that they look for a *real* expert,
so that they may all discover where they have gone wrong.

As this summary reveals, the *Laches* is a skilful combination of the
dramatic and the philosophical. How are we to understand the work as a
whole? There have been three main answers.[1]

A. The first might be termed the *dramatic* interpretation.[2] At one time it
was not uncommon to study the *Laches* more as a piece of literature than
as a philosophical work in its own right. The dialogue was thought to
provide a useful and entertaining introduction to Socrates and his method
of argument, and there were hints of the contribution he had made to the
development of Greek ethical thought. Yet it seemed that the primary
purpose of the *Laches* was the defence and commemoration of a respected
friend and teacher. It was a dialogue about a philosopher rather than
itself a significant piece of philosophy; it was the work of a youthfully
enthusiastic Plato who had not yet settled to serious philosophical contemplation.

Three points could be made in defence of this judgement:

1. The *Laches* has a much more dramatic flavour than some of Plato's
other dialogues, particularly those thought to belong to a late stage of his
career. The characters are sketched firmly, and the twists and turns of the
conversation are skilfully presented. Among the more notable moments
are Lysimachus' recognition of Socrates as a friend of his family (180c–
181d); the humorous account of Stesilaus' embarrassment when serving

1. The following account makes no claim to originality, and as it is impossible in a short
introduction to do justice to all that has been written on the *Laches*, it should be taken as no
more than a general survey. Acknowledgement is due to all those whose work is cited in notes
and in the bibliography. For a view somewhat different from those discussed below, see Buford.

2. For examples of this view see J. Burnet, *Platonism* (Berkeley 1928), pp. 3–15; A. E.
Taylor, *Plato: The Man and His Work* (London 1926), p. 58; U. von Wilamowitz-Moellendorff,
Platon: Sein Leben und seine Werke (Berlin 1959), p. 141; cf. Croiset, p. 88, who calls the *Laches*
'une simple exposition de méthode'.

in the marines (183c–184b); and in the later pages, Socrates' tactful control of Laches' frustration and irritability (e.g. 196a–c). However, as Plato preferred the dialogue form to the systematic exposition of a treatise, the particular dramatic merits of the *Laches* are not in themselves incompatible with a purpose that is primarily philosophical.

2. Powerful tributes to Socrates' personal bravery and intellectual ability are woven into the conversation. There is indeed little doubt that Plato intended to arouse the reader's admiration for his teacher; but it does not follow that the *Laches* is primarily an apologetic work.

3. The *Laches* appears to be inconclusive. A problem is posed, but no solution is reached. This ought not, however, to damage the credibility of the dialogue as a work of serious philosophy, since a number of important issues are raised. In the course of the discussion distinctions are made between bravery and recklessness, and between 'technical' knowledge and knowledge of moral value.[1] There are also no fewer than three different accounts of bravery, the first of which is framed in terms of *behaviour* (190d–192b), the second in terms of a trait of *character* (192b–193d), and the third in terms of a special kind of *knowledge* (194c–196c). Moreover, the last of these accounts is shown by Socrates to be equivalent to a definition of goodness as a whole (*sumpasa aretē*), and as this was originally to be the goal of the discussion (190b), it might be argued that the *Laches* is not so inconclusive after all. Neither of the two remaining interpretations (B and C below) regard the apparently aporetic conclusion as a problem: it is taken to be an invitation for the reader to use the material in the dialogue to make the next moves in the argument for himself.

B. The second interpretation is the *philosophical* one. On this view drama is secondary to philosophy. The first half of the dialogue is seen as no more than an attractive backdrop to an important philosophical debate, namely the attempt to define bravery (189d ff.), and hence critical attention is concentrated upon the two key passages in which the generals' rival definitions are developed, Laches' in terms of a trait of character (192b–193d), and Nicias' in terms of a special kind of knowledge (197e–199e). It is at once apparent that this interpretation is open to the objection that by failing to take account of what it sees as a purely introductory section it makes no sense of the dialogue as a whole.[2] In reply, however, it could be said that an examination of the debate about bravery in isolation might at least lead to a proper understanding of the philosophical point Plato

1. The concepts of bravery and recklessness or daring are distinguished at 184b and 196e–197d. For the kinds of knowledge see 194c–196c.

2. Thus Kohak, p. 123, protests against any view which entails a 'twelve-page preface introducing a seven-page dialogue'.

intended to make in writing the *Laches*. On the basis of the two key passages noted above it has often been suggested that Socrates' conversation with Laches is simply a device to prepare the reader for the more sophisticated account of bravery given by Nicias, and that it is this last definition that the *Laches* is intended to endorse. The dialogue is thus held to provide an intellectualist account of bravery and to raise, for perhaps the first time, the problem of the unity of the virtues.¹ However, it seems that this is not the only, or even the best, way in which these passages can be understood.²

For consider first the discussion of Laches' second account of bravery (192b–193d). Laches believes that bravery is a trait of character, namely endurance; but this definition soon proves to be inadequate, since it permits the unacceptable conclusion that even foolhardy stubbornness is to be included under the heading of bravery. In order to overcome the problem Socrates introduces the qualification that bravery is endurance *with wisdom*, but this only leads to a further problem: he finds he can produce examples in which the conditions of endurance and wisdom appear to have been fulfilled, but in which Laches is adamant that there is no question of bravery being shown. It seems that the definition is too wide, but without waiting to reflect on that possibility, Socrates continues to produce examples for Laches to consider. In these new examples the more foolish of two people appears to be the braver, and Socrates and Laches find that they are now trying to hold three contradictory propositions:

(a) Bravery is good
(b) Endurance with foolishness is bad
(c) Endurance with foolishness is bravery.

It has often been suggested that the reader is to respond to the problem by rejecting the current definition, namely that bravery is endurance with wisdom, *and* Laches' original definition, namely that bravery is simply endurance. However, this would be to misunderstand the nature of the problem. The difficulty arises not from the element of endurance, but from that of wisdom. How can it be that a fool can be braver than a wise man? That seems to be the equivalent of saying that a bad man is better than a good man. The discussion, therefore, has shown that there is a problem for any account of bravery which has a cognitive element; it has *not* shown that such an account cannot contain any reference to endurance

1. See pp. 22–3.

2. For examples of this view see Irwin and Vicaire; also G. Grote, *Plato and the Other Companions of Socrates* (London 1885), vol. 2, p. 149; cf. C. Ritter, *Platon: Sein Leben, seine Schriften, seine Lehre* (Munich 1910), vol. 2, pp. 295–7, and H. Raeder, *Platons Philosophische Entwickelung* (Leipzig 1905), p. 210. For a contrasting view of the dialogue's purpose see, for example, E. Horneffer, *Platon gegen Sokrates* (Leipzig 1904), p. 35 ff.

or a trait of character. Laches' insight is never explicitly rejected in the dialogue itself, and indeed Socrates continues to treat it as a possible basis for further discussion (194a).

Secondly, to turn to the final argument against Nicias' account (197e–199e),[1] there can be no intellectualist account of bravery unless the problem raised by the discussion of Laches' revised second account (endurance with wisdom) is solved. Nicias, however, succeeds in overcoming the difficulty by insisting on a greater precision in the use of terms (194c–196c; cf. 197a–b). He clears the way for his own definition by distinguishing between different *kinds* of knowledge, technical knowledge and knowledge of moral value. Yet, even so, he faces a problem. Socrates shows him that this new definition is equivalent to saying that bravery is the knowledge of good and evil, and hence they now find themselves in their turn trying to hold three contradictory propositions:

(a) Bravery is a *part* of goodness
(b) Bravery is the knowledge of good and evil
(c) The knowledge of good and evil is *goodness*.

The suggestion has often been made that the reader is intended to reject (a) and reconcile (b) and (c) by accepting the notion of the unity of the virtues. However, it might be objected that Socrates effectively rules out (b) when he claims that Nicias has *failed* to find the definition of bravery. Moreover, at the conclusion of the discussion both he and Nicias seem to reaffirm their support for (a). It has been argued in defence that Nicias' definition, 'bravery is knowledge of what is fearful and of what is encouraging', is based on a remark of Socrates (194d); but it is unreasonable to maintain that Plato could not have intended to modify any view which he chose to label as Socrates' own, particularly when, as in the present case, that view seems to be criticized by the character of Socrates himself.

It seems that the two key philosophical passages, considered in themselves, do not suggest any single solution to the problem of defining bravery; instead there is a range of possibilities. On the one hand, the *Laches* may be intended to support the notion of the unity of the virtues, or at least the weaker claim that one cannot have one virtue unless one has them all; on the other hand, there may be a suggestion of some account which differs from the intellectualist account offered by Nicias, or simply an inconclusive debate. The philosophical interpretation provides no means of deciding between these options, and we are brought back to the criticism that it fails to make sense of the dialogue as a whole. Is there any

1. Vlastos, pp. 266–9, discusses this passage in detail and argues for a conclusion different from that suggested below; cf. Irwin, pp. 88–9, with notes.

other way of looking at the *Laches* which might shed some light on Plato's intentions?

C. The third interpretation is the *philosophico-dramatic* one. This is an attempt to see the dialogue as a unified whole. The *Laches* is regarded as 'a balanced work of art, in which character and action illuminate the thought, and the thought is in turn a judgement on the characters'.¹ On this view critical study of the key philosophical passages is combined with an understanding of the dialogue which depends on the structure of the work and the role of the leading characters. Those who have studied the *Laches* in this way suggest that the dialogue rejects an account of bravery in terms of endurance alone, and an account in terms of knowledge alone, in order to point the reader towards a compromise in which bravery is defined in terms of knowledge *and* endurance. Such a solution to the problem is close to the revised version of Laches' second account, namely that bravery is endurance with wisdom; and although this definition is criticized in the dialogue itself, the suggestion that it is Plato's preferred solution can be supported from both the philosophical and the dramatic points of view.

Firstly, if we recall the results of the discussion of the key philosophical passages, we will see that there is nothing in the argumentation of the *Laches* which explicitly excludes the suggested compromise definition. It was not clear that the dialogue endorsed Nicias' intellectualist account, nor that it revealed any difficulty in regarding endurance as at least a necessary condition for bravery. Moreover, we saw that the problem which Socrates and Laches encountered over their definition in terms of endurance with wisdom was one which Nicias overcame in order to validate his own account of bravery as a special kind of knowledge. Nicias was able to draw a distinction between technical knowledge and knowledge of moral value, and it was by failing to note this distinction that Socrates and Laches had gone astray. It seemed, for example, that they were committed to the paradox that a fool could be braver than a wise man; but in fact they need only have argued that a (technical) novice could indeed be braver than a (technical) expert if the qualification 'with wisdom' were interpreted as 'provided he has a correct understanding of the moral nature and consequences of his action', and not as referring merely to technical competence. Could it not be, therefore, that Plato intended the reader to see the relevance of Nicias' distinction and so come to the view that bravery might be endurance with the knowledge of good and evil?

1. O'Brien (1963), p. 135. For other examples of this view, see Hoerber and Santas (1969).

Secondly, as a dramatic work, the *Laches* is said to fall into two balanced halves, in each of which are opposed two contrasting points of view:[1]

1. In the first half the generals tackle Lysimachus' question about the value of military training. Nicias offers what could be termed an intellectualist answer (181d–182d), and puts his emphasis on the advantages to be gained from the possession of knowledge. He refers in passing to his belief that the training promotes bravery, but otherwise confines his attention to commending the professional and 'scientific' approach to warfare. Laches then replies with a weak attempt to belittle the practical benefits of which his colleague has spoken (182d–184c), but astutely points out that there is more to a successful soldier than a knowledge of the art of war. Military training cannot promote bravery, he asserts, it can only inspire confidence, and without the right *temperament* such confidence in one's own expertise is potentially dangerous.

2. The conflicting attitudes of Nicias and Laches are picked up again in the second half of the dialogue, where Socrates is pursuing a definition of bravery. This time it is Laches who goes first. Guided by Socrates, he makes a creditable attempt at a definition, despite a false start which was caused by his inexperience in learned debate. As he begins with the belief that bravery is primarily a matter of sticking to one's guns, Laches is drawn to describe it in terms of a trait of *character*, a kind of endurance (*karteria*), but is prepared to concede that there could also be an element of wisdom involved. Nicias, however, believes bravery must be more than recklessness or the willingness to take risks. He is far more interested in the cognitive aspect, which is for him the distinguishing mark of a virtue, and defines bravery as a special kind of *knowledge*.

The two views opposed in both halves of the dialogue reflect traits within the personalities of the two generals. Each, it is argued, typifies the strengths and weaknesses of the position he adopts: Plato has provided a commentary on the debate through the characters of the participants.[2]

Laches is clearly brave and determined as a soldier, but his bravery is confined to action: he is ready to abandon the intellectual discussion when the going becomes hard. Nicias, in contrast, is a thoughtful and intelligent man, perfectly at home with academic conversation and resolved to carry on the inquiry to the end. His contemporaries, however, were aware that this resolution did not extend beyond his intellectual pursuits. His record as a general reveals a tendency to caution which is often excessive, and in the *Laches* there seem to be several veiled anachronistic references to the demise of the Sicilian expedition in 413, when Nicias' failure to retreat

1. See in particular Hoerber, p. 98 f., and O'Brien (1963), pp. 139–40.
2. See O'Brien (1963), p. 141 ff.

quickly enough from the blockade of Syracuse brought an Athenian army to disaster.[1]

The ideal, of course, would be a man who could combine the strengths of both Nicias and Laches, a man such as Laches describes at the pivotal point of the dialogue as a 'true musician' whose words are in harmony with his actions (188d). Both generals are united in regarding the third main character, Socrates, as such a person. He is the perfect compromise, praised by Laches for his bravery in action and by Nicias for his wisdom in debate. The 'dramatic' interpretation, it is suggested, is to this extent correct: the *Laches* is in certain respects a eulogy of Socrates, for in the character of Socrates Plato offers a clue to solving the problem posed in the discussion. The inconclusive ending invites the reader to supply the missing piece of the jigsaw, and if it is to match Socrates' character, that piece must also be a combination of the strengths to be found in the definitions of both Nicias and Laches. Thus the structure of the work, together with the character sketches, is thought to point, independently of the philosophical arguments, to an account of bravery which combines both *endurance* and *knowledge*.[2]

Therefore, of the three ways in which our question of the relation of the dramatic and philosophical elements in the *Laches* has been answered – (A) dramatic, (B) philosophical and (C) philosophico-dramatic – (A) would not now generally be accepted for the reasons stated above, but both (B) and (C) are still strongly supported. It would seem, however, that (C) best fits an analysis of the philosophical sections, and also respects the artistic integrity of the dialogue.[3]

The differing interpretations have inevitably given rise to divergent opinions on the relationship between the *Laches* and other Platonic dialogues.[4] The dramatic interpretation (A) assumes that the *Laches* is an early work without direct relevance to the philosophical issues raised in the more mature studies. The philosophical interpretation (B) also favours an early date on the grounds that it reflects the thought of the historical Socrates, and is the point of departure for the more developed account of his views found in the *Protagoras* (349e–351b). There Socrates' partner in

1. See 195e and especially 198e–199a with p. 112 n. 1.

2. See 192d, 'wise endurance', i.e. a combination of the kind indicated above in the discussion of interpretation (B).

3. *Pace* Guthrie, p. 133 n. 1, who briefly dismisses this view.

4. A word of caution is needed here, for there is a danger in all these views that the philosophical relationship of the ideas expressed in various dialogues is being confused with the chronological order of composition. In the absence of a certain word on the purpose and intended audience of Plato's work, it cannot be assumed that whichever of two dialogues appears to contain the more developed philosophical theories is necessarily the later and more mature.

the discussion, the sophist Protagoras, denies that knowledge is sufficient for virtue and maintains that there are further requirements, namely the constitution of the people concerned, and the proper training of their characters. These additional elements will produce, in the case of bravery, the appropriate degree of *endurance* to avoid either inactivity or reckless-ness. Socrates attacks this position, arguing for the intellectualist defi-nition offered by Nicias in the *Laches*, and accepts the consequence that all the virtues must collapse into one undifferentiated virtue.

The philosophico-dramatic interpretation (C), however, has often been thought to place the *Laches* later than the *Protagoras* and to regard it as correcting the earlier work by advocating against Socrates a position closer to that of Protagoras.[1] On this view the *Laches* corresponds closely to Book IV of the *Republic*, where another account of bravery is found. In the *Republic* Plato develops the doctrine of the tripartite division of the soul. The human soul is said to be formed of three distinct parts: reason, spirit and appetite. Reason may conflict with appetite, and to prevail against appetite it must have the support of the spirit. Bravery consists in the alliance of reason and the spirited part against desire, and it is therefore defined in terms of both cognitive and non-cognitive elements.

The account of bravery found in the *Republic* and, according to the philosophico-dramatic interpretation, also in the *Laches*, is an advance on Socratic intellectualism in two main ways. First, it escapes from the paradoxical claim that all the virtues are really one; second, it allows for weakness of will (*akrasia*),[2] which the Socratic view cannot explain, by introducing the possibility of internal conflict between reason and appetite.

There is, however, at least one respect in which the *Laches* continues to share a difficulty with the Socratic account. In the *Laches* Socrates introduces a very broad concept of bravery,[3] namely that it is the virtue shown in pursuing a chosen course of action in the face of opposition, internal or external. This is an extension of the usual concept, and leads to the problem of how to distinguish bravery from self-control (*sōphro-sunē*), since resistance to certain desires, for example for food, would not generally be regarded as bravery. It is worth noting that, to avoid such problems, Aristotle confined bravery in the strict sense to the battlefield,

1. The *Protagoras seems* ignorant of the distinction between moral and technical knowledge drawn in the *Laches*, and this might be thought to offer some support for the later dating of the *Laches* relative to the *Protagoras*.

2. See pp. 27–8.

3. In his list of examples given in the course of the discussion of Laches' first definition, 190d–192b.

treating all other usages of the word as metaphorical, and similarly regarded self-control as displayed primarily in the checking of certain basic appetites.[1]

The *Laches* poses, as we have seen, a particular problem of interpretation: what is the relation between the philosophical and dramatic elements of the dialogue? This, however, is only one aspect of a more general problem which is fundamental to the way we think and talk about the world – the problem of the relation between drama and philosophy, science and art. We are accustomed to think of the artist and the scientist in quite different terms: their work seems to have different purposes, to use different kinds of language and to be assessed by different standards; but within the Platonic dialogues such polarization is less evident. Protagoras, for example, in the dialogue named after him, asks whether he should defend his view that virtue can be taught by a story or myth (*muthos*, not so narrow or pejorative a word in Greek), or by a reasoned exposition (*logos*), and both he and his audience clearly regard these as genuine alternatives. A philosophical drama, such as the *Laches*, will use both *logos* and *muthos* to achieve its purpose, blending reasoned argument and dramatic techniques in an appeal to both rational and intuitive faculties. It is, therefore, a challenge to the way in which we distinguish art and science. The *Laches* should make us think again about the nature of our language (not only verbal, but musical and graphic and indeed all other kinds), and prompt us to ask whether the technical language of science is really 'truer' or more valid than the imaginative and metaphorical language of art. It should also cause us to think about the purpose of artistic endeavour and consider whether art, like science, is not ultimately the pursuit of truth.

---

1. *Nicomachean Ethics* 1115a10–35 on bravery, and 1118a23–26 on self-control. It is well worth reading Aristotle's account of bravery alongside that of the *Laches*.

SUMMARY OF *LACHES*

A. *Education and the Value of Military Training*

[1] Has Military Training a Place in Higher Education?
[2] Laches Introduces Socrates to the Discussion
[3] Nicias on the Virtues of Military Training
[4] Laches on the Futility of Military Training
[5] The Need for Expert Advice: Are the Generals Qualified to Speak about Education?
[6] The Generals Agree to Cooperate with Socrates and Put Their Expertise to the Test

B. *An Inquiry into the Nature of Bravery*

[1] The Need to Define Bravery
[2] Laches' First Definition: To be Brave is to Stand and Fight
[3] Laches' Second Definition: Bravery is Endurance
[4] Impasse: Nicias is Asked to Help
[5] Nicias' Definition: Bravery is a Special Kind of Knowledge
[6] Implications of Nicias' Definition: Can Animals and Children be Brave?
[7] Nicias Has Defined Goodness, Not Bravery
[8] The Discussion Breaks Up: Socrates Suggests They All Have Much to Learn

LACHES

Speakers

SOCRATES

LYSIMACHUS: Son of the statesman Aristides. An
Athenian gentleman reputed to have been given the
best education his city could provide (*Meno* 94a).

MELESIAS: A friend of Lysimachus. Son of the
politician Thucydides (not to be confused with the
historian), but unable to follow his father's distinguished career. He was trained to be one of the
best wrestlers in Athens (*Meno* 94c), and is known
to have been a member of the oligarchic council set
up to rule the city in 411 (Thucydides VIII.86.9).

NICIAS: Son of Niceratus. A prominent Athenian politician who opposed the policies of the extreme democrats. Although frequently elected as general, his
record was marred by a disastrous defeat in Sicily in
413, which cost him his life.

LACHES: Son of Melanopus. An Athenian general
prominent in the Peloponnesian War until his death
in action at the battle of Mantinea in 418.

ARISTIDES: Son of Lysimachus. At the time of this
dialogue he was still a young boy. He is mentioned
in the *Theaetetus* (151a) and in the *Theages* (130a ff.)
as a pupil of Socrates who left his studies too early
and lapsed from his teacher's high standards.

LACHES

A. Education and the Value of Military Training

A[1]. Has Military Training a Place in Higher Education?

The main purpose of this first section is to set the scene and the subject of the dialogue. Lysimachus and Melesias have a problem: how are they to ensure that their sons will grow up to be good men and do well for themselves? They see the solution in some kind of higher education, perhaps including military training, and so seek the advice of two generals, Nicias and Laches.

To be good (agathos) a man had to possess goodness (aretē), which was identified with a set of virtues (aretai), including bravery (andreia): cf. 198a. Lysimachus assumes (a) that these virtues can be taught, or at least that education is necessary to acquire or develop them, and (b) that the generals are suitable men to advise him on the value of military training, being experienced soldiers and fellow parents. Socrates is to question both these assumptions as the dialogue proceeds.

LYSIMACHUS: Well, Nicias and Laches, you have watched our man at his military training,[1] and since my friend Melesias and I didn't explain at the time our reason for asking you to come and watch him with us, we'll explain it now. In your case, we believe we ought to be perfectly frank. There are, you see, some people who scoff at men like yourselves, and if someone asks for advice, they won't say what they really believe. They aim at what they think the person consulting them wants to hear, and offer him something quite different from their real opinion. But you, we thought, were not only capable of forming an opinion, but having done so would speak your minds straightforwardly: that's why we invited you along to ask your advice on the problem we're now going to put to you.

This is all by way of a long preamble to the following problem. The two boys here are our sons: this is Melesias' son, who is called Thucydides after his grandfather, and this is mine, also named after his grandfather, my father – we call him Aristides.[2] Now, we have decided to take these

178a

b

179a

1. 'Military training' (*hoplomachia*), literally 'fighting in armour': simulated combat with sword, spear and shield to develop skill, strength and agility. On Greek arms and armour, and warfare in general, see A. M. Snodgrass, *Arms and Armour of the Greeks* (Ithaca, N.Y., 1967) and J. K. Anderson, *Military Theory and Practice in the Age of Xenophon* (Berkeley 1970).

2. The Greeks did not have surnames, but family connections were reflected in the choice of name and it was common practice, in Athens at least, for a boy to be called after his grandfather.

boys in hand, in so far as we possibly can, and not – as most parents do when their children have reached their teens – let them do whatever they want; now is the time to start doing our utmost to take care of them. Well,

b we knew that you both had sons too, and it occurred to us that you, if anyone, would have been concerned about the kind of education which would make first-rate men of them: but if by any chance you don't happen to have given any thought to such a question, may we remind you that it isn't something you should neglect, and invite you to join us in arranging some way to take care of our children?

Now, you must let us tell you, Nicias and Laches, what made us reach this decision, even if it is a slightly long story. The fact is, you see, that Melesias here and I are in the habit of having dinner together, and the

c boys dine with us. Well now, as I said to begin with, we'll be perfectly frank with you. We can each tell these young men a great many stories about our own fathers' impressive record of wartime and peacetime achievements in the administration of the allied cities and the government at home;[1] but neither of us can tell them about anything we've achieved ourselves. So, of course, we feel ashamed that the boys should realize this, and we blame our fathers for allowing us to run wild once we became

d teenagers, while they were busy with other people's affairs.[2] We explain all this to the boys, telling them that if they fail to take themselves in hand, and ignore our advice, they'll be complete nonentities; on the other hand, if they do take care of themselves, they'll probably turn out to be worthy of their names.

They say, in fact, that they will do as they're told; so we're now considering what discipline or occupation would make the best possible men of

e them. Someone suggested this discipline to us, on the grounds that for a young man to undertake military training is a fine thing. He spoke highly of the man you've just seen giving the display, and urged us to watch him in action. So we decided that we should go and see the man for ourselves and take you along too, partly so that you could watch him with us, and partly also so that you could share our discussion – if you're willing – on the care of our sons.

180a   That's the problem we wanted to share with you. Now it's up to you to give us your advice – both on this particular discipline, as to whether or not you think one ought to study it; and on others, if there's any other

1. Thucydides (not to be confused with the historian, who may have been a relation) was the leading opponent of Pericles in the mid fifth century. Aristides, renowned for his honesty and plain dealing, was a general and statesman prominent in the wars against the Persians (490–479), and architect of the Delian league (an anti-Persian alliance of Greek cities formed in 478 and administered from the sacred island of Delos).

2. Cf. p. 69 n. 2.

discipline or activity you can recommend for a young man – and to tell us
what you'll do about sharing our discussion.

A[2]. Laches Introduces Socrates to the Discussion

*The generals willingly agree to help Lysimachus and Melesias. Laches, noticing
Socrates close by, introduces him as something of an expert on education, a
view which Nicias confirms. His credentials are excellent: not only has he
considerable experience of higher education in various forms, but he is also an
outstandingly brave man in his own right. Moreover, it transpires that Socrates
is under an obligation to help out, as his father was a close friend of Lysimachus.
This passage (cf. A(6)) can be read purely as a defence of Socrates against the
kind of criticism which led to his execution (see pp. 33–4). Adherents of the
philosophico-dramatic interpretation treat it as serving to establish Socrates as
a man who combines moral worth with intellectual ability, in contrast to Nicias
and Laches who are each depicted as relatively one-sided characters. The
relation of these character sketches to the purpose of the dialogue is discussed on
p. 75ff. It is typical of Socrates' philosophical approach, as revealed by Plato,
that he should plead ignorance of the matter in question and invite the others to
state their opinions first.*

NICIAS: I certainly have nothing but praise for what you intend to do,
Lysimachus and Melesias, and I'm quite prepared to join you; I may say
the same, I think, for Laches here?

LACHES: Yes, you're quite right, Nicias. The remark Lysimachus   b
made just now about his father and Melesias' father was very apposite, in
my opinion, not only to their situation, but to ours and that of everyone
involved in affairs of state. As he says, it's almost always the case, whether
it's a question of their children or whatever else it might be, that their
private affairs are handled carelessly and neglected. So in that respect I
can agree with you, Lysimachus; but I'm surprised that you're asking *us*
for advice on your sons' education and you aren't asking Socrates here: c
because, in the first place, he comes from your own township,[1] and, in
the second, he always spends his time in places where one might find the
kind of thing you're in search of for the children – some creditable discipline or pursuit.

LYSIMACHUS: Do you mean to say that Socrates here has taken an
interest in this kind of thing, Laches?

LACHES: Yes, he certainly has, Lysimachus.

NICIAS: I might perhaps be in as good a position as Laches to vouch

1. Township, Greek *dēmos*: originally a natural village, but became the smallest political
division of Attica under the reforms of Cleisthenes (late sixth century).

for that. As a matter of fact, quite recently I myself was introduced by him
d to a music-teacher for my son – a student of Agathocles called Damon,[1] not
only a very accomplished musician, but all in all as valuable a companion
for children of that age as one could hope for.

LYSIMACHUS: Socrates, and Nicias and Laches, people of my age really
can't keep in touch with the younger generation any more, we just potter
around at home most of the time feeling our age. But Socrates, son of
Sophroniscus, if you can also give some good advice to this man from your
e home town, you ought to do so. And it's only right that you should, when
in fact you're a friend of the family through your father. Your father and
I, you know, were always close friends, and to the day he died we never
had an argument.

In fact, I did remember one thing while these gentlemen were talking
just now: when the boys are discussing things together at home, they often
mention someone called Socrates and speak very highly of him, but I
181a never asked them if they meant Sophroniscus' son. Well now, boys, tell
me, is this the Socrates you were for ever talking about?

ARISTIDES: Certainly, he's the one, father.

LYSIMACHUS: By all that's wonderful,[2] Socrates, it's good to know
you're a credit to your father – he was a fine man[3] – and also to discover
that we'll both be treating each other's family affairs as our own!

LACHES: What's more, Lysimachus, you mustn't let him slip away.
I've seen him in a quite different context proving a credit not just to his
b father, but also to his country. He marched back with me in the retreat
from Delium[4] and, I assure you, had the rest of the troops been prepared
to follow his example, our city would now have its head held high and
would never have taken such a terrible fall.[5]

LYSIMACHUS: When your conduct wins the praise of men of such
authority, this is praise indeed, Socrates! It's a joy to hear, let me tell you.
I'm delighted to know you're so well respected and I'd like you for your
c part to think of me as one of your closest friends. You really ought to have
come calling on us before now, you know; you should have made yourself

---

1. Agathocles was a sophist (see p. 94 n. 1) of whom nothing is known. Damon was a major
early Greek writer on musical theory: he was known for an interest in the moral and social
effects of musical modes (see 188d and p. 96 n. 3).

2. The Greek has 'By Hera!', the wife of Zeus and goddess of marriage and birth.

3. καὶ ἄλλως omitted (Badham).

4. In 424 the Boeotians decisively beat the Athenians at Delium, thus ending an ambitious
attempt to overthrow the Boeotian government. The story is told by Thucydides IV. 91–6.

5. It is impossible in English to render the extended pun in this passage on the different
senses of the Greek orthos, 'upright' or 'straight' ('head held high'), and its related verba
meaning 'raise up', 'restore' or 'be a credit to'.

LACHES

at home with us, as you had every right to. But, as it is, starting from today, now we've recognized each other, you must make a point of taking us into your confidence and get to know us and these youngsters of ours, and then you and they can continue our friendship. However, I'm sure you'll see to that and we'll remind you about it later; but what do you say about the problem we had started to tackle? What do you think? Is it a suitable discipline for these young men or not – doing some military training, I mean?

SOCRATES: Well, Lysimachus, on that matter I'll certainly try to give you any advice I can, and I'll also try to do everything you invite me to d
do. But I think it's only right that since I'm younger than these gentlemen and rather inexperienced in the field, I should listen to what they have to say first and learn from them. Then, if I have anything else to add to what they've said, I should explain my position and try to convince you and our friends here. Well now, Nicias, won't one of you start us off?

A[3]. Nicias on the Virtues of Military Training

Nicias makes a number of points in favour of military training, which he believes (a) promotes physical fitness, (b) prepares a man for the military duties of a citizen, (c) gives one the edge over unskilled opponents, (d) promotes an interest in military science, (e) makes one braver, and (f) encourages a soldierly appearance.

Nicias emerges as a thoughtful and intelligent man. His case is primarily theoretical, and is indicative of the growing professionalism which entered Greek warfare in the latter part of the fifth century. In relation to the rest of the dialogue, the most significant point is (e), which assumes that bravery can be taught: for the Greeks, what could be taught was knowledge, hence (e) is an anticipation of Nicias' definition of bravery as a special kind of knowledge in B(5).

NICIAS: There's no difficulty about that, Socrates. You see, I take the view that for young men to have a firm understanding of the subject in question is an advantage in many ways. First of all, although they usually e
like to fritter away their free time on other activities, as you know, it's a good idea for them to spend their time doing this instead, which is bound to make them fit and healthy, since it is at least as serious, and requires just as much hard effort, as any other physical exercise. Moreover, it's 182a
also a kind of exercise which, like riding, should be very much the business of a free man:[1] we are athletes taking part in a contest, you see, and the

1. There were, as yet, no professional armies, so it was a vital duty of every adult male citizen to fight as a foot soldier or, in the case of the wealthy, as a cavalryman.

87

only people who get training for the conditions under which we have to compete are those who are trained in the use of military equipment. So later on this discipline will be of some benefit in an actual confrontation, when the army is drawn up in ranks and you have to fight as part of a large body of men; but its greatest benefit will be felt when the ranks are broken, and you suddenly have to fight man to man, either in chasing and attacking a man who puts up a defence, or in retreating and warding off

b attack yourself. A man with a good grasp of this discipline would come to no harm if he had only one opponent to deal with, and perhaps not even if he had more than one; and it would give him the edge, whatever the situation. Then again, this kind of training provides men with the incentive to pursue another worthwhile discipline, because anyone who has done military training will be keen to progress to the next stage and learn about the deployment of troops; and when he has mastered that and taken a pride in it, he'll hurry on to discover all there is to know about strategy.

c Now, it's clear that it is both honourable and worthwhile to study and practise all the disciplines and activities related to those, and that this particular discipline may serve as a starting-point for them. And we can make this additional point, which is not unimportant, that the possession of this same knowledge will make any individual a great deal braver and more daring in battle than he would otherwise be. And, even if some people think it's rather a trivial point, we shouldn't regard it as too insignificant to mention that it will produce a rather smart appearance in the

d very situations in which a soldier ought to look smart, and in which, at the same time, a smartly turned-out appearance will make more of a formidable impression on the enemy.

So my opinion is, Lysimachus, as I say, that these subjects ought to be taught to our young men, and I've explained why I think so. But I'll certainly be glad to listen to Laches if he has anything different to say.

A[4] Laches on the Futility of Military Training

Laches argues that there is little point in taking a course in military training as (a) the foremost military power in Greece, Sparta, has no truck with it; (b) experience suggests that the instructors themselves do not profit from their knowledge; and (c) it could only cause a coward to take foolish risks, and make a brave man into the butt of criticism.

Laches has no academic training, and his argument rests entirely on personal observation and experience. Point (a) is not strong, as Sparta had long possessed something similar to the training on offer; (b) is a little unfair, and though cautionary, is scarcely an argument in itself. Point (c), however, is crucial to the structure and meaning of the dialogue: a direct contradiction of Nicias' point (e), it exemplifies Laches' belief that bravery depends on what you are and not on what you know; for him it is not a kind of knowledge, but a certain kind of behaviour or a certain trait of character (see B[2] and B[3]).

LACHES: Well, Nicias, it's hard to say of any discipline that it shouldn't be studied, because it seems to be a good idea to know everything. And if this business of weapon training *is* a discipline, as the instructors maintain, and as Nicias says, of course it ought to be studied. On the other e hand, if it's *not* a discipline, and the claims made for it are fraudulent, or if it is a discipline, but not a very serious one, why should we really need to study it?

I say this because I've been struck by the following thought: in my opinion, if this training had anything in it, it wouldn't have escaped the Spartans, whose sole concern in life is to search out and practise whatever 183a disciplines and pursuits will give them military superiority over others.[1] And if it has escaped them, it certainly can't have escaped these military instructors that no one else in Greece takes such matters as seriously as the Spartans, and hence that if anyone gained the Spartans' respect in this sphere, he would make a great deal of money in other countries. It's the same when *we* honour a tragic poet – which is why no one who thinks he has a flair for tragedy displays his talents by doing the rounds of the other cities outside Attica: he makes straight for Athens, naturally, and stages a performance for an audience here. When it comes to these fighting men, b however, it's my observation that they regard Sparta as a sort of Holy of Holies and they won't put so much as a toe in the place. They prefer to skirt around it and put on displays for all and sundry, and especially for people who would be the first to agree that their own military standing is far lower than most.

And another thing, Lysimachus: I've come across quite a number of c these instructors when they've been faced with the real thing, and I know the stuff they're made of. We can see right away how the land lies: not one man who has done this weapon training has ever made a name for himself on active service. It looks almost deliberate! And yet in every other subject the men with high reputations come from the ranks of those who have gone through the appropriate training: by comparison with others, these instructors of ours appear to have been remarkably unfortunate in this respect.

1. The Spartan army, known and feared as the finest in Greece, was the product of a ruthless regime of training which began for all male citizens at the age of seven. On Sparta, see P. Cartledge, *Sparta and Lakonia* (London 1979); W. G. Forrest, *A History of Sparta*, 2nd ed. (London 1980); and J. F. Lazenby, *The Spartan Army* (Warminster 1985). cf. Socrates' example at 191c, which derives its force, and a certain irony, from Laches' admiration of Sparta.

Take Stesilaus:[1] we've all stood in that huge crowd and watched him
d giving an exhibition of his skill, and blowing his own trumpet as he did,
but I've once had a better view of him[2] when he made a proper exhibition
of himself without intending to! When he was serving as a marine, his
ship collided with a merchantman and he went into action carrying a spear
with a sort of sickle fastened on the end – the weapon was in a class of its
own, of course, like the man himself.[3] Now the fellow has never really
done anything else worth mentioning, but you must hear the upshot of
e his clever stunt with his spear-cum-sickle. As he was fighting, the weapon
somehow got caught in the other ship's rigging and it stuck fast; so Stesilaus tugged at it, wanting to pull it free, but with no success – and meanwhile the ships were moving past each other. For a time he dashed along
on deck clutching the shaft; but when the other ship began to slip away
and pulled him after it, still hanging on to the spear, he let the shaft slide
through his hands until he was gripping the very end of the butt. When
184a they noticed his antics, the crew of the merchantman started laughing at
him and clapping; then, when someone hurled a stone on to the deck close
to his feet, he let go of the spear and his own ship's company couldn't stop
themselves from laughing any longer: what a sight it was, that sickle-
spear of his dangling from the merchantman! Well now, perhaps there is
something in this training after all, as Nicias says; but that's the sort of
b experience that I've always had.

So, as I said at first, either it is a discipline, but of no great use, or it's
not, and people merely claim it is under false pretences; but, whichever
way, it's not worth trying to study. And it would be true to say, I think,
that if someone who was a coward were to imagine that he knew all about
it, he would become over-confident and then make it all the more obvious
what his true colours were. If, on the other hand, he were a brave man,
people would watch his every move, and if he made even the slightest
c mistake, he would have to put up with a great deal of abuse. People have
a grudge against men who profess to know such things, so unless a man
is strikingly braver than the rest, there's no way he can avoid becoming a
laughing-stock if he claims this kind of knowledge.

That's my opinion, Lysimachus, on the interest taken in this subject.
However, you had better do what I suggested at the beginning: don't let

1. We know no more about Stesilaus than we learn from this passage, and Laches' anecdote
could be an invention on the part of Plato. If Stesilaus is a historical figure, he may be compared
with the brothers Euthydemus and Dionysodorus (*Euthydemus* 271d and 273e).
2. ἐν τῇ ἀληθείᾳ omitted (Schanz).
3. As merchant ships were propelled by sail alone (warships had oars as well), a weapon
devised to cut rigging, leaving the ship helpless, was by no means a foolish idea.

our friend Socrates slip away; ask him to share *his* thoughts on the issue with us.

A[5]. The Need for Expert Advice: Are the Generals Qualified to Speak about Education?

Socrates convinces Lysimachus and Melesias that they need expert advice. Military training is only at issue in so far as it may help to educate the boys to their best advantage, so the expert required is an expert in education. Socrates denies such knowledge in his own case and suggests that Lysimachus should challenge Nicias and Laches to prove their title to it by stating (a) those known experts who had trained them, and/or (b) their own record as successful teachers.

Socrates picks up Lysimachus' assumption that the generals, qua generals, are suitable advisers. Their experience qualifies them to speak on the technical knowledge and practical skills to be derived from military training, as both had done, but not on what was for Lysimachus the real issue, that of developing the boys' soul or character (psuchē). In speaking of bravery, both generals had touched on this issue, but for Socrates it is as yet unclear whether their opinions are properly grounded in moral knowledge.

LYSIMACHUS: But I *am* asking you, Socrates, because it seems as if our council[1] needs someone to act as umpire. Had our two friends agreed, we wouldn't have been so much in need of such help; but as it is, since Laches has voted for the opposite to Nicias, as you can see, it's as well that we should hear your opinion too, and see which of them you vote with.

SOCRATES: What, Lysimachus? Do you intend to follow whatever course the majority of us recommends?

LYSIMACHUS: Yes, what alternative is there, Socrates?

SOCRATES: And how about you, Melesias? Would you do the same? Imagine there was some discussion about the kind of athletic training your son should practise: would you be influenced by the majority of us, or by the man who happened to have trained and exercised under a good coach?[2]

MELESIAS: By the man who'd been trained, I suppose, Socrates.

SOCRATES: Would he have more influence on you than four of us put together?

MELESIAS: Probably so.

1. Perhaps a joking comparison of the present company with the Council (Greek *boulē*), the keystone of Athenian democracy; a body of five hundred members who prepared business for the popular assembly, in addition to administrative and judicial duties.

2. 'Coach', Greek *paidotribēs*: a teacher of gymnastics and games, one of the three basic elements in Athenian primary education along with music and the three Rs.

SOCRATES: Yes, because I think that if a decision is to be made properly, then it must be made on the basis of knowledge and not numbers.

MELESIAS: Of course.

SOCRATES: So, what we should do now, first of all, is consider whether
185a we have among us an expert in the subject we're discussing or not. If we have, we should take his advice, albeit his alone, and ignore other people; and if we haven't, we should look for somebody else. Or is it that you and Lysimachus think that all there is at stake here is something that doesn't really matter, rather than what is in fact the most precious thing you possess? I take it, you see, that a man's sons may turn out to be good, or they may turn out to be the opposite; but his entire household's way of life is going to depend on the sort of characters they turn out to be.

MELESIAS: That's true.

SOCRATES: So we ought to give the matter considerable thought.

MELESIAS: Certainly.

SOCRATES: To follow on from what I was just saying, then, if we were
b wanting to consider which of us had the most expertise in athletics, how would we go about it? Wouldn't we choose the man who'd learnt about athletics, who'd practised, and who'd been trained in the sport by top coaches?

MELESIAS: I think so.

SOCRATES: So, even before we consider that, we should ask in what *subject* we're looking for teachers, shouldn't we?

MELESIAS: How do you mean?

SOCRATES: Perhaps it'll be clearer for you if I put it like this. It strikes me that here we are discussing which of us has become an expert and has had teachers to this end, and which hasn't, when right from the start
c we've failed to agree what subject it is we're talking about.

NICIAS: Why, Socrates, isn't it military training we're considering, and whether or not young men ought to learn it?

SOCRATES: Yes, of course, Nicias. But when someone is considering whether or not to put some drops in his eyes, what do you suppose he's thinking about at the time, the drops or his eyes?

NICIAS: His eyes.

SOCRATES: And whenever someone is considering whether or not he
d should introduce his horse to a bridle, and when he ought to do it, I suppose that then it's the horse and not the bridle that he's thinking about, isn't it?

NICIAS: True.

SOCRATES: So, in a nutshell, whenever someone is considering something for the sake of something else, it's the latter that he's actually think-

ing about – the thing for the sake of which the consideration was made –
and not the thing for which he was searching for the sake of the other.

NICIAS: It must be.

SOCRATES: And so we must consider our adviser too, and ask whether
he's an expert in the care of the 'thing for the sake of which' we're considering the subject we are.[1]

NICIAS: Certainly.

SOCRATES: So, we can now say that we're considering a subject, and
that it's for the sake of young men's characters we're considering it, can't   e
we?

NICIAS: Yes.

SOCRATES: So what we have to consider is this: is any of us an expert
in caring for the character, and able to care for it properly, and which of
us has had good teachers?

LACHES: Why, though, Socrates? Haven't you ever seen people who
have become greater experts in some subjects without teachers than others
with them?

SOCRATES: Yes, I have, Laches; but in their case you'd be reluctant to
accept any claim they might make to be good craftsmen, unless they could
show you not just one, but several well-made pieces of work as examples
of their skill.   186a

LACHES: You're right there.

SOCRATES: And so we're under the same obligation, Laches and
Nicias. Lysimachus and Melesias have invited us to discuss their sons,
because they're anxious for the boys' characters to develop in the best way
possible. So, what we must do, if we claim we can, is to point out to them
teachers who are known firstly to have been upstanding men in their own
right and to have cared for many young men's characters, and secondly
to have taught us also. Alternatively, if one of us can't claim to have had   b
a teacher, but can describe his own achievements, he'd better point out
the men, Athenian or foreign, slave or free, whose characters by common
consent have benefited from his efforts. And if we're not in a position to
do either of these things, we ought strongly to recommend that they look
for advice elsewhere. When our friends' sons are at stake, we can't risk
corrupting them, and then having to face the bitter reproaches of people
we're close to.

I'll be the first to explain my position, then, Lysimachus and Melesias,   c
and I may say I've not had any instruction on the subject, although it's
true that it has been a passionate interest of mine ever since I was a boy.

1. Reading σκοποῦμεν ὃ σκοποῦμεν (Cron).

But I've never been able to pay fees to the sophists[1] – the only ones who professed to be able to make a good and honest man of me – and I can't discover the art for myself even now. However, if Nicias or Laches had learnt or discovered it, I wouldn't be at all surprised: they're wealthier than I am, so they can afford to be taught by other people, and they're

d older too, so they've had time to discover it. They certainly give me the impression they're able to educate a man – for they'd never have made such a confident display of their opinions on activities that are useful for the young, or are no good at all, unless they were convinced that their knowledge was equal to it. So in general I've every confidence in them; but they don't agree with each other and that has surprised me.

I have in consequence a request to make of you in return, Lysimachus. Laches urged you just now not to let me slip away, but to ask me some questions, and now I urge you not to let Laches or Nicias slip away, but to ask *them* some questions. Say to them, 'Socrates says he doesn't understand this subject in the slightest and isn't competent to decide

e which of you is right: he hasn't been taught, or discovered for himself, anything about that kind of thing at all. And now you, Laches and Nicias, are each to tell us if you've met anyone who was highly skilled in bringing up the young, and whether you learnt what you know from someone else or discovered it for yourselves. If you learnt it, could you tell us who

187a taught each of you, and who is in the same profession? Then, if you haven't the time yourselves because of affairs of state, we can approach them and offer them a fee, or do them a favour, or both, to persuade them to look after our sons and yours too: otherwise they might turn out to be good for nothing and a disgrace to the family name. But, if you discovered something of the kind for yourselves, could you give us an example of others who have turned under your care from being good-for-nothings into fine, upstanding men? If this is going to be your first venture into the field of education, you see, you must take care that you don't experiment

b on your own sons and your friends' children rather than on a guinea-pig, and that you don't just prove to be trying to run before you can walk, as the saying goes.[2] So, could you tell us how much of all this you claim, or don't claim, matches your record and resources?'

1. Itinerant professional teachers lecturing on a variety of subjects, but generally offering advice on how to succeed in public life: see p. 215.

2. 'Guinea-pig': the Greek has 'put a Carian at risk'. Caria, in south-west Turkey, was a traditional source of slaves and mercenary soldiers, both of which classes were regarded as expendable relative to citizens; cf. *Euthydemus* 285c. 'Run before you can walk': the Greek has 'begin pottery by making a wine jar', too large a piece for a novice.

There, Lysimachus, that's what you must find out from our friends here, and don't let them off!

LYSIMACHUS: Well, gentlemen, to my mind Socrates' suggestion is admirable: but whether you're willing to have such questions put to you c and are prepared to give an account of yourselves in reply, that you must decide for yourselves, Nicias and Laches. Melesias and I, as I'm sure you must realize, would be delighted if you were willing to give a full answer to all Socrates' questions: as I began by saying at the outset, the reason we invited you to give us advice was that we thought, naturally, you'd taken an interest in this kind of thing, especially as your sons, like ours, are almost old enough to start their education. So, if it's all the same to d you, could you join Socrates in discussing the issue and exchange your views with one another? After all, he is right in saying that we're now discussing our most precious possession. Think about it, and decide whether you agree that this is the right way to go about it.

A[6]. The Generals Agree to Cooperate with Socrates and Put Their Expertise to the Test

Both generals agree to comply with Socrates' suggestion: Nicias because, as he explains to Lysimachus, it is Socrates' usual procedure, and one with which he is greatly in sympathy; Laches because, to judge from his exceptional conduct at Delium, Socrates should be well worth hearing. Lysimachus then asks Socrates to put the questions to them on his behalf.

The section is in many ways an 'apology' for Socrates and a justification of his philosophical method. Here again, Nicias' primary concern is for what men know and say, whereas Laches, by no means so familiar with the intellectual world, is more concerned with what they are and do.

NICIAS: Lysimachus, my friend, it definitely looks to me as though you only know Socrates from what you knew of his father, and that you've never had anything to do with him personally. Well, I suppose you might have met him as a boy with his father in your home town, at the temple e or at some other gathering of local people, but since he became older you've never come across the man, that's quite clear.

LYSIMACHUS: What exactly makes you think so, Nicias?

NICIAS: You seem not to know that whenever anyone comes face to face with Socrates and has a conversation with him, what invariably happens is that, although they may have started on a completely different subject at first, Socrates will keep heading him off as they're talking until he has him trapped into giving an account of his present life-style, and of the 188a way he has spent his life in the past. And once he has him trapped, Socrates won't let him go before he has well and truly cross-examined him on every angle. Now I'm well acquainted with him, and I know that putting up with this treatment from him is inevitable; and what's more, I'll get the same treatment myself, I'm sure of that. I enjoy his company, you see, Lysimachus, and I don't think there's anything wrong in suggesting that we haven't acted properly in the past, or that we're not doing so now. On b the contrary, you're bound to be more careful about your way of life in future if you don't shrink from this treatment, but believe, as Solon said,[1] that it's right to go on learning as long as you live, and are prepared to do so because you don't assume that wisdom is an automatic consequence of old age. To me there's nothing unusual, or annoying either, about being cross-examined by Socrates; in fact, I was fairly certain some time ago that with Socrates here it wouldn't be the boys we'd be talking about, but c ourselves. So, what I'm saying is that, as far as I'm concerned, there's no reason why I shouldn't spend the time with him as he wants; but you'd better see what Laches feels about this kind of thing.

LACHES: I'm very single-minded, Nicias, when it comes to discussions, or if you like, I'm not so much single-minded as in two minds about them.[2] Sometimes you'd think I was fond of discussions, but on other occasions it would look as though I hated them. You see, whenever I hear a man talking about goodness or any kind of wisdom – a real man, that d is, who lives by his principles – I'm overjoyed, because I can see that the speaker is in tune with his words and that the two go together. Such a man really is, I think, a true musician: he uses the finest mode and has tuned to it not just a lyre or some other entertaining instrument, but he has tuned his own life so that his words harmonize with his actions; and it's done fairly and squarely in the Dorian mode, the one native mode of Greece, not in the Ionian or, I'll warrant, in the Phrygian or Lydian modes either.[3] In any event, a man like that fills me with pleasure when he speaks, e and everyone would assume that I was fond of discussions – I'm so keen to take in what he has to say. But it pains me to hear someone who is quite the opposite, and the more eloquently he seems to speak, the worse it becomes, and then it looks as though I hate discussions.

1. Solon was an Athenian statesman and poet of the sixth century. His poetry, mainly reflections on social, political and moral themes, survives only in fragments. Nicias refers to the line, 'I grow older learning ever more and more' (fragment 18 in J. M. Edmonds (ed.), *Elegy and Iambus*, I (Cambridge, Mass., and London 1931; Loeb edition).

2. The Greek contains a pun on two senses of the word *haploun*, which could ...ean both 'single' and 'straightforward'.

3. Various modes or scales (*harmoniai*) were associated with distinct emotions and held to influence the character permanently. In the *Republic* Plato approves only of the brave and sober Dorian and Phrygian modes, the others being weak and dissolute (400a–c, 424c).

In Socrates' case I'm not familiar with his conversation, but I believe I do have prior experience of his conduct, which I found worthy of a man of high principles and total frankness. So, if he has these gifts too, his 189a wish is mine. I'd be delighted to be questioned by such a man, and I wouldn't find it at all annoying to learn a lesson or two. I also agree with Solon, adding just one condition: as I grow older, I'm willing to learn a great many things, but only from good men. Let Solon concede that my teacher is himself a good man, otherwise I'll hate my lessons and seem a slow learner; whereas if my teacher is younger than I am, or isn't well known as yet, or anything of that sort, I don't mind at all. So, Socrates, b I promise you can teach me and examine me on whatever point you want, and learn whatever I know in return. That's how I've thought about you ever since that day the two of us came through a dangerous experience together, and you proved your mettle in the way any man has to, if he's going to justify his reputation. So say whatever you like, and don't take the slightest account of our difference in age.

SOCRATES: It seems we shan't have to complain that *you're* unwilling c to think it over and share your thoughts with us!

LYSIMACHUS: Well then, it's up to us now, Socrates – I say 'us', since I'm including you on our side. Could you take my place and consider on behalf of the boys what we need to find out from our friends here, and give us your own advice as you talk things over with them? For myself, you see, the problem is my age: I forget most of the questions I mean to ask – and for that matter most of the answers I hear as well – and if a conversation changes tack in the middle, I don't remember at all. So could d you discuss matters between the three of you and go through what we proposed? I'll listen, and then Melesias and I will both do whatever you think is best.

B. *An Inquiry into the Nature of Bravery*

B[i]. The Need to Define Bravery
Socrates now raises what he believes to be a further, and more fundamental, qualification for a teacher. He holds as a general principle that if one knows one can improve x by adding to it y, and also knows how to add y to x, one must know what y is, and hence be able to say what it is. As educating the boys amounts to adding goodness to them, Nicias and Laches must be able to define goodness if they are to offer any advice on education. Socrates will test them by asking for a definition of bravery, the constituent part of goodness that is particularly relevant to military training.

Socrates has not yet made it clear what 'to say what it is' will actually involve. It seems true that a teacher must have some grasp of the result he is trying to achieve, and that he will have some ability to communicate this to other people. However, when Socrates goes on to discuss Laches' first attempt at a definition, it becomes clear that he has in mind something far stricter than these minimum requirements.

SOCRATES: Well, Nicias and Laches, we'd better do as Lysimachus and Melesias have asked. Now possibly, it wouldn't be a bad idea for us to examine ourselves thoroughly on the kinds of question we've just attempted to consider – the questions regarding the men who have taught
e us in this branch of education, or those others we've turned into better people. However, in my opinion, the following line of inquiry also has a bearing on the same problem and is, if anything, more fundamental to it. You see, if we know that we can improve something by adding something else to it, and we can, moreover, cause the one to be added to the other, clearly we know what it is we're adding, and we could advise people on the best and easiest means of acquiring it. Now you probably don't understand what I mean, but if I put it like this, you'll understand it more
190a easily. If we know that we can improve someone's eyes by adding sight to them, and we can, moreover, cause sight to be added to that person's eyes, clearly we know what sight is, and we could advise people on the best and easiest means of acquiring it. You see, if we didn't even know what sight is, or what hearing is, then as doctors we'd hardly be worth consulting for advice on ears and eyes and the best way of acquiring
b hearing and sight.

LACHES: You're right, Socrates.

SOCRATES: In the present case, Laches, our friends are inviting us to advise them on the means of adding goodness to their sons and so improving their characters, aren't they?

LACHES: Certainly.

SOCRATES: So the qualification we need is this: we need to know what goodness is, don't we? Because if we hadn't a clue what goodness actually is, there'd be no way in which we could possibly give anyone any
c advice on the best way of acquiring it, would there?

LACHES: No, I don't think there would, Socrates.

SOCRATES: So, we claim that we do know what it is, Laches.

LACHES: Yes, we do.

SOCRATES: So, since we know what it is, we could also, presumably, *say* what it is, couldn't we?

LACHES: Of course.

SOCRATES: Well, in that case, my good friend, let's not look at goodness as a whole straight away – it might well be a rather lengthy business. Let's examine part of it first of all and see whether we're in a position to know about that. We'll probably find this makes our inquiry easier.   d

LACHES: By all means, Socrates, let's do as you wish.

SOCRATES: So which part of goodness are we to choose? Clearly, I think, the one to which the subject of military training belongs – and that, I imagine, is generally supposed to be bravery. Isn't that so?

LACHES: Yes, it certainly is.

B[2]. Laches' First Definition:
To be Brave is to Stand and Fight

Laches answers the request to define bravery by describing the behaviour of a brave infantryman. Socrates, however, points out that a soldier could behave in quite the opposite way and still be thought of as brave; moreover, bravery is by no means confined to the army. What he really requires is a definition that holds good for each and every occasion on which someone could be said to be brave, and he illustrates his meaning by defining quickness.

By giving several examples of the kind offered by Laches, it would be possible to convey an intuitive grasp of the nature of bravery. Socrates, however, goes beyond what it seems reasonable to require of a teacher: firstly, he delimits the usage of the word by citing all the different occasions on which one could be brave (it is worth noting how broad a concept of bravery he is using), and secondly he requires an analytical capacity to produce a definition that holds good for each and every occasion mentioned. It is to be noted that in Socrates' example quickness and bravery are not truly analogous kinds of quality: being quick is behaving in a certain kind of way, but being brave is a matter of one's behaviour being caused by a certain mental state (see Irwin, p. 45).

SOCRATES: First of all, then, let's try to say what bravery is, Laches; and after that we'll investigate any ways of adding it to young men, in so far as it may be possible to do so by means of various activities and disciplines. So, as I say, try to put into words what bravery is.   e

LACHES: My word, Socrates, that's not difficult! If a man is prepared to stand in the ranks, face up to the enemy and not run away, you can be sure that he's brave.

SOCRATES: You've got a good point there, Laches. But it's probably my fault: I didn't make myself clear, and the question you've answered isn't the question I meant to ask, but a different one.

LACHES: What do you mean by that, Socrates?

SOCRATES: I'll explain, if I can. I'm assuming that this man you men-   191a tioned – the one who stands in the ranks and fights the enemy – is a brave man.

LACHES: I certainly think so.

SOCRATES: Yes, and so do I. But what about another man, a man who still fights the enemy, but runs away and doesn't make a stand?

LACHES: How do you mean, 'runs away'?

SOCRATES: Well, I suppose just like the Scythians[1] are said to fight every bit as much in retreat as in pursuit, and perhaps just like Homer
b   says in praise of Aeneas' horses that they know how 'quickly to cover the ground in flight or in pursuit, it makes no odds', and pays tribute to Aeneas himself for his knowledge of fear, and says he's a 'contriver of fear'.[2]

LACHES: And very properly too, Socrates, because he was talking about chariots, and your point about the Scythians applies to *cavalry* – that's the way cavalry go into action, but infantry operate as I described.

SOCRATES: With the possible exception, Laches, of the Spartan infan-
c   try. At the battle of Plataea,[3] so the story goes, the Spartans came up against the troops with wicker shields,[4] but weren't willing to stand and fight, and fell back. The Persians broke ranks in pursuit; but then the Spartans wheeled round fighting like cavalry and so won that part of the battle.

LACHES: That's true.

SOCRATES: Well, this is what I meant just now when I said it was my fault you didn't give a proper answer, because I didn't phrase the question properly; you see, I wanted to find out not just what it is to be brave as
d   an infantryman, but also as a cavalryman, and as any kind of member of the forces; and not just what it is to be brave during a war, but to be brave in the face of danger at sea; and I wanted to find out what it is to be brave in the face of an illness, in the face of poverty, and in public life; and what's more not just what it is to be brave in resisting pain or fear, but
e   also in putting up stern opposition to temptation and indulgence – because

1. The Scythians were a nomadic people of southern Russia. Among the first to master the art of horsemanship, their military success was based on skilled light cavalry, armed with bows, not unlike the Indians of the NorthnAmerican plains.

2. An instance of gentle intellectual humour. The quotations are from the *Iliad* V, 222–3 and VIII, 106–8, but in that context they refer to the ability to put an opponent to flight, rather than to the use of feigned flight as a tactic. Plato was fond of such witty allusions to Homer.

3. In 479 the Persian army led by Mardonius was defeated at Plataea, on the border between Attica and Boeotia, by the united Greek army under the Spartan king Pausanias. Herodotus (IX.53) gives a notably different account of the battle from Socrates'.

4. The élite native Persian infantry were armed with spear, bow and distinctive wicker shield.

I'm assuming, Laches, that there are people who are brave in all these situations.

LACHES: Very much so, Socrates.

SOCRATES: So, all these people are brave, but some possess bravery in the face of indulgence, others in the face of pain, temptation or fear; and others in the same circumstances, I imagine, possess cowardice.

LACHES: Certainly.

SOCRATES: What *is* each of these two qualities – that's what I wanted to know. So try again, and tell me with respect to bravery first of all what the constant factor in all these situations is – or do you still not understand what I mean?

LACHES: No, not entirely.

SOCRATES: Well, what I mean is this: it's as if I were asking what quickness is, which is a quality present to us in running, playing the lyre, speaking, learning and many other activities, and which we possess in virtually any pursuit worth talking about, in the actions of our hands or legs, or mouth and voice, or mind. Wouldn't you put it like that too? 192a

LACHES: Certainly.

SOCRATES: Suppose, then, someone asked me this question: 'Socrates, what do you say it is, this quality which in each instance you term quickness?' I'd reply that for me quickness is the ability to do a lot in a short space of time, whether one is speaking, running or engaged in any other activity. b

LACHES: And you'd be quite right.

SOCRATES: Now then, you try, and say what bravery is in the same terms, Laches: what ability is called bravery and is the same in pleasure, pain and all the situations in which we said just now that it was to be found?

B[3]. Laches' Second Definition:
Bravery is Endurance

Laches now identifies bravery with endurance (karteria). *Socrates' reply falls into two parts. In the first (192c–d), adopting premises which could for the Greeks be assumed without argument, he moves by deduction to the conclusion that only endurance* with wisdom *can be a virtue. Then in the second part (192e–193d), he brings forward counter-examples which seem to show not only that endurance with wisdom might not always be brave, but also that it might be braver to show endurance with foolishness. However, the first two examples are really no more than an alternative way of asking* what kind *of wisdom must be added to endurance to produce bravery: will it be commercial acumen, for instance, or medical science? Laches' reaction shows that it will be no such thing; but no attempt is made to suggest any further possibilities. In the later examples, he assumes at once that it is foolish, though brave, to face a danger for which one is ill prepared. However, one cannot judge the issue unless one knows what is at stake: it is foolish to take unnecessary risks, but it is not foolish to go forward to almost certain death if, for example, it is known that such action will save the lives of others. Moreoever, a man who is ill prepared merely has more opportunity to show his bravery than a man backed by great resources, and it does not follow that one can judge which of the two is braver in absolute terms.*

What Socrates and Laches need is the distinction between different kinds of knowledge which Nicias offers when he is asked to help (B[4] and B[5]). Nicias distinguishes between the kind of knowledge a doctor or farmer might have (of what will happen) from the kind of knowledge necessary for bravery (of whether a thing is good or bad). If the revised definition, endurance with wisdom, were to be changed to read 'endurance with knowledge of good and evil', the difficulties raised by the counter-examples would disappear; and indeed those who hold the philosophico-dramatic interpretation of the dialogue believe that it is intended to endorse exactly such a definition of bravery (see p. 75 ff.).

LACHES: I take it, in that case, to be a certain endurance present in one's character, if I have to mention the element essentially present in all cases.

c   SOCRATES: Well of course you have, if we're going to give ourselves an answer to our question! Now, this is how it appears to me: by no means every kind of endurance, I think, can appear to you to be bravery. I make that surmise because I'm almost certain, Laches, that you think of bravery as one of the finer things.

LACHES: One of the finest, you can be sure of that.

SOCRATES: So endurance accompanied by wisdom would be both fine and good, wouldn't it?

LACHES: Certainly.

d   SOCRATES: But what of it when accompanied by foolishness? Surely it's quite the opposite, damaging and detrimental?

LACHES: Yes.

SOCRATES: Then are you going to say such a thing is fine, if it's a detrimental and damaging thing?

LACHES: No, at least not with any justice, Socrates.

SOCRATES: So you won't agree that this kind of endurance is bravery, on the grounds that it's not fine, whereas bravery is a fine thing.

LACHES: That's right.

SOCRATES: So, according to your account, *wise* endurance will be bravery.

LACHES: So it seems.

SOCRATES: Let's see now: wise, but wise in what respect? Perhaps in   e
every respect, great or small? Suppose, for instance, someone showed endurance in spending his money wisely, because he realized that if he spent it, he'd make a profit: would you call him brave?

LACHES: Good heavens, I certainly wouldn't!

SOCRATES: Well, what if a doctor, whose son, or someone else, was suffering from pleurisy and asking for something to eat or drink, showed endurance in refusing to give way?

LACHES: No, there's no way I'd call that bravery either.   193a

SOCRATES: Well then, suppose during a war a man showed endurance by being prepared to fight: he has calculated his chances wisely and realized that others will support him, that he'll be fighting an enemy outnumbered and outclassed by his own side, and that he has the stronger position – now, which would you say is the braver, the man showing endurance with the benefit of this kind of wisdom and these resources, or a man from the opposing camp willing to show endurance in standing against him?

LACHES: I'd say the man in the opposing camp, Socrates.   b

SOCRATES: But surely his endurance is more foolish than that of the other?

LACHES: Yes, you're right.

SOCRATES: Then you'll say that if a man who knows about horseman-ship shows endurance in a cavalry action, he won't be as brave as a man without such knowledge.

LACHES: Yes, I think so.

SOCRATES: And the same goes for a man who shows endurance with a   c
knowledge of slinging, archery or any other skill.

LACHES: Certainly.

SOCRATES: And you'll say that anyone willing to go down into a well,[1] and to dive, and show endurance in this or in some similar activity, will be braver than the experts, although not an expert himself.

LACHES: What else can one say, Socrates?

SOCRATES: Nothing, provided one thinks so.

LACHES: Well, I do.

SOCRATES: Moreover, Laches, when such people take risks and show

[1]. Plato refers to this curious activity elsewhere (*Republic* 453d, *Protagoras* 350a), but it is not clear what exactly it was, or whether it had some practical purpose, as opposed to being simply a dangerous stunt.

endurance, they're perhaps more foolish than those who do the same things with skill.

LACHES: Apparently so.

d   SOCRATES: Now, we've previously shown that *without knowledge* endurance and daring are disgraceful and damaging, haven't we?

LACHES: Certainly.

SOCRATES: And bravery, we agreed, is a fine thing.

LACHES: Yes, we did.

SOCRATES: But now we're claiming, on the contrary, that this disgraceful thing, endurance without knowledge, is bravery.

LACHES: Apparently so.

SOCRATES: Then do you think we've given a good account?

LACHES: Good heavens, Socrates, I certainly don't.

B[4]. Impasse: Nicias is Asked to Help

Socrates finds that Laches is keen to continue searching for the definition of bravery, but suggests that they invite Nicias to help them get over their difficulty. Although Nicias subsequently diverts his attention towards a purely intellectualist account of bravery, Socrates seems not to abandon entirely a definition in terms of endurance. Indeed, he appears to suggest that such a definition may still turn out to be true, despite the problems which he and Laches have encountered (194a). If it is right to read the section in this way, it may be a clue to the interpretation of the dialogue as a whole, for perhaps Plato did not so much intend to reject Laches' definition in favour of Nicias' as to show that no definition of bravery could be adequate unless it incorporated the insights of both the generals.

SOCRATES: So I suppose, to use your words, that we're not tuned in

e   the Dorian mode, you and I, Laches, since what we do doesn't harmonize with what we say. If people judged us by our actions, they might well say that we had our share of bravery; but to judge from this conversation, I don't think they would if they could hear us discussing it.

LACHES: You're quite right.

SOCRATES: Well now, do you think it's good that we're in this position?

LACHES: No, not at all.

SOCRATES: So do you mind if we abide by part of what we said?

LACHES: What part, and what did we say?

SOCRATES: We said we were to show endurance. So, if you don't mind,

194a let's stick to the search and show some endurance, in case Bravery herself pokes fun at us for not bravely searching for her, when perhaps endurance actually is bravery after all.

LACHES: I'm not prepared to give up too soon, Socrates. It's true I'm not used to this kind of discussion, but hearing what has been said has made me feel like fighting it out. I'm really annoyed because I can't find the words to say what I'm thinking – I'm sure I can *see* what Bravery is,   b
but somehow or other she has escaped me for the moment, so I can't find the words to catch her and actually say what she is!

SOCRATES: Well, my friend, the good huntsman must follow the trail and not give up the chase, mustn't he?

LACHES: Yes, without a doubt.

SOCRATES: Then do you mind if we invite Nicias here to join the hunt? He may be more resourceful than we are.

LACHES: Of course I don't mind.   c

SOCRATES: Come on then, Nicias, your friends are floundering in a sea of words! We've got ourselves hopelessly confused, so you'd better give us some help, if there's anything you can do. The hopelessness of our predicament is obvious; but if you tell us what *you* think bravery is, you'll get us out of this hopeless state, and you'll also confirm your own thoughts by putting them into words.

B[5]. Nicias' Definition: Bravery is
a Special Kind of Knowledge

Nicias believes that goodness depends on knowledge, and so for him bravery must be some kind of knowledge, and more specifically the knowledge of which situations are fearful and which are encouraging. Laches is totally opposed to the idea and cites what he believes to be counter-examples. Nicias defends his definition by claiming that Laches has failed to distinguish between two different kinds of knowledge. Laches in turn regards this as splitting hairs, but Socrates persuades him not to abandon the discussion.

It may be significant that Nicias' definition is said to be derived from Socrates' own beliefs (see p. 74). Laches' attitude is exactly what one would expect, given his views on military training, but Nicias' distinction between knowing what will happen and knowing whether it will be good or bad is perfectly valid, and would have helped to solve the problems of Laches' second definition (see p. 75).

NICIAS: Well, I've been thinking for some time now, Socrates, that you two aren't defining bravery in the right way. You see, you aren't making use of a very good point I've heard you make in the past.

SOCRATES: What sort of point, Nicias?

NICIAS: I've often heard you saying that we're each good in so far as   d
we're clever, but in so far as we're ignorant, we're bad.

SOCRATES: You're certainly right there, Nicias.

NICIAS: So if a brave man is a good man, it's obvious that he's clever.

SOCRATES: Did you hear that, Laches?

LACHES: I did, and I don't really understand what he means at all.

SOCRATES: Well, I think I do, and I think he's saying that bravery is some sort of cleverness.

LACHES: What sort of cleverness, Socrates?

e   SOCRATES: You're asking *him* that, I take it?

LACHES: I am.

SOCRATES: Come on, then, Nicias, tell him what sort of cleverness bravery would be on your account. It wouldn't, I suppose, be cleverness at playing the flute.

NICIAS: Of course it wouldn't.

SOCRATES: Nor at playing the lyre.

NICIAS: Not at all.

SOCRATES: Well, what is it, then? What subject is it knowledge *of*?

LACHES: That's the right question to ask him, Socrates: let him tell us what sort of knowledge he says it is.

NICIAS: This is the knowledge I mean, Laches: knowledge of what
195a is fearful and what is encouraging, both in wartime and in all other situations.

LACHES: What a peculiar thing for him to say, Socrates!

SOCRATES: What makes you say that, Laches?

LACHES: What makes me say that? Surely cleverness has nothing to do with bravery!

SOCRATES: Nicias doesn't agree.

LACHES: I'll say he doesn't! But he's talking gibberish!

SOCRATES: Then let's put him straight; let's not get abusive.

NICIAS: No; but it strikes me, Socrates, that Laches is keen to have it proved that I'm talking nonsense, because he has just been proved to be doing the self-same thing!

b   LACHES: You're absolutely right, Nicias, and I'll certainly try to prove it, because you *are* talking nonsense! For instance, in the case of ill health, doctors are the ones who know the dangers, aren't they? Or do you think brave men are the ones who know? Or perhaps you'd call doctors brave?

NICIAS: No, not at all.

LACHES: No, and I don't suppose you'd say the same about farmers either; but they're surely the ones who know the dangers that are part of agriculture. Other skilled people, moreover, all know what is fearful and

what is encouraging in their own crafts; but they're no more brave for   c
that.

SOCRATES: What do you think Laches' argument is, Nicias? He certainly does seem to have a point.

NICIAS: Yes, he certainly has a point, but it isn't right.

SOCRATES: How so?

NICIAS: Because he thinks doctors know more about their patients than what is healthy and unhealthy for them.[1] But that is surely all they do know: to be healthy might be more dangerous for some people than being ill – but do you think doctors are the ones who know that, Laches? Don't you think many people would be better off never recovering from an illness? Tell me, do you believe it's always better to live? Wouldn't it often   d be better for some to die?

LACHES: That much I'll agree.

NICIAS: So do you think that what is fearful is the same for those who'd be better off dead as for those who'd be better off alive?

LACHES: No, I don't.

NICIAS: Well, do you attribute this knowledge to doctors or to any other skilled person apart from the one who knows what is fearful and what is not – the man I call brave?

SOCRATES: Do you see what he means, Laches?

LACHES: I do indeed: he's saying brave men are prophets,[2] because   e who else will know whether it's better for a man to live or die? But what about yourself, Nicias? Are you admitting you're a prophet, or are you saying you're neither a prophet nor brave?

NICIAS: What? Prophets? Now you think it's *their* business to know what is fearful and what is encouraging, do you?

LACHES: Yes, I do: who else could it be?

NICIAS: The man I'm talking about is a much more likely candidate, my good friend. A prophet's only duty is to understand the signs of future events – to know whether someone is going to die, fall ill, go bankrupt, or be on the winning or losing side in a war or some other contest. But   196a deciding which of these it's better for someone to suffer or not is surely no more the business of a prophet than it is of anyone else!

LACHES: Well, I don't understand this fellow, Socrates; I don't see what he's driving at. He isn't letting us know whom he calls brave: it's

---

1. εἰπεῖν οἷόν omitted (Badham).

2. Prophet, Greek *mantis*: a seer or augur who claimed to foretell the future either through direct divine inspiration (as, for example at Delphi) or by interpretation of supposedly ominous natural occurrences. Traditionally accorded great respect, their influence was declining by the latter part of the fifth century; see p. 112 n. 1.

not a prophet or a doctor, but he isn't saying who else it might be, unless
he means it's some god. So it looks to me as though Nicias is not prepared
b   to be a gentleman and admit when he's talking nonsense: he's twisting
and turning to hide the fact that he's baffled. You and I could have twisted
in the same way just now if we'd wanted not to look as though we were
contradicting ourselves. If we were arguing in court, there'd be some
excuse for such behaviour, but when we're having a friendly conversation
like this, why would anyone waste time dressing himself up with such
frippery?

c   SOCRATES: I can't see any reason for that either, Laches. But let's see:
it may be that Nicias does think he has a point, and perhaps he isn't just
arguing for argument's sake. So let's ask him for a clearer explanation of
what he has in mind: if it looks as though he has got something, we'll
concede the point; if not, we'll tell him why.

LACHES: In that case, Socrates, if you'd like to ask the questions, please
go ahead: I rather think I've heard enough.

SOCRATES: Well, I've no objection to that, Laches; I'll ask the questions on behalf of us both.

LACHES: Very well, then.

B[6]. Implications of Nicias' Definition:
Can Animals and Children be Brave?

*If bravery is a kind of knowledge, how can Nicias account for the fact that
certain animals are often said to be brave? Socrates can see two possible replies:
either Nicias is flying in the face of accepted usage and denying that animals
can be brave, or he accepts that certain animals are brave, and in so doing
attributes to them a level of understanding not attained by many human beings.
Nicias takes the former alternative, finding fault with what he sees as a general
failure to distinguish between cases of bravery and cases of recklessness or
fearlessness. Animals and children may sometimes behave as if brave, but they
cannot actually be brave, or properly be described as such, because they do not
appreciate the danger they face.*

*In this section Nicias identifies a common intuition that an action can only
be virtuous if the agent is aware of what he is doing. However, it is not clear
that this awareness must be the strict kind of knowledge which Nicias claims
in his definition; it might simply be a matter of realizing the danger, and thus
well within the abilities of children and animals. What is really required is an
argument to prove that our common usage of the word 'bravery' is at fault: it
must be shown that bravery, and other virtues, need a rational element which
would exclude animals. In other Platonic dialogues, e.g.* Meno *and* Phaedo,

various arguments are evaluated which aim to prove that knowledge is necessary for virtue; but in the Laches *Nicias is allowed to evade the issue. The difficulty of proving the proposition was a constant problem for Socrates and Plato.*

SOCRATES: Now, Nicias, tell me – or rather, tell us, since Laches and I are sharing the discussion between us – your argument is that bravery is knowledge of what is fearful and what is encouraging, isn't it?

NICIAS: Yes.

SOCRATES: And this isn't something everyone is aware of, since doctors and prophets won't be aware of it, and won't be brave, unless they supplement their own knowledge with this particular kind. Isn't that what you said?

NICIAS: Yes, it was.

SOCRATES: So, it's actually not something any pig would know, as the saying goes,[1] and a pig couldn't be brave.

NICIAS: No, I think not.

SOCRATES: It's obvious, Nicias, you don't believe even the Crommyonian pig[2] could have been brave. I don't mean to be flippant by that remark; I think that if one puts forward this theory, one is forced either to deny that any animal whatsoever is brave, or else to allow that an animal like a lion, or a leopard, or even a wild boar, is clever enough to know things which all but a few human beings find too difficult to understand. And if one has the same concept of bravery as you, one is bound to admit that as far as being brave is concerned, lions, stags, bulls and apes are all in this same position.

LACHES: My word, that's an excellent point, Socrates! Now let's have an honest answer to this, Nicias: are they more intelligent than us, these animals we all agree are brave? Is this what you're saying? Or have you the nerve to contradict everyone else and not call them brave at all?

NICIAS: Yes, I have, Laches. 'Brave' is not a word I use to describe animals, or anything else that's not afraid of danger because of its own lack of understanding; I prefer 'fearless' and 'foolish'. Or do you suppose I call every little child brave because it doesn't understand, and so is not afraid of anything? No, I think to be unafraid and to be brave are two quite different things. Bravery and foresight are, in my opinion, things a very small number of people possess; whereas being reckless, daring, fearless and blind to consequences is the norm for the vast majority of

1. 'Any pig would know' is the Greek equivalent of 'Any fool would know'.

2. Theseus, the legendary early king of Athens, was reputed to have killed a large and ferocious sow called Phaea at Crommyon in Attica. Plutarch gives the story in his *Life of Theseus*, 9.

men, women, children and animals. So you see, what you and most people
c call brave, I call reckless: brave actions are those coupled with wisdom,
as I said.

LACHES: Look how well this fellow thinks he has dressed himself up
with an argument, Socrates! There are men everyone agrees are brave,
and he's trying to take this honour away from them.

NICIAS: I'm not referring to you, Laches, so cheer up! I admit you're
clever, and Lamachus too,[1] since you're both brave; and the same goes
for plenty of other Athenians.

LACHES: I could say something to that, but I won't, in case you call me
a real son of Aexone![2]

d SOCRATES: No, don't say anything, Laches. You see, you don't seem
quite to have realized that he has acquired this cleverness from Damon,
a friend of ours, and that Damon spends a great deal of time with Prodicus,[3] who is thought, of course, to be the best of the sophists at distinguishing terms like these.

LACHES: Yes, Socrates, and it's appropriate for a *sophist* to deal in this
sort of subtlety, but hardly for a man the country thinks fit to govern it!

e SOCRATES: Surely, my friend, it's appropriate for a man with the greatest responsibilities to have the greatest wisdom. However, I think it's
worth examining Nicias, to see what he has his eye on in his attempt to
pin down this term 'bravery'.

LACHES: In that case, *you* consider the point, Socrates.

SOCRATES: I intend to, my dear sir; but don't think I'm excluding you
from sharing the discussion. Do give it your attention, and join me in
considering the arguments that are put forward.

LACHES: Very well, then; if you really think it's necessary.

SOCRATES: Indeed I do.

B[7]. Nicias Has Defined Goodness, Not Bravery

*In this section Socrates raises a difficulty for Nicias by showing that his defi-
nition of bravery actually contradicts their initial assumption that bravery is a
part of goodness (190c–d). First, Nicias is brought to see that his definition is
equivalent to the proposition that bravery is the knowledge of future evil and*

1. Lamachus was a respected Athenian general; the colleague of Nicias on the Sicilian
expedition, he was killed in a skirmish before Syracuse in 414.

2. Aexone was Laches' township (see p. 85 n. 1); its inhabitants had a proverbial reputation
for abusive wit.

3. Prodicus was a sophist (see p. 94 n. 1) and contemporary of Socrates from Ceos. His
work concentrated on linguistic usage and undoubtedly included semantic distinctions between
ethical terms; he also wrote on the origin of religion and on natural science. On Damon see
p. 86 n. 1.

*future good or non-evil. Next, Socrates points out that knowledge is not subject
to temporal restrictions: if a doctor knows that a particular drug will cure a
particular illness, then he knows that it could have done so yesterday, and will
be able to do so tomorrow. Socrates seems to be suggesting that one difference
between knowing something and merely having an opinion that happens to be
true is that knowledge must be founded on general principles and observed
regularities. It follows that the knowledge which Nicias holds to be bravery is
none other than the knowledge of some such principles: if one knows about
future good and future evil, one must know certain general principles about the
nature of all good and evil things, which is, in short, the knowledge of good
and evil. Having gained Nicias' agreement for this step, Socrates then brings
out the inconsistency in Nicias' position. Nicias believes that being virtuous is
a matter of possessing certain kinds of knowledge, so he readily agrees that
goodness itself is the possession of the ultimate moral knowledge, which is the
knowledge of good and evil. It seems that within the terms of his definition
Nicias cannot distinguish between bravery and goodness, yet he also wishes to
say that there is a difference between them, since bravery is merely a part of
goodness. How is the dilemma to be resolved? The* Laches *offers no explicit
answer, but it has often been thought to contain clues to Plato's own view: the
merits of the various suggestions are discussed in the introduction, p. 72 ff.*

SOCRATES: Now, Nicias, could you explain it to us again from the
beginning? You know we started our discussion by considering bravery   198a
as a part of goodness?

NICIAS: Yes, I do.

SOCRATES: So you did agree with our answer that it's a *part*, and hence
that there are other parts, which are known collectively as goodness, didn't
you?

NICIAS: Yes, of course.

SOCRATES: Now, you mean the same by these parts as I do, don't you?
For me, besides bravery, the list includes self-control, fairness and other
similar qualities. Isn't it the same for you?

NICIAS: Certainly.   b

SOCRATES: Hold on a minute: so far we're in agreement, but now let's
consider what is fearful and what is encouraging, and make sure that you
don't think they are one thing, while we think they're another. Let me
tell you what we think, and if you don't agree, you can explain why. We
think that the things which are fearful are simply those which cause fear,
and that the things which are encouraging are those which do not; and
fear is caused not by past or present evil, but by the evil that one expects

to come, because fear is the expectation of future evil. You do agree with that, don't you, Laches?

c   LACHES: I agree entirely, Socrates.

SOCRATES: So there it is, Nicias: our view is that what is fearful is future evil, and what is encouraging is the good, or the absence of evil, that is yet to come. Now, is that how you describe them, or have you some other way?

NICIAS: No, that's how I describe them.

SOCRATES: And it's knowledge of *these* things you call bravery?

NICIAS: Absolutely.

SOCRATES: Then let's see if you agree with us on yet a third point.

NICIAS: What point is that?

d   SOCRATES: I'll explain. It seems to your friend and me, taking account of all objects of knowledge, that it's never one thing to know how a past event took place, another to know how events are unfolding in the present, and another to know how future events will come about and what the best course for them would be: it's the same knowledge throughout. For example, health, regardless of time, is the exclusive province of medicine, a single science which reviews the present state of things, and the events
e   of the past, and the way things will develop in the future; and agricultural science is in the same position as regards the produce of the land. And, of course, regarding military affairs, you yourselves would bear me out that it is generalship which always takes the best stock of any situation, particularly one lying in the future: generalship does not expect to be subordinate to prophecy, but to take precedence, because it has a better understanding of a current military situation and the way it will develop –
199a   hence the provision in law that the general has authority over the prophet, rather than the prophet over the general.[1] Are we agreed, Laches?

LACHES: Yes, we are.

SOCRATES: Well now, Nicias, do you agree with us that, when the subject is the same, it's one and the same kind of knowledge that understands future, present and past?

NICIAS: Yes, that is my view, Socrates.

SOCRATES: And bravery, my friend, is knowledge of what is fearful
b   and what is encouraging, as you say – isn't that so?

NICIAS: Yes.

1. Prophets or seers (see p. 107 n. 2) formed part of a general's staff. Plato may intend an allusion to Nicias' excessive reliance on his prophets, notably when in the summer of 413 he delayed the retreat from Syracuse for three weeks on their advice, a move which led to the destruction of the Athenian army and Nicias' own death. Thucydides VII.50, and Plutarch, *Life of Nicias* 23, have the story.

SOCRATES: And we've agreed that what is fearful and what is encouraging are, respectively, future evil and future good.

NICIAS: Certainly.

SOCRATES: And that it's the same knowledge that covers the future and all the other stages of the same subjects.

NICIAS: That's so.

SOCRATES: Then bravery can't only be knowledge of what is fearful and what is encouraging, because like other kinds of knowledge it understands not only the future stages of good and evil,[1] but also the present c and the past.

NICIAS: Apparently so.

SOCRATES: So the answer you gave us, Nicias, covers only about a third part of bravery, whereas we asked what bravery is as a whole. And so now, it seems, on your own admission, bravery is knowledge not only of what is fearful and what is encouraging, but according to the way you describe it now, of pretty well the whole subject of good and evil, regardless of time. Does that reflect your change of mind, or would you put it d differently, Nicias?

NICIAS: No, that's how it seems to me, Socrates.

SOCRATES: Then does it seem to you, good sir, that a man would in any way lack goodness, if he understood all the different kinds of good, and had an exact knowledge of the course of these in the past, present and future, and a similar understanding of evil? Moreover, do you suppose he'd lack self-control, or fairness and holiness, when because of his knowledge of how to behave properly towards the gods and his fellow men, he alone has it in him to avoid what is to be feared and gain what is e good?[2]

NICIAS: I think you have a point there, Socrates.

SOCRATES: So, what you're now describing, Nicias, won't be a *part* of goodness, but goodness in its entirety.

NICIAS: So it seems.

SOCRATES: But we did say that bravery is only *one* of the parts of goodness.

NICIAS: Yes, we did.

SOCRATES: But what you're now describing appears not to be so.

NICIAS: No, it seems not.

SOCRATES: So we've *not* discovered what bravery is, Nicias.

NICIAS: No, apparently not.

---

1. καὶ πάντως ἐχόντων omitted (Stallbaum).
2. καὶ τὰ μή omitted (Badham).

B[8]. The Discussion Breaks Up: Socrates Suggests
They All Have Much to Learn

All the generals can agree is that Lysimachus and Melesias should ask Socrates if he is willing to undertake their sons' education himself. Socrates, however, feels that he has not emerged from the discussion with greater credit than the others, and declines the invitation. He suggests that when a teacher is found, they should all take lessons, and not just send the boys. The dialogue concludes because all concerned have failed to prove themselves suitably qualified to speak on education.

LACHES: And there was I thinking you'd find it, my dear Nicias – you
200a were so disdainful of the answers *I* gave Socrates. In fact, with that expertise you picked up from Damon I quite expected you to make the discovery!

NICIAS: That's marvellous, Laches, I must say! A moment ago you were shown to know nothing at all about bravery, and now you don't think it matters any more: so long as I'm shown up in the same light, that's all that bothers you. We're both totally ignorant of things any self-respecting man ought to know, but apparently it won't make any differ-
b ence to you now! It strikes me you're behaving in a typically human way – you keep an eye on others, but you never take a good look at yourself. Now, I think I've spoken fairly well for the moment on what we were discussing, and if there's anything unsatisfactory in what has been said, I'll correct it later with Damon's help (a man you want to ridicule without ever having met) and with the help of others. And once I have the matter settled, I'll explain it to you; I won't begrudge you that – I think you have
c a lot to learn!

LACHES: And you're such a clever fellow, I know, Nicias! All the same, as far as the education of their boys goes, my advice to Lysimachus here and Melesias is to dispense with you and me, but not to let our friend Socrates slip away, as I said from the beginning. If my sons were old enough, that's exactly what I would do.

NICIAS: On that even I agree with you: if Socrates is willing to take charge of the boys, they shouldn't look any further – I'd be only too
d pleased to entrust Niceratus to him,[1] if he should be willing. But, you see, every time I mention anything about it, he recommends other people and isn't willing to do it himself. However, why don't you see if Socrates will take more notice of you, Lysimachus?

1. Niceratus: Nicias' son, said by Aristotle (*Rhetoric* 1413a8; cf. Xenophon, *Symposium* III. 5, IV. 6) to have been made to learn all of Homer by heart and compete in rhapsodic competitions (on which see pp. 39–40). He was executed in 404/3 by the Thirty Tyrants, a group of radical oligarchs who seized power in Athens immediately after the Peloponnesian War.

LYSIMACHUS: It's only right he should, Nicias: I'd be willing to do a great deal for him that I'd not be willing to do for scores of other people. What do you say, then, Socrates? Will you do as I ask and wholeheartedly help the boys make the best of themselves?

SOCRATES: It would certainly be a terrible thing, Lysimachus, not to   e
be willing wholeheartedly to help someone make the best of himself. So, if it had become apparent in the course of our discussions just now that I had some knowledge of the matter which our two friends do not, it would be right to make a point of inviting *me* to do them this kindness; but we've all become equally confused. Why opt for any particular one of us? I don't   201a
think any of us is to be preferred; and since that's the case, you're to consider whether my advice sounds any good. My suggestion, gentlemen – tell it not in Gath[1] – is that we should all cooperate in looking for the best teacher we can find, primarily for ourselves – we need one – and secondly for the boys, and we shouldn't spare the expense or any other efforts we can make. What I don't advise is that we allow ourselves to remain in the same condition we're in now. And if anyone finds it amusing that men of our age think fit to go back to school, I think we should appeal to Homer,   b
who said that 'modesty sits ill upon a needy man'.[2] Let's not take any notice of what anyone else may say, and let's all cooperate in seeing to our own needs as well as the boys'.

LYSIMACHUS: Yes, I like that idea of yours, Socrates. I'm the oldest, and I'll be the keenest to learn with the youngsters! But what you must do for me is this: tomorrow morning I'd like you to call round at my house so we can discuss the matter further – don't let me down. But for now   c
let's draw the meeting to a close.

SOCRATES: I'll do that, Lysimachus. God willing, I'll call on you tomorrow.

---

1. The Greek seems to mean 'between ourselves', and may be a loose quotation: cf. Euripides, *Hippolytus* 295 and Aristophanes, *Thesmophoriazousai* 472.
2. The quotation is from *Odyssey* XVII, 347; it is given in its original form at *Charmides* 161a.

LYSIS

INTRODUCTION TO *LYSIS*

The *Lysis* is on the face of it difficult to the point of perversity. It asks a question – 'What is friendship?' – which is in all conscience hard enough, but does so in such a way as to generate confusion. Why? Was Plato simply muddled, or did he have some deep purpose?

But first, a word on the key terminology. The theme of the *Lysis* is *philia*. 'Friendship' is the customary, but inadequate, translation of the Greek. 'Liking' hardly covers the range of connotations of the concept any better:[1] parents cannot be said to feel mere 'friendship' or 'liking' for their children. Consequently 'love' is in many cases a preferable rendering, so long as it is remembered that in general fond affection is the major component of the love that is *philia*, whereas the love which is character-ized by passionate sexual desire is, in Greek, *erōs*; and *erōs* constitutes the subject of two of Plato's later and more elaborate dialogues, the *Phaedrus* and the *Symposium*.[2] It is, however, impossible to put *philia* in one seman-tic compartment and *erōs* in another: some instances of *erōs* may manifest elements of *philia* and vice versa.[3]

In the introductory section of the dialogue, which deals with the youth Hippothales and his love for the boy Lysis, the terms used are without exception[4] 'erotic': Hippothales is referred to as the *erastēs*, the older, sexually active partner (*erōn*) in a male homosexual relationship; Lysis is the *paidika*, the younger, sexually passive partner (*erōmenos*)[5] – though Hippothales has not as yet managed to consummate his love (*erōs*). His *erōs* for Lysis stands in relation to and in contrast with the simple *philia*

1. See Guthrie, IV, pp. 136–7.

2. The *Lysis* is generally agreed to be among the latest of the early dialogues: see Guthrie, IV, pp. 134–5; C. H. Kahn, 'Did Plato Write Socratic Dialogues?', *Classical Quarterly*, 31 (1981), pp. 305–20; G. Vlastos, 'The Socratic Elenchus', *Oxford Studies in Ancient Philosophy*, I (1983), p. 27 n. 2 and pp. 57–8, and 'Socrates' Disavowal of Knowledge', *Philosophical Quarterly*, 35 (1985), p. 1 n. 1. For the dramatic date of the work, see p. 120 n. 4.

3. For fuller discussion of *philia*, see Dirlmeier, Fraisse and Ferguson, pp. 53–75; also Robin and Gould. For a discussion of *erōs* and *philia* with special reference to homosexual relationships (the context in which *erōs* and *philia* are examined in the *Lysis*), see K. J. Dover, *Greek Homosexuality* (London 1978), pp. 49–54. Compare also Hyland.

4. At 206a Socrates addresses Hippothales as 'my friend' (*phile*). This is the only occurrence of any *philia*-related term before the entry of Lysis and Menexenus into the dialogue, but it has no connection with Hippothales' relationship with Lysis.

5. See Dover, op. cit., p. 16.

(friendship) which the two boys, Lysis and Menexenus, when they are subsequently introduced into the dialogue, are seen to feel for each other, and with the higher sort of *philia* which Socrates will exhibit in his treatment of the two boys and Hippothales. That is to say, Hippothales embodies the one-sided sexual love (*erōs*) felt by the lover (*erastēs*)[1]; in Lysis and Menexenus we have an instance of natural, reciprocal friendship (*philia*); while Socrates gradually reveals a higher *philia*, educative *philia*.[2] On a practical level Hippothales is taught how a lover (*erastēs*) should treat his boy (*paidika*); on an intellectual and moral level Lysis, Menexenus and Hippothales (and of course all the others present) are given a lesson in philosophy.[3]

In this way the dramatic framework[4] of the dialogue provides arresting illustrations of *philia* and *erōs* before the actual philosophical inquiry into the nature of *philia* is begun.[5] Next, the preliminary inquiry (207d–211a), which Plato uses to smooth the transition from the obvious charms of his scene-painting to the greater demands of the philosophical problems of the dialogue proper, offers in the choice of its theme yet another example of *philia*, parental love; this is simple natural love (which, however, is shown later on (212e–213a) sometimes to be unreciprocated by the child, when very young). Here too the connection between *philia* and education (*paideia*) is implicit in the argument. For *philia* is the wish to make someone as happy as possible.[6] Happiness consists in possessing the freedom to do what one likes.[7] One is granted the freedom to do what one likes in those spheres of action in which one possesses greater knowledge. This is, of course, because it is to everyone's advantage to entrust the power to act in a given sphere to those with greater knowledge of that sphere. But according to Socratic doctrine, knowledge is knowledge of the good, whether in morals or any other sphere of conduct, and if one knows the good, one will do only good, since no one deliberately does wrong. That is to say, knowledge brings one the freedom to do what one likes, which in turn brings happiness. Happiness is therefore dependent on knowledge;

1. Cf. *Phaedrus* 238c–241d.
2. See further Friedländer, pp. 92–104.
3. It has been argued that one of the aims of this dialogue was to rescue Socrates' reputation as an educator of the young from the charge of corrupting them, for which, along with the charge of impiety, he was condemned to death in 399: see Levin, p. 250 n. 20.
4. No indication of the dramatic date of the dialogue can be gleaned from it, unless one is to take the reference to 'Darius' gold' at 211e to refer specifically to Darius II, who was king of Persia from 424 to 405, rather than as a general allusion to the proverbial wealth of the kings of Persia, notably of Darius I, who reigned from 521 to 486. See Schoplick, p. 28 n. 1.
5. See also Hoerber, pp. 15–28.
6. At this stage of the dialogue, this is simply a 'working definition'.
7. cf. *Republic* 557b–c, 561c–e.

and if one wants someone to be as happy as possible, one must give that person as much knowledge as possible: one must *educate* him.[1]

It is while the dialogue is still in its preliminary stages that what is perhaps the most striking feature of the Socratic conception of *philia* is brought out: the view that the basis of friendship is utility or, as it is seen later in the dialogue (215b, 221d–e), need or deficiency: one man is useful to another because he meets a need which that man has. What makes a man useful is knowledge, which, according to Socratic belief, is to be identified with the good: one man feels *philia* for another because that other possesses relevant knowledge which makes him useful to the first man.[2] But the utilitarian motive is not so utterly selfish as it might at first glance seem: what is useful is what produces good for one, so to love what is useful is to love what is good, albeit what is good for oneself. The utilitarian view of *philia* leads to the general conclusion that everyone will feel *philia* for the man who is wise (i.e. who possesses knowledge), because he will be useful and good (210d).[3]

With the dramatic and philosophical background now set, one would have expected Socrates to start the philosophical inquiry proper with the question 'What is *philia*?' The other early 'definition' dialogues all ask their respective questions in this form. Before dealing with the primary question of the dialogue, however, Plato toys with the problem of the ambiguity inherent in the terms to be discussed, by having Socrates ask,[4] 'When one man loves (*philei*) another, which is the friend of which?' Like the English 'friend', the Greek *philos* may be active, passive, or both: it may mean 'a man who loves another', 'a man who is loved by another', or 'a man who both loves another and is loved by that other'. Is the friend the man who loves (but is not necessarily loved in return by the man he loves), or the man who is loved (but does not necessarily love in return the man by whom he is loved), or the man who both loves a man and is loved by him in return? At first sight the third alternative would seem the obvious answer, but it is correct only so far as it goes. It is incomplete in

1. One of the major benefits which the younger partner (*paidika*) was considered to derive from his older lover (*erastēs*) was education (*paideia*): see Dover, op. cit., pp. 202–3.

2. *Philia* based on utility is one of the sorts of friendship which Aristotle recognizes in his analysis of the term in *Nicomachean Ethics* VIII and IX.

3. See Guthrie, III, pp. 462–7, on Socratic utilitarianism.

4. Socrates first says (212a) that what he wants to ask is 'how one man becomes the friend of another'. This is not, of course, the main question of the dialogue. It is immediately superseded by the more specific question, 'Which is the friend of which?', but is later addressed in the investigation of the cause and goal of friendship (217a ff.). It arises from Socrates' musing on his inability to find a real friend and is, in a sense, transitional, in that it leads directly to the first question of the main part of the dialogue.

that it fails to account for unreciprocated *philia*. Conventional usage allows us to talk of *philia* when only one of the parties involved actually loves. In such a case one may call either the man who loves or the man who is loved the friend, according to one's point of view. If A loves B but B hates A, A can be called the friend because he loves B (who hates him), or B can be called the friend because he is loved by A (whom he hates).

What is Plato's purpose in devoting so much attention to the ambiguities of the word *philos*? Perhaps, conscious of the difficulties inherent in the word under consideration and unable to offer a solution to a question which, in the terms in which it is couched, must remain insoluble, he wished to bring the difficulty out into the open and to do so in as entertaining a manner as possible, in a passage of dazzling eristics, even if it meant perplexing his readers as deeply as Socrates bewildered the two boys.

Plato now turns to the dialogue's main question: 'Who are friends?',[1] or rather, as it is put later in the dialogue, when the emphasis has shifted from *philia* as an interpersonal relationship to *philia* as the pursuit of a loved object,[2] 'What is a "friend"?', that is to say, 'What is "that which is a friend" (neuter)?'[3] But the dialogue ends (223b) with Socrates' assertion that they have been unable to discover what a 'friend' (masculine) is. In fact it is not the masculine *ho philos*, 'the friend', but the neuter *to philon*, 'that which is a friend', which has been the term under investigation throughout the main part of the dialogue. This shift from the masculine plural ('Who are friends?') is not difficult in Greek, where the use of the neuter singular imports a greater degree of universality or abstractness into the term. The neuter singular of the adjective is in general in Greek virtually synonymous with its cognate abstract noun. In the *Euthyphro*, for example, the term to be defined shifts between *to hosion* ('that which is pious') and *hosiotēs* ('piety'). But the substitution of *to philon* for *philia* brings with it a complication peculiar to the concept. *Philia* may be, indeed in general usage properly is, reciprocal, whereas *to philon* is naturally passive, meaning 'that which is loved'. *Philia* too usually refers to human relationships, while *to philon* is a non-human object, or an abstraction. In substituting *to philon* for *philia* Plato is in fact narrowing the scope of the investigation. We move from considering friendship as a relationship between two persons to investigating an impersonal object

1. 213c, 214a, 214d. This is investigated in the form, 'Who is friend to whom?', that is to say, in the specific form, 'Is like friend to like?', etc. Inasmuch as *philia* in the human sphere is the relationship between *philoi* or friends, it is appropriate for the search for the definition of the abstract *philia* to be framed in terms of an attempt to define the members of that relationship.

2. See Robinson (1970), pp. 70–72.

3. 216c, 218b, 218d and 222b.

which receives love, and thence indeed to investigating the primary object of love (*prōton philon*).

Indeed, it is only at the end of the dialogue that, by an abrupt change, Plato returns to the concept of mutual friendship.[1] The basic problem of the dialogue lies in Plato's failure to distinguish between *philia* as a loving human relationship and *philia* as the pursuit of a loved object. These are essentially separate questions, but Plato treats them as if they were the same. He starts off by investigating the former, moves without warning at 216c to considering the second, and then abruptly embraces the first again at 221e. He can hardly have been unaware that he was attempting to investigate two complex questions in the same dialogue. Why, then, did he choose to do this? Was it because he wished to stress the intimate connections between the two? Or has he allowed himself to be diverted from his original aim of explaining mutual friendship by his desire to show that the 'first loved object' (*prōton philon*) was the good, because the latter was for him philosophically more important?

It is interesting to see how in his analysis of *philia* in the *Nicomachean Ethics*[2] Aristotle avoided the pitfalls in which Plato let himself be caught in the *Lysis*. He first of all limits his discussion to *philia* as a relationship between human beings, explicitly excluding any excursion into the realm of the abstract; he then introduces the terms *philētos* and *philēton*, which are exclusively passive in meaning ('who is loved' and 'which is loved'), thereby avoiding the confusion of active and passive meanings of *philos* and *philon*. And he dismisses the notion of *philia* for inanimate objects: they are incapable of reciprocating the *philia* and one feels no wish for their good. He divides friendship into three kinds: first, that based on utility (or benefit); second, that based on pleasure; and third, that based on goodness. The first and second kinds are merely 'accidental', in that the person who is loved is not loved for what he is but for the benefit or pleasure he can provide, and are easily dissolved; the third, perfect friendship, is of those who are good, and alike in their goodness. Each loves the other for his goodness, and their friendship lasts as long as their goodness (which is a long time, since goodness is an enduring quality). Further, such friendship *entails* mutual benefit and pleasure (the first two kinds). For Aristotle, therefore, mutuality is an essential component of any friendship: his definition of friendship is *mutual* goodwill (*eunoia*) and a wish for each other's good that is recognized by both parties. Without reciprocation and without recognition of the friendly disposition, there is only goodwill, not friendship.

1. See Robinson (1970), pp. 70–72.
2. See especially 1155b–1156a.

With his insistence on mutuality, his theory of goodwill and his distinguishing of an object or recipient of love (*philētos*, *philēton*), Aristotle provides an answer to the problem which Plato raises at the beginning of the discussion of *philia*, in his question, 'Which is friend of which?': how is it that the man who both loves and is loved can be called a friend, when neither the man who only loves (but is not also loved), nor the man who is only loved (but does not also love), can be called a friend? For Aristotle, only the first can be called a friend or *philos*; the second is only well disposed (*eunous*); the third is only an object of love (*philētos*). Aristotle answers the question by limiting the meaning of *philos*; Plato, by confronting the term as it is actually used in Greek, makes himself a prisoner of its ambiguities.

The whole discussion of reciprocity at the beginning of the main part of the dialogue is quite mercilessly sophistic in nature, in its bewildering examination of the problem of 'Which is friend of which?' And when Socrates goes on to examine the two most prevalent traditional explanations of the phenomenon of friendship – the attraction of likes and the attraction of opposites or unlikes – his general treatment is again sophistic, especially in his championing first one hypothesis and then its opposite. He achieves refutation of these hypotheses by forcing 'like' and 'unlike' to mean 'absolutely identical' and 'absolutely opposite',[1] rather than merely 'similar' and 'dissimilar'. Such absolutes are, of course, unattainable in the human sphere.

Why does Socrates argue in this way in the *Lysis*? It is hard to believe that Plato was unaware of the eristic nature of the argumentation.[2] The most plausible explanation[3] is that he intends to satirize the methods of the sophists. But why, then, are there no sophists present in the dialogue, to act as dramatic and philosophical foils? Why adopt such an approach with two young boys? One would have expected such arguments as Socrates puts forward to have come *from* a sophist, whom he would have proceeded to refute, as in the *Euthydemus*, or to have been used by Socrates *against* a sophist, as in the *Protagoras*.[4] Perhaps Menexenus is meant to represent the sophists in our dialogue. He is explicitly characterized as 'eristic' or 'argumentative' and as a 'formidable opponent in debate' (211b–c); yet he hardly lives up to either description. Indeed, in this

1. And 'good' and 'bad' to mean 'absolutely good' and 'absolutely bad': see Hoerber, pp. 22–3; Guthrie, IV, p. 147; Levin, p. 246.

2. cf. 216a–b; see also Guthrie, IV, p. 145 ff.

3. So G. Stallbaum, *Platonis Opera Omnia*, IV, ii (2nd ed., Gotha and Erfurt 1857), p. 114; see also Guthrie, IV, p. 146.

4. See Guthrie, IV, pp. 143–4.

dialogue, all the theses which are proposed for consideration are proposed by Socrates himself, just as all the refutations of them are Socrates' own. Menexenus, like Lysis, is permitted little more than to say 'Yes' or 'No', as Socrates requires.[1]

There is, however, much that is both positive and valuable to be gleaned from the *Lysis*, even from the more eristic passages. The recognition of an intermediate state between good and bad[2] is a major step forward from the primitive dichotomies of the Presocratic philosophers and of the sophists, who made such unscrupulous use in their eristic of the 'either-or' split.[3] This recognition assumes greater importance later in Plato, when he develops the notion of *doxa*, opinion, as a state intermediate between knowledge (of the forms) and ignorance.[4] The distinction is in a sense prefigured in the *Lysis* itself, where Socrates speaks of an intermediate state for philosophers between wisdom (i.e. knowledge) and ignorance,[5] though here there is no mention of *doxa* or hint of the theory of forms.

In drawing, in the course of the argument, the important distinction between property and accident, Socrates introduces the concept of *parousia* or 'presence' (*of* the property or accident *to* the object). This concept is used later in the theory of forms, where the relation of forms to particulars is frequently termed 'presence': the form is 'present to' the particulars (and the particulars 'share in' or 'partake of' (*metechein*) the form). But there is no need to import subsequent Platonic doctrine into this relatively simple context.[6] Nor should one try to see the theory of forms in the *prōton philon*, 'the first object of love', though here the temptation is greater. For it is spoken of in the language which Plato later uses of the forms, and indeed does prefigure the form of the good in the *Republic*,[7] since it is 'what every soul pursues and that for the sake of which everything is done'. But the relation of the *prōton philon* to the other *phila* or objects of love is not the same as that of the form to the particulars: the *prōton philon* is not the form which is present to all *phila* and by which they are *phila*.[8]

What positive conclusions can be drawn from the *aporia* with which the

1. See G. Vlastos, 'The Socratic Elenchus', *Oxford Studies in Ancient Philosophy*, 1 (1983), p. 58, and McTighe, p. 69; see also Guthrie, IV, p. 147.

2. See also *Gorgias* 467e ff.

3. See Guthrie, IV, p. 148, and cf. *Euthydemus* often, e.g. 276b. On eristic in general, see pp. 32, 299–303.

4. See pp. 27–8 with references there, and *Symposium* 201e ff., *Republic* 476e ff.

5. 218a–b; cf. also *Symposium* 204a ff.

6. 217c–218c: see Guthrie, IV, pp. 148–9, 150–53, and Vlastos, op. cit., pp. 35–7.

7. 505d–e; see Guthrie, IV, p. 151, and Schoplick, p. 55.

8. See further Guthrie, IV, pp. 151–2.

dialogue ends? Plato leaves one hypothesis of the final piece of argumentation unexamined and consequently unrefuted. 'What is good is akin to everything, whereas what is bad is alien to everything' would have meant that the good is akin to the good, to the bad and to what is neither good nor bad, and that the bad is not akin to the good, or to the bad, or to what is neither good nor bad. Since nothing is friend to bad and bad is friend to nothing (214b–d, cf. 216b), the formulation leaves: the good is akin to the good; the good is akin to what is neither good nor bad; and, correspondingly, since kinship has been shown to be reciprocal (221e–222d), what is neither good nor bad is akin to the good. The good, however, in being self-sufficient, is friend to *nothing* (214e–215c), so that only the correspondent statement can remain: what is neither good nor bad is akin to – and so a friend to – the good. This is in accord with the good's being the first object of love (*prōton philon*), but cannot easily be reconciled with *philia* as a reciprocal, loving, human relationship, unless one is to assume that a man, who, *qua* man, is neither good nor bad (since no human being can be absolutely good or absolutely bad), loves the good in another man, who, *qua* man, is neither good nor bad, and is loved by that other for the good in himself.

This promising train of thought brings us to the good's being a friend of the good, a doctrine which Plato elsewhere accepts much more readily. In the *Phaedrus* (255b; cf. *Laws* 837a ff.), Socrates explicitly states that fate has decreed that good man be friend to good man (and that bad man not be friend to bad man). In *Republic* 387d–e Plato links the self-sufficiency of good men (in the non-absolute sense, i.e. men who are good but not absolutely or completely good) and their friendship for each other: one good (*epieikēs*) man will not think death a terrible thing for another good man who is his friend (*hetairos*), or mourn him as having suffered something terrible; and he is himself most self-sufficient in regard to living a good life, and, of all men, least needs another. And Aristotle who, of course, makes the friendship of good men the highest kind of friendship (*Nicomachean Ethics* 1156b7 ff.), is at pains to show that good men do need each other as friends; their self-sufficiency is not absolute (1169b3–1170b19). In the *Lysis* Plato is, in effect, a victim of his own terminology and of his attempt to explore the two questions of the primary object of love and reciprocal friendship simultaneously. He has accounted for the former satisfactorily, but lost sight, to some extent, of the latter in the process.[1]

Is the dialogue a success? Opinions differ,[2] but the *Lysis* has too many

1. See Robinson (1970), pp. 70–72.
2. See Guthrie, IV, p. 143, for a brief review.

splendid features for us to count it a failure. The scene-setting and characterization (especially of the besotted Hippothales) are first-rate; the eristic
fireworks are as instructive as they are dazzling. With its discussion of
the problems of reciprocity and 'viewpoint' in considering the question
'Which is friend of which?', in its examination of the utilitarian motive
for friendship and the possibility that its cause lies in a feeling of lack or
deficiency, in its investigation of traditional theories of *philia*, such as the
attraction of likes or opposites, and in hinting at a new one in *oikeiotēs* or
kinship, the *Lysis* raises fundamental issues about the nature of personal
friendship, in addition to answering the essential question of what the
primary object of *philia* is: the good.

SUMMARY OF *LYSIS*

A. Depiction of Simple *Erōs* (Sexual Love) and *Philia* (Friendship)

B. Knowledge is the Source of Happiness

C. Reciprocal and Non-reciprocal Friendship

D. Like is Friend to Like

E. Unlike is Friend to Unlike

F. The Presence of Bad is the Cause of Love (*Philia*)

G. The Possession of Good is the Goal of Love (*Philia*)

H. The First Thing That is Loved

I. Desire is the Cause of Love

J. What is Akin is Friend to What is Akin: *Aporia*

LYSIS

SOCRATES

CTESIPPUS: From the deme of Paeania, the cousin of
Menexenus, with whom he was present at the death
of Socrates (*Phaedo* 59b). Also appears in the *Euthydemus*. At the time of this dialogue, he is in his midteens.

HIPPOTHALES: Of approximately the same age as Ctesippus. Does not appear elsewhere in Plato, but is
mentioned as a follower of his by Diogenes Laertius
(III.46).

LYSIS: Eldest son of Democrates, from the deme
Aexone, in his early teens. Unknown apart from this
dialogue.[1]

MENEXENUS: Son of Demophon; of the same age as
Lysis. In all likelihood, he is the Menexenus who
gave his name to another Platonic dialogue.

---

1. But see J. K. Davies, *Athenian Propertied Families, 600–300 B.C.* (Oxford 1971),
pp. 359–61.

LYSIS

A. *Depiction of Simple* Erōs *(Sexual Love) and* Philia *(Friendship)*

The first section sets the scene, introduces the characters and provides two contrasting pictures of love and friendship. The first is the unreciprocated sexual love (erōs) of the lover (erastēs) for the boy with whom he is in love (erōmenos) in the romantic infatuation of Hippothales with Lysis; the second, the simple reciprocal friendship (philia) of the two boys, Lysis and Menexenus.

I was on my way from the Academy,[1] making straight for the Lyceum,[2] along the road which runs outside the city wall, close under the wall itself. At the little gate by the spring of Panops[3] I came across Hippothales, Hieronymus' son, Ctesippus from Paeania[4] and a number of other young men standing in a group with them. As I approached them, Hippothales spotted me and said, 'Socrates, where are you off to? Where are you coming from?'

'I'm on my way from the Academy and going straight to the Lyceum,' I replied.

'You should come here,' he said, 'straight to us. Aren't you going to join us? It'll be worth it, you know.'

'Where do you mean?' I asked. 'And to whom? Who's "us"?'

'Here,' he replied, showing me a sort of enclosure and an opened door directly opposite the wall. 'We spend our time there,' he went on, 'and we're not the only ones. Lots and lots of other young men do too, handsome young men.'

'What *is* this place? What do you do here?'

'It's a wrestling-school,' he said, 'built not long ago. We spend most of our time there having discussions. We'd be glad to have you join us in them.'

'That's very kind of you,' I said. 'Who's the teacher there?'

'A crony and admirer of yours,' he replied, 'Miccus.'[5]

1. A park and gymnasium just outside Athens, to the north-west of the city. Plato established his 'Academy' there, *c.* 385.

2. A gymnasium to the north-east of the city, where Aristotle later (*c.* 335) founded his 'Lyceum'; cf. *Euthydemus ad init.*

3. An obscure local Athenian deity.

4. An Athenian 'deme' or local administrative unit.

5. Nothing else is known of him.

'Heavens!' I exclaimed. 'He's no lightweight, but an able master of his craft.'[1]

'Will you follow us in, then,' he asked, 'to see for yourself who's there?'

b   'First I wouldn't mind hearing what my going in will entail, and which handsome young man is the favourite amongst you.'

'Each of us has his own opinion about that, Socrates,' he said.

'And what's yours, Hippothales? Tell me that.'

He blushed at the question, so I said, 'Hippothales, you don't need to tell me whether or not you're in love with someone. I can see that you're not just in love, but that you're already far gone in it. I may not know c   much else, I may be useless at other things, but somehow God's given me the power to recognize in an instant a man in love *and* the boy he's in love with.'

Hearing this made him blush more than ever. Ctesippus then said, 'How sweet of you to blush, Hippothales, and to be too shy to tell Socrates his name! Still, if Socrates spends even a short time with you he'll become a nervous wreck hearing you go on and on about him. He's certainly made d   us quite deaf, Socrates, dinning the name "Lysis" into our ears. He only has to have a little to drink, and we're pretty sure to wake up thinking we're hearing that name. And while what he says of him in conversation is awful, it's not absolutely awful; but when he tries to drown us in a flood of poetry and prose he's composed . . . ! What's even more awful is that he actually sings of his boy in an amazing voice which we have to put up with hearing. And now when you ask him the boy's name he blushes!'

e   'I should think Lysis must be someone young,' I said. 'I'm only guessing, though, because I didn't recognize the name when I heard it.'

'Yes,' he said, 'people don't use his own name very much. He's still identified by means of his father's who is very well known. And yet I'm positive you must know what the boy looks like. His looks alone are enough to get him recognized.'

'Tell me whose son he is,' I said.

'He's the eldest son of Democrates from Aexone,'[2] he replied.

'Well,' I said, 'what an absolutely noble and splendid love it is you've found, Hippothales! Come on, give me a demonstration of what you've 205a been giving these fellows here. I want to find out whether you know what a lover ought to say about his boy, to his face or to others.'

'Surely you're not taking seriously anything Ctesippus has been saying, Socrates?' he asked.

1. Literally 'wise man' (*sophistēs*).
2. Another Athenian deme; see p. 131 n. 4, and *Laches* 197c.

'Do you deny being in love with the boy he says you're in love with?'
I asked.

'No, I don't,' he replied, 'but I do deny writing poems or prose pieces
about my boy.'

'He's insane,' said Ctesippus. 'Raving mad.'

So I said, 'Hippothales, I don't want to hear any of your verses or any
song you've written about the young man, but rather their general tenor,   b
so that I'll know how you behave towards your boy.'

'No doubt Ctesippus will tell you,' he replied. 'His knowledge and
recollection of it all must be quite perfect if, as he says, he's bored to death
hearing me ranting all the time.'

'Right then,' said Ctesippus, 'I certainly shall. The fact is, Socrates, it's
a ridiculous business. How isn't it ridiculous that a man who is a lover
and thinks of virtually nothing but the boy he's in love with should have
nothing original to say that even a boy himself might not come up with?   c
He just puts into his poems and prose pieces things that the whole city
sings of about Democrates and the boy's grandfather, Lysis, and all his
ancestors – their wealth, their horse-breeding, their victories at the Pythian, Isthmian and Nemean Games[1] in the chariot-races and horse-races,
and as well as that even hoarier stuff. Indeed, the day before yesterday he
described to us in a poem of his the entertainment of Heracles – how,
because he was related to Heracles, their ancestor, being himself   d
descended from Zeus (and the daughter of the founder of the deme[2]), duly
made Heracles welcome – just the sort of thing old women sing of, and a
lot of other stuff like that, Socrates. That's what he puts into his prose
pieces and songs and forces *us* to listen to.'

When I heard that I said, 'You *are* ridiculous, Hippothales! Are you
composing and singing a eulogy in your own honour before you've won
your victory?'

'But it's not in my own honour, Socrates, that I either compose or sing
it,' he objected.

'You *think* it's not,' I said.

'How's that?' he asked.

'Those songs,' I said, 'concern you most of all. If you catch the sort of   e
boy you're talking of, what you've said and sung of him will bring you
glory and be in effect eulogies in honour of you as victor, in that you got

1. Three of the four great Greek games, the fourth and most important being the Olympic
Games held at Olympia in Elis. The Pythian Games, second in importance to the Olympic,
took place at Delphi; the Isthmian, which were especially patronized by the Athenians, at
Corinth; and the Nemean at Nemea in the Argolid.

2. See p. 131 n. 4.

such a boy. However, if he slips through your fingers, the greater the eulogies you've pronounced on your boy have been, the greater will the blessings of beauty and goodness seem to be of which you've been 206a deprived, and so you'll seem to be ridiculous. Any man who knows what's what when it comes to love, my friend, does not praise the boy he's in love with until he's caught him, for fear of how the future will turn out. Also, when a man praises or compliments handsome boys, they become filled with pride and conceit. Don't you think so?'

'I do,' he said.

'And the more conceited they are, the harder they become to catch?'

'Probably.'

'What sort of a hunter do you think a man would be then if, when hunting, he scared off his quarry and made it harder to catch?'

b 'Obviously a pretty poor one.'

'And to employ speeches and songs not so as to make him amenable but so as to make him wild shows considerable crassness, doesn't it?'

'I suppose so.'

'Well, watch out that you don't expose yourself to all those charges with your poetry-writing, Hippothales. Still, I don't imagine you'd readily agree that a man who harms himself by the poetry he writes can ever be a good poet, since he's harmful to himself.'

'Heavens, no,' he replied. 'That would be quite absurd. But it's for c precisely that reason that I'm taking you into my confidence, Socrates. If you've any further advice to give, do tell me what a man ought to say and do to endear himself to his boy.'

'It's not easy to say,' I replied. 'But if you wouldn't mind getting him to have a talk with me, I could perhaps give you a demonstration of what you ought to talk to him about, instead of the things these fellows tell me you say and sing.'

'Well,' he said, 'that's not difficult. If you go in with Ctesippus here, and sit down and start talking, I imagine he'll come over to you without any prompting – he's exceptionally fond of listening to people, and also, d since it's the festival of the Hermaea,[1] the young men and boys are mixed in together in the one spot. So he *will* come over to you, but if he doesn't, Ctesippus knows him well through his cousin Menexenus who happens to be Lysis' best friend. Let Ctesippus call him over, if he doesn't come without prompting.'

'That's what we should do,' I said. So I immediately took Ctesippus e into the wrestling-school. The others came after us.

Inside we found the boys. They had just finished making their sacrifice,

1. A festival in honour of Hermes, the patron of wrestling-schools and gymnasia.

and the ceremony was already almost over. In fact, they were all having
a game of knuckle-bones, and were still dressed in their finest clothes.
Though most of them were playing outside in the court, some were in a
corner of the changing-room, playing at odds and evens with a large
number of knuckle-bones which they took out of little baskets. Around
them stood others watching them. Lysis belonged to the latter group. He
stood among the boys and young men with a garland on his head. He was   207a
easily the best-looking, and deserved to be called not just handsome but
rather handsome and good. We went over to the opposite side of the room
and sat down – it was quiet there. We started to talk amongst ourselves.
Lysis kept turning round and looking at us, obviously wanting to come
over to us. For a while, however, he was at a loss about what to do, and
hesitated to come over to us on his own; but then Menexenus came in
from the court in the middle of the game he'd been playing, and when he   b
saw Ctesippus and me, came to sit beside us. Lysis saw him, followed and
sat down beside us with him. Then the others came over to us as well.
And, when Hippothales saw more people standing there, he hid himself
behind them, where he thought Lysis wouldn't notice him, since he was
afraid of annoying him. From there he listened to us.

I looked at Menexenus and said, 'Menexenus, which of you is the elder?'   c
'We disagree about that,' he replied.
'Would you also dispute which of you is the nobler, then?' I asked.
'Of course,' he said.
'And the same goes for which is the more handsome.'
They both laughed at that.
'Anyway, I shan't ask which of you is the wealthier,' I said, 'because
you're friends, aren't you?'
'Of course,' they replied.
'And friends are supposed to have all things in common, so in that at
least there will be no difference between you, provided you're telling the
truth about your friendship.'
They agreed.
I was then going to ask which of them was the juster and which the   d
cleverer, when someone came over and got Menexenus to leave with him,
claiming that the trainer wanted him. I presumed he was to take part in
the sacrifice.

B. *Knowledge is the Source of Happiness*

The description of how not to treat the boy one is in love with is now contrasted with a practical demonstration by Socrates of the right way to do it. His treatment of Lysis exemplifies a superior kind of love/friendship (philia): the educative kind. Socrates is, in fact, educating both Lysis and Hippothales simultaneously: Hippothales is being taught how to be a true friend (philos) and educate his boy himself; Lysis (and, of course, Hippothales and the rest) is being taught that he must acquire knowledge in order to be allowed to do what he likes and so gain happiness; and that he must be humble.

Socrates implicitly defines philia as 'wanting to make someone as happy as possible'; happiness (eudaimonia) is to consist in possessing freedom and being allowed to do what one likes. Taking as an example parental love (philia), he shows that it is the possession of knowledge in a certain sphere or spheres of action which wins the child freedom and the licence to do what he likes. Hence, by implication, knowledge gives happiness. The conclusion is reached that a man will be trusted by everyone in those matters in which he possesses greater knowledge, but that he will be trusted by no one in those in which he does not. Utility is introduced as an essential factor in philia: people will defer to someone with greater knowledge because it is to their advantage to do so; knowledge makes one useful and good (i.e. good for someone); and if one is useful and good one is universally sought after as a friend (philos).

Since Menexenus had gone off, then, I put my questions to Lysis instead: 'I suppose, Lysis, your father and mother love you very much?'

'Of course,' he replied.

'Then they'd want you to be as happy as possible?'

'Naturally.'

e 'Do you think that a man is happy when he's a slave and allowed to do nothing he desires?'

'Heavens, no, I don't,' he said.

'Then if your father and mother love you and desire your happiness, it's absolutely clear that they must do their best to make you happy.'

'Of course,' he said.

'So they let you do what you want and don't scold you at all or stop you doing what you desire?'

'Heavens, no, Socrates, there are lots and lots of things they stop me doing.'

'What do you mean?' I asked. 'They want you to be perfectly content, 208a but still stop you doing what you want? Well, tell me this: if you desire to ride in one of your father's chariots and take the reins in a race, they wouldn't let you, but would stop you?'

'Heavens,' he said, 'indeed they wouldn't let me.'

'Well then, whom would they?'

'My father has a charioteer who's paid to do that.'

'What do you mean? They trust a hired servant rather than you to do what he wants with the horses and, what's more, they actually pay this fellow money for doing just that?'

'Why, of course,' he replied.   b

'But they do trust you, I imagine, to be the master of the mule-pair. If you wanted to take the whip and flog them, they'd let you.'

'No, they certainly would not.'

'What!' I exclaimed. 'Is no one allowed to flog them?'

'Yes,' he said, 'the mule-driver is.'

'Is he a slave or a free man?'

'A slave,' he said.

'Do they really think more highly of a slave than of you, their son, and trust their property to him rather than you, and let him do what he wants, but stop you? Tell me this too: do they let you be your own master, or   c don't they trust you with even that?'

'Of course they don't,' he replied.

'But you do have a master?'

'My tutor here,' he said.[1]

'He's not a slave, is he?'

'Indeed he is. One of ours,' he replied.

'It *is* strange,' I said, 'that a slave should be the master of a free man. What is it this tutor does that makes him your master?'

'He takes me to school, of course,' he replied.

'Surely they're not your masters as well, your teachers?'

'They most certainly are.'

'So your father deliberately sets lots and lots of bosses and masters over   d you. But when you go home to your mother, she lets you do what you want with her wool or her loom when she's weaving, so that she can see you perfectly content. I don't suppose she stops you touching her weaving-blade or shuttle or any other of her spinning implements.'

Lysis laughed and said, 'Heavens, Socrates, not only does she stop me, but I'd actually be beaten if I touched any of them.'   e

'Goodness,' I said, 'surely you haven't done anything wrong to your father or mother?'

1. The tutor or *paidagōgos* was a slave of the family who looked after a boy's general welfare during the time he was not under the eye of his parents or teachers.

'Heavens, no, I haven't,' he replied.

'Well then, what have you done to make them behave so oddly and stop you being happy and doing what you want, and bring you up by keeping you all day long in a state of constant subjection to someone else and in short doing virtually nothing you desire? The result would appear to be that neither is all that great wealth any use to you, but everyone rather than you is master of it, nor is your own person, which is so noble, any use to you, but even that is tended and taken care of by someone else; whereas you, Lysis, are master of nobody and do nothing you desire.'

'It's because I'm not yet of age, Socrates,' he said.

'I'm not sure it's that that stops you, Lysis, since both your father, Democrates, and your mother trust you to *some* extent, I imagine, without waiting until you're of age. For example, when they want things read to them or written for them, I imagine they give that job to you before anyone else in the house. Don't they?'

'Of course,' he replied.

'So in that instance you're allowed to write whichever of the letters you want first, and whichever second; and you're allowed to do the same in reading them. And, I imagine, when you pick up your lyre, neither your father nor your mother stops you tightening or slackening whichever of the strings you want, or plucking or striking them with your plectrum. Or do they?'

'No, they don't.'

'So, Lysis, what on earth can be the reason for their not stopping you in those cases, whereas they do stop you in the ones we were speaking of just now?'

'I suppose it's because I know about those things but not the others,' he replied.

'Well,' I said. 'Excellent! So your father is not waiting for you to come of age to trust everything to you, but on the day he considers that you know better than himself, he'll trust both himself and his property to you.'

'I expect so,' he said.

'All right,' I said, 'but what about the man next door? Doesn't the same criterion about you apply to him as to your father? Do you think he'll trust you to run his house, as soon as he considers that you have a better knowledge of running a house than he does himself? Or will he retain charge of it himself?'

'I imagine he'll trust me with it.'

'What about the Athenians? Do you think they'll trust you with their affairs, as soon as they realize that you know enough?'

'I do.'

'Heavens,' I said, 'what about the Great King, then?[1] Would he trust his eldest son, the heir to the throne of Asia, to put what he wanted into the sauce for the meat he was having cooked, or would he rather trust us, if we came to his court and showed him that we had a finer knowledge than his son of the preparation of fancy dishes?' e

'Us, obviously,' he replied.

'He wouldn't let his son put in even a pinch of anything, but would let *us*, even if we wanted to chuck in salt by the handful.'

'Naturally.'

'What if his son had an eye-complaint? Would he let him touch his own eyes if he considered him to be no doctor, or would he stop him?' 210a

'He'd stop him.'

'But if he supposed we were skilled in medicine, even if we wanted to open his eyes and sprinkle ashes in them,[2] I don't think he'd stop us, so long as he considered we knew the right treatment.'

'That's true.'

'So he would trust *us* rather than himself or his son with everything else as well in which we seemed to him to be more expert than they?'

'He'd have to, Socrates', he replied.

'Then it's like this, my dear Lysis,' I said. 'As regards matters of which we possess knowledge, everyone, both Greeks and foreigners, men and b women, will trust them to us and we shall do what we want with them, and no one will deliberately thwart us, but we for our part shall be free in those matters and masters of other people, and those things will be our business, since we shall profit from them. Whereas, as regards matters of which we have no understanding, not only will no one trust us to do what c we please in them, but everyone, not just strangers, but even our fathers and mothers and anyone closer to us than they, will do their best to thwart us, and we for our part shall be subject to others in those matters, and they will not be our business, since we shall not profit from them. Do you agree that it's like that?'

'Yes.'

'Shall we be dear to anyone, and will anyone love us, in matters in which we are of no benefit?'

'Certainly not,' he replied.

'So now, your father doesn't love you, nor yet does anyone else love anyone else, in so far as that other is useless?'

'It would appear not,' he said.

---

1. 'King' or 'Great King' meant, from the time of the Persian Wars, the king of Persia.
2. Ashes were used as a salve in the treatment of eye-complaints.

d   'So if you become wise, my boy, everybody will be a friend to you,
everybody will be close to you, since you'll be useful and good; but if you
don't, neither your father nor your mother nor your close kin nor anyone
else at all will be a friend to you. And is it in fact possible, Lysis, to pride
oneself on things of which one has not as yet any knowledge?'

'How could it be?' he asked.

'And if you need a teacher, you do not as yet possess knowledge.'

'True.'

'So you don't pride yourself on your knowledge, if you are in fact
without any as yet.'

'Heavens, Socrates,' he said, 'I don't think so.'

e   When I heard him admit that, I looked at Hippothales and almost put
my foot in it. It was on the tip of my tongue to say, 'There, Hippothales,
that's how one ought to talk to one's boy, making him humble and unaffected, not, as you do, making him conceited and spoiled.' Well, I noticed
he was squirming with embarrassment at what we'd been saying and I
remembered that, though he was standing near by, he wanted to avoid
being seen by Lysis, so I checked myself and said nothing.

C. *Reciprocal and Non-reciprocal Friendship*

*Difficulties are caused in this passage and in the rest of the dialogue by Plato's
ambiguous use of the word* philos: *he shifts to and fro, without warning or
explanation, from the masculine* philos *to the neuter* philon. *More confusingly,
he shifts from the active sense of the masculine noun* philos ('*friend (of)*', i.e.
'*he who loves*') *and the active sense of the masculine adjective* philos ('*friendly
(to)*', i.e. '*who loves*') *to the two respective passive senses* ('*friend (of)*', i.e.
'*who is loved*', and '*dear (to)*', i.e. '*who is loved*'); *and from the passive sense
of the neuter adjective* philon ('*dear (to)*', i.e. '*which is loved*') *to the active
sense of the same neuter adjective* ('*friendly (to)*', i.e. '*which loves*'). *A further
complication is caused by his use of both the masculine and the neuter to denote
reciprocal friendship, i.e. '*friend*' meaning '*he who/that which both loves and
is loved*'.*

*At 212a, Socrates asks: 'How does one man become the friend of another?'
This question is immediately modified to: 'When a man loves* (philein) *someone,
which is the friend of which?'*

*First step (212b1–3). The possibilities are: (i) the one who loves is the friend
of the one who is loved; (ii) the one who is loved is the friend of the one who
loves; (iii) there is no difference. Possibility (iii) is accepted.*

Second step (212b3–d4). Socrates then considers the case of unreciprocated love: the one who loves is not loved in return, or is hated, by the one who is loved; the one loves and the other is loved. Which is the friend of which in this case? The possibilities are: (i) the one who loves is the friend of the one who is loved; (ii) the one who is loved is the friend of the one who loves; (iii) neither is the friend of either. Possibility (iii) is accepted.

Third step (212d4–e6). This leads to Hypothesis 1, that nothing that does not love in return is dear to what loves it. For example, (i) I love wine; (ii) wine cannot love me in return; (iii) therefore, wine is not dear to (i.e. loved by) me. This absurd conclusion is rejected on the authority of a quotation from Solon.

Fourth step (212e6–213b5). Hypothesis 2, which corresponds to the second possibility of the second step, is that what is loved is dear to what loves it, whether it loves or hates what loves it. This is refuted as follows: (i) the one who is loved is the dear one, i.e. friend; (ii) the one who is hated is the enemy (the hated one). From these, two conclusions follow: (iii) the friend (the one who is loved) may be loved by his enemy (the one who is hated); and (iv) the enemy (the one who is hated) may be hated by his friend (the one who is loved). These conclusions in turn lead to the paradoxes: (v) one may be a friend to one's enemy; (vi) one may be an enemy to one's friend.

Fifth step (213b5–c5). Hypothesis 3, which corresponds to the first possibility of the second step, that what loves is the friend of what is loved, is now considered. This hypothesis is refuted as follows: (i) what loves is the friend of (loves) what is loved; (ii) what hates is the enemy of (hates) what is hated. From these, two conclusions follow: (iii) the friend (the one who loves) may be the friend of (love) his enemy (the one who hates him); and (iv) the enemy (the one who hates) may be the enemy of (hate) his friend (the one who loves him). These conclusions in turn lead to the paradoxes: (v) the friend may be the friend of his enemy; (vi) the enemy may be the enemy of his friend.

Summary (213c5–7). Socrates summarizes the rejected answers to the question 'Who are friends?' These are Hypothesis 3 (those who love), Hypothesis 2 (those who are loved) and Hypothesis 1 (those who both love and are loved).

Socrates' point is that reciprocated love is not the whole answer. We can still talk of philia where only one of the pair loves – in which case it is impossible to say whether it is the one who loves or the one who is loved who is the friend.

Meanwhile Menexenus had come back and taken his seat beside Lysis   211a
again. Lysis then whispered to me in a very boyish and friendly way, so that Menexenus should not hear, 'Socrates, say what you've been saying to me to Menexenus too.'

So I said, 'You can tell him that, Lysis. I'm sure you were paying close attention.'

'I certainly was,' he replied.

'Well then,' I said, 'try to remember it as well as you can in order to
b tell him it all clearly, and if you forget any of it, ask me again the next
time you run into me.'

'I'll most definitely do that, Socrates,' he said. 'Rest assured. But talk
about something else with him, so that I too may hear some more, until
it's time to go home.'

'Well, I can hardly say no to *you*,' I replied. 'But see that you come to
my rescue if Menexenus tries to refute me. You know how argumentative[1]
he is, don't you?'

c 'Heavens, he is indeed. That's why I want you to talk to him.'

'For me to make a fool of myself?' I asked.

'Heavens, no,' he replied, 'for you to teach him a lesson.'

'How?' I asked. 'It's not easy. He's a formidable opponent, a pupil of
Ctesippus. Look, he's here himself – don't you see him? – Ctesippus.'

'Don't worry about anybody, Socrates,' he said. 'Come on, talk to him.'

'If I must, I must,' I said.

While the two of us were having this *tête-à-tête*, Ctesippus interrupted:
'Is this a private party you two are having, or can we take part in the
d conversation?'

'Yes, indeed you must,' I replied. 'Lysis doesn't understand something
I've been saying, but tells me he thinks Menexenus knows, and demands
that I ask him.'

'Why don't you ask him, then?' he said.

'All right, I will,' I replied. 'Menexenus, be ready to answer whatever
questions I put to you. Ever since I was a boy I've always desired to
acquire a certain thing. You know how different people desire different
things: for example one man desires to acquire horses; another, to acquire
e dogs; another, gold; another, honours. I'm quite indifferent to those
things, but I do passionately love acquiring friends. I'd rather get a good
friend than the best quail or cock in the world. By heaven, I'd prefer that
to the best horse or dog. I think, by the Dog,[2] I'd much rather acquire a
real friend than Darius' gold[3] – I'd much rather acquire Darius himself:[4]
that's how much I love friends. When I see you two, you and Lysis, I'm
212a amazed, and think you must be very happy because, though you are so
young, you've been able to acquire that possession quickly and easily:
you've acquired Lysis as a friend so quickly and firmly; and he, you.

1. Literally, 'eristic': see pp. 32 and 299–303.
2. See p. 204 n. 1.
3. The wealth of the king of Persia was proverbial: see also p.120 n. 4.
4. Omitting ἤ.

Whereas I'm so far from acquiring one that I don't even know how one man becomes the friend of another. *That's* what I want to ask you about, in view of your experience.

'Tell me, when a man loves someone, which is the friend of which? Is it the one who loves who is the friend of the one who is loved? Or is it the b one who is loved who is the friend of the one who loves? Or is there no difference?'

'I don't think there's any difference,' he replied.

'What do you mean?' I said. 'Both of them become friends of each other if only one loves the other?'

'I think so,' he said.

'What? Isn't it possible for a man who loves someone not to be loved in return by that someone he loves?'

'It is.'

'And is it possible for a man who loves someone actually to be hated by him? Lovers certainly do sometimes seem to experience something of that sort with their boys. However much they may love them, some think c they're not loved in return; others, that they're actually hated by them. Don't you think that's true?'

'Yes, very true indeed,' he replied.

'In such a case, then,' I went on, 'the one loves and the other is loved?'

'Yes.'

'Then which of them is the friend of which? Is it the one who loves who is the friend of the one who is loved, whether he's loved in return or whether he's actually hated? Or is it the one who is loved who is the friend of the one who loves? Alternatively, in such a case is neither the friend of either, unless both of them love each other?'

'It would certainly appear to be so.'

'So we now think differently from how we thought earlier. *Then* we d thought that if one loved, both were friends; whereas *now*, unless both love, neither is a friend.'

'That may well be right,' he said.

'So nothing that does not love in return is dear to what loves it.'

'It would appear not.'

'So they're not horse-lovers either whom the horses don't love in return – or quail-lovers, or dog-lovers, wine-lovers, sports-lovers, or wisdom-lovers, if wisdom doesn't love them in return. Or does each group love those things which are nevertheless not friendly to them? Was the e poet lying who said:

143

"Happy the man to whom his children are dear, and his horses with
    hoofs uncloven,
his hunting-dogs, and his guest from a foreign land"?'[1]

'I don't think he was,' he replied.

'You think he was speaking the truth?'

'Yes.'

'Then, Menexenus, it would appear that what is loved is dear to what
loves it whether it loves what loves it or whether it actually hates it. For
example, some newly born children do not yet love, while others actually
hate their mother or father when they are punished by them. None the
less they are most dear to their parents at the time they actually hate them.'

'I think that's so,' he said.

'So it's not the one who loves who is the friend according to this line of
argument, but the one who is loved.'

'It would appear so.'

'And the one who is hated is the enemy, not the one who hates.'

'Apparently.'

'Then many men are loved by their enemies and hated by their friends,
and are friends to their enemies and enemies to their friends, if it is what
is loved that is the friend, not what loves. And yet it's quite absurd, my
dear fellow – or rather, I think, impossible, in fact – to be an enemy to
one's friend and a friend to one's enemy.'

'What you're saying would appear to be true, Socrates,' he said.

'If that's impossible, it must be what loves that is the friend of what is
loved.'

'Apparently.'

'And it is what hates that is the enemy of what is hated.'

'It must be.'

'That will mean, then, that we must allow exactly what we allowed
earlier in our discussion, that a man is often the friend of what is not his
friend, and often of what is actually his enemy, when he either loves what
doesn't love him, or loves what actually hates him; and that a man is often
the enemy of what is not his enemy, or of what is actually his friend, when
he either hates what does not hate him, or hates what actually loves him.'

'That may well be right,' he said.

'What are we to do, then,' I asked, 'if neither those who love, nor those
who are loved, nor those who both love and are loved are to be friends?

213a

b

c

1. Solon, Fragment 23 in J. M. Edmonds, *Elegy and Iambus*, I (Cambridge, Mass., and
London 1931; Loeb edition). See also p. 179 n. 1.

Shall we say any others remain, over and above these, who become friends to one another?'

'Heavens, Socrates,' he said, 'I don't know what to say.'

'Can it be that we were not conducting our investigation properly at all, d Menexenus?' I asked.

'I don't think we were, Socrates,' said Lysis. As soon as he said that he blushed. I thought that he'd let those words slip out unintentionally, because of the extreme concentration with which he'd obviously been listening to what we'd been saying.

D. *Like is Friend to Like*

Socrates now suggests another answer to the question 'Who are friends?': like is friend to like. This is refuted by considering men who are alike in being bad, and those who are alike in being good.

A bad man, it is argued, cannot be friend to another bad man, because (i) if one bad man associates with another, he wrongs him; (ii) wronger and wronged cannot be friends; therefore (iii) bad cannot be friend to bad.

Step (i) is explained by Republic *351c7–352d2, where Plato argues that unjust men are capable of undertaking joint action only if they are not com-pletely bad: it is precisely the presence of some portion of justice in them that enables them to cooperate; if they were completely unjust, they would be unable to stop themselves wronging one another in any joint undertaking, and so would never achieve anything together.*

Moreover, Socrates goes on (214d), bad men are unstable; therefore a bad man is never like even his own self, much less like any other bad man.

The idea that a good person is friend to another good person now looks attractive. But (i) if two things are alike (and by this Socrates means completely alike, i.e. identical), the one cannot do anything good or bad to the other which that other cannot do to itself, because the two are identical; therefore (ii) neither will be useful to the other; therefore (iii) neither will feel affection for the other, since philia is dependent on considerations of utility; therefore (iv) like (i.e. identical) will not be friend to like.

Socrates ignores the fact that if two people are alike only in some respects (i.e. similar, rather than identical), friendship could exist between them, since the one could be useful to the other in the respects in which the other was deficient, but in which he himself was not.

Socrates now argues: (i) the good man is self-sufficient; therefore (ii) the good man needs nothing; therefore (iii) the good man will hold nothing in affection;

*therefore (iv) the good man will be friend to no one. Again, in this argument,
good must mean completely good, in that to be completely self-sufficient, one
must be completely good.*

So, wanting to give Menexenus a rest and delighted with Lysis' interest
e in philosophy, I took up the discussion with him instead and said, 'Lysis,
I think what you're saying is true. If we were looking at the question
properly, we should never be lost like this. Well, let's change our
approach. Our method of looking at the question seems to me to be taking
us along a rather difficult sort of road. I think we ought to follow the path
which we turned along before, and look at the question according to the
214a precepts of the poets, who are, so to speak, our fathers and guides in
wisdom. They, of course, express themselves impressively on the subject
of people who are friends. Indeed they say that God himself makes them
friends by bringing them to one another. I think the sort of thing they say
is this: "God always brings like to like"[1] and makes them acquainted.
b Haven't you come across that line?'

'I have,' he said.

'Then have you also come across the writings of our wisest men, which
say just the same: like must always be friend to like? These are, of course,
the men who discuss and write about nature and the universe.'[2]

'That's true,' he said.

'Well,' I said, 'are they right?'

'Possibly,' he replied.

'Possibly half-right,' I said, 'but possibly even wholly right, only we
don't understand them properly. We think that the closer one wicked
c man gets to another wicked man and the more he associates with him, the
more he becomes hated by him, because he wrongs him; and it is, of
course, impossible for wronger and wronged to be friends, isn't it?'

'Yes,' he replied.

'Well then, according to that, half of the statement would be untrue, if
wicked men are like one another.'

'That's true.'

'But I think that what they mean is that good men are like one another
and therefore friends, whereas bad men (as is in fact said of them) are
never like even their own selves, but are capricious and unstable, and

1. Homer, *Odyssey* XVII, 218.
2. e.g. Empedocles (*c.* 493–*c.* 433), fragments 22.4–5, 62.6, 90, 107, 109, 110.9, and Democritus (born *c.* 460), fragment 164, in H. Diels and W. Kranz, *Die Fragmente der Vorsokratiker*,
(6th ed., Berlin 1951–2). See also Aristotle, *Nicomachean Ethics* 1155b1 ff.

anything which is unlike and at variance with itself would hardly become   d
like or friend to anything else. Don't you think so too?'

'I do,' he said.

'Well then, in my opinion, Lysis, this is what people mean when they say, in their cryptic way, that like is friend to like: friendship exists only between good men, whereas the bad man never achieves true friendship with either a good or a bad man. Do you agree?'

He nodded assent.

'So, we can now tell who are friends. Our argument shows us that the answer is those who are good men.'

'Yes,' he said, 'it does indeed seem so.'   e

'I agree,' I said. 'And yet I'm not happy with a part of the answer. Come on then, by heaven, let's look at what it is I suspect. Are two people who are alike friends in so far as they are alike, and are two such people useful to each other? To put it another way, what benefit could *any* two things which were alike hold for each other, or what harm could they do to each other, that they could not do to themselves too? What could be done to them that could not be done to them by themselves too? How would such   215a
things be held in affection by each other when they could give each other no assistance? Is it possible?'

'No.'

'How could what is not held in affection be a friend?'

'It's not possible.'

'Well then, two people who are alike are not friends; but would one good man be a friend to another good man in so far as he is good, not in so far as he is like him?'

'Possibly.'

'But again, wouldn't the good man, in so far as he is good, be, to that extent, sufficient for himself?'

'Yes.'

'And the man who is sufficient needs nothing because of his being sufficient.'

'Naturally.'

'And the man who needs nothing would not feel affection for anything either.'

'No, he would not.'

'And what he doesn't feel affection for he wouldn't love either.'   b

'Certainly not.'

'And the man who doesn't love is no friend.'

'Apparently not.'

'How can we say, then, that good men will be friends to good men at all, if they neither miss one another when they're apart (they're sufficient for themselves even when they're separated), nor have need of one another when they're together? How can such people put a high value on one another?'

'There's no way.'

c 'And they wouldn't be friends, if they didn't put a high value on one another.'

'True.'

E. *Unlike is Friend to Unlike*

The opposite thesis is now examined: unlike is friend to unlike. It is argued that like is not friend to like: in fact, like is enemy to like because of the spirit of envy and rivalry that their being alike engenders between them; unlike will be friend to unlike because they will find each other useful, in that the one will be able to supply what the other needs.

This is quickly refuted: (i) enmity is the opposite of friendship; therefore (ii) the inimical cannot be friend to the friendly; and (ii) the friendly cannot be friend to the inimical.

This argument can work only if 'unlike' means 'opposite', not 'dissimilar': philia might be possible between, for example, someone who was only partly inimical and someone who was only partly friendly, since, though not opposites, they would still be unlike, qua dissimilar.

'Look where we're going wrong, Lysis. Aren't we in fact entirely mistaken?'

'How?' he asked.

'I once heard someone say – I've just remembered it – that like was the greatest foe to like,[1] and so were good men to good men. What's more, he brought forward Hesiod as a witness, saying that:

> "Potter feuds with potter, bard with bard,
d > beggar with beggar."[2]

And he said it was the same in all other cases. It was inevitable that things which were most like one another should be most filled with envy, contentiousness and hatred, and that things which were most unlike one another, with friendship. The poor man was forced to be friend to the

---

1. cf. Heraclitus (floruit *c.* 500), fragment 51 in Diels-Kranz (see p. 146 n. 2); see also Aristotle, *Nicomachean Ethics* 1155b4–6.
2. Hesiod, *Works and Days* 25–6.

rich; the weak, because of his need for assistance, to the strong; the sick
man, to the doctor; and everyone who was ignorant felt affection for and
loved the man who possessed knowledge. In fact he pursued his theme
even more impressively, saying that the last thing that like would be was   e
friend to like. It was the very opposite of that: the most *opposed* was the
greatest friend to the most opposed; each thing desired that sort of thing,
not its like. For example, the dry desired the wet; the cold, the hot; the
bitter, the sweet; the sharp, the blunt; the empty, filling; the full, empty-
ing; and the rest likewise on the same principle, because opposite was
food to opposite; and like would derive no advantage from like. What's   216a
more, Lysis, it seemed clever of him to say that. He did speak well. But
how do you boys think he spoke?' I said.

'I think he did put it well,' replied Menexenus, 'to judge from your
account of it, at any rate.'

'So, are we to say that opposite is greatest friend to opposite?'

'Of course.'

'Well,' I said, 'isn't that monstrous, Menexenus? Won't those terribly
clever fellows, those experts in disputation,[1] leap on us at once in delight
and ask whether enmity is not the most opposite thing to friendship?
What answer shall we give them? Are we not forced to agree that they're   b
right?'

'We are.'

'So then, they'll say, is the enemy friend to the friend or the friend
friend to the enemy?'

'Neither.'

'Well, is the just friend to the unjust or the self-controlled to the undisci-
plined or the good to the bad?'

'I don't think so.'

'But yet,' I said, 'if it is because of their being opposite that one thing
is friend to another, those things too must be friends.'

'They must.'

'So, neither like is friend to like nor opposite to opposite.'

'It would appear not.'

F. *The Presence of Bad is the Cause of Love* (Philia)

*The remaining possibility is that what is neither good nor bad is the friend of
the good (and not of the bad, since nothing would be friend to the bad, or of*

1. i.e. sophists (see pp. 213–6); such 'experts in disputation' (*antilogikoi*) are satirized in the
Euthydemus.

what is neither good nor bad, since like cannot be friend to like). Here it must be noted that 'friend' is no longer reciprocal, but only active: it means 'friend to', i.e. 'loving', because, as was argued earlier, the good man is friend to no one (215a–c).

This remaining possibility is illustrated and developed by the common Socratic means of a medical analogy. What is neither good nor bad (the body) becomes the friend of the good (medicine) because of the presence of bad (disease); and this happens before what is neither good nor bad itself becomes bad through the presence of the bad in it.

That is to say, bad may be present in two ways: first, in such a way that it makes what is neither good nor bad desire good; second, in such a way that it has made what was neither good nor bad become wholly bad – and the wholly bad is no friend to good.

The example of philosophy, the love of wisdom, is used to illustrate and summarize the results: (i) those who are already wise no longer love wisdom: like (good) is not friend to like (good); there is no presence of bad. (ii) those who are so ignorant that they are bad do not love wisdom: opposite (bad) is not friend to opposite (good); the bad is present in the second way described above; (iii) those who possess ignorance (a bad thing), but have not yet been rendered stupid (bad) by it (i.e. those who are neither good nor bad), do love wisdom: what is neither good nor bad is the friend of the good because of the presence of bad (in the first way described above). Socrates concludes that (iii) gives the answer to the question of what a friend is.

c 'Let's consider the possibility which is left, that we're even more mistaken, and the truth is that what a friend is is none of these, but that it is what is neither good nor bad that becomes, in some cases, the friend of the good.'

'What do you mean?' he said.

'Heavens,' I said, 'I don't know. In fact my head's spinning with the difficulties of the argument. It may well be that "the beautiful is the friend",[1] as the old proverb has it. It certainly resembles something soft,

d smooth and shiny; which is why, being that sort of thing, it can easily give us the slip and escape from us. Well, I say that the good is beautiful. Don't you think so?'

'I do.'

'Well then, I have a feeling that what is neither good nor bad is the friend of the beautiful and good. Listen and I'll tell you what gives me

1. The proverb really means 'What is beautiful is loved.' Socrates is attempting a rather feeble, donnish joke.

that feeling: I think there are, as it were, three categories of things: the good, the bad, and what is neither good nor bad. What do you think?'

'I agree,' he said.

'Also, the good is not friend to the good, or the bad to the bad, or the good to the bad. Our earlier argument showed that those were ruled out. We're left, then, with the possibility that if anything is friend to anything, it is what is neither good nor bad that is the friend either of the good or of the sort of thing it is itself, since nothing surely would be a friend to the bad.'

'True.'

'Nor indeed, as we said just now, is like friend to like. Is it?'

'No.'

'So, what is neither good nor bad will not be a friend to the sort of thing it is itself.'

'Apparently not.'

'It follows, then, that only what is neither good nor bad becomes a friend to the good, and only to the good.'

'It must be so, it would appear.'

'Is what we're now saying leading us in the right direction then, boys?' I asked. 'Just suppose we were to take the instance of the healthy body. It needs no medical care or any other form of assistance, since it is sufficient, which means that no one, when healthy, is a friend to a doctor, *because of* his health. Is he?'

'No.'

'But the sick man is, I imagine, because of his disease.'

'Naturally.'

'And disease is a bad thing, medicine a beneficial and good thing.'

'Yes.'

'And a body, of course, as a body, is neither good nor bad.'

'That's so.'

'And a body is forced to welcome and love medicine because of disease.'

'I think so.'

'So, what is neither bad nor good becomes the friend of the good because of the presence of bad –'

'It would appear so.'

'– but obviously *before* it becomes bad itself through the bad it possesses. Once it had become bad it would certainly not desire the good or be its friend any longer, because we said it was impossible for bad to be friend to good.'

'It is impossible.'

'Now consider what I'm saying: some things are of the same sort themselves as whatever is present to them is. For example, suppose one were to smear something with a certain colour. What has been smeared *on* is, in a sense, present *to* what has been smeared.'

'Of course.'

'At that time, then, is what has been smeared of the same colour as what is on it?'

'I don't understand,' he said.

d   'Well, let me put it this way,' I said. 'Suppose someone smeared your fair hair with white lead. Would it then be white, or just seem so?'

'Just seem so,' he replied.

'And yet whiteness would be present to it.'

'Yes.'

'All the same, your hair wouldn't be any whiter at all as yet. Though whiteness is present to it, it is not more white than it is black.'

'True.'

'But when, my friend, old age brings that same colour to your hair, it becomes at that time of the same sort as what is present to it is – white, by the presence of white.'

'Of course.'

e   'Well, that's the question I'm asking you now. When one thing is present to another, will what possesses what is present to it be of the same sort as it? Or only if it is present in a certain way, but not if it is not?'

'The latter, rather,' he said.

'So sometimes, when bad is present, what is neither bad nor good is not bad as yet, but there are times when it has already become bad.'

'Of course.'

'When it's not yet bad, then, though bad is present, this presence of bad makes it desire good; whereas the presence of bad which actually makes it bad deprives it of both its desire and its feelings of friendship for

218a   the good, because it is no longer neither bad nor good, but is now bad. And bad was found to be no friend to good.'

'No, indeed.'

'That's why we'd say that those who are already wise, whether they are gods or men, no longer love wisdom,[1] and that those who are so ignorant that they are bad do not love wisdom either, because no bad or stupid man loves wisdom. So, we're left with those who possess that bad thing, ignorance, but have not yet been rendered foolish or stupid by it, in that

b   they still believe they don't know what they don't know. Consequently those who are still neither good nor bad do, in fact, love wisdom; whereas all those who are bad, as well as all those who are good, do not, because,

1. 'Philosophy' is, of course, literally 'the love of wisdom'.

as we decided earlier in our discussion, neither is opposite the friend of opposite, nor like of like. Don't you remember?'

'Of course,' they said.

'So now, Lysis and Menexenus,' I said, 'we've done it! We've discovered what a friend is and what it is not. We say that in the soul, in the body and anywhere else, it is what is neither bad nor good that is the c friend of the good because of the presence of bad.'

The two of them agreed wholeheartedly, admitting that it was so.

G. *The Possession of Good is the Goal of Love* (Philia).

The definition is now modified: what is neither good nor bad (the body) is the friend of the good (medicine) because of the bad (disease) for the sake of (another) good (health). Medicine, a good thing, is a friend (loved by what is neither good nor bad) for the sake of health, a good thing and also a friend.

We now begin to find philon *being used ever more frequently in its passive sense instead of the active. The shift begins in this section and gathers momentum as we move into Section H where the use of* philon *in its passive sense becomes predominant. Consequently, when, for example, Socrates say that 'medicine is a friend', what the Greek really means is 'medicine is something that is loved'. From 218d until 220e great care must be taken to distinguish between the active and passive uses of the word.*

And what's more I felt quite delighted, like a hunter, in the satisfaction of getting in my grasp what I'd been hunting. Then, unaccountably, a most absurd suspicion came into my head that what we'd agreed was not true, and I said at once in annoyance, 'Unfortunately, Lysis and Menexenus, it may well be that we've been building castles in the air.'

'What makes you say that?' asked Menexenus.

'I'm afraid,' I said, 'that we've run into certain arguments about what d a friend[1] is which are, as it were, impostors.'

'How's that?' he asked.

'Let's look at it this way,' I said. 'Is the man who's to be a friend[1] a friend[1] *to* someone or not?'

'He has to be,' he replied.

'Is it for the sake of nothing or because of nothing, then, or for the sake of something and because of something?'

'For the sake of something and because of something.'

1. Active sense.

'Is that thing for the sake of which the friend[1] is friend[1] to the friend[2] a friend,[2] or is it neither a friend[2] nor an enemy[3]?'

'I'm not quite with you there,' he said.

e   'That's not surprising,' I said. 'But perhaps you will follow me if I put it like this – and I think I'll understand what I'm saying better too. The sick man, we said a minute ago, is the friend[1] of the doctor, isn't he?'

'Yes.'

'Is it because of disease and for the sake of health, then, that he's the friend[1] of the doctor?'

'Yes.'

'Disease is a bad thing?'

'Of course.'

'What about health?' I asked. 'Is it a good thing or a bad one or neither?'

'A good thing,' he said.

219a 'So it appears that we were saying that the body, which is neither good nor bad, is, because of disease – that is, because of a bad thing – the friend[1] of medicine, and medicine is a good thing; and it is for the sake of health that medicine has acquired the friendship, and health is a good thing, isn't it?'

'Yes.'

'Is health a friend[2] or not a friend[2]?'

'A friend[2].'

'Disease is an enemy[3].'

'Of course.'

b   'So what is neither bad nor good is, because of what is bad and an enemy,[3] friend[1] of what is good, for the sake of what is good and a friend[2].'

'Apparently.'

'What is a friend[1] is the friend[1] of what is a friend[2] for the sake of what is a friend[2] because of what is an enemy[3].'

'It would appear so.'

H. *The First Thing That is Loved*

Since medicine (a 'friend' in the sense of a 'loved object') is loved for the sake of health (another 'friend' or 'loved object'), then health, in being itself a 'friend' or 'loved object', must be loved for the sake of yet another 'friend' or 'loved object', and so on to infinity, or until one reaches the 'first friend' or the 'first thing that is loved' (prōton philon), for the sake of which all other things that

1. Active sense.
2. Passive sense.
3. Passive sense: 'hated'.

are 'friends' are loved. The 'first thing that is loved' is not loved for the sake of another 'friend', so that what is really loved (or a 'friend') is not loved for the sake of another 'friend', in contrast to all other 'friends'.

Socrates next examines the qualifying phrase 'because of the bad'. Since the good is a 'friend' or 'loved object' because of the bad, then if the bad is removed, the good becomes useless to what is neither good nor bad: if there is no disease (bad), the body (what is neither good nor bad) needs no remedy (good). Therefore the good is loved because of the bad and is useless in itself.

The identification of the good with what is a 'friend' enables Socrates to argue that the 'first friend' or the 'first thing that is loved' is loved because of an 'enemy' or 'hated object'; and if the 'enemy' is removed, the 'first friend' will no longer be a 'friend'.

'All right then,' I said. 'Now that we've got as far as this, boys, let's be careful not to be deceived. I'm willing to ignore the difficulty that what is a friend[1] has become the friend[3] of what is a friend,[2] and therefore like becomes the friend[3] of like,[4] which, we say,[5] is impossible. Anyway, to avoid being deceived by that point, let's consider the following one: medicine, we say, is a friend[6] for the sake of health.'

c

'Yes.'

'Is health a friend too, then?'

'Of course.'

'If it is a friend, it is so for the sake of something.'

'Yes.'

'And that something is a friend, if it is to be consistent with what we admitted earlier.'

'Of course.'

'And that too, in its turn, will be a friend for the sake of a friend?'

'Yes.'

'Well then, aren't we bound to get tired going on like that and give up, or else arrive at some point of origin which will not refer us to yet another friend, but which will constitute the first thing that is a friend, for the sake of which we say that all the others too are friends?'

d

'We are.'

'My fear about this is that all the other things, which we said were

1. Active sense.
2. Passive sense.
3. Reciprocal sense.
4. But this is not really a case of like being friend to like. Rather it is a case of 'what loves' being a 'friend to' (active, not reciprocal) 'what is loved'.
5. 214a–215c.
6. From here until the end of the section 'friend' is always passive.

friends for the sake of that thing, being as it were phantoms of it, may deceive us, and that that first thing may be what is really and truly a friend. Let's look at it this way. When a man values something highly, as, for example, a father prizes his son more than all his other possessions,

e would such a man value anything else highly because of his considering his son most important? For example, if he found that his son had drunk hemlock, wouldn't he value wine highly, if he believed that that would save his son?'

'Why, he certainly would!' he replied.

'*And* the jar which contained the wine?'

'Of course.'

'So does he *then* value his son no more highly than he values an earthenware cup or three measures of wine? Or perhaps it's like this: all concern of that sort is shown not for those things which are procured for the sake of something, but for that thing for the sake of which all things of that

220a sort are procured. Admittedly, we do often say that we value gold and silver highly, but that hardly comes any nearer the truth. What we value most highly is that thing (whatever it may reveal itself as being) for the sake of which both gold and everything else that is procured are procured. Shall we settle for that?'

'Of course.'

'May the same thing be said of what is a friend as well? All the things we say are our friends for the sake of some other thing that is a friend are

b clearly friends in name only; whereas what is really a friend should be that thing in which all those so-called friendships terminate.'

'That should be the case,' he said.

'What is really a friend, then, is not a friend for the sake a friend.'

'True.'

'Well then, that's settled: it is *not* for the sake of a friend that what is a friend is a friend. So, is the good a friend?'

'I think so.'

'Then is the good loved because of the bad? Is the following the case?

c Suppose of the three categories we were speaking of a minute ago – namely good, bad, and what is neither good nor bad – two were allowed to remain, and the bad were removed and did not interfere with anything, body, soul, or the other things which we say are in themselves neither bad nor good. Wouldn't the good be of no use at all to us in that case, but have become useless? You see, if nothing harmed us any more, we'd have no

d need of any benefit, and in this way it would then become obvious that we felt affection and love for the good because of the bad, the good being a remedy for the bad, the bad being a disease; and if there is no disease,

156

a remedy is not needed. Is that the nature of the good? Is it because of the bad that the good is loved by us, who are between the bad and the good? Is it of no use itself for its own sake?'

'It would appear that's the case,' he replied.

'So that thing that is a friend of ours in which all the others terminated – we said those things are friends for the sake of something else that is a e friend – is quite different from them. *They've* been called friends for the sake of a friend, but what is really a friend seems of the completely opposite nature to that, because we showed that it is a friend because of¹ an enemy, and if the enemy were removed, it would appear to be no longer a friend.'

'I'm inclined to agree,' he said, 'at least according to what we're saying now.'

I. *Desire is the Cause of Love*

Socrates now argues that desires may be harmful (bad), beneficial (good) or neither (neither good nor bad). If all bad things, including bad desires, are removed, there will still be those desires which are neither bad nor good. Building on this, Socrates asserts: (i) if a man desires (epithumein) or adores (eran) something, he also loves (philein) it; (ii) even if bad things are destroyed, there will still be some things which will be loved; (iii) if a man still loves something after the bad has been removed, it cannot be because of the bad that he loves it, since once the cause has been removed, there can be no consequence of it. Therefore (iv) it must be desire that is the cause of philia.

The conclusion that desire is the cause of philia *is hardly justified by the argument. Socrates has shown that the cause of love need not be the bad, or is not the bad, and that in ordinary parlance love and desire imply each other; but he has not demonstrated why desire must be the* cause *of love.*

'By heaven,' I exclaimed, 'if the bad is destroyed, will it be impossible to be hungry any more, or thirsty, or anything else of that sort? Or will 221a there still be hunger, as long as there are men and other animals, but not *harmful* hunger? And thirst and the other desires, except that they won't be bad, since the bad will have been destroyed? Or is the question of what there will or will not be then ridiculous, because who can know? Well, anyway, we do know this, that as things are, it *is* possible to be harmed by being hungry, though it is possible to be benefited by it too. Isn't that so?'

1. Plato has in fact written *heneka* ('for the sake of ', which he has hitherto in this passage reserved for speaking of the goal, not the cause, of love), instead of the expected *dia* ('because of'), by a sort of rhetorical confusion. *Heneka* can, however, also mean 'because of', and this is how the sense demands it be translated here. For a discussion, see Shorey.

'Of course.'

'Then it's possible, when one experiences thirst or any other such
b desire, for that desire sometimes to be beneficial, other times to be harmful, and other times to be neither?'

'Yes, definitely.'

'If bad things are destroyed, is there any reason why things which are
not in fact bad should be destroyed along with the bad things?'

'None at all.'

'So there will still be the desires which are neither good nor bad, even
if bad things are destroyed.'

'Apparently.'

'Is it possible, then, for a man who desires and adores something not
to love what he desires and adores?'

'I don't think so.'

'So, it would appear that even if bad things have been destroyed, there
c will still be some things which will be loved.'

'Yes.'

'But not if the bad were the cause of something being a friend. The one
thing would not be a friend to the other, once the bad had been destroyed,
because once the causal factor had been destroyed, it would surely be
impossible for the thing of which it was the cause to exist any longer.'

'You're right.'

'And we have allowed that what is a friend loves something, and does
so because of something? Didn't we think at that stage that it was because
of the bad that what was neither good nor bad loved the good?'

'True.'

d 'But now, it would appear, there seems to be another cause of loving
and being loved.'

'It would.'

'So really, as we were saying just now, desire is the cause of friendship,
and that thing which desires is a friend to which it desires, and at the time
it desires it. Whereas what we said before about what was a friend was a
piece of nonsense, like a poem spun out at length.'

'That may well be the case,' he said.

J. *What is Akin is Friend to What is Akin:* Aporia

*Socrates argues that desire is felt for what one is in need of; that what one is in
need of is what has been taken away from one; that what has been taken away*

from one is what is akin to one; and therefore the object of sexual love (erōs), love/friendship (philia) and desire (epithumia) is what is akin.

The reciprocal nature of this is now brought out: if A is akin to B, then B is akin to A. This means that if A loves B, since B is akin to A, then since A is also akin to B, it must be loved by B. This is, in effect, to say that what is akin is the friend of what is akin. But this may stand only if what is akin is different from what is like, since like cannot be friend to like. On the assumption that akin and like are not the same, Socrates now suggests: either (a) what is good is akin to everything (good, bad and neither good nor bad), and what is bad is alien to everything; or (b) the bad is akin to the bad, the good is akin to the good, and what is neither good nor bad is akin to what is neither good nor bad.

Menexenus and Lysis favour accepting (b); but it has already been shown that bad cannot be friend to bad, and good cannot be friend to good. Instead of examining (a) as formulated, Socrates argues that what is akin cannot be the same as what is good, because this would mean that one good man is a friend only to another good man – a statement thought to have been refuted earlier (Section D).

Socrates now sums up the rejected arguments and admits defeat. If he had examined (a) as formulated, what conclusions might he have reached? What is good is akin to everything (and what is bad is alien to everything) would have meant: (i) the good is akin to the good; (ii) the good is akin to the bad; (iii) the good is akin to what is neither good nor bad; and, since kinship is a reciprocal relationship, (iv) what is neither good nor bad is akin to the good. Since the good is self-sufficient and so a friend to nothing (214e–215c) and the bad is incapable of enjoying philia (214b–d; see also 216b), then only (iv) can remain. Assuming, then, for the sake of argument, that this is the conclusion that Plato is leaving us to draw from the aporia, namely that what is neither good nor bad is akin to – and so friend to – the good, can we reconcile this statement, which satisfactorily accounts for the object of philia (namely, the good), with reciprocal friendship? Does each man, who, as a human being, is neither absolutely good nor absolutely bad, love the good in another man, who is also neither absolutely good nor absolutely bad?

'But surely,' I went on, 'that thing which desires desires what it is in need of, doesn't it?'

'Yes.'

'So the thing which is in need is the friend of what it is in need of?' e

'I think so.'

'And it finds itself in need of what is taken away from it.'

'Of course.'

'It would appear, then, Menexenus and Lysis, that the object of passionate love, friendship and desire is, in fact, it seems, what is akin.'

Both of them said yes.

'So if *you* are friends to each other you are in a way akin to each other by nature.'

'Definitely,' they said.

222a 'And boys,' I said, 'if one man desires another or adores him, he'd never desire or adore or love him, if he weren't in some way in fact akin to the man he adored, either in his soul, or in some disposition of his soul, or in his conduct, or in his looks.'

'Yes, certainly,' said Menexenus. Lysis stayed silent.

'All right,' I said. 'We've shown, then, that we must love what is akin by nature.'

'It would appear so,' he said.

'So the genuine lover, though not the fake one, must be loved by his boy.'

b To that Lysis and Menexenus gave a rather grudging nod of assent; Hippothales turned all the colours of the rainbow with delight.

I now wanted to review the course of the discussion, so I said, 'If what is akin is in any respect different from that which is like, I think, Lysis and Menexenus, we'd be saying something significant about what a friend is; but if what is like and what is akin are in fact the same thing, it is not easy to reject the earlier argument, that like is useless to like by virtue of their being alike; and it's wrong to allow that what is useless is a friend.

c Well then,' I said, 'since we've got rather woozy with the argument, shall we come to an agreement and say that what is akin is something different from what is like?'

'Yes, of course.'

'Shall we assume, then, that what is good is akin to everything, whereas what is bad is alien to everything? Or is the bad akin to the bad; the good to the good; and what is neither good nor bad to what is neither good nor bad?'

They said they thought it was so: each was akin to its counterpart.

d 'In that case, boys,' I said, 'haven't we fallen back into those first statements of ours about friendship, which we rejected, since one unjust man will be a friend to another unjust man, and bad man to another bad man, no less than one good man to another good man?'

'It would appear so,' he said.

'What's more, if we say that what is good and what is akin are the same

160

thing, is that anything other than to say that one good man is a friend only to another good man?'

'True.'

'All the same, we thought we'd refuted ourselves in that too. Don't you remember?'

'We do.'

'What more can we do with the argument, then? Or is it obvious that   e
we can do nothing with it? I beg to be allowed to recapitulate all that we've said, then, like the clever fellows in the courts. If neither those who are loved nor those who love, nor the alike nor the unlike, nor the good, nor those who are akin, nor all the other cases we went through – I can't remember them all now, there were so many – well, if none of those is a friend, I don't know what more to say.'

With that I was intending to provoke another of the older men into   223a
speaking. Just then, like evil spirits, Lysis' and Menexenus' tutors came over with the boys' brothers, called to them, and told them to come home; it was already late. At first, with the support of those standing around us, we tried to chase them away; but since they took no notice of us, but began to shout angrily in their rather foreign accents and went on calling the boys (we were of the opinion they'd had a bit to drink at the festival of   b
the Hermaea, which made them impossible to handle), we then conceded defeat to them and broke up our party. However, I did say, just as they were leaving, 'Lysis and Menexenus, we've now made utter fools of ourselves, an old man like me and you, since these people will go away and say that we think that we're friends of one another – for I consider myself one of your number – though we were not as yet able to find out precisely what a friend is.'

CHARMIDES

INTRODUCTION TO *CHARMIDES*

Ostensibly the *Charmides* is a 'definition' dialogue in the classic mould; but it is much more than that. It goes far beyond the limited concern of searching for the definition of a particular moral term. For in the course of his attempt to define the peculiarly Greek virtue of *sōphrosunē*, Plato develops his investigation so as to cover the great Socratic paradox that virtue is knowledge.[1] What is under examination in the *Charmides* is not so much *sōphrosunē* as knowledge, in particular the strange and problematic concept of 'knowledge of knowledge'.[2] But before considering the latter, we must first address ourselves to the question of what *sōphrosunē* is.[3]

Wisdom, courage and justice are an instantly recognizable trinity of major virtues. To add a fourth, 'self-control' or 'self-knowledge', would seem to us today unnecessary and rather strange. But translate the four into ancient Greek and you have a naturally cohesive foursome: they are, for instance, the four cardinal virtues of the state at *Republic* 427e. For a Greek of Plato's day, *sōphrosunē* was just as important a virtue as the other three. How this came to be is a long story, which need not detain us here. But in reading the *Charmides* one must never forget that Plato is investigating one of the cornerstones of the Greeks' cultural and moral heritage.

The etymological meaning of *sōphrosunē* is 'soundness of mind';[4] but what it meant in the popular usage of Socrates' and Plato's day was primarily 'self-control', and this is how the word has been rendered in this translation, despite the manifest inadequacy of such a rendering.[5] What

1. See Cornford, quoted in J. Gould, *The Development of Plato's Ethics* (Cambridge 1955), p. 37; Guthrie, IV, pp. 156, 173–4; Sprague, p. 53; and North, p. 158.

2. The difficulty of this concept has been thought to indicate a more advanced stage in Plato's philosophical development than that of the other early 'Socratic' dialogues and has consequently been used to argue that the *Charmides* is one of the latest of the early dialogues. See Guthrie, IV, p. 155, and C. H. Kahn, 'Did Plato Write Socratic Dialogues?', *Classical Quarterly*, 31 (1981), pp. 305–20.

3. The best comprehensive treatment of the concept is by North.

4. Cf. *Cratylus* 411e.

5. Older translations have tended to favour 'temperance', but that word now has rather different connotations. 'Moderation', 'soberness', 'temperateness', 'chastity', 'modesty', 'restraint'   -restraint', 'self-discipline', 'self-respect', 'discretion', 'wisdom', 'prudence', 'humility', are among the large array of alternatives, all of which cover at least some of the aspects of *sōphrosunē*. 'Sense', meaning 'good sense', perhaps best conveys the wealth of conno-

the term really points to *in this dialogue* is 'self-knowledge';[1] but since 'knowledge of oneself' (*epistēmē heautou*) is one of the *definitions* proposed in the course of the investigation of *sōphrosunē*, this obvious rendering of the term must reluctantly be abandoned.

For Plato, Socrates was the embodiment of *sōphrosunē*, as he was of the other virtues.[2] The aspects of *sōphrosunē* displayed *par excellence* by Socrates were self-knowledge and self-mastery (*enkrateia*). Knowledge of oneself was in fact the kernel of Socrates' teaching. He believed that his primary duty in life was to persuade everyone to 'tend his soul' in order to make it as good as possible;[3] a man had to know himself, which meant knowing his soul (*psuchē*), before he could 'tend' it.[4] A memorable illustration of the second and minor aspect, self-mastery, or self-control in its popular meaning, is provided in Plato's description of how Socrates masters his passion when he catches a glimpse of Charmides' beautiful body beneath his cloak (155d–e).

Why is the everyday meaning restricted to the scene-setting in this dialogue?[5] The answer might be found in a wish to highlight by contrast the aristocratic prejudices[6] of Socrates' interlocutors, Charmides and Critias, who ignore the meaning given to *sōphrosunē* by the common man and instead give Socrates the benefit of their philo-Laconian education.[7] But the real reason must be that, for the purposes of developing the highly intellectual and moral interpretation of the virtue at which the dialogue is aiming, the everyday usage needs to be kept in the background. The two are connected, as in the case of any of the particular virtues; but the connection is not the focus of the dialogue.

tation of the Greek word, and is probably immediately recognizable as a major virtue in the English-speaking world; but since it fails directly to connote 'self-control', which is the primary meaning the word held for Greeks of the fifth and fourth centuries, it has been rejected in favour of that primary meaning.

1. This is the definition of *sōphrosunē* in *Alcibiades I* 131a–b, 133c–e.

2. His wisdom and justness pervade the dialogues; his courage too is exemplary, and is indeed mentioned at the beginning of this dialogue (see also *Symposium* 219e ff., *Laches* 181b).

3. See *Apology* 29d–30b.

4. Cf. *Alcibiades I* 132c.

5. 155d–e and 162c–d.

6. See Witte, p. 39.

7. Charmides' first definition of *sōphrosunē*, as 'quietness' (or 'slowness'), is that of the conventional young Athenian aristocrat who had received the traditional education of his class, which had taken over various Spartan ideals of conduct, such as *hēsuchia* (quietness) and *eunomia* (good order, orderly behaviour); his second definition of *sōphrosunē*, as 'modesty', also betrays his conservative upbringing, while the third, 'doing one's own job', points to a form of social organization with minimal class mobility. Similarly, the fifth definition of *sōphrosunē*, which Critias embraces so readily, 'knowledge of oneself', has its foundations in the strongly conservative Apolline religion so dear to the Spartans.

Charmides[1] and Critias[2] were not simply Athenian aristocrats but were, more importantly, members of Plato's own aristocratic family. Charmides was his uncle on his mother's side; Critias, his mother's cousin. Both belonged to Socrates' circle, though Critias had mixed with the sophists,[3] and in this dialogue, to some extent, he represents their ethical standpoint and methods of argumentation.

Why should Plato have chosen these two members of his own family to be Socrates' interlocutors in this dialogue? Why should he have honoured them with such praise of their noble ancestry, which was also his own ancestry, as he does at the beginning (157e–158b)? The answers lie in the two men's subsequent careers.[4] Critias went on to become the extremist leader of the Thirty Tyrants, who imposed a reign of terror on Athens at the end of the Peloponnesian War in 404–403, in their attempt to impose their oligarchy on the citizen body. Charmides too became one of the Thirty, meeting his death, with Critias, in battle against the democrats. Part of Plato's purpose in this dialogue is to exculpate Socrates from any responsibility for the crimes of his former companions. Xenophon, in *Memorabilia* I. 2.12 ff., also comes to Socrates' defence against the same charge, stating that Socrates had taught Critias *sōphrosunē* in his youth and had spoken out so strongly against his later behaviour that he had taken grave offence. By showing Critias as both quite lacking in *sōphrosunē* and quite ignorant of its meaning beyond a superficial acquaintance with its conventional use within his aristocratic circle; by representing Charmides as equally unaware of its true purport, despite his possession of the natural *sōphrosunē* of youth, which he will lose when he reaches adulthood; and by portraying Socrates as trying his best to discover with them the true meaning of *sōphrosunē*, and as failing to elicit the answer from them, though possessing the virtue himself – by all these means Plato is endeavouring to show that Socrates tried to educate Critias and Charmides in *sōphrosunē*, but failed. But by trying, he saved himself from any possible accusation of responsibility for their later crimes.

If that, then, is the wider, personal motive for writing the dialogue, what are its philosophical purposes? First of all, Plato wishes to show the Socratic *elenchus* in action, and the first two definitions of this dialogue offer excellent examples of this.

A prominent feature of Socrates' method is to elicit from his respondent

---

1. Cf. *Protagoras* 315a and *Symposium* 222b.

2. He also appears in the *Timaeus* and in the *Critias*, to which he gives his name.

3. See pp. 213–6.

4. The dramatic date of the dialogue is established as 432 by the mention of the fighting at Potidaea (153b).

the admission that the virtue in question, or virtue itself, is necessarily a good (*agathon*)[1] or admirable (*kalon*)[2] thing. This is simply assumed to be true. No attempt is made to prove that a virtue, or virtue itself, *is* necessarily *agathon* or *kalon*. For Socrates, as for his interlocutors, it is an accepted truth; and a proposed definition must be rejected if it is found to be incompatible with it.[3] Thus the refutation is built, not on a fact already proved to be true, but on something that everyone merely intuitively 'knows' to be true. The refutation of a proposed definition of V (a virtue) as *x* proceeds as follows: V is necessarily *agathon/kalon*: *x* is sometimes not *agathon/kalon*; therefore V is not *x*.

The bulk of the refutation of the first definition, '*sōphrosunē* is quietness', is, as so frequently in these early dialogues, *epagōgē* or inductive argument by means of analogical cases.[4] Socrates enumerates cases in which *x* is agreed to be bad (*kakon*), not good.[5] By accumulating negative cases[6] he convinces his interlocutor that his position is untenable. The enumeration is of course incomplete; every case is not, indeed cannot be, considered. A few are adduced, and he then intuits a general rule. A specious air of completeness is sometimes achieved, as here, by dividing the induction into two: to refute this first definition, the one set of cases is concerned with the body, the other with the soul. Socrates reviews some cases pertaining to the body and then states that what has been agreed to be true for these cases is true for all cases pertaining to the body. He then does the same for cases pertaining to the soul. By adding both together he gives a more convincing impression of having considered every case. If it is too great a leap to intuit the general rule from just a few cases, divide the induction into two, make two smaller leaps by intuiting two sub-rules from two (still incomplete) sets of cases, and then add them together to reach the general rule itself.[7]

The long analogical *epagōgē* of the first definition enables Socrates to telescope the argumentation in the second refutation. One negative case is enough to dispatch the proposed definition, '*sōphrosunē* is modesty'.

1. Cf. *Meno* 87d and *Protagoras* 349c.

2. Cf. *Laches* 192c. The regular meaning of *kalon* is 'beautiful' or 'fine'. Alternatively, the virtue may be 'beneficial' (*ōphelimon*).

3. See Santas, pp. 127–8.

4. See pp. 19–20.

5. In the refutation of this first definition, *x* is sometimes 'contemptible' (*aischron*), not 'admirable' (*kalon*).

6. See R. Robinson, *Plato's Earlier Dialectic* (2nd ed., Oxford 1953), pp. 42–5.

7. In refuting the first definition Socrates is careful to argue not that the universal, quietness, is bad, or rather contemptible, but that it is no more *kalon* than its opposite. This relieves him of any danger of having to deal with the argument that, if quietness is contemptible, its opposite, quickness, must be admirable, and therefore quickness is *sōphrosunē*.

CHARMIDES

The point of these refutations is to demonstrate how difficult it is to formulate for complex ethical terms such as *sōphrosunē* definitions of universal application. For Socrates, the term to be defined was univocal[1] and its definition had to be coextensive; it had to provide an equivalent. But a mere synonym would not be sufficient, nor would a pat 'dictionary' definition such as we might be tempted to think of. Socrates' search for definition was a search for the *ousia*, the essential nature, of the term under consideration. Socratic definition aimed at explicating the essential constitution or structure of the term he was examining.[2]

If the first two definitions illustrate the formal Socratic *elenchus*, the third and fourth certainly do not. This is because Socrates does not want so much to refute these definitions completely as to build on them. They are both part of a focusing process (as, to a lesser extent, were the first two refuted definitions[3]), by which a definition of *sōphrosunē* gradually emerges, despite the *aporia* with which the dialogue ends. The first two definitions are in some degree merely preliminary and dispensable. The third, with its change of advocate from Charmides to Critias, marks, as does a similar change of interlocutor in the *Laches* and the *Lysis*, the turning-point of the dialogue, a rise in the level of the discussion.[4]

To dispose of the third definition Socrates shamelessly resorts to a sophistic trick, playing on the ambiguity of the Greek verb *poiein*, which may mean either 'do' or 'make'. The proffered definition of *sōphrosunē*, 'doing one's own job', or, more literally, 'doing one's own things', is indeed a major advance on the first two, and not, in fact, too far from what one might consider an acceptable answer, as the course of the dialogue and later Platonic pronouncements make clear.[5] Socrates, however, perverts the natural sense of the phrase and insists on interpreting it as 'making one's own things'. Critias rightly attacks this ludicrous twisting of the meaning and reasserts the natural sense of the words. Socrates avoids taking issue with him, seizing instead on one of his incidental points in order to introduce a fourth definition himself: '*sōphrosunē* is the doing of good things.' Again he does not attempt a formal refutation. Instead, he sidesteps the problem by bringing the crucial missing element, knowledge, into the discussion. At a stroke, essential intellectual and

1. See Robinson, op. cit., p. 56 ff.
2. See Robinson, op. cit., pp. 49-60, especially p. 58.
3. These are not rejected out of hand, since, though manifestly extremely inadequate, they do contain part of the truth of *sōphrosunē*.
4. See Guthrie, IV, pp. 167-8.
5. Cf. *Republic* 433a: 'doing one's own job' is given as a definition of justice (*dikaiosunē*), with the meaning of 'each man performing the one function in the state for which his nature most suits him'.

religious elements are introduced. Self-knowledge[1] and moderation[2] were the watchwords of the Apolline religion. Indeed it was from the temple of Apollo at Delphi that Chaerephon, a friend of Socrates who appears briefly at the beginning of this dialogue, had received the famous message that Socrates was the wisest of men, a message which Socrates interpreted as meaning 'the wisest of men in that he knew that he did not know'.[3] The introduction of these religious and intellectual factors by Socrates leads to the longest and most significant section of the discussion, the examination of *sōphrosunē* as knowledge of *one*self (the fifth definition) and, more importantly, as knowledge of *it*self, that is to say, as knowledge of knowledge.

It is noteworthy that, throughout the dialogue, Socrates' contributions to the process of definition of *sōphrosunē* are essentially concerned with introducing psychical and moral considerations. In each of the two groups of definitions, 1–2 and 3–6, one can discern a movement, instigated by Socrates, from the external to the internal.[4] This is most easily shown as follows:

	EXTERNAL (body)	INTERNAL (soul)
Charmides	(1) Quietness	(2) Modesty
Critias	(3) Doing one's own job	(5) Knowing oneself/ knowledge of knowledge
Socrates	(4) Doing of good	(6) Knowledge of good

In modifying Critias' definitions to 'doing of good' and 'knowledge of good' respectively, Socrates goes somewhat beyond the scope of *sōphrosunē* itself. Plato is leading the reader on to confront the Socratic concepts of the unity of the virtues and the identification of virtue with knowledge – in particular, with knowledge of good and bad.

The interrelationships between (3) and (5) and between (4) and (6) are expressions of the Socratic belief that to possess knowledge is to act upon it: the man who knows himself will do his own job, or rather, more literally, 'the things of himself'; and the man who knows the good will do what is good.

Socrates sets about testing the fifth definition, 'knowledge of oneself', by his customary means of analogical argument, and here, for the first

1. *Gnōthi sauton*, 'know thyself': see 164d–165b.
2. *Mēden agan*, 'nothing in excess': see 165a–b.
3. See *Apology* 20d–21d.
4. 160d and 164a. See further Friedländer, pp. 79–80.

time, we see Plato questioning this aspect of Socratic dialectic.[1] Even at this comparatively early stage of his philosophical career Plato was conscious of the shortcomings of his mentor's methods. The general criticism which he puts into Critias' mouth is valid and apposite: argument from analogy too often relies on specious similarities to make its point, while ignoring important differences; as a dialectical tool analogy is useful, but it has its limitations.

More important for the dialogue as a whole, however, than the questioning of the validity of analogical arguments as a class, significant though that undoubtedly is, is the specific setting of crucial limits to the operation of the favourite Socratic *technē*-analogy.[2] Socrates constantly treated the virtues or virtue itself as a *technē*, a skill, craft, or art – that is to say, as a body of precisely attainable knowledge (*epistēmē*), and, more importantly, as analogous to the other *technai*, for instance, shoemaking or weaving, in every respect. But the analogy can only be drawn up to a point, and no further. Knowledge of oneself can be shown to be different from the other *technai* in some extremely significant respects. Unlike the other knowledges (*epistēmai*) or skills (*technai*), knowledge of oneself has no product, as, for example, medicine has health; and self-knowledge has no object which is different from itself, as, for example, arithmetic has numbers. Plato is here confronting a crucial assumption of Socrates' moral philosophy, that the knowledge attainable in professional skills (*technai*) can also be attained in moral conduct by the examination of moral language. By demonstrating that there are major respects in which knowledge of knowledge is not analogous to professional skills, Plato is able to show that a man should attempt to attain that moral knowledge or virtue which will emerge, albeit darkly, as the true definition of *sōphrosunē*, not just by considering the similarities between the *technai* and morality, but also by analysing their differences.[3]

In the course of the argument the definition of *sōphrosunē* has been modified, without comment, from knowledge of *oneself* to knowledge of *itself*, i.e. to knowledge of knowledge. What is in effect a fallacy has arisen as a consequence of the terms in which the argument has been couched.[4] But Plato does in fact seem to see no difficulty in considering knowledge of oneself as equivalent to knowledge of knowledge (in that it is knowledge of one's own knowledge), i.e. in equating one's own self and one's own

---

1. cf. *Phaedrus* 262b; and see Guthrie, IV, p. 168 and n. 1, and T. Irwin, *Plato's Moral Theory: The Early and Middle Dialogues* (Oxford 1977), pp. 75–6.
2. See pp. 20, 22–3, 41, 267 ff. and Irwin, op. cit., pp. 71–7.
3. See J. Gould, *The Development of Plato's Ethics* (Cambridge 1955), pp. 37–41.
4. See introduction to Section F.

knowledge. By this small but crucial shift from 'oneself' to 'itself' we arrive at the philosophical core of the dialogue: the examination of 'knowledge of knowledge'.

The first question to be faced about knowledge of knowledge is its logical possibility. Can knowledge know itself? No other perceptional, emotional or mental activity appears to be self-relational. Can anything in the physical world, such as motion or heat, relate its own faculty to itself? This last point prefigures an important tenet of Plato's later philosophical thought, the belief in self-motion, in a self-moving soul (*psuchē*), which is the prerequisite for life itself.[1]

If we assume for the sake of argument that knowledge of knowledge *is* possible, what will it mean? Socrates interprets it in two ways: first, as the knowledge of itself and of the other knowledges and of ignorance, or rather, (i) the knowledge of *what* one knows and *what* one does not know and of *what* another man knows and does not know. As such it will mean knowledge of the *extent* or *limit* of one's own knowledge (and that of others). Subsequently, the interpretation is scaled down to (ii) the knowledge *that* one knows something and *that* one does not know something (and *that* another man knows something and does not know something). All this was of especial interest to Plato because of Socrates' famous insistence that he was wiser than other men in knowing the limits of his own knowledge, i.e. he claimed to know that he did not know, and did not think that he knew.[2]

If, then, knowledge of knowledge is taken to mean (ii) knowledge *that* one knows something, then it can only recognize *that* some state or condition constitutes knowledge; it cannot recognize *what* that knowledge is knowledge *of* (i.e. the objects of the knowledge, or the facts known). If knowledge of knowledge, *qua* knowledge *that* one knows, is going to know *what* a given 'ordinary' knowledge is knowledge *of*, it has to have added to it that 'ordinary' knowledge (*epistēmē*) or skill (*technē*) – such as medicine, the knowledge of what is healthy.

So knowledge of knowledge, in the sense of (ii) knowledge *that* one knows, seems of limited use. But before reconsidering knowledge of knowledge in the sense of (i) knowledge of *what* one knows, Socrates briefly discusses knowledge of knowledge as (iii) merely a general acquaintance with the concept of knowledge, a sort of knowing *how* to

---

1. cf. *Phaedrus* 245c ff., *Timaeus* 89a and *Laws* 895e–896a. See also Guthrie, IV, p. 171.

2. *Apology* 20d–21d. For discussions of the meaning of this assertion, see N. Gulley, *The Philosophy of Socrates* (London 1968), pp. 62–74, and G. Vlastos, 'Socrates' Disavowal of Knowledge', *Philosophical Quarterly*, 35 (1985), pp. 1–31.

know.[1] But such knowledge will presumably serve only to make easier the learning of the objects of each 'ordinary' knowledge to which it is applied, and to give a clearer understanding of the 'ordinary' knowledge learned: one will know *how* to have that ordinary knowledge as well as *that* one has it.

Socrates accordingly reverts to knowledge of knowledge in sense (i), and now interprets it as (iv) a sort of 'super-knowledge' which oversees the operation of the other, 'ordinary' knowledges and ensures that each is performed efficiently. The way to this interpretation has been opened up by (iii), knowing *how* to know. But 'super-knowledge' would be useful only in so far as it would tell a person what to do for a given purpose. It would not tell him in what circumstances it would be good or beneficial to do it in order to ensure his happiness. It could only ensure the technically correct performance of an action, not the happiness to be derived from any possible act. It would be for the knowledge of good and bad to tell him that. And even if a superordinate knowledge of knowledge presided also over the knowledge of good and bad, it would still have no product. Benefit, the product of the putative relationship, is in fact the product of the knowledge of good and bad, not of the knowledge of knowledge, which is therefore not beneficial.[2]

The refutation of the fifth definition in this developed form, 'super-knowledge', leaves the dialogue ending in the customary *aporia*. The real answer to the question 'What is *sōphrosunē*?' is, however, there, though not made explicit. *Sōphrosunē* is beneficial; the knowledge of good and bad is beneficial; so *sōphrosunē* is the knowledge of good and bad (in effect, the sixth and final definition). But this implicit definition is the definition of virtue itself, rather than the particular aspect of virtue which is *sōphrosunē*. Since Socrates believed that all the virtues are one,[3] the dialogue ends with a clear but unstated assertion of the Socratic principle that virtue is knowledge, more specifically the knowledge of good and bad.

The main purpose of the dialogue now becomes clear. It has not been the ostensible reason for the investigation, to define *sōphrosunē* by itself. It has rather been to examine the Socratic paradox that virtue is knowledge. Right from the start it has been stated unequivocally that *sōphrosunē* is a virtue: first it is called an admirable (*kalon*) thing (159c); then (160e) explicitly a good (*agathon*) thing (and we are reminded of this

1. See Guthrie, IV, pp. 162 and 174, and Robinson, pp. 37–8.
2. The refutation is strikingly similar to those of the first two definitions. Once again a generally accepted truth, this time that virtue is necessarily beneficial, is not satisfied, with the result that the definition must be abandoned.
3. Compare the end of the *Laches*.

in the final *aporia* where *sōphrosunē* is called 'the most admirable of all things' (175a) and 'a great good' (175e)); and the fourth definition of *sōphrosunē* is 'the doing of good things'. When, with the fifth definition, Plato devotes the major part of the inquiry to attempts to define *sōphrosunē* in terms of knowledge, the real purpose of the dialogue begins to emerge and the conclusion, that virtue is knowledge, becomes inevitable.

What has this examination of virtue as knowledge in the *Charmides* to offer us? Its most original and memorable feature is the discussion of the concept of 'knowledge of knowledge'. Though doubts are voiced as to the very possibility of its existence, and though it is unique in having neither a product nor an object different from itself, and in being the only mental activity to be self-relational, Plato refuses to abandon it. But dissatisfied with the apparently meagre benefits to be derived from *sōphrosunē* in sense (ii), knowledge *that* one knows, he examines it as knowledge of *what* one knows, in two versions: (i) as knowledge of the extent or limits of one's knowledge, with obvious reference to Socrates' claim to know more than other men in knowing the limits of his knowledge (that, in fact, he did not know), and to his exhortation to all men to examine themselves in order to discover the limits of their own knowledge;[1] and then as (iv), some sort of 'super-knowledge' which oversees the other knowledges or skills. This latter hypothesis is left undeveloped presumably because its closer investigation would take us too far from the goal to which Plato is leading. For all its attractions, knowledge of knowledge must not be allowed to overwhelm or disrupt the firmly Socratic definitional framework within which the problems are discussed, and so divert us from reaching the important main conclusion of the *Charmides*, the equation of virtue and knowledge.

As a 'definition dialogue' the *Charmides* is eminently a success. Though it ends in the usual *aporia*, the 'real' answer can be rescued from the confusion without too much difficulty. But it is in its examination of a great Socratic paradox, and in particular in its raising of the fascinating question of knowledge of knowledge, that the dialogue transcends the more limited preoccupations of the simpler 'definition dialogues': it introduces us to some of the most important wider concerns of Socratic philosophy and gives notice of the more complex and demanding issues which Plato will confront when he moves on from writing 'Socratic dialogues' of definition.

---

1. See *Apology, passim.*

SUMMARY OF *CHARMIDES*

CHARMIDES

Speakers

SOCRATES

CHAEREPHON: From Sphettus in Attica. A fanatical disciple of Socrates, who went to Delphi to ask the famous question of the oracle – whether there was any man wiser than Socrates. Sent into exile with the leading democrats by the Thirty Tyrants, returned with Thrasybulus in 403, but died before Socrates was brought to trial in 399.

CHARMIDES: The son of Glaucon and the brother of Plato's mother, Perictione. Belonged to Socrates' circle. Socrates himself urged him to take up politics (Xenophon, *Memorabilia* III.7). Became one of the Thirty Tyrants of the oligarchical revolution in Athens in 404. Killed, along with Critias, early in 403 at Munychia in the Piraeus, fighting against the democrats led by Thrasybulus.

CRITIAS: Born *c.* 460, died 403. The son of Callaeschrus and the cousin and guardian of Charmides (and cousin of Plato's mother). Became associated with Socrates early, and also with the sophistic movement. Was a literary as well as a political figure, composing elegiac poetry and tragedies, fragments of which are extant. Achieved infamy as the extremist leader of the Thirty Tyrants.

CHARMIDES

A. *Health of Body is Dependent on Health of Soul*

The introductory conversation establishes the dramatic date, setting and speakers. The subject of the dialogue is introduced through Socrates' asserting that it is impossible to heal the part without also setting oneself to heal the whole: to heal a diseased part of the body the doctor must treat not only that diseased part, but the body as a whole and the soul, since all things, both good and bad, originate in the soul; and the soul is to be treated with charms, i.e. beautiful words, which will produce self-control (sōphrosunē) in it. Socrates is, therefore, even before he begins the search for a definition of self-control (sōphrosunē), implicitly defining it as 'health of soul'. Thus two basic Socratic tenets may be discerned in this passage: (i) the importance of tending the soul, and (ii) the parallelism of the health of the body and the health of the soul.

We'd got back yesterday from the camp at Potidaea.[1] I'd been away a long time, so I was glad to return to my old haunts. I went to Taureas'[2] wrestling-school opposite the temple of Basile,[3] where I found a large crowd of people, some unknown to me, the majority acquaintances of mine. I had not been expected, and as soon as they saw me coming in they shouted over to me from all sides. Chaerephon, who is quite mad, sprang from their midst, ran towards me, grabbed me by the hand and exclaimed, 'Socrates, how did you manage to escape from the battle?' (Shortly before we came away there had been a battle at Potidaea, of which the people here had only just learned.)

'Just as you see,' I replied.

'But a report has reached us,' he said, 'that the battle was very hard-fought and that many people we knew have died in it.'

'The report is reasonably accurate,' I said.

'Were you actually in the battle?' he asked.

'I was.'

153a

b

c

---

1. A Corinthian colony in Chalcidice. It was a tributary ally of Athens and revolted in 432. After the battle referred to here, in which Socrates saved Alcibiades' life (see *Symposium* 219e ff.), the Athenian army laid siege to the city until it fell in 430.

2. Presumably the 'chorēgos' or producer of choruses who was once assaulted by Alcibiades: see Demosthenes, *Against Midias* 147, Plutarch, *Life of Alcibiades* 16.4 and J. K. Davies, *Athenian Propertied Families, 600–300 B.C.* (Oxford 1971), p. 29.

3. *Basilē* (Queen), apparently a personification of Athenian royalty, was worshipped at a sanctuary to the south of the Acropolis.

'Come and sit down here, then,' he said, 'and tell us all about it. We haven't heard the whole story properly yet.' With that he took me over to Critias, Callaeschrus' son, and sat me down beside him.

I sat down, said hello to Critias and the others, and proceeded to tell them all the news from the camp, answering whatever questions I was d asked; and each had a different question.

When we'd exhausted that subject I asked them about things here: what was happening in the field of philosophy; had any of the young men become pre-eminent for wisdom or beauty or both? At that Critias looked 154a towards the door where he'd seen a number of young men coming in, squabbling noisily with one another, and another crowd following them. 'I think you're going to get an answer to your question about the handsome young men right away, Socrates,' he said. 'Those young men coming in just now are, as it happens, the advance guard and lovers of the young man who is thought to be our most handsome at present; and it looks to me as if the young man himself is already getting quite close.'

'But who is he?' I asked. 'Who's his father?'

'I'm sure you must know him,' he replied, 'although he hadn't come of b age before you went away. He's Charmides, my cousin, the son of my uncle Glaucon.'

'Heavens, I do indeed know him,' I exclaimed. 'He was very promising when he was still a child. As it is, I suppose by now he must be quite the young man.'

'You'll know right away how old he is and what he's like,' he said. Just as he was saying that, Charmides came in.

Now, my friend, I'm no judge. I'm simply a blank ruler[1] when it comes to gauging how handsome young men are. Very nearly all men of that age c seem handsome to me. All the same, at that moment Charmides seemed to me amazingly tall and handsome. All the others present appeared to me to be in love with him, they were so startled and disconcerted by his entrance; and there were many more of his lovers among those who came behind him. The reaction of the grown men was not so surprising, but I watched the boys and saw that none of them, not even the smallest of them, had eyes for anyone else. Every one of them looked at him as if he d were a statue. Chaerephon called to me and said, 'What do you think of our young man, Socrates? Hasn't he got a lovely face?'

'Extraordinarily lovely,' I replied.

'But just let him be persuaded to strip and you won't notice he's got a face at all, his body is so perfectly beautiful.'

1. Literally, 'I'm a white measuring line.' A line rubbed with coloured chalk was used for measuring white marble; a line rubbed with white chalk was proverbially useless for this.

Well, the others said exactly the same as Chaerephon, and I said, 'Goodness, how irresistible you make him sound, provided that he happens to have just one other little thing.'

'What's that?' asked Critias.

'Provided that he happens to be endowed with a fine soul,' I said. 'He e should, of course, have such a soul, since he does belong to your family, Critias.'

'Why,' he said, 'he's very beautiful and noble in that respect too.'

'Then why don't we strip that part of him,' I said, 'and look at it, before we look at his body? He must now be of an age to be willing to engage in discussion.'

'Indeed he is,' said Critias. 'He's a philosopher, you know, and in the opinion of others, as well as in his own, quite a poet too.' 155a

'That's an accomplishment that has been in your family for a long time, Critias, thanks to its kinship with Solon.[1] But why don't you call the young man over here and show him to me? Even if he happened to be even younger than he is, it wouldn't be improper for him to talk to us in your company: you're his guardian as well as his cousin.'

'You're quite right,' he said. 'We'll call him.' With that he turned to his attendant. 'Boy,' he said, 'call Charmides. Tell him I want to have b him see a doctor about the complaint he spoke to me of the day before yesterday.' Critias then turned and said to me, 'You see, he said recently he'd been having headaches when he got up in the morning. Now what's to stop you pretending to him that you know of some remedy for a headache?'

'Nothing,' I said. 'Just let him come.'

'He'll be here,' he replied.

Which is just what happened. He came, and he caused a great deal of laughter: each of us who were sitting down tried to make room for him c by pushing his neighbour away in a frantic attempt to have the boy sit next to him, until we forced the man sitting at one end of the row to stand up and tipped the man at the other off sideways. In the event Charmides came and sat between me and Critias. Well, by then, my friend, I was in difficulties, and the self-assurance I'd felt earlier that I'd talk to him quite easily had been knocked out of me. When Critias told him I was the man who knew of the remedy, he gave me a look that is impossible to describe d and made ready to ask me something. Everyone in the wrestling-school swarmed all round us. That was the moment, my noble friend, when I saw what was inside his cloak. I was on fire, I lost my head, and I

1. A great Athenian statesman and poet of the early sixth century who introduced important constitutional, legal and economic reforms. Plato too was related to him through his (Plato's) mother (Diogenes Laertius, III. 1).

considered Cydias[1] to be the wisest man in matters of love. When speaking of a handsome boy, he said, by way of advice to someone, 'Take care not to go as a fawn into the presence of a lion and be snatched as a portion of
e meat.' I felt I'd been caught by just such a creature. All the same, when Charmides asked me whether I knew the remedy for his headaches, I somehow managed to answer that I did.

'What is it, then?' he asked.

I replied that it was a leaf, but that there was a charm that went with the remedy: if one chanted the charm at the same time as one employed the remedy, the remedy cured one completely; without the charm, the leaf was of no use.

156a Charmides said, 'Well then, I'll take down a copy of the charm from you.'

'Whether you can persuade me to divulge it or not?' I said.

He laughed at that and said, 'If I can persuade you, Socrates.'

'All right,' I said. 'And you're quite sure that's my name?'

'Yes, unless I'm quite mistaken,' he replied. 'There's a great deal of talk about you among the boys of my age, and I remember your being with Critias here when I was a child.'

'That's very flattering of you,' I said. 'That means I'll feel less inhibited
b about telling you what the charm actually is. Just now I was in difficulties as to how to show you its power. You see, Charmides, it's the sort of charm which cannot cure the head alone. Perhaps you too have heard what good doctors say when a patient comes to them with sore eyes. They say, I think, that they cannot attempt to heal his eyes alone, but that they must treat his head too at the same time, if his sight is to recover. They
c say too that to think that one could ever treat the head by itself without the whole body is quite foolish. On that principle, then, they apply their regimens to the entire body and attempt to treat and heal the part in conjunction with the whole.[2] You do realize that this is what they say and that this is in fact the case, don't you?'

'Yes, certainly,' he said.

'Do you think that's right, then? Do you accept the principle?'

'Most definitely,' he said.
d When I heard him agree to that, I regained my confidence, all my self-assurance gradually returned, my spirits began to rise again, and I said, 'Well, it's like that with this charm too. I learned it when I was away on

---

1. Lyric poet whose floruit was c. 500; fragment 2 in J. M. Edmonds, *Lyra Graeca*, III (Cambridge, Mass., and London 1940; revised Loeb edition), p. 68.
2. At *Phaedrus* 270c Plato ascribes this doctrine to Hippocrates.

an expedition with the army from one of Zalmoxis'[1] Thracian doctors, the ones who are said actually to be able to give men immortality. This Thracian said that the Greeks were right in saying what I was telling you a minute ago. "Our king Zalmoxis," he said, "who is a god, says that just as one shouldn't try to heal the eyes without the head, or the head without the body, so one shouldn't try to heal the body without the soul either; and that this is the reason why many diseases baffle doctors in Greece – because they ignore the whole, which they ought to take care of, since if the whole is not well, it is impossible for part of it to be so." He said all things, both good and bad, in the body and in the whole man, originated in the soul and spread from there, just as they did from the head to the eyes. One ought, then, to treat the soul first and foremost, if the head and the rest of the body were to be well. He said the soul was treated with certain charms, my dear Charmides, and that these charms were beautiful words. As a result of such words self-control came into being in souls. When it came into being and was present in them, it was then easy to secure health both for the head and for the rest of the body. Now, when he taught me the remedy and the charms, he said, "See that no one who has not first surrendered his soul to be treated by you with the charm persuades you to treat his head with this remedy. In fact," he said, "this is the mistake that is made with people today. Some men try to be doctors and try to produce either health or self-control, the one in isolation from the other." He gave me very strict orders that there should be no one, no matter how rich or noble or beautiful, who could persuade me to do otherwise. Now I – you see I gave him my word and must obey him – I shall obey him, and if you'd like, in accordance with the stranger's orders, to surrender your soul to me to charm with the Thracian's charms first, I shall apply the remedy to your head. But if not, there's nothing we can do for you, my dear Charmides.'

When Critias heard me say that, he said, 'The head complaint would prove to be a godsend for the young man, Socrates, if he's going to be forced to improve his mind as well because of his head. All the same, I can tell you that Charmides is generally considered to surpass those of his own age-group not just in his looks but also in that very quality for which you say you have the charm. You do mean self-control, don't you?'

'I most certainly do,' I said.

'Well then, rest assured that he is regarded as far and away the most

---

1. A god of the dead worshipped by the Getae, a Thracian tribe. See Herodotus IV.93–6, where he also gives an account of Zalmoxis (or Salmoxis, as he knows him) whereby he is a mortal who pretended to be immortal.

self-controlled of the present generation and, for his age, second to none in everything else too.'

'Indeed it's only right, Charmides,' I said, 'that you should surpass the
e rest in all things like that. I don't think there is anyone else here who could easily point to any two Athenian families, apart from those from which you come, whose union might be expected to produce anyone better or more noble. Your father's family, that of Critias, Dropides' son, has been eulogized by Anacreon,[1] Solon and many other poets, and has been presented to us by tradition as pre-eminent for beauty, virtue and every-
158a thing else that is called happiness. The same is true of your mother's family too: no one in the continent of Asia is said to have been considered more handsome or taller than your uncle Pyrilampes,[2] whenever he went as ambassador to the Great King[3] or anyone else in the continent. That whole side of the family is in no way inferior to the other. So it's natural that, coming from such people, you should be first in everything. Now,
b from what I've seen of your looks, dear son of Glaucon, I don't think you fall short of any of your forebears in anything; and if you are sufficiently endowed with self-control and the other qualities, as Critias maintains, your mother bore a blessed son in you, my dear Charmides. Well, anyway, this is how things stand: if self-control is already present in you, as Critias here says, and you are sufficiently self-controlled, you no longer need the charms of Zalmoxis or of Abaris the Hyperborean,[4] but I'd have to give
c you the headache remedy itself right away. But if you think you're still lacking in those respects, I must employ the charm before giving you the remedy. Tell me yourself, then, whether you agree with Critias and say that you already have enough self-control, or whether you say that you are deficient in it.'

At first Charmides blushed, looking even more handsome – his bashful-ness suited his years. Then he gave a not ignoble answer. He said it wasn't easy in the present circumstances either to confirm or to deny what was
d being asked. 'If,' he said, 'I say I'm not self-controlled, it's absurd that one should say such things against oneself, and at the same time I'll make a liar of Critias here and of many others too, who, according to him, think I'm self-controlled. On the other hand, if I say I am, I praise myself,

1. A famous lyric poet, born in Teos c. 570.
2. A friend of Pericles, famed for his breeding of peacocks, who became Plato's stepfather.
3. See p. 139 n. 1.
4. A servant of Apollo, the god of healing. He was said to travel all over the world, carry-ing an arrow and never eating (Herodotus IV.36), and to have shown the Spartans how to perform sacrifices which put an end to the plagues in their land (Apollonius (2nd cent. B.C.?), *Mirabilia* 4).

which will perhaps seem rather bad form. So I don't know what answer to give you.'

To that I replied, 'What you're saying seems reasonable to me, Charmides. I think,' I went on, 'that together we ought to consider whether or not you do possess what I'm asking about, to make sure that you're not e forced to say things you don't want, and that I don't resort to medicine without due consideration. So if it's all right with you, I'd like to consider the question with you; but if it's not, we'll leave it be.'

'But it's most definitely all right,' he said. 'So far as that's concerned, consider the question as you yourself think best.'

'Well,' I said, 'it seems to me to be best to consider the question in this way. Obviously if self-control is present in you, you can give an opinion about it, since it must, of course, by being in you (if indeed it is), be 159a perceptible, thus enabling you to form an opinion about it – about *what* self-control is, and what *sort* of a thing it is. Don't you think so?'

'I do,' he replied.

'And since you know how to speak Greek,' I said, 'you could, of course, also state what you think, just as it appears to you?'

'Possibly,' he said.

'Well then, so that we can guess whether it is in you or not, tell me,' I said, 'what you say self-control is in your opinion.'

B. *First Definition: Quietness*

Charmides' first definition, which describes the outward manifestation of the virtue in a social context, as a sort of 'good conduct', is typical of a young Athenian aristocrat. Socrates refutes this definition by gaining agreement that self-control is kalon (admirable, beautiful, fine), whereas quietness is not always kalon; therefore self-control is not quietness.

At first he hesitated and was quite unwilling to answer, but then he said b that in his opinion self-control was doing everything in an orderly and quiet way – walking in the streets and talking and doing everything else in the same way. 'In my opinion,' he said, 'what you're asking about is, in short, a sort of quietness.'

'Well, are you right?' I asked. 'Certainly they do say, Charmides, that quiet people are self-controlled. Let's see whether they have a point, then. Tell me, isn't self-control one of those things which are admirable?' c

'Yes, certainly,' he said.

'Is it more admirable, then, in a writing-lesson, to copy the letters quickly or quietly?'

'Quickly.'

'What about reading? Quickly or slowly?'

'Quickly.'

'And playing the lyre quickly and wrestling nimbly are much more admirable than doing these things quietly and slowly?'

'Yes.'

'What about boxing and the pancration?[r] Isn't it the same with them?'

'Yes, certainly.'

d 'And with running and jumping and all the activities of the body, isn't it the nimble and quick performance of these which is the mark of the fine body, whereas the laborious and quiet performance of them is the mark of the contemptible one?'

'So it seems.'

'Then it seems to us,' I said, 'that with regard to the body at least, it is not what is quiet, but what is quickest and most nimble that is most admirable. Isn't that so?'

'Yes, certainly.'

'Was self-control an admirable thing?'

'Yes.'

'With regard to the body at least, then, it isn't quietness but quickness that would be the more self-controlled thing, since self-control is an admirable thing.'

'So it would appear,' he said.

e 'Again, is facility in learning the more admirable thing, or difficulty in learning?' I asked.

'Facility in learning.'

'And facility in learning is learning quickly, whereas difficulty in learning is learning quietly and slowly?'

'Yes.'

'And isn't it a more admirable thing to teach someone quickly and vigorously, rather than quietly and slowly?'

'Yes.'

'Again, is recalling to mind and remembering quietly and slowly the more admirable thing, or vigorously and quickly?'

'Vigorously and quickly,' he replied.

160a 'And isn't readiness of mind a sort of nimbleness of the soul, not quietness?'

1. A regular event in athletic contests. It was a violent form of wrestling, in which kicking and punching were allowed, though biting and gouging were forbidden.

'True.'

'And again, isn't it understanding what is said in a writing-lesson or lyre-lesson or anywhere else, not as quietly but as quickly as possible, that is most admirable?'

'Yes.'

'And further, in the investigations of the soul and in deliberating, it isn't, I think, the man who is quietest and deliberates and discovers with great effort who is accounted worthy of praise, but the man who does it most easily and quickly.'   b

'That's so,' he said.

'Then, Charmides, in everything to do with the soul and the body we find speed and nimbleness more admirable than slowness and quietness.'

'That may well be the case,' he said.

'So self-control won't be a sort of quietness, and the self-controlled life won't be a quiet one either, at least according to this argument, since if it is self-controlled, it must be an admirable thing. Indeed, there are two possibilities: it's either never or probably very rarely in life that quiet c actions prove more admirable than quick and forceful ones. But, my friend, if at the most there are in fact as many quiet actions which are more admirable as there are vigorous and quick ones, it still wouldn't mean that doing things quietly would be self-control any more than doing them vigorously and quickly would, whether in walking or talking or anything else; or that the quiet life would be more self-controlled than the non-quiet, since we assumed in our discussion that self-control was one d of the admirable things, and we've shown that quick things are just as admirable as quiet ones.'

'I think you're right in what you've said, Socrates,' he said.

C. Second Definition: Modesty

Charmides' second definition is an advance on his first in that it attempts to describe the inner condition which might produce such an outward manifestation as quietness. Socrates' refutation is achieved by arguing that self-control is not only admirable, but also good, whereas modesty is not always good; therefore self-control is not modesty.

'Well then, Charmides,' I said, 'this time concentrate harder and look into your own self. Consider what sort of a person the presence of self-control makes you, and what it would have to be like to produce such an

effect on you. Think it all through and then tell me plainly and manfully:
e what does it seem to you to be?'

He paused and, examining himself with a most manly effort, said,
'Well, I think that self-control makes a man feel shame and be bashful,
and that self-control is the same thing as modesty.'

'All right,' I said. 'Didn't you agree just now that self-control was an
admirable thing?'

'Yes, certainly,' he said.

'Self-controlled men are good men too, then?'

'Yes.'

'Can a thing be good which does not produce good men?'

'Certainly not.'

'Then self-control is not only an admirable thing but a good thing too.'

161a 'I think so.'

'Well then!' I exclaimed. 'Don't you believe that Homer is right when
he says: "Modesty is not a good companion for a needy man"?'[1]

'I do,' he replied.

'So modesty, it would appear, is not a good thing and is a good thing.'

'So it seems.'

'And self-control is a good thing if it makes men in whom it is present
good and not bad.'

'Why, yes, I do think it's as you say.'

'So self-control can't be modesty, if it really is a good thing, and if
b modesty is no more a good thing than a bad one.'

'Well, Socrates,' he said, 'I think that's right.'

D. *Third Definition: Doing One's Own Job*

*'Doing one's own job' or, more literally, 'doing (prattein) one's own things',
is the definition of justice given at Republic 433a. There it means 'each man
performing the one function in the state for which his nature most suits him'.
Here, however, Socrates takes it to mean the opposite, by interpreting the phrase
as 'each man doing (or making) everything for himself': each man should weave
his own clothes, wash his own clothes, make his own shoes, etc. (This is the
form of social organization rejected at Republic 369e ff.) On the basis of this
interpretation, Socrates refutes the definition by arguing that self-control is good,
yet there are times when doing one's own job is bad; therefore self-control is not
doing one's own job.*

The more experienced Critias now takes over from Charmides, and Socrates

1. Homer, *Odyssey* XVII, 347. The same line is quoted at *Laches* 201b.

*makes explicit for the first time his equation of 'doing' (prattein) with 'making'
(poiein, which may also mean 'doing' – this is the ambiguity exploited by
Socrates). Critias rejects this equation: 'doing' one's own things is not the same
as 'making' one's own things. A craftsman may make his own things and those
of other people, and still be self-controlled in that he is merely doing his job; it
is people who do other people's jobs who are not self-controlled.*

*Critias in fact draws a distinction between making (poiein), on the one hand,
and doing (prattein) and working (ergazesthai), on the other: only noble and
beneficial 'makings' (poiēseis) can be called 'workings' (ergasiai) and 'doings'
(praxeis); only these are a man's 'proper business' (oikeia). Critias then
abruptly concludes from this that self-control must be doing one's own job.*

*Socrates' comments on this lead on to the fourth definition: one's proper
business and one's own job are good things; self-control is, on the current
hypothesis, the doing of one's own job; therefore self-control is the doing of good
things (this is the fourth definition).*

[*Charmides speaks*] 'But give me your considered opinion of this statement about self-control, which I've just remembered I heard from someone once: that self-control might be doing one's own job. Give me your
considered opinion. Was the man who said that right?'

'You wicked boy,' I replied, 'you heard that from Critias here or from
another of our clever fellows.'   c

'It must have been from someone else,' said Critias. 'It certainly wasn't
from me.'

'But what difference does it make, Socrates,' said Charmides, 'who I
heard it from?'

'None at all,' I replied. 'In any case, the question we've got to consider
is not who said it, but whether or not the statement is true.'

'You're quite right,' he said.

'Of course,' I said. 'All the same, I should be surprised if we actually
will discover what exactly its status is. It appears to have a sort of cryptic
meaning.'

'How is that?' he asked.

'Because presumably,' I replied, 'he did not really mean quite what his   d
words conveyed when he said that self-control was doing one's own job.
Or do you believe that the writing-master does not *do* something when he
reads or writes?'

'No,' he said, 'I do believe he does something.'

'Then do you think that it's only his own name that the writing-master
reads and writes, or teaches boys to? Or did you write your enemies'
names just as much as your own and your friends'?'

187

'Just as much.'

'Well then, were you meddling – that is, were you without self-control
e in doing that?'

'Not at all.'

'And yet you were not doing your own job if reading and writing are
"doing something".'

'They most certainly are.'

'And, my friend, healing, building houses, weaving and producing any
piece of skilled work whatsoever, by any skill whatsoever, are all presumably "doing something".'

'Of course.'

'Well then,' I said, 'do you think a state would be well run by a law like
this, which commands each person to weave his own coat and wash it,
and make his own sandals and oil-flask and scraper[1] and everything else
162a on the same principle of each person's keeping his hands off what is not
his own, and working at and doing his own job?'

'No, I don't,' he replied.

'Nevertheless,' I said, 'a state run on the principle of self-control would
be run well.'

'Certainly,' he said.

'Then,' I said, 'self-control would not be doing one's own job when it's
of that sort and done in that way.'

'Apparently not.'

'Then it looks as if, as I was saying just now, the man who said that
doing one's own job was self-control was speaking cryptically, since I
b don't suppose he was so simple-minded as that. Or was it some fool that
you heard saying this, Charmides?'

'Far from it,' he said. 'He seemed to be a pretty clever fellow, you
know.'

'Well, as far as I can see, he propounded this as a deliberate puzzle for
us, for no other reason than that he thought it would be difficult for us to
find out what on earth doing one's own job is.'

'Possibly,' he said.

'So what on earth would doing one's own job be? Can you tell me?'

'Heavens, I don't know,' he said. 'I dare say there is no reason why
even the man who said it should have the slightest idea of what he meant.'
As he said that, he gave a little smile and looked at Critias.

c   Now Critias had clearly long been champing at the bit in his eagerness
to impress Charmides and the others present. He had only with great

---

1. After exercise, it was customary to cover the body with oil, which was then scraped off,
taking the dirt and sweat with it.

difficulty managed to restrain himself up to then, and this was the last straw. I think it's absolutely certain – as I assumed at the time – that it was from Critias that Charmides had heard this answer about self-control. So Charmides, who did not want to explain the answer himself, but to have Critias do it, kept trying to provoke him and pointing out that he had been refuted. This was too much for Critias. It appeared to me as though he had got irritated with Charmides, just as a poet might do with an actor who treated his poetry badly. So he gave him a look and said, 'Is that what you think, Charmides? That if *you* don't know what on earth the man meant who said that doing one's own job was self-control, *he* doesn't know either?'

'Why, Critias, my dear fellow,' I said, 'it is not at all surprising that at his age Charmides doesn't understand it; but, of course, it's natural for you to possess that knowledge in view of your age and your devotion to study. So if you agree that self-control is what Charmides says it is, and are willing to take the argument over, I'd much rather investigate with you whether what we said is true or not.'

'Well, I do agree,' he said, 'and am willing to take it over.'

'That's very good of you,' I said. 'Tell me, do you also agree with what I was asking a minute ago, that all craftsmen make something?'

'I do.'

'Well then, do you think they make only their own things or other people's things too?'

'Other people's things too.'

'Then are they self-controlled in so far as they're not making only their own things?'

'What objection is there?' he asked.

'None as far as I'm concerned,' I replied. 'But watch that there is not one for the man who assumes that doing one's own job is self-control, and then says that there is no objection to those who do other people's jobs being self-controlled too.'

'I suppose,' he said, 'I've agreed that those who *do* other people's jobs are self-controlled, by agreeing that those who *make* other people's things are.'

'Tell me,' I said, 'don't you call "making" and "doing" the same thing?'

'No, I don't,' he replied, 'nor for that matter "working" and "making". I learned that from Hesiod, who said, "Work is no disgrace."[1] Now, do you suppose that if he had been calling the sorts of thing you were speaking of a minute ago "works" and "working" and "doing", he would have said there was no disgrace in being a cobbler or selling salt fish or being

1. *Works and Days* 309.

employed in a brothel? Don't you believe it, Socrates. Hesiod too, in my opinion, considered making to be different from doing and working. A

c thing which was *made* sometimes brought disgrace when it lacked beauty; while a *work* could never be any disgrace at all. Things that are beautifully and beneficially made he called "works", and such "makings" he called "workings" and "doings". It must be stated that he believed only things like that to be a man's proper business, while everything that was harmful was other people's business. So we must conclude that both Hesiod and any other knowledgeable person call the man who does his own job self-controlled.'

d 'Critias,' I said, 'the minute you began to speak I was pretty sure of your thesis – that you called what is proper to a man and what is his own job good things, and that you called the "makings" of good things "doings". I have heard Prodicus[1] drawing his innumerable distinctions between names, you know. But I give you my permission to assign each name as you wish; only do make it plain to what you are applying whichever name you use. Now then, go back to the beginning again and give us a clearer definition.'

E. *Fourth Definition: The Doing of Good Things*

Socrates does not, as one might expect, examine what Critias means by 'good things'; instead he turns to the question of whether it is possible for the self-controlled man to be ignorant of his being self-controlled. His argument is as follows: (i) self-control is doing what one should; (ii) doing what one should is doing good; therefore, by implication, (iii) self-control is doing good; but (iv) one may do good without knowing it; therefore (v) one may be self-controlled without knowing it.

Critias consequently abandons this line of argument. The implication of this section, of course, is that self-control is doing good knowingly: self-control is the knowledge of (the doing of) good.

e [*Socrates speaks to Critias*] 'Are you saying that this doing or making, or whatever you like to call it, of good things is self-control?'
'I am,' he said.

1. Prodicus of Ceos, a sophist and contemporary of Socrates, lectured on the necessity for a precise use of language, drawing nice distinctions between synonyms. He appears in the *Protagoras*. See also *Laches* 197d.

'So it's not the man who does bad things, but the man who does good things who is self-controlled?'

'Don't you think so, my good fellow?' he asked.

'Never mind,' I said. 'Let's not consider what I think just yet, but rather what you're saying now.'

'Well,' he said, 'I'm saying that it is not the man who doesn't do good things but does bad who is self-controlled, but that it is the man who does good things and not bad who is. That is, I define self-control quite plainly as the doing of good things.'

'There's probably no reason why that shouldn't be true. However, I am surprised,' I said, 'that you believe that men who are self-controlled do not know that they are self-controlled.' 164a

'But I don't,' he protested.

'Weren't you saying a short while ago,' I said, 'that there was no reason why craftsmen shouldn't be self-controlled, even when making other people's things?'

'I was,' he said. 'But what of it?'

'Nothing. But tell me whether you think that a doctor, when making someone healthy, does what is beneficial not only to himself but also to the man he is curing?' b

'I do.'

'Is the man who does that doing what he should?'

'Yes.'

'Isn't the man who does what he should self-controlled?'

'He certainly is.'

'Then must a doctor know when his curing is beneficial and when it's not? Must every craftsman know when he's likely to profit from whatever work he does and when he's not?'

'Perhaps not.'

'So sometimes,' I said, 'the doctor does something beneficial or harmful without knowing which he has done.[1] And yet, according to what you say, in doing what is beneficial, he has done what is self-controlled. Wasn't that your point?' c

'Yes, it was.'

'Then it would appear that sometimes, when he does what is beneficial, he does what is self-controlled and is himself self-controlled, though he does not know that he *is* being self-controlled?'

'But that could never happen, Socrates,' he said. 'Still, if you think that

---

1. Sometimes it may be better for a man to die than to be cured. The doctor will know that he has cured a man, but not whether his curing of him will have benefited him; cf. *Laches* 195b–e and *Gorgias* 511e–512b.

that must follow as a result of what I admitted earlier, I'd rather retract
d part of that admission – and I'd not be ashamed to say that I was wrong –
than ever allow that a man who does not know himself is self-controlled.'

F. Fifth Definition: Knowing Oneself

*The refutation of this definition is attempted, in the first place (165c–166a), by
analogy with a 'productive' knowledge: sōphrosunē has no product, as medicine (the knowledge of what is healthy) does: it produces health. Critias counters
by showing that there are other knowledges, such as arithmetic, which also
do not have products; so Socrates has not shown that sōphrosunē cannot be
knowledge of oneself.*

*Socrates accordingly attempts a second refutation, which again uses analogy:
every knowledge is the knowledge of something, and this something is different
from the knowledge itself. Arithmetic, for example, is the knowledge of numbers, but numbers are not arithmetic itself. So what is sōphrosunē the
knowledge of in the same sense? What object different from itself does it have?
Critias denies the analogy, and replies that this is precisely the difference
between sōphrosunē and all other knowledges.*

*As a result of all this, the definition of sōphrosunē is modified to 'knowledge
both of the other knowledges and of its own self (and of ignorance)'. Sōphrosunē is no longer knowledge of oneself, but knowledge of itself (and of the
other knowledges and ignorance): in other words, it is knowledge of knowledge.
The move from 'oneself' to 'itself' appears to be an unwitting fallacy (see
Tuckey, pp. 32–6, and Guthrie, IV, pp. 169–70). It arises as a natural
consequence of the structure and movement of the argument which, by setting
out to demonstrate the uniqueness of sōphrosunē, has driven itself into saying
that, if all the other knowledges have objects which are different from themselves, then sōphrosunē (which is already unique in having no product) must,
if it is to be unique in this respect too, have itself as its object. In effect, Plato
seems to be treating one's knowledge as equivalent to oneself. This emerges most
clearly at 169e, where knowledge of knowledge is made to correspond to a man's
knowledge of himself: what it should in fact correspond to is a man's knowledge
of his own knowledge.*

*Next the definition is reformulated in terms of the sōphrōn man: he is the
man who knows himself and knows what he knows and what he does not know
(and what another man knows and does not know).*

*Finally part of the definiens (the defining expression, i.e. 'knowing oneself')
is added to the definiendum (what is to be defined, i.e. sōphrosunē and the
sōphrōn man): at 167a–b it is said that being sōphrōn, and sōphrosunē, and*

knowing oneself, are knowing what one knows and what one does not know.
(This is expanded in 167b to 'knowing (that one knows and that one does not
know) what one knows and what one does not know'.) By all this Plato is
leading up to an interpretation of knowledge of knowledge as knowledge of the
extent or limits of one's knowledge.

[*Critias speaks*] 'Indeed, I'd almost say that is what self-control really
is, knowing oneself. I agree with the man who dedicated the inscription
to that effect at Delphi.[1] The fact is, I think that the inscription was
dedicated to serve instead of "Hail", as a greeting from the god to the
people entering the temple, as though the god felt that this form of greeting   e
wasn't correct, and that they ought not to recommend *that* to one another,
but rather self-control. So this is how the god speaks to the people who
enter his temple, and not in the way men do. At least, that's what I think
the man who dedicated the inscription intended by the dedication. He
says to whoever enters nothing other than "Be self-controlled". Or rather,
he expresses himself more cryptically, as a prophet would, because, as the
inscription implies and as I maintain, "Know yourself" and "Be self-
controlled" are the same thing, though one might perhaps think that they   165a
are different, as, I believe, the people who dedicated the later inscriptions,
"Nothing in excess" and "A pledge is the next thing to ruin", actually
did. In fact, they thought that "Know yourself" was a piece of advice, not
a greeting from the god to the people entering. Consequently, because
they themselves wanted to dedicate pieces of advice that were no less
useful, they inscribed those words and dedicated them. The reason why
I'm saying all this, Socrates, is this: I let you have all we've said before –
perhaps you were more right there, perhaps I was, but nothing of what   b
we said was absolutely clear. Now, however, I'm willing to explain this
fully to you, unless you do agree that self-control is knowing oneself.'

'But, Critias,' I said, 'you're treating me as if I'm maintaining that I
know what I'm asking about, and as if I'll agree with you if I really want
to. But it's not like that. In fact, I'm going along with you in investigating
whatever proposition is made, because I myself am in ignorance. So, when
I've considered it, I'm prepared to tell you whether or not I agree with   c
you. But wait until I've considered it.'

'Consider it, then,' he said.

'I am,' I said. 'If indeed self-control *is* knowing something, it will
obviously be *a* knowledge and a knowledge *of* something, won't it?'

'Yes,' he said. 'Of oneself.'

1. The temple of Apollo at Delphi was the seat of the Pythian oracle, the most famous and
influential in Greece.

'Now, isn't medicine the knowledge of what is healthy?'

'Yes, certainly.'

'Well then,' I said, 'if you asked me, "What use is medicine to us, inasmuch as it is the knowledge of what is healthy? What does it
d produce?", I'd say that it is of considerable benefit in that it produces health, a splendid product, for us. Do you accept that?'

'I do.'

'Well, if you then asked me what product I say the art of building, which is the knowledge of building, produces, I'd say buildings; and the same for the other arts. Now, since you say that self-control is the knowledge of oneself, you ought to be able to tell me the answer in the case of self-control, when I ask, "Critias, what splendid product worthy
e of the name does self-control, in so far as it is the knowledge of oneself, produce for us?" Come on then, tell me.'

'But Socrates,' he said, 'your method of investigating the question is wrong. It isn't like the other knowledges, and they aren't like one another either; but you're conducting the investigation as if they were. For tell me,' he went on, 'what is the product of the art of arithmetic or geometry, in the way that a house is the product of the art of building, a cloak of the art of weaving, or many other such products of many arts which one could
166a point to? Can you point to any such product of those arts? You won't be able to.'

I said, 'That's true, but I can point to this – what each of these knowledges is the knowledge of, that thing being different from the knowledge itself. For example, arithmetic is the knowledge of the even and the odd, of the way in which members of the one group are numerically related to one another and to members of the other group, and vice versa, isn't it?'

'Yes, certainly,' he said.

'Aren't the odd and the even different from arithmetic itself?'

'Of course.'

b 'And again, weighing is the weighing of the heavier and the lighter weight; but the heavy and the light are different from weighing itself. You admit that?'

'I do.'

'Tell me, then, what is self-control the knowledge of, that thing being different from self-control itself?'

'That's just it, Socrates,' he said. 'You've come in your investigation to the question of what the difference is between self-control and all the other knowledges. You're trying to find some similarity between it and the
c others. There isn't any. All the others are knowledges of something else,

not of themselves. Self-control alone is the knowledge both of the other knowledges and of its own self. You're well aware of that. Indeed I think you're doing what you said just now you were not doing: you're ignoring the real point at issue in our discussion in your efforts to refute me.'

'How can you believe,' I exclaimed, 'that if I'm trying my hardest to refute you, I'm doing it for any other reason than that for which I'd investigate what I say myself! You see, my great fear is that I may some   d
time not notice that I'm thinking I know something when in fact I don't. And this, I tell you, is what I'm doing now: looking at the argument mostly for my own sake, but perhaps for the sake of my friends as well. Or don't you think that it is a common good for almost all men that each thing that exists should be revealed as it really is?'

'I do indeed, Socrates,' he said.

'Well then, Critias, don't be discouraged, and give me the answer, as you see it, to the question. Never mind whether it's Critias or Socrates who is the one refuted. Just concentrate on the argument itself, and con-   e
sider what on earth will become of it if it is examined.'

'I'll do that,' he said, 'because I think that what you're saying is quite reasonable.'

'Well then,' I said, 'tell me, what do you say about self-control?'

'Well,' he said, 'I say that it alone of the knowledges is the knowledge both of itself and of the other knowledges.'

'Would it be a knowledge of ignorance too,' I asked, 'if it is a knowledge of knowledge?'

'Yes, certainly,' he replied.

'So the self-controlled man alone will know himself and be able to   167a
examine what he in fact knows and what he doesn't, and he will be capable of looking at other people in the same way to see what any of them knows and thinks he knows, if he *does* know; and what, on the other hand, he thinks he knows, but does not. No one else will be able to do that. In fact, that is being self-controlled and self-control and knowing oneself – knowing what one knows and what one doesn't. Is that what you're saying?'

'Yes,' he replied.

'Well then,' I said, 'third time lucky.[1] Let's go back to the beginning again, as it were, and consider – whether or not it is possible for that to   b
be the case – to know that one knows and that one does not know what

1. Literally, 'the third (libation) to (Zeus) the Saviour'. The third cup of wine of a libation was dedicated to Zeus the Saviour. To drink this third cup was to pray for good luck.

one knows and what one does not know; and secondly, if it *is* perfectly possible, what benefit our knowing that would bring us.'

'Indeed we ought to look at that,' he said.

G. *Is Knowledge of Knowledge Possible?*

Socrates again proceeds by means of analogies. First, a sense such as vision sees colour – it does not see itself and the other visions and non-visions – and an emotional/mental activity such as desire desires pleasure – it does not desire itself and the other desires.

Second, Socrates adduces comparative terms; but these are not true analogies at all. The preceding analogy employed things which, though not knowledges, were all mental activities of some sort and consequently, to a limited extent, analogous to knowing; but comparatives are analogous only in being of something. Plato can attempt the analogy with comparatives only because of a peculiarity of the Greek language, which may express, by the use of the genitive case, 'greater than' as 'greater of'. Thus (i) knowledge is the knowledge of something; (ii) what is superior is the superior of something; (iii) if a thing is the superior of itself, it will also be the inferior of itself.

All this leads to the general conclusion that whatever relates its own faculty to itself will also have that essential nature to which its faculty was related. That is, (a) the superior is the superior of the inferior: if the superior relates its faculty of superiority to itself, it will also have the essential nature (inferiority) to which its faculty was related; so if the superior is the superior of itself, it must simultaneously be the inferior of itself. And (b) vision sees colour: if vision relates its faculty of vision to itself, it will also have the essential nature (colour) to which its faculty was related; if vision sees itself, vision must be coloured. (a) is rightly pronounced impossible, but (b) is left as a (remote) possibility.

'Come on then, Critias,' I said, 'look at it, and see whether you can be shown to be closer to a solution in these matters than I, because I am at a loss. Shall I tell you where I find myself in difficulties?'

'Yes, certainly,' he said.

'Well then,' I said, 'if what you were saying a moment ago really is the case, won't it all amount to this, that there is some one knowledge which
c is the knowledge of nothing but itself and the other knowledges, this same knowledge being the knowledge of ignorance too?'

'Yes, certainly.'

'See what a strange thing we're trying to say, my friend. If you look at that same proposition in other cases, it'll come to seem to you, I think, that it is impossible.'

'How? In what cases?'

'In these. Consider whether you think there is a vision which is not the vision of what the other visions are visions of, but is the vision of itself and the other visions, and non-visions in the same way: and though it is a vision, it sees no colour, only itself and the other visions. Do you think d there is such a vision?'

'Heavens, no, I don't.'

'What about a hearing which hears no sound, but hears itself and the other hearings and non-hearings?'

'No, not that either.'

'Take all the senses together. Do you think there is some sense of the senses and of itself which, however, senses nothing of what the other senses sense?'

'No, I don't.'

'Do you think there is some desire which is the desire for no pleasure, e but for itself and the other desires?'

'Certainly not.'

'Nor indeed, I think, is there a wish which wishes for no good, but which wishes for itself and for the other wishes.'

'No, definitely not.'

'Would you say there was some love of that kind, which is actually the love of no beautiful thing, but of itself and the other loves?'

'No, I'd not,' he said.

'Have you ever observed a fear which fears itself and the other fears, but fears none of the things which are frightening?' 168a

'No, I haven't,' he replied.

'Or any opinion which is an opinion of opinions and of itself, but which holds no opinion about what the other opinions hold opinions about?'

'Not at all.'

'But it would appear we're saying that there is some such knowledge, which is the knowledge of no branch of learning, but is the knowledge of itself and the other knowledges?'

'Yes, we are!'

'Isn't it strange, then, if it really does exist? In fact, let's not state categorically just yet that it doesn't exist, but let's keep on investigating whether it does exist.'

'You're right.' b

'Come on, then. This knowledge is the knowledge of something, and it has some such *faculty*, so as to be *of something*, hasn't it?'

'Yes, certainly.'

'For example, we say that that which is superior has some such *faculty*, so as to be the superior *of something*, don't we?'

'Yes. It does.'

'Then that something is inferior, if the other is to be superior.'

'It must be.'

'Now, if we were to find some superior thing which is the superior of those things which are superior and of itself, but the superior of none of those things of which the other superior things are the superiors, I'm quite

c   sure that what would be the case with it would be this: if it *were* the superior of itself, it would also be the inferior of itself, wouldn't it?'

'It would certainly have to, Socrates,' he said.

'And if something is the double both of the other doubles and of itself, it would itself constitute a half, as would the others, if it were double, since there is not, I'm sure, a double of anything but a half.'

'True.'

'That which is the superior of itself will be the inferior of itself too, and

d   what is heavier, lighter, and what is older, younger, and so on. Whatever relates its own faculty to itself will also have that essential nature to which its faculty was related, won't it? I mean something like this: hearing, for example, we say is the hearing of nothing other than sound, isn't it?'

'Yes.'

'If it is to hear itself, it will hear itself as possessing a *sound*, since it couldn't hear otherwise.'

'Most definitely.'

'And vision, of course, my good friend, if it is to see itself, must have some colour, since vision will certainly never see anything that is colour-

e   less.'

'No, it definitely won't.'

'Do you see, then, Critias, that of all the examples we've gone through, for some it seems to us absolutely impossible, while in the case of the others it is very difficult to believe, that they could ever relate their own faculty to themselves? For instance, it is absolutely impossible for magnitudes and numbers and the like, isn't it?'

'Yes, certainly.'

'Whereas hearing and vision, and also motion moving itself and heat burning itself and everything like that, would excite disbelief in some

169a   people, though perhaps not in others. What we need, my friend, is some great man to determine satisfactorily for all instances whether none of the things which exist relates its own faculty to itself naturally, but to something else instead, or whether some do, but others don't; and if there are things which relate it to themselves, whether the knowledge which we say is self-control is one of them. I don't believe I'm competent to settle these questions, which is why I cannot state categorically whether it is b possible for there to be a knowledge of knowledge, and why I do not accept that, if it definitely does exist, it is self-control, until I have considered whether a thing like that would benefit us or not, since I do have the feeling that self-control is something beneficial and good. Right, then, son of Callaeschrus, since you maintain that self-control is the knowledge of knowledge and indeed of ignorance too, show first, as I said a minute ago, that it is possible, and then that in addition to being possible it is beneficial as well; and you may perhaps satisfy me that you're right in c what you say self-control is.'

H. *Knowledge of Knowledge as Knowing* That *One Knows*

It is now assumed for the sake of argument that knowledge of knowledge is possible. Critias makes the point that if a man possesses knowledge of itself (heautēs), he will know himself (heauton). Though this is in fact a fallacy (see p. 192), in that the man should know, not himself, but his own knowledge, Socrates agrees. But he protests against equating knowing oneself with knowing what it is that one knows and what it is that one does not know: knowledge of knowledge will be able to determine only that one thing is knowledge and another is not; a man knows what is healthy by medicine (which is the knowledge of what is healthy), not by the knowledge of knowledge; indeed, knowledge of knowledge will enable a man to know only that he knows something and that he does not know something (and that another man knows and does not know something), but not what he knows.

Knowledge of knowledge will not enable a man to tell a real doctor from a quack. The sōphrōn man will know that the doctor possesses some knowledge, but he will not know what it is knowledge of; it is medicine that tells him that it is knowledge of what is healthy and what is diseased. Further, the doctor himself knows only what is healthy and what is diseased: he does not know about medicine (i.e. medical knowledge) qua knowledge, since knowing about knowledge is the province of the sōphrōn man. Consequently, one can tell a real doctor from a quack only by being a doctor in addition to being sōphrōn: one must possess both sōphrosunē (knowledge that one knows) and technē (professional skill), in order to know what one knows or what another knows in any given technē.

When Critias heard this, and saw that I was in difficulties, he seemed to me to be forced by *my* being in difficulties to fall into difficulties himself, in the way people who see others yawning in their faces are affected similarly. Well, conscious that he had a reputation to keep up, he felt ashamed in front of the others and was unwilling to admit to me that he was unable to determine the points on which I was challenging him. He

d said nothing clear, in an attempt to conceal his difficulties. So, to get on with our investigation, I said, 'Well, if you like, Critias, let's grant for the moment that it is possible for there to be a knowledge of knowledge. We'll consider whether or not this is the case later on. Come on then, let's suppose it is perfectly possible: how does that increase one's chances of knowing what one knows and what one doesn't – which, of course, we said[1] was knowing oneself, that is, being self-controlled, didn't we?'

'Yes, certainly,' he said. 'And it does, I think, follow, Socrates. If a

e man possesses knowledge which knows itself, he would himself be like what he possesses. For example, when a man possesses swiftness, he is swift; when he possesses beauty, he is beautiful; when he possesses knowledge, he is knowing: and when a man possesses knowledge which is knowledge of itself, he will then, of course, be knowing himself.'[2]

'I don't doubt,' I said, 'that when a man possesses that which knows itself he will know himself; but why, when he possesses that, must he necessarily know what he knows and what he doesn't know?'

170a 'Because, Socrates, the one is the same as the other.'

'Perhaps,' I said, 'but I don't really think I've changed at all, because I still don't understand how knowing what one knows and knowing what one does not know are the same as that.'

'What do you mean?' he asked.

'This,' I replied. 'Supposing there is a knowledge of knowledge, will it be able to determine anything more than that one thing is knowledge and another is not?'

'No, just that.'

'Is it the same thing as knowledge and ignorance of what is healthy? Is

b it the same as knowledge and ignorance of what is just?'

'Not at all.'

'The one is, I think, medicine, the other public affairs, while this one is nothing other than knowledge.'

'Of course.'

'If a man doesn't know in addition what is healthy and what is just, but

1. 167a–b.
2. This is inaccurate: he will not be 'knowing *himself*', but 'knowing his own knowledge': see pp. 171–2, 192.

knows only knowledge, inasmuch as he possesses knowledge only of that, he would in all probability know, both about himself and about others, that he or they know something and possess some knowledge, wouldn't he?'

'Yes.'

'How will he know by that knowledge *what* he knows? For example, he knows what is healthy by medicine, not by self-control; what is har- c monious, by music, not by self-control; what makes a building, by the art of building, not by self-control; and so on. Doesn't he?'

'So it seems.'

'How will he know by self-control, if it is only the knowledge of knowledge, that he knows what is healthy or what makes a building?'

'He won't at all.'

'So the man who is ignorant of that won't know what he knows, but only that he knows.'

'It would appear so.'

'Being self-controlled, or self-control, wouldn't be knowing what one d knows and what one doesn't know, but only, it would appear, that one knows and that one doesn't know.'

'It may well be.'

'Nor will that man be able to examine another man who claims he knows something, to see whether he knows what he says he knows or whether he does not. All he'll know, it would appear, is that the man possesses some knowledge. Self-control will not make him know what it is *of*.'

'It seems not.'

'So he won't be able to distinguish the man who pretends to be a doctor, e but isn't, from the man who really and truly is one, or indeed to distinguish any other of those who know from any other of those who don't. Let's look at it this way. If the self-controlled man, or anyone else at all, is to know the difference between the man who is really and truly a doctor and the man who is not, he won't proceed as follows, will he: he certainly won't talk to him about medicine – because, as we said, a doctor understands nothing but what is healthy and what is diseased – will he?'

'That's so.'

'He knows nothing about knowledge. We allocated that to self-control alone.'

'Yes.'

'Then the medical man doesn't know medicine[1] either, since medicine 171a is a knowledge.'

1. From here till the end of the section, 'medicine' renders *iatrikē*, which is short for *iatrikē epistēmē* or *iatrikē technē*, 'medical knowledge' or 'medical skill'.

'True.'

'So the self-controlled man will know that the doctor possesses some knowledge; but when he has to try to find out what it is, won't he consider what it is knowledge *of*? Hasn't each knowledge been defined not just as *a* knowledge, but also as a specific one, by reference to what it is *of*?'

'Yes indeed.'

'Medicine, then, is distinguished from the other knowledges by being defined as the knowledge of what is healthy and what is diseased.'

'Yes.'

b 'Then the man who wants to look at medicine must look at whatever things it is concerned with, and surely not at things with which it is *not* concerned.'

'Certainly.'

'The man looking at it properly, then, will consider the doctor *qua* medical man, in relation to what is healthy and what is diseased.'

'It would appear so.'

'As regards what is said or done in such a case, he'll consider whether what is said is true and whether what is done is right?'

'He must.'

'Could anyone follow up either of those questions without medicine?'

'Certainly not.'

c 'No one could, it would appear, except a doctor; nor could the self-controlled man either, unless he were a doctor in addition to being self-controlled.'

'That's so.'

'So inevitably, if self-control is only the knowledge of knowledge and of ignorance, it won't be able to distinguish the doctor who knows his art from one who doesn't, but pretends he does or thinks he does, or any other of those people who know anything at all, except for the man who practises the same art as itself, in the way other craftsmen do.'

'So it seems,' he said.

I. *Benefits of Knowledge of Knowledge*

(a) *Let* sōphrosunē *be knowledge of* what *one knows and* what *one does not know (and of* what *another knows and does not know). In that case, error would be removed from human life, because each person would do only what he knew and would leave what he did not know to those who did. But such knowledge does not exist.*

(b) *Let* sōphrosunē *be knowledge of knowledge in the sense of a general acquaintance with the concept of knowledge (see Guthrie, IV, pp. 162 and 174, and Robinson, pp. 37–8), a sort of 'knowing how to know', as well as that one knows. This will make the learning of any 'ordinary' epistēmē (knowledge) or technē (skill, craft, art) easier, and will produce a clearer grasp of the knowledge. And knowledge of knowledge in this sense will enable someone who has learned an 'ordinary' knowledge to examine anyone else with that 'ordinary' knowledge better than someone without this knowledge of knowledge. But this is not a grand enough conception of knowledge of knowledge.*

(c) So let sōphrosunē be knowledge of what one knows and what one does not know, in the sense of being a sort of 'super-knowledge', a knowledge which presides over the performance of the 'ordinary' knowledges, and ensures their correct functioning. There will be technical perfection in every knowledge or skill and no bogus practitioners of any knowledge or skill. But technical perfection is no guarantee of the good and happy life.

'What benefit would we get from self-control in that case, Critias,' I asked, 'if it is like that? If, as we assumed in the beginning, the self-controlled man knew what he knew and what he didn't know – that he knew the former but did not know the latter – and was able to examine anyone else in the same position, it would be a great benefit to us, we maintain, to be self-controlled. We'd live all our lives without making any mistakes, and not just those of us who possessed self-control, but all those other people who were governed by us as well, because we'd neither try ourselves to do what we didn't know, but would find those who did and hand the matter over to them, nor trust those whom we governed to do anything except what they were likely to do properly – and that would be what they possessed knowledge of. In that way a house run on the principle of self-control would be likely to be run admirably, as would a state that was run on that principle and everything else that self-control governed. When error has been removed and correctness leads the way, people in those circumstances must do admirably and well in their every activity, and people who do well must be happy. Isn't that what we said about self-control, Critias,' I asked, 'when we said what a good thing it was to know what one knows and what one doesn't know?'

'It certainly was,' he replied.

'But as things are,' I went on, 'you can see that there is obviously no knowledge like that anywhere.'

'I can,' he said.

'Well,' I said, 'does knowing knowledge and ignorance, which is what we are now discovering self-control to be, bring the following advantage,

203

that the man who possesses this knowledge will more easily learn whatever else he learns, and everything will appear clearer to him inasmuch as he will see, in addition to each thing he learns, its knowledge? And will he examine other people better in things he has learned himself, whereas people who examine others without that knowledge will do so more feebly and incompetently? Aren't those the sorts of benefit we'll derive from self-

c control, my friend? Haven't we got our eye on something grander, and aren't we demanding that it should be something more than it actually is?'

'That may perhaps be so,' he replied.

'Possibly,' I said, 'but possibly what we demanded it should be isn't anything useful. What makes me suspect this? It's that there seem to me to be certain strange consequences which follow if self-control is something like that. Let's see: if you like, let's agree that it's possible to know knowledge, and let's not reject what we assumed in the beginning, that self-control is knowing what one knows and what one doesn't know. Let's

d grant it for the sake of argument. Having granted all that, let's consider even more carefully whether something like that will in fact benefit us, because I don't think that we were right in allowing what we were saying a minute ago, that self-control would be a great good if it were a thing like that, and organized the running of both house and state.'

'Why?' he asked.

'Because,' I replied, 'we readily allowed that it was a great good for men if each group of us were to do what it knows and were to hand over what it doesn't know to others who do know.'

e 'Then we weren't right in allowing that?' he asked.

'I don't think so,' I replied.

'What you're saying is really strange, Socrates,' he said.

'By the Dog,'[1] I exclaimed, 'I think so too, you know. That's what I was referring to just now when I said that there appeared to me to be certain strange consequences which would follow and that I was afraid we weren't looking at the question properly. The truth is, even supposing

173a self-control actually is like that, I don't think it's at all obvious what good it produces for us.'

'How is that?' he said. 'Explain! We too want to know what you mean.'

'I'm sure I'm talking nonsense,' I said. 'All the same, one must examine any thought that occurs to one and not dismiss it without due consideration, if one has even a little respect for oneself.'

'Quite right,' he said.

1. A favourite oath of Socrates. It was considered milder than an oath sworn by the name of a god, and somewhat whimsical.

'Listen to my dream, then,' I went on, 'and see whether it's come through the Gate of Horn or of Ivory.[1] Supposing self-control were as we now define it, and did govern us completely – wouldn't everything be done as the various knowledges directed? No one who claimed to be a   b pilot, but wasn't, would deceive us; no doctor, no general, or anyone else who pretended to know something he didn't know, would escape our notice. Under those circumstances, wouldn't the result be that we should be healthier of body than now, that when in danger at sea or in war we should escape unharmed, and that all our utensils, clothing, footwear, indeed all our possessions and many other things too, would be works of   c skill and art, because we employed true craftsmen? If you liked, we might concede that the art of the seer was the knowledge of what is to be, and that self-control, presiding over it, could deter impostors and appoint the true seers as foretellers of the future. Now, I agree that the human race, given this, would do things and live as knowledge directed – because self-   d control would mount guard and wouldn't let ignorance creep in and be a partner in our work. But that by doing things as knowledge directed we'd do well and be happy, that is something we can't as yet be sure of, my dear Critias.'

'On the other hand,' he said, 'you won't easily find any other complete form of success, if you disregard doing things as knowledge directs.'

J. Sixth Definition: The Knowledge of Good and Bad

Critias defines sōphrosunē *as knowledge of good and bad. Socrates responds that the efficient functioning of the other knowledges, such as medicine, is in no way impaired by the absence of the knowledge of good and bad, but that nothing can function well and beneficially without it. Hence, if* sōphrosunē *is the knowledge of knowledge and ignorance, but it is the knowledge of good and bad that is beneficial, then* sōphrosunē *is not beneficial.*

Critias objects that sōphrosunē, *conceived as a 'super-knowledge' presiding over the other knowledges, could still be beneficial, by governing the knowledge of good. But Socrates replies that the knowledge of knowledge and ignorance cannot produce the products* (erga) *of the other knowledges or skills, and therefore cannot produce benefit, which is the product of the knowledge of good.*

'There's just one more little thing I'd like you to explain to me,' I said. 'As knowledge of *what* directs, do you mean? Of cutting leather for shoes?'

1. In *Odyssey* XIX, 563–7, true dreams are said to come to men through the Gate of Horn, false ones through the Gate of Ivory.

e 'Heavens, no!'
'Of working in bronze?'
'Not at all.'
'Of wool or wood or something like that?'
'Certainly not.'

'So,' I said, 'we no longer adhere to the doctrine that the man who lives as knowledge directs is happy. You don't allow that those people who live as knowledge directs are happy; rather you seem to me to make a distinction and define the happy man as one who lives as the knowledge of some particular things directs. Perhaps you mean the man I was speak-

174a ing of a minute ago, the man who knows everything that is to be, the seer. Do you mean him or someone else?'

'Both him and someone else.'

'Who else?' I asked. 'Can it be that you mean the kind of man who knows all the past and the present in addition to the future, and is ignorant of nothing? Let's assume that such a man exists. I don't imagine you'd say that there was anyone who lived more as knowledge directs than he.'

'Certainly not.'

'There's just one more thing I want to know. Which of the knowledges is it that makes him happy? Or do all of them alike?'

'Definitely not all of them alike,' he said.

b 'Well, which *most* makes him happy? The one by which he knows – *what* past, present or future thing? Is it the one by which he knows the game of draughts?'

'What! Draughts indeed!' he exclaimed.

'The one by which he knows arithmetic?'

'Not at all.'

'Is it the knowledge by which he knows what is healthy?'

'You're getting closer,' he said.

'The closest one I can get to is the one by which he knows – *what*?' I said.

'Good and bad,' he replied.

'You wretch,' I said, 'you've been leading me round in a circle all this time, keeping from me that it was not living as knowledge directed that made one do well and be happy, not even if it were knowledge of all the

c other knowledges put together, but only if it were knowledge of this on. alone, that of good and bad. Because, Critias, if it's your intention to remove that knowledge from the other knowledges, will medicine make us healthy any the less; shoemaking make shoes any the less; weaving make clothes any the less? Will piloting prevent death at sea any the less, or generalship death in war?'

'No,' he said.

'But, my dear Critias, we'll be unable to ensure that each of these is performed well and beneficially if that knowledge is absent.'

d

'That's true.'

'But it would appear that *that* knowledge isn't self-control, but rather the knowledge whose function is to benefit us. It's not the knowledge of knowledges and ignorances, but of good and bad; so that if *that* knowledge is beneficial, our self-control must be something else.'

'Why wouldn't self-control benefit us?' he asked. 'If self-control is in the fullest sense the knowledge of knowledges and presides over the other knowledges too, it would certainly govern the knowledge of good too and consequently benefit us.'

e

'Would *it* make us healthy too,' I asked, 'not medicine? Would it make the products of the other arts, instead of each of them making its own? Weren't we solemnly declaring all this time that it was knowledge only of knowledge and ignorance and of nothing else? Isn't that so?'

'Apparently.'

'So it won't be the producer of health?'

'Certainly not.'

'Because health belonged to another art, didn't it?'

175a

'Yes.'

'So it won't be the producer of benefit either, my friend, since we allocated that product to another art a minute ago, didn't we?'

'Yes, certainly.'

'How will self-control be beneficial, then, when it is the producer of no benefit?'

'It won't at all, it would appear, Socrates.'

K. *Aporia*

The conclusion is reached that sōphrosunē is not beneficial, though it is agreed to be the most admirable of all things. Socrates finds this unacceptable, and all the more disappointing in that a number of important concessions were made in the course of the investigation to allow the argument to proceed. These were: (i) that there was knowledge of knowledge; (ii) that knowledge of knowledge knew the products of the other knowledges; (iii) that the sōphrōn man knew that he knew what he knew and that he knew he did not know what he did not know (despite the impossibility of a man's knowing what he does not know – cf. Meno 80d–e, and Euthydemus passim, e.g. 276d ff.).

Socrates blames this outcome on his shortcomings as an investigator and states his belief that sōphrosunē *is beneficial. This is a strong hint of the 'real' definition:* sōphrosunē *is the knowledge of good and bad. Since this would be the definition, not of a virtue, but of virtue itself, then, as in the* Laches, *Socrates is underlining the essential unity of the virtues. The 'real' conclusion of the dialogue, which emerges from the* aporia, *is an affirmation of the Socratic paradox that virtue is knowledge.*

'Do you see, Critias, how all this time I had good reason to be apprehensive, and was quite right to accuse myself of not conducting a worthwhile inquiry into self-control? Something that is agreed to be the most admir-

b able of all things wouldn't have seemed to us to be of no benefit if I had been any use at making a proper investigation. As it is now, we're defeated on all fronts, and are unable to discover to which actual thing the lawgiver[1] gave that name of self-control. And yet we have conceded many points which did not follow from our argument. We conceded that there was a

c knowledge of knowledge, although the argument denied it and claimed there wasn't. We conceded that this knowledge knew the products of the other knowledges too (although the argument denied this as well), just to have the self-controlled man in possession of the knowledge that he knows what he knows and that he does not know what he does not know. We made that terribly generous concession without even considering the impossibility of a man's knowing in some sort of way what he does not know at all; for we allowed that he knows what he does not know, and yet I think nothing would seem stranger than that. All the same, although the

d investigation has found us so very good-natured and compliant, it has still been no more able to discover the truth, but has made such sport of it as to demonstrate to us quite brutally the uselessness of self-control as we defined it in those fictions we agreed on for so long. I'm not annoyed so much for myself as for you, Charmides,' I said, 'because you, who have such good looks and are in addition very self-controlled of soul, will not

e profit from that self-control, and because despite its presence in you, it won't bring you any benefit at all in life! I'm even more annoyed about the charm I learned from the Thracian[2] – that I went on taking great pains to learn the charm for a thing which is worth nothing. In fact, I really don't think that this is the case at all, but that I'm an awful investigator – because I do think that self-control is a great good, and that if you do

176a possess it, you are fortunate. See whether you do possess it and have no need of the charm – because if you do possess it, I'd advise you instead

1. A reference to the belief that names were given to things by a sort of primeval legislation, rather than by arising from a consensus of usage; see *Cratylus* 388d ff.
2. See 156d.

to consider me a fool, incapable of investigating anything in a reasoned argument, and yourself the happier the more self-controlled you are.'

Charmides said, 'But heavens, Socrates, I don't know whether I possess it or whether I don't. How can I know it, when, on your own admission, not even you and Critias are able to discover what on earth it is? Still, I don't really believe you at all, Socrates, and I really do think I need the b charm; and as far as I am concerned, there's no reason why I shouldn't be charmed by you every day, until you say I've had enough.'

'All right,' said Critias. 'But, Charmides, by doing that, you'll prove to me that you are self-controlled – if you turn yourself over to Socrates for charming, and don't disappoint him in anything either great or small.'

'Rest assured that I will follow him and won't disappoint him. I'd be behaving terribly if I didn't obey you, my guardian, and didn't do what c you tell me.'

'I am telling you,' he said.

'Well then, I'll do it,' said Charmides, 'starting today.'

'What are you two plotting to do?' I asked.

'Nothing,' said Charmides. 'We've done our plotting.'

'Are you going to resort to the use of force, without even giving me a preliminary hearing in court?' I asked.

'I certainly am,' he replied, 'since Critias here orders me to – which is why *you* should plot what *you'll* do.'

'But there's no time left for plotting,' I said. 'Once you're intent on d doing something and are resorting to the use of force, no man alive will be able to resist you.'

'Well then,' he said, 'don't you resist me either.'

'I won't,' I said.

HIPPIAS MAJOR
AND
HIPPIAS MINOR

INTRODUCTION TO *HIPPIAS MAJOR*
AND *HIPPIAS MINOR*

Plato's two dialogues which have Hippias as the chief interlocutor are distinguished as *Hippias Major* and *Hippias Minor* by virtue of their relative lengths. Though they are both works of the early period of Plato's philosophical writing, we will find reasons to believe that *Hippias Major* belongs on the borderline with the middle period, when Plato began to develop Socrates' philosophy in a more idiosyncratic manner. There is some controversy about the authenticity of *Hippias Major*: the inclusion of the dialogue in this volume reflects what I think may now be called the majority opinion (a notable exception is Kahn) that it is a genuine work of Plato's; indeed, as Platonic scholarship progresses, the same aspects of the dialogue which once seemed to point to its spuriousness can now be seen as relevant to the development of Plato's thought (see further pp. 218–23).

Although the two dialogues may have been written some years apart, Plato chose to tie them together with the same dramatic date (see p. 275 n. 1), which cannot certainly be decided, but is possibly about 420 B.C., since Gorgias' famous visit to Athens is a past event (*Hippias Major* 282b) and Hippias' words at 281a–b imply that he is not visiting Athens in an official capacity as ambassador for Elis and perhaps that it is a time of peace: Gorgias' visit was in 427, and there were a few years of uneasy peace between Athens and Sparta after 421. But apart from this dramatic date, the two dialogues have little in common, except their badinage at the expense of Hippias. Socrates' 'affected deference mingled with insulting sarcasm', as it was once described by the Victorian scholar George Grote, is a feature not only of our two dialogues, but also of Xenophon's report of a meeting between Socrates and Hippias (*Memorabilia* IV.4, which is worth comparing with *Hippias Major* on other points too); so perhaps this was the historical Socrates' attitude, though Xenophon may simply be imitating Plato.

Hippias of Elis (*c*.470–*c*. 395) was a prominent member of the Greek sophistic movement of the fifth century – the 'age of enlightenment', as it is sometimes known, since an increase in intellectual activity is taken to constitute an enlightenment. His particular philosophical theories and attitudes, in so far as they are recoverable from the second-hand reports that remain, need not concern us here (but see Guthrie, III, and Kerferd), since they do not play a part in our dialogues: there is only an elusive mention of some theory at *Hippias Major* 301b–e. Rather, Hippias in our dialogues is representative of the sophists in general, as, to some extent, are Protagoras in much of *Protagoras* and Gorgias in *Gorgias*, for instance. Using individual sophists as representatives in this way inevitably results in superficial criticism: general characteristics of the movement are attacked, rather than the sophist's particular thought and argument. With hindsight we may regret this, since it is noticeable that when Plato does turn to more substantial criticism, as in *Euthydemus* or *Theaetetus*, our knowledge respectively of a type of sophistic argumentation and Protagoras' thought is greatly increased. But it must immediately be said that it is not Plato's purpose in *Hippias Minor*, *Protagoras* and so on to provide detailed criticism of sophistry, but rather to use this movement as a dramatic background: to show how Socrates confronted and confuted it by superior philosophical assumptions and methods. The main reason for choosing such a background is that Plato wished to distinguish his master from the sophists: as is clear from his *Apology of Socrates*, he believed that confusion of Socrates with the sophists was a prime cause of his execution in 399.

The background to our dialogues, then, is this. Prior to the fifth century B.C., the prevailing Greek view of man's lot in relation to the gods had been pessimistic: man was in the hands of fickle beings whose minds were impenetrable, since the good might suffer while the wicked prospered. In a sense the mainstream of Greek philosophy at this time, though to a degree counter-religious, had been part and parcel of this mood, since it concentrated on trying to understand macrocosmic events beyond man's control. But during the fifth century a more optimistic mood began to be expressed. Encouraged, no doubt, by their almost miraculous defeat of the Persians by 479, and by an increase in proficiency in all areas of art and science, Greek tragedians and other thinkers stressed how much man on his own could achieve (see, in this context, *Hippias Major* 281d–282a).

This shift of mood was partly generated by a change in social and political conditions. This is certainly the case in fifth-century Athens, where most of our evidence comes from; but this limitation of the evidence need not worry us in this context, since Athens was the centre of the sophistic movement. Socially, the upper classes acquired more money and correspondingly less need to work – that is, they acquired more leisure. Leisure always allows more time to concentrate on cultural achievements: the Greek word for leisure, *scholē*, is also the word for learned discussion, and hence school. Politically, Athens was by now a direct democracy, where the rewards for persuasive public speaking could be very great for an ambitious young man (see also p. 264 n. 2).

The sophists (the term originally had no pejorative connotations, but had much the same reference as our 'teacher' – someone who is clever, knows his stuff and is prepared to impart it) arose in response to these circumstances, as itinerant teachers of the arts and sciences, from fighting to astronomy. In particular, in Athens they claimed to teach the science of government, which generally meant the ability to speak (*Euthydemus* 272a; *Protagoras* 318e–319a; *Gorgias* 449a–b, 452d–e). The sophists, then, were professional teachers, catering to the upper classes. Some specialized in one or two fields, others (like Hippias: see *Hippias Major* 285c–e; *Hippias Minor* 368b–d; *Protagoras* 318d–319a) cast their net wider. They were all offering an education to supplement what a young man could get at school. In order to attract pupils they gave *epideixeis*, a term which has been translated 'lecture' in these two dialogues, but which literally means 'display' (see p. 32), and covered not only their formal lectures, but also question-and-answer sessions (see Thucydides III. 38.7; *Euthydemus* 274a; *Hippias Minor* 363d; *Gorgias* 449c; *Protagoras* 329b, 334e–335a). Pupils were also taught in seminars (*Protagoras* 314e–316a).

It must be appreciated that there is far more to individual sophists than this outline of the general characteristics of the movement might suggest. Individual sophists made important contributions to philosophy, mathematics, rhetoric, linguistics and so on, but, as remarked above, Plato is not concerned in our dialogues with these particulars.

Plato's dislike of the sophistic movement as a whole, though there are signs elsewhere of respect for certain individuals, shows in his portrayal of Hippias as stupid and vain (I trust that this picture of Hippias emerges from almost every page of both dialogues, but it has been challenged recently by Woodruff (1982)). He was not alone in this dislike, but why did he feel it? The main reason is his judgement that their values were misplaced. Not only does he portray Hippias as being overly concerned with money (*Hippias Major* 282b–283b), but he sees the sophists as teaching rhetoric, the appearance of truth, rather than the truth itself (*Hippias Major* 304a–e; *Hippias Minor* 369b–c; *Euthydemus* 289d–290a; *Gorgias* 464b–466a, 471e–472a); and indeed the contrast between rhetoric and philosophy is a recurrent theme throughout Plato's dialogues. It was Protagoras' boast to teach his pupils the ability to present either side of a case with equal plausibility, and indeed this is the purpose of all rhetoric. This became mistrusted as the ability 'to make the weaker argument defeat the stronger' (*Apology* 23d). Parallel to this is the repeated portrayal of Hippias as more concerned with a favourable audience reaction than the truth (*Hippias Major* 288a, 289e–290a, 291e–292a, 292e; cf. *Republic* 493a). In short, Plato feels that Socrates, with his disciplined method of inquiry, was a true moral teacher, while the sophists were not.

Secondly, Plato felt that the sophists perpetuated an inadequate political system. Within a democratic system of which Plato was at least suspicious, they offered political training to anyone who had the money to pay for their instruction. But in Plato's view the best politician is not necessarily the most persuasive speaker who happened to be rich enough to have gained instruction, but the philosopher who knows the truth. In this context, at *Hippias Major* 282c–d, he compares the sophists unfavourably with other philosophers, because the former teach all and sundry (cf. Xenophon, *Memorabilia* I.6.13).

Finally – and this is especially apparent in our dialogues – he seems to feel that they have no right to set themselves up as teachers, since when questioned by Socrates they are soon shown to be incoherent on the very subjects in which they profess to be experts. In *Hippias Minor* Socrates lampoons the sophists' literary studies and ties Hippias' thesis into knots (see Socrates' concluding words at 376c); in *Hippias Major* Hippias fails to satisfy Socrates' requirements of definition and so cannot be said to know what he initially claimed confidently to know. Here, however, the main contrast is with the greater validity, as Plato sees it, of Socratic philosophy, and it is to this, as it emerges from our two dialogues, that we must now turn: this, not criticism of Hippias, is after all the main purpose of the dialogues.

Hippias Major belongs to a group of dialogues (the 'dialogues of search') in which Socrates is shown discussing some moral concept with the ostensible purpose of attempting to define it (see also in this volume *Laches*, *Lysis* and *Charmides*). The pattern of these dialogues is that various definitions are proposed but all are found to be lacking, so that the discussions are aporetic (see pp. 30–31). The reasons for this apparent failure, as we now judge, are partly the caustic nature of Socrates' inquisition, partly his belief in what is known as 'real definition' (definition not of words – 'nominal definition' – but of things), coupled with his belief in the significant univocality of terms: he believes that however wide the usages of a term, they still reflect some single, definable core.

The reason Socrates places so much emphasis on definition is apparent in our dialogue (286c–d, 304d–e): one cannot incorrigibly use a term, let alone preach about it, unless it is known what that term refers to. This is a reasonable stricture where complex or ambiguous terms are involved, and all the terms Socrates discusses are complex or ambiguous. Nevertheless, it might be thought that the stricture is exaggerated. One line of argument might be that a term acquires a certain meaning or family of meanings within a culture, and that anyone brought up within that culture, having inherited this meaning, will be able to communicate meaningfully with anyone else from the same background, even if he cannot *define* the term. Socrates, however, would carp at this cultural limitation: his search is for a *universal*, which transcends boundaries of any sort. He would claim that all such limited meanings are species of the generic meaning which he is after. His only exaggeration, in these terms, is to fail explicitly to acknowledge even the limited usefulness of such limited meanings (for further discussion of Socrates and definition, see pp. 21–2, 223–4).

The concept being discussed in *Hippias Major* is *to kalon* or *kallos*. It is a term of commendation wherever it is used, and its range is very wide. A glance at *Hippias Major* shows it being used to praise soup and argumentation on the one hand, and to describe the beauty of girls and the moral propriety of certain behaviour on the other. Given the extent of the reference of the term, it is no wonder that Socrates' assumption of univocality runs into difficulties and the dialogue is aporetic. As an attempt to cover this vast range, I have chosen to translate the abstract substantives *to kalon* and *kallos* as 'fineness' and the adjective *kalos* as 'fine'. These English terms are suitably vague and work well for the majority of the cases in the dialogue, though they are somewhat awkward in the case of beauty. What is perhaps lost, however, and so must be mentioned here, is the aesthetic connotation of the Greek term, which is a telling feature of Greek mentality: for a sensitive Greek a fine argument or achievement was a thing of beauty; their works of art and their analyses of beauty reflect this in emphasizing order, symmetry and so on (we still today describe a proof as 'elegant'). What is gained is that it is crucial for the English reader of the dialogue as a whole that the same term be used throughout; otherwise Socrates' assumption of univocality is lost.

Briefly, the course of the dialogue is as follows. After some preliminary banter and scene-setting (Section A), Socrates asks a typical question: 'What is fineness?' At first, Hippias misunderstands the question altogether, and responds by asserting that a fine-looking girl is fine (Section B). However, under Socrates' coaxing, he later comes up with two further suggestions which, though unsatisfactory, are more plausibly definitional in nature: fineness is gold, and fineness is health, wealth and a variety of traditional Greek good things (Sections C and D). Socrates and his *alter ego* (see 286c–287c for the introduction of this *alter ego*) now take over to suggest three further definitions: fineness is appropriateness, or benefit, or aesthetic pleasure (Sections E, F and G). None of these stand up to Socrates' probing, however, and the dialogue ends in the usual *aporia* (compare *Laches*, *Lysis*, *Charmides*).

The dialogue thus falls broadly into two parts; in the first Hippias is the proposer of ideas and definitions, and in the second Socrates or his *alter ego* takes over this role. The dialogue's treatment of the ideas and definitions that arise is discussed in the running commentaries which introduce each section in the text, but these two natural parts respectively offer a convenient means of raising the two questions of this introduction: first, is the dialogue authentic? This question will take us further afield than it might seem to suggest. Secondly, are there constructive thoughts about fineness in the dialogue, despite its negative conclusion? Between them, the answers to these two questions should allow the reader an overview of the chief issues of the dialogue, and we will end with some thoughts on its wider purposes.

Socrates' arguments against Hippias, and some other assumptions he makes about fineness, plunge us into questions of the development of

Plato's metaphysics and of the authenticity of the dialogue. It has been argued both that the dialogue contains recognizable signs of Platonic as opposed to Socratic thought, and that it does not; and it has been argued both that the thought and style of the dialogue are incompatible with Platonic authorship, and that they are not. I shall assume that the style can tell us very little about the dialogue's authenticity; I make this assumption not just for the sake of Greekless readers, but also because the arguments from the style of the dialogue have not proved conclusive either way. This brings the thought of the dialogue to the fore, and the interpretation of certain passages becomes important.

These passages require a brief introduction (see further pp. 32–3). The issue is this. In the early Platonic dialogues of search, Socrates attempts to define moral properties such as justice, courage and so on, but is not committed to any special ontological status for these properties. (The reader should be aware, however, that this orthodox 'minimalist' view of the early dialogues has been attacked, especially by Allen.) His search for a definition never succeeds, but we learn that the definition must be unitary and applicable to all relevant cases, that it must explain why all relevant cases have the properties they have, and that the defined property must never be liable to characterization as its opposite. No ontology is intended: these are merely requirements of Socratic definition. Later, Plato himself, reflecting that there must *be* some stable entities (otherwise we could never assign properties even to things which only deserve them for a short while), was led to postulate an existence for the moral properties Socrates was concerned with, and others like them, as entities separate from the world of changing phenomena. He called these entities 'forms' (*eidē, ideai*) and believed that they alone have the true, stable existence – they really are what they are (fine, just or whatever) – necessary for objects of knowledge and definition. The contrast is with the things of this world which 'participate in' or 'imitate' these forms (or in which the forms may be said to be present), about which one can only have beliefs. Forms are responsible for whatever qualities phenomena have.

This sketch, though necessarily curt, should be enough to set the background for deciding the question of *Hippias Major*: is the thought of the dialogue Socratic, Platonic, or transitional?

In the course of Socrates' arguments against Hippias' three ideas about fineness he makes the following points. Fineness is 'something' (287c), an 'actual entity' (287c–d), a form (*eidos*, 289d), which, because it is 'fineness itself' (286d etc.) and absolutely, not relatively, fine (*passim*), is responsible for the relatively fine particular things being fine (*passim*), by being present in them (289d–e etc.). Do these ideas contain no more than

Socratic requirements of definition (the 'minimalist' view, whose clearest recent proponent is Guthrie, IV, pp. 183–91), or is the dialogue transitional between Socratic and Platonic thought (here views vary according to how close the commentator finds that the thought is to Plato's; Woodruff (1982) contains the best account – he finds the dialogue to be minimally transitional), or is it fully fledged Platonism (Tarrant, Moreau)?

We may begin by conceding to the minimalist interpretation that there are no phrases or ideas here which cannot be paralleled here and there in the Socratic dialogues (see Grube, *CQ* 1926, for a catalogue), or which, at least, are not in themselves significant. This consideration, however, seems to me to miss the point, which is that in *Hippias Major* we come across all these phrases and ideas in close conjunction, frequently reiterated, and in a single dialogue. Moreover, it is no great task to put them together into a coherent paragraph, as I have just done; this smacks of some systematic theorizing, whereas Socrates, as almost everyone agrees, was not systematic in this regard. We will find that this general impression of systematization is corroborated in the case of each doctrinal point.

Fineness is *something* (287c). This is not in itself significant. Though the phrase is used by Plato to describe forms (e.g. *Phaedo* 65d4–7, 74a9–12; *Republic* 476c9), it is basically a premiss: only if it is used to develop a theory of forms does it become ontologically significant. Otherwise it may be no more than a prerequisite of definition: there is something which Socrates can reasonably hope to define. But the phrase becomes more telling when taken in context: it is glossed by 'fineness is an actual entity' (literally, 'an existing something') in the context of stating that it (and justice, wisdom, etc.) are responsible for particular things being fine (just, wise, etc.). Again, the statement that fineness *exists* says no more in itself than we have already seen: in a similar vein, Woodruff (1982, p. 164) points out, anyone might inveigh against injustice without hypostatizing it as a Platonic form: 'Any discussion presupposes the existence of what it discusses.' True, but not every discussion makes that presupposition explicit, nor does Socrates (*Protagoras* 330c–d is a notable exception; *Euthyphro* 5d and 6d come close, as does *Meno* 72b–c). Furthermore, Socrates is here made to generalize his point into a theory: anything which is responsible for other things having some characteristic is an existing entity. It would be quite incorrect to read back into this the dichotomy between being and becoming found in fully fledged Platonism, but Plato is on the verge of claiming that only existing entities can be responsible in this way, because 'becoming' things may be responsible for even the opposite characteristic. The non-relativity of fineness is stressed in *Hippias Major*: in conjunction with the emphasis on its existence, the idea is very close to the independence of Platonic forms. So we find here, at the least, that *Hippias Major* is more systematic and reflective than is usual in early dialogues.

In this context we should glance at one other phrase, 'fineness itself' (286d etc.). The phrase is literally 'the fine itself' (*auto to kalon*): the literal translation shows up a Platonic tendency. The addition of 'itself' basically does no more than pinpoint, stress or isolate whatever is being discussed, and it is used as such in Socratic contexts, and even outside the Platonic corpus (Isocrates, *Antidosis* 130, written in 353 B.C.). But in a Platonic or even quasi-Platonic context the phrase feeds the tendency to distinguish fineness and similar concepts from their instances, as each being a thing in itself. The phrase occurs nine times in *Hippias Major*, whereas it is very rare in other early dialogues, which suggests that Plato might, consciously or unconsciously, be nourishing that tendency.

What about the notion that fineness is responsible for fine things being fine? As mentioned before, Socrates assumes that a definition must explain why all relevant cases have the property or properties they have, and he uses the same formula that we find in *Hippias Major* ('F things are F thanks to F-ness') to get across this idea of logical responsibility (for instance, at *Euthyphro* 6d). But Plato too uses the formula in expounding his notion of *forms* as 'causes' (*Phaedo* 100d). In *Hippias Major*, is there any way of telling whether the mood is Socratic or Platonic on this point? No, there is not. All we can say is that since the formula first appears in a context of virtual hypostatization of fineness, it is part of that transitional mood, and this is corroborated by the frequency of the idea in *Hippias Major* (287c–d, 288a, 290d, 294a–d, 299d–e, 300a–b, 302c–e), which again suggests the germs of quite systematic reflection on the matter.

The same conclusion is all that can be said about another recurring idea in *Hippias Major*, that fineness may be said to 'be present in' fine things (289d, 293e–294a, 294c, 299e, 300a, 303a). This materialistic image is intended to describe how fineness is responsible for fine things being fine, and as such it is equally undecidable to which mood it belongs. The idea crops up in both Platonic (*Phaedo* 100d etc.) and Socratic (*Charmides* 158e, *Laches* 189e, *Lysis* 217b, *Euthydemus* 301a) contexts, but the frequent occurrence of the image in our dialogue suggests that it is now a theory rather than just a way of explaining the relationship between the concept in question and its instances. It is accordingly relevant to remember that *theories* about the relationship between a universal and its instances become particularly germane if some ontological significance is attributed to the universal. That is, once the idea has taken root that fineness may be an entity of a different order, it needs a theory to explain how such an entity relates to fine things.

Finally, what about the idea that fineness itself is absolutely fine, as contrasted with the relative fineness of particular fine things? I am not here concerned with the knotty problem of what exactly Plato meant by self-predicative statements like 'Fineness is fine' (on which see Woodruff (1982), pp. 153–6, 157–9, 172–5, with his further references): statements of this form occur in both Socratic and Platonic contexts. Our concern here is the contrast with the inadequacy of fine things. In a Socratic context this contrast rules out proposed definitions which name examples of a concept, because they are no more fine than not-fine, and therefore cannot be the items Socrates wants true definitions to name, nor can they be responsible for fineness or whatever. To Plato the contrast is ontological: the things of this world have this ontological inferiority to forms, which purely and eternally are what they are (this is his famous 'degrees of reality' theory). In *Hippias Major* what we once again find is that the idea is expressed more frequently and systematically than in any other early dialogue, but falls short of overt ontological commitment. Overt ontological commitment would be something like *Symposium* 210e–211b, which I take to echo *Hippias Major*:

[The form, fineness] is eternal: it is subject neither to generation and destruction, nor to increase and decrease. It is not partly fine but partly contemptible; nor sometimes fine but sometimes not; nor fine in one relation but contemptible in another; nor fine in one place but contemptible elsewhere, depending on how people perceive it . . . it is absolute, self-sufficient, single and eternal, and all other fine things participate in it, but it is neither increased nor decreased by their generation and destruction, but remains unaffected.

Clearly, there is nothing like this in *Hippias Major*, but it does seem to be the case that as a result of reflection and systematization of the usual Socratic requirements of definition, Plato is on the verge of developing his famous theory. In particular, the seeds of hypostatization of fineness, combined with the contrast with fine things, provide a missing link with Plato's developed theory as found in *Republic*, in such a way that Plato seems to be capable there of merely *assuming* points made in *Hippias Major*. At the end of *Republic* V, in a famous argument designed to convince us of his theory, he merely assumes that fine things in this world have the inadequacy argued for by Socrates against Hippias' definitions in *Hippias Major*. The same assumption, that only the form is absolutely fine, occurs in the passage of *Symposium* quoted above; again, the thing to notice is that, as distinct from merely making an assumption, *Hippias Major* argues the point.

Scholars will think my discussion of this crucial topic too brief; others may think it too lengthy, but it is a necessary preamble to the question of authenticity, to which I now turn, assuming that the metaphysics of the dialogue is mid-way between the positions of Socrates and of Plato (this is also the conclusion of Morgan, though he reaches it from an entirely different approach): this will make possible a brief resolution of the question.

Given that we have dismissed arguments from style (the reader is referred to Kahn as the best recent example of this type of approach), the conclusion that the dialogue is transitional removes the remaining prop to the view that it is spurious. Moreau, for instance, argues that the dialogue presupposes the full Platonic ontology, but is stylistically immature: unable to reconcile these two conclusions, he argues that the dialogue was written by a student of Plato's who was familiar with the theory of forms. But it should by now be clear that the Platonic ontology in the dialogue is fledgling, not fully fledged: there is little sign of the crucial dichotomies that characterize mature Platonism. So far from there being any reason to reject the dialogue as spurious, it actually fills a gap in the written works between the early Socratic dialogues and the middle-period Platonic ones. (And it is worth noticing here that Aristotle seems to have *Hippias Major* in mind on several occasions (see pp. 250 n. 1, 256 n. 1, 259 n. 1), which increases the possibility that the dialogue was written by Plato himself rather than some pupil; and the quantity of echoes of *Hippias Major* in the fourth book of Xenophon's *Memorabilia* also increases the likelihood of its authenticity.) All this implies a relative date for the dialogue just prior to, say, *Phaedo*; more precise dating relative to dialogues such as *Gorgias* and *Meno* would be tricky. My feeling is that, given the tentatively transitional theories of *Hippias Major*, it post-dates *Gorgias* and precedes *Meno*; but I would not like to argue the point in detail. It was probably written, then, *c.* 385.

We must now consider particularly the latter part of the dialogue with a view to answering the question: What can we learn from *Hippias Major* about the Socratic/Platonic theory of fineness? But there is a prior question: What justification is there for looking in the dialogue for any positive view of fineness at all? For in the first place, the dialogue is aporetic: it ends negatively with Socrates professing just as much puzzlement about fineness as he had at the start of his discussion with Hippias. Secondly, his strictures on definition (p. 217) make certain usage of a term depend on knowledge of its definition, and, as just mentioned, *Hippias Major* does not make known the definition of fineness.

There is no short answer to either of these much-discussed problems. It will have to be enough here if I simply state conclusions, without the argument and evidence which lead me to endorse them. First, then, though the dialogues of search are formally aporetic, it is sometimes possible to reconstruct some positive points from clues scattered throughout the dialogue. It would be jejune, in my opinion, to expect to be able to reconstruct a *definition*: this expectation would entail the belief that Plato does not intend us to believe his arguments. It has often been stated, for instance, that where an argument contains an obvious fallacy, Plato expects his readers to notice it and reject the argument. This approach is methodologically unsound, at the least: barring very strong evidence to the contrary, we have to suppose that Plato intended the arguments he used, or at least the conclusions they support. Nevertheless, we might reasonably expect to gain information by default: if fineness is *not* such-and-such, what might it be? And what assumptions control the argument?

Secondly, his reasons for wanting a definition, in *Hippias Major* at any rate, fall into the categories Santas has called 'diagnostic' and 'aetiological' (pp. 115–26). He wants to know what fineness is so that he can tell what things are fine (304d–e) and so that he can support beliefs that certain things are fine (286c–d with 288a). Neither reason precludes his having not only beliefs that certain things are fine, but also the ability to make judgements about fineness, for instance that it is beneficial. The first reason is sometimes taken to preclude this, but does not: the diagnostic use of definitions only claims that a definition would be an invaluable tool for diagnosis, not that it is the *only* possible tool.

We see from the start, then, that we should not expect *Hippias Major* to provide a definitive Platonic or Socratic theory of fineness – Plato was rarely this kind of discursive philosopher – but we might expect to be pointed in certain directions. Some pointers of a logical nature have already emerged from our discussion of Hippias' 'definitions', for instance that fineness is fine and is the single entity which makes all fine things fine; but we are now concerned less with logic than with the descriptive pointers that may arise from the attempted definitions put into Socrates' own mouth in the latter part of the dialogue.

Socrates' first two proposals link together in a way that makes it reasonable to consider them together. When Socrates touches on the topic of appropriateness in Section C, he takes it to be synonymous with usefulness. So his first proposal, in Section E, that fineness is appropriateness, naturally leads on to his second, in Section F, that it is usefulness or benefit. It is argued in Section E that fineness is not appropriateness *if* appropriateness only makes things *appear* fine (that is, we may add 'appropriate' to our quiver of attributes of fineness if we understand it as 'making things *actually* fine'); fineness must make things actually fine, and may then be benefit, or the cause of goodness, as Section F considers.

The rejection of the definition of fineness as appropriateness tells us no more than we already know: that fineness cannot be contextually determinable, and is the cause of things really being fine. But what about the idea that fineness is benefit? Even if Plato does not believe that this is its definition (as we have to suppose, despite the weakness of his argument against it), he does not rule out the possibility of *describing* fineness as beneficial. In fact, it is telling that at 296c–d the idea that fineness may have harmful consequences is rejected: it must be beneficial. And the final attempted definition, of fineness as aesthetic pleasure, reduces in Plato's view to describing fineness as beneficial (303e–304a). The conclusion is inescapable that, in Plato's view, the notions of fineness and benefit are closely linked, even if not interchangeable. This conclusion is fortunate because elsewhere (especially at *Gorgias* 474d–e and by Xenophon, *Memorabilia* III.8.4–7) the idea that fineness is beneficial is attributed to Socrates without refutation; and fineness is constantly linked to benefit (and goodness) in the Socratic dialogues as the three firm attributes of the virtues that are his main concern.

We can go one stage further. If fineness is beneficial, it is productive of good (296e ff.). But by the rules of Socratic/Platonic causation, only something good can be productive of good. Thus the assumption underlying much of the second half of the dialogue, and especially (paradoxically) the rejection of the definition that fineness is benefit, is precisely that fineness is good. If goodness produces good, and fineness produces good, is fineness then not definable as goodness? By the Socratic assumption of univocality (that distinct terms have distinct definitions), the answer must be negative; still, some very close connection is being suggested here, which Plato is either unwilling or unable to try to expound. Since goodness is the goal of life, the idea that fineness is good can be seen to be more than the mere truism that it sounds.

Finally, what can the last attempted definition, that fineness is aesthetic pleasure, tell us about fineness? First, since this is presumably meant to be the most plausible attempt at defining fineness in aesthetic terms, and since it is rejected, it tells us not to limit fineness to the aesthetic and sensible. This may be thought to have seemed obvious to a Greek, for whom the term covered moral as well as aesthetic qualities. But notice that Hippias' second definition (Section D), in which he apparently moves away from the aesthetic and into the area of common Greek morality, still strongly emphasizes display and being seen to have admirable possessions. Very probably this was an inherent way of thinking, handed down from Homer, whose thought was still influential in Plato's day, and whose heroic code valued visible prowess and the esteem of one's peers. Socrates was always the enemy of this ingrained Homericism, and hence a revolutionary: we will see this at work to some extent in *Hippias Minor*. Secondly, but connectedly, the rejection of this definition tells us that fineness cannot be assessed by the apparent pleasure it produces (or rather, in view of the ideal philosophic pleasures of other dialogues, by even the best of what is commonly taken to be pleasant).

This direct attack on the presuppositions of his contemporaries is actually, in my view, a satisfactory end to the dialogue. The dialogue is aporetic, but it is not therefore negative. Any educator has to rid his audience of misconceptions in order to make room for what he sees as the truth. Socrates has less certainty about what the truth is than many more misguided and dogmatic moral teachers, but he has, he feels, a valid method of inquiry. The positive potential of this method, which may at times seem pointlessly destructive, is that what we learn about fineness in *Hippias Major*, even if not much in itself, may be used as premisses for prospective future inquiry or action.

If the dialogue is scarcely informative on the nature of fineness, why did Plato write it? There is no single answer to this question; I mention the four possible reasons which strike me; they are not mutually exclusive. First, as mentioned on p. 214, he wished to distinguish Socrates from the sophists who are epitomized in Hippias. Second, given the somewhat systematic manner in which the quasi-ontological issues are broached, we cannot rule out the notion that Plato wanted to use the dialogue to communicate these budding ideas of his. Third, the definitions of fineness that are put into Socrates' mouth are no doubt ones that Plato wanted to explore either for themselves or to clear them out of the way. Fourth – and I reserve this until last, because it seems to me to be the dominant reason – Plato appears to have used the dialogue to air certain formal issues connected with Socratic definition. Each stage of the argument can be seen to raise a separate issue. If the raising of such issues *was* the dominant reason for the writing of the dialogue, it would explain why the attempts to define fineness sometimes sound implausible: they are introduced as much for reasons of logical rigour and completeness as for their possible virtues as definitions. It is arguable that the course of the arguments is somewhat pedantic and tortuous precisely because they are designed to raise such logical points in as clear and thorough a manner as possible: I am thinking particularly of 297e–303d, on aesthetic pleasure, on whose purpose see below. To be specific, the points raised in the dialogue are as follows. (Notice that in a definition of the form *A* is *x*, *A* is the *definiendum* ('what is to be defined'), *x* is the *definiens* ('definer').)

   1. If the *definiendum* is a universal, the *definiens* must be

     (a) neither a particular, like a girl (287e–289d)

     (b) nor a mass substance, like gold (289d–291c).

These are relatively straightforward points, as the relevant sections of the dialogue show: if *Hippias Major* is an exercise in logic, it makes sense to start by eliminating obvious errors before moving on to more abstruse ones. Both these first points are subordinate to the fundamental principle of definition, which is stressed in other early dialogues, and has been called the principle of coextensivity (Kahn, p. 275): 'The *definiens* must be true of all and only those cases which are cases of the *definiendum*.' The *definiens* must be neither too narrow nor too broad.

   2. A true definition must be timelessly true (especially 291d–293c). For this to be the case

     (a) the *definiens* must be the cause of things having the property which the *definiendum* has or is (288a etc.);

     (b) the *definiendum* must be absolutely what it is (288c etc.);

     (c) definitions must state the reality of the case, not the appearance (293e–294e).

   3. The *definiens* must have unity (297e–303d): only then can it encompass the unity of the *definiendum*. The supposed problem with the definition of fineness as visual *and* auditory pleasure is that if one of them is fineness, the other cannot be fine, since visual pleasure, for instance, cannot be responsible for the fineness of auditory pleasure.

These issues we would class as formal or even logical. Two others, arising from Section F of the dialogue, are particularly interesting in the context of Socrates' and Plato's concern with virtue.

   4. Intuitively good properties cannot be defined in neutral terms (296b–d). Thus it is a mistake to think of fineness simply in terms of ability because ability may have negative consequences.

   5. Intuitively good properties cannot be defined in isolation from goodness (296d–297d; see p. 225).

If it is right to think of *Hippias Major* as making these statements about Socratic definitions, then the dialogue is not unimportant. It is virtually a handbook on Socratic definition. It is interesting that Plato, having stood back from his master's and his own early work enough to formulate these propositions, was at the same time, as I have argued, working towards his own metaphysical response to the issues Socrates raised. This makes good sense: he feels that such a list of features required in a *definiendum* can only be satisfied by a Platonic form, which *ex hypothesi* has the necessary properties. This is obvious enough in the case of (1)–(3); on (4) and (5) it must be remembered that in *Republic* Plato declares that all forms participate in the form of the good (507b–509b).

It must also be added, however – though it is a pity to end on a downward beat in the case of such a lively dialogue – that if the dialogue is seen as a record of Plato's early thoughts about definition, it is ultimately disappointing and perhaps even muddled. One argument in particular – that of Section F, on the difference between causes and their products – raises problems. Plato has stymied himself, in two respects. First, the argument would forbid even the statement that *goodness* produces good, since it denies that a cause can have the same properties as its product; yet the core of *Hippias Major*, as of dialogues containing more developed Platonic theory, is that the forms *are* the causes of things having their qualities. Secondly, Plato implicitly rules out any meaningful definition whatsoever: the final position (see p. 225) entails that one can only make tautologous statements like 'Fineness is fineness', when attempting definition. No wonder we are given no clear definition of fineness in the dialogue and receive only pointers. There is no sign that Plato recognized these difficulties at the time; but it is true that in the dialogues immediately following *Hippias Major* Plato begins more fully to develop his own solutions to the problems posed by Socrates' search for definitions.

SUMMARY OF *HIPPIAS MAJOR*

HIPPIAS MAJOR

Speakers

SOCRATES

HIPPIAS: From Elis in the Peloponnese. Born *c.* 470, died *c.* 395 – in other words, a more or less exact contemporary of Socrates. He was a prominent sophist, offering tuition in a vast range of subjects (see *Hippias Major* 285c–e, *Hippias Minor* 368b–d, *Protagoras* 318d–319a).

HIPPIAS MAJOR

A. Introduction

The introductory conversation is lively and full of characterization: Socrates teases Hippias more and more obviously, but Hippias is so full of his own importance that Socrates' sarcasm is lost on him. Plato enjoys portraying Socrates making a fool of sophists: see Protagoras, Gorgias, Euthydemus. Much of the argument, as a consequence of this characterization, is conducted at the level of implication. It may be seen as hostile to the sophistic movement as a whole, embodied in Hippias in this dialogue. The sophists claimed to offer the best education, but this is an incoherent generalization: is it best for everyone everywhere? So Hippias is led to the absurd conclusion that the Spartans, in not wishing to be educated by him, are acting illegally. In order to reach this conclusion Socrates trades on an ambiguity in the term 'law', which is either law as actually established, or law as it ought to be established. Only in the latter sense (and also only on the assumption that Hippias' education is beneficial) could the Spartans conceivably be said to be contravening law.

SOCRATES: Here's that fine[1] expert Hippias! It's ages since you descended on Athens![2] 281a

HIPPIAS: I've been busy, Socrates. You see, whenever Elis needs to negotiate with some other city, I'm the first of her citizens she turns to when she chooses a representative, since she thinks that I am best able to judge and report each city's communications.[3] Though I've often b
been sent to other cities too, Sparta's where I've represented Elis most often and on the most crucial and important issues.[4] So, to answer your question, that is why I don't frequent this region.[5]

SOCRATES: Well, Hippias, this is the sort of thing a true all-round expert must expect. I say 'all-round' because not only are you capable, in the private sphere, of giving the young men who pay you so much their

1. *Kalos*, so the ostensible subject of the dialogue is present from the start. Hippias' fineness is re-emphasized at 291a – but he fails to know what fineness is, just as Charmides in *Charmides*, for all his *sōphrosunē*, fails to know what that is.
2. On the dramatic date of the dialogue (*c.* 420), see p. 213. His previous visit may have been that of *c.* 433, mentioned in *Protagoras*.
3. Hippias is sometimes portrayed as vain (e.g. 286a, 286e), but in this case his claim may not be unjustified, and we know of other sophists who acted as ambassadors for their cities.
4. Elis was situated in the north-west of the Peloponnese, much of which was dominated by Sparta in the later fifth century B.C..
5. This sort of pompous phrase is typical of Hippias; see further p. 232 n. 6.

c money's worth and more in terms of benefit,[1] but also, in the public sphere, you are able to help your own city, which is only right and proper for someone who intends to gain the public's esteem and avoid their contempt.[2] But tell me, Hippias, why those men of old, with great reputations for wisdom – Pittacus, Bias, Thales and his school, and more recent thinkers too, up to and including Anaxagoras – why does it turn out that they all, or most of them, abstained from state affairs?[3]

HIPPIAS: Why else do you think, Socrates, apart from a complete
d inability to use their wisdom for accomplishments in both spheres, the public and the private?

SOCRATES: Is it really the case that just as all other areas of expertise have progressed, and their former practitioners are inferior to the present ones, so also your own field, sophistry, has progressed, and some of the ancients who were concerned with wisdom are inferior to you and your colleagues?

HIPPIAS: That's quite right.

SOCRATES: So if Bias were resurrected,[4] Hippias, he would be a source
282a of amusement to you and your colleagues, just as sculptors say that Daedalus[5] would be ridiculous if he had been born nowadays and were to produce the work for which he became famous.

HIPPIAS: That is so, Socrates, just as you say. But *I* tend to praise the men of old who came before us, before and more than my contemporaries, because while I try and avoid the malice of the living, I am frightened of the wrath of the dead.[6]

b SOCRATES: Fine words, Hippias, and fine thoughts, in my opinion.

1. See 282c ff., *Apology* 20a–b. In Plato's view to offer learning for sale was despicable in itself, and also dangerous: see *Protagoras* 313a–314b.

2. Socrates, on the contrary, tends to despise the opinion of the public: see especially *Crito* 47a–48a.

3. Pittacus, Bias and Thales are three of the seven Wise Men of Greece (see *Protagoras* 343a for a full list) who are attributed with various gnomic sayings. Thales (fl. *c.* 585) is traditionally seen as the first of the Presocratic philosopher-scientists: his 'school' presumably refers to his fellow Milesians, Anaximander and Anaximenes. The 'more recent thinkers' are the other Presocratics; Anaxagoras' floruit was *c.* 450. Pittacus, Bias and Thales, however, were all concerned with political matters (as were others of the seven Wise Men), so their inclusion is odd, but Socrates is presumably thinking in terms of the traditional contrast between intellectuals and men of action.

4. There is a pun in the Greek *Bias anabioiē* which is untranslatable into clear English. Plato was fond of such slight puns.

5. Daedalus was a legendary founder of sculpture whom Socrates, himself a sculptor, occasionally refers to in admiration: *Euthyphro* 11d ff., *Alcibiades I* 121a, *Meno* 97d–e, *Ion* 533a.

6. The sophists were often practitioners and teachers of rhetoric: Hippias was no exception (see *Hippias Minor* 368d). This sentence of Hippias' is typical of the style affected especially

And I am in a position to confirm that you are not mistaken: in fact your area of expertise *has* progressed towards the ability to combine private with public business. I mean, Gorgias, the famous sophist from Leontini,[1] came here on public business as the representative of his native city, because he was thought to be the most competent of the Leontinians to conduct their state affairs; and not only was he popularly regarded as the best speaker ever to have addressed the Assembly,[2] but he also gave lectures[3] as a private individual and met with our young men, and earned and received a lot of money from our city. Or take our eminent friend   c
Prodicus,[4] who often came here on public business; but the high point was his recent visit on public business from Ceos when he gained considerable fame in the Council as a speaker, as well as earning an incredible amount of money from giving lectures as a private individual and meeting with our young men. On the other hand, none of those men of old ever thought it right to be remunerated or to display his wisdom by lecturing to all sorts of people. That's how simple they were: they didn't realize   d
how valuable money is. Either of the men I've mentioned, however, has earned more money from his expertise than any other practitioner of any craft. And even before them there was Protagoras.[5]

HIPPIAS: You don't realize just how fine the situation is, Socrates: you'd be astonished if you knew how much money *I* have earned. Here's just one example: once, on a trip to Sicily while Protagoras was living there, despite his prestige and greater age, it took me, his junior by far,   e
hardly any time to earn at least 150 *minae*;[6] yes, and from a single place, Inycum,[7] which is pretty small, I got more than twenty *minae*, which I

---

by Gorgias of Leontini: we find antithesis ('living . . . dead'), balanced length of clauses ('I try . . . living, I am frightened . . . dead'), verbal play ('before . . . before') and poetic vocabulary ('wrath'). In Greece the souls of the dead were held to be fearful entities who had to be propitiated.

1. A reference to the famous visit of Gorgias (c. 485–c. 395) in 427.

2. In the Athenian democratic system there were two main organs of the people: the Council of 500 members annually chosen by lot from the ten tribes into which citizens were divided, and the Assembly which every male citizen over eighteen could attend.

3. *Epideixeis:* see p. 32. Socrates mistrusted these displays as superficial and as inaccessible to *elenchos* (on which see pp. 29–32).

4. Prodicus (c. 465–c. 390), from the island of Ceos, another sophist: see *Laches* 197d.

5. Protagoras of Abdera (c. 490–c. 420), the first and most famous of the professional sophists.

6. There is evidence that an average wage for an artisan at the end of the fifth century B.C. was about four *minae* a year. On the size of the fees received by the sophists, see Kerferd, pp. 26–8.

7. Inycum is not otherwise known. Its present obscurity reflects its ancient unimportance, which is precisely Hippias' point.

took home with me and gave to my father, much to his astonishment and that of the rest of my fellow-citizens. I would go so far as to suppose that *my* earnings are more than the total earnings of any other two sophists you care to mention.

283a   SOCRATES: Well, that *is* fine, Hippias, and powerful evidence both of your expertise and of how much more clever our contemporaries are than men of old. To your way of thinking, Anaxagoras and his predecessors[1] were pretty dense, in view of the stories that are told about them. For instance, they say that Anaxagoras had the opposite experience to you: once he inherited a lot of money, but wasn't concerned about it and lost it all – so little intelligence was there in his philosophizing;[2] and there are other similar stories about other men of old. So I think this is a fine piece of evidence you've produced about the wisdom of our contemporaries as

b   compared to their predecessors; and the common view too is that wisdom begins at home.[3] And, of course, you can define the wise man by seeing who has earned the most money. But enough on that. Now tell me this: from which of the cities you've visited did you earn the most? Obviously Sparta, I suppose, since you've been there most often.

HIPPIAS: Good heavens, no, Socrates!

SOCRATES: What? Do you mean you've earned the least there?[4]

c   HIPPIAS: In fact I've never earned anything there at all.

SOCRATES: That's preposterous, Hippias! I can hardly believe my ears! What you're good at, surely, is improving the morals of those who come to you as students, isn't it?[5]

HIPPIAS: Yes, very much, Socrates.

SOCRATES: Well, were you only able to improve the sons of Inycans, not of Spartans?

HIPPIAS: Far from it.

SOCRATES: Is it, then, that Sicilians desire to be improved, but Spartans don't?

d   HIPPIAS: No, Socrates, the Spartans certainly want to as well.

SOCRATES: So they couldn't afford your teaching?

HIPPIAS: No, they have enough money.

1. Reading μέχρι Ἀναξαγόρου λέγεται with Grube.

2. There is a joke here: Anaxagoras postulated Intelligence as the prime mover of the universe, so there *was* Intelligence in his philosophy!

3. Literally, 'the expert should above all be expert for himself', a proverb.

4. See also *Protagoras* 342a–e and *Laches* 182e–183b for Spartan resistance to the sophists.

5. Many sophists claimed to teach *aretē* (excellence, virtue), which meant being good at whatever skill the sophist was imparting, but especially the art of government (see *Protagoras* 318d–319a). But here I have translated *aretē* in moral terms, as the context demands (see 284a) and because, as 286a–b shows, this too is part of Hippias' repertoire.

SOCRATES: Why then, if they have the desire and the money, and if you are able to give them the greatest benefit, did you not leave them with your coffers full? Could it be – no, surely the Spartans can't educate their own children better than you can? Is that to be our conclusion? Would you endorse it?

HIPPIAS: Not at all.

e

SOCRATES: Were you, then, unable to persuade the young men in Sparta that if they attended your classes they would make better progress towards virtue than if they went to their own teachers? Or were you unable to persuade their fathers that, if they have their sons' interests at heart at all, they should entrust them to you rather than take care of them themselves? I assume that they weren't deliberately preventing their sons becoming as good as possible.[1]

HIPPIAS: I don't think they were.

SOCRATES: Well now, Sparta has an orderly constitution.

HIPPIAS: Of course.

SOCRATES: And in cities with orderly constitutions virtue is highly thought of.

284a

HIPPIAS: Certainly.

SOCRATES: And you know better than anyone else how to impart virtue.

HIPPIAS: Yes, far better, Socrates.

SOCRATES: Well, consider the expert teacher of horsemanship: in Greece, wouldn't he receive especially high regard and earnings in Thessaly, and wherever else this skill is cultivated?

HIPPIAS: Presumably.

SOCRATES: So won't the expert teacher of the subjects which are most valuable for virtue receive especially high regard and earnings in Sparta, if he wants, and in any other Greek city which has an orderly constitution? Do you think he will do better in Inycum, Sicily?[2] Is that what we are to believe, Hippias? We must take your word for it, if you say so.

b

HIPPIAS: The thing is, Socrates, the Spartans are conservative about their laws and won't educate their sons in an unusual manner.

SOCRATES: What? Surely it's not the Spartan tradition to do wrong rather than right?

c

HIPPIAS: I wouldn't think so, Socrates.

SOCRATES: Would they be doing right in educating their younger generation better rather than worse?

1. Only male children were educated in Sparta, as in other Greek states.
2. Sicily was proverbially luxurious and therefore contrary to the discipline of the Spartan way.

HIPPIAS: Yes, but a foreign education is illegal there. Otherwise you may be sure – to judge by the pleasure my teaching gives them and the praise I receive – that I would have been the foremost recipient of any money that there was to be had for teaching. But, as I say, it's illegal.

d   SOCRATES: Hippias, do you think law harms or benefits a city?

HIPPIAS: I imagine it's established to be beneficial, but sometimes it is harmful, if a bad law gets passed.

SOCRATES: But surely legislators establish the law because it is the greatest good for a city, and is the *sine qua non* of an orderly community?

HIPPIAS: True.

SOCRATES: So any legislator who proposes a law without a grasp of what is good falls short of legality and law. Do you agree?

e   HIPPIAS: Strictly speaking, Socrates, that is so; but it strains normal language.[1]

SOCRATES: Do you mean a knowledgeable or an ignorant use of language, Hippias?

HIPPIAS: A popular one.

SOCRATES: Is it the populace that knows the truth?

HIPPIAS: No, of course not.

SOCRATES: But men of knowledge, anyway, hold that in truth, the more beneficial a thing is, the more it is lawful for all men. Don't you agree?

HIPPIAS: Yes, I suppose I agree that this is the truth of the matter.

SOCRATES: And the facts are and remain as men of knowledge hold them to be?

HIPPIAS: Certainly.

285a   SOCRATES: Now, *you* claim that the education you offer, though foreign, is more beneficial for the Spartans than their native one.

HIPPIAS: Yes, and I'm right too.

SOCRATES: And do you also maintain that the more beneficial a thing is, the more lawful it is, Hippias?

HIPPIAS: Yes, as I've already said.

SOCRATES: So in your view it is more lawful for the young men of Sparta to be educated by Hippias than by their fathers, assuming that they will in fact get greater benefit from you.

HIPPIAS: But they will.

---

1. The historical Hippias (see *Protagoras* 337d and especially Xenophon, *Memorabilia* IV. 4.5–25) would probably have maintained that no man-made law can encompass the good, which is the province of natural law. For the fifth-century debate on this and related issues, see Guthrie, III, pp. 117–31; Kerferd, Chapter 10.

SOCRATES: So, in failing to offer you money and entrust their sons to   b
you, the Spartans are on the wrong side of the law.

HIPPIAS: I agree – I mean, I think your argument is in my favour and
I see no reason to resist it.

SOCRATES: We find, then, my friend, that the Spartans, who are
thought to be the most law-abiding people, are in contravention of law,
and on the most important of matters at that.

B. *Fineness and a Fine-looking Girl*

*After some more teasing of Hippias, the main subject of the dialogue, 'What is
fineness?', is introduced. Socrates gains Hippias' agreement that there is such
a thing as fineness, and asks him to define it. But Hippias avoids the question –
he seems to acknowledge his inability to answer it – and gives instead, as an
example of fineness, a fine-looking girl. He does not make the gross mistake of
saying that fineness is a fine-looking girl – that is, of offering this as a definition
of fineness – as the passage has often been interpreted. But he has admitted the
existence of fineness, so the point Socrates has to get across in this section is that
an example of F can never be the F itself: Hippias must first learn how to distinguish between the general and the particular. In this section, then, Socrates
provides two criteria which fineness itself must satisfy and which any example
of fineness, such as a fine-looking girl, fails to satisfy. First, any example of
fineness cannot be responsible for fineness in other fine examples, and so cannot
tell us how to recognize fineness elsewhere. Second, any fine thing in this world
is only relatively fine and may in another contrast be seen as contemptible.
Therefore it cannot stand as the paradigm, fineness, which, since it is supposed
to be responsible for the fineness of fine things, cannot be described under any
circumstances as less than fine. So the two criteria which an F itself must satisfy
are that it must be responsible for other things being F, and it must never be
not-F. If Hippias can come up with an answer which tries to satisfy these
criteria, he will be on the road to defining fineness. He attempts a definition
based on the first of these criteria in the next section, and on the second in the
section after that; thus the first part of the dialogue is carefully structured.*

SOCRATES: But what do they praise you for, and enjoy hearing about?[1]
I suppose it must be your special branch of knowledge, astronomy.[2]   c

1. See 284c.
2. Compare *Hippias Minor* 368b–d and *Protagoras* 318e with regard to the following list of
Hippias' accomplishments.

HIPPIAS: Not at all. That's a subject they don't even tolerate.[1]

SOCRATES: But does geometry give them any pleasure?

HIPPIAS: No. It's barely an exaggeration to say that many of them can't even count![2]

SOCRATES: Then they won't put up with you lecturing on arithmetic.

HIPPIAS: Certainly not.

SOCRATES: Then they must enjoy the subject in which your analytical
d abilities are so exceptional, the significance of letters, syllables, rhythms and intonations.[3]

HIPPIAS: My dear Socrates! Intonations and letters! Ha!

SOCRATES: So *which* lecture-subject of yours gives them pleasure and wins you their praise? You'll have to tell me yourself, because I'm stuck.

HIPPIAS: The genealogies of heroes and men, and how cities were founded in the distant past: in short, antiquarianism in general is what
e they most enjoy hearing about, and so I was obliged to make a thorough study of the whole subject until I'd mastered it.

SOCRATES: Well, Hippias, you're certainly lucky that the Spartans don't enjoy the enumeration of Athenian *archontes* from Solon onwards,[4] otherwise you'd have had a job mastering it.[5]

HIPPIAS: Why, Socrates? I can reel off fifty names after hearing them only once.

SOCRATES: You're right: I wasn't taking your mnemonic technique into account.[6] *Now* I understand the situation: the Spartans treat you as
286a children do old women, to tell them pleasant stories; so naturally they enjoy you and your vast store of knowledge.

HIPPIAS: Yes, and I tell you, Socrates, I acquired quite a reputation

1. Those who studied the heavenly bodies from the standpoint of physical science were liable to be thought atheistic (cf. p. 18). This would have been particularly the case in a conservative society such as Sparta.

2. Spartan education was notoriously geared towards military rather than cultural expertise.

3. It is unclear whether the subject is music or rhetoric.

4. Each year in Athens nine *archontes* ('leaders') were elected by lot, with mainly administrative duties. One of them, the eponymous *archōn*, gave his name to the year: Socrates is referring to a list of these eponymous *archontes*. The office had been in existence before Solon (*archōn* 594/3), but his reforms lessened its power, so Socrates takes him as the founder of the democratic office.

5. Socrates seems to think such antiquarianism consists in mechanical memorizing and, as he says shortly, in weaving stories. As a matter of fact, it was often embryonic historiography and also led some fifth-century thinkers (perhaps including Hippias) to fascinating views on human progress and the origins of civilization: see Guthrie, III, pp. 63–84; Kerferd, Chapter 12.

6. Hippias' mnemonic technique is also referred to at *Hippias Minor* 368d and Xenophon, *Symposium* 4.62. Mnemonic techniques were part of an orator's training. On the whole subject, in classical and medieval times, see Yates.

by an exposition I gave there recently of the fine practices to which a young man ought to devote himself. I've got an exceedingly fine lecture composed on the subject; its use of words is particularly good. The scene is subsequent to the sack of Troy and I start the lecture off with Neoptolemus asking Nestor[1] which fine practices bring fame to a young man, and then Nestor gives him plenty of advice on the finest rules of life. This is the lecture I delivered there and, at the request of Eudicus the son of Apemantus,[2] I'm going to give it here too, in two days' time, in Pheidostratus' school. It's worth hearing and there'll be more besides, so make sure you come, and bring other competent critics.

SOCRATES: Yes, I'll do that, God willing, Hippias. But while we're on the subject, I've got a small question to which I'd appreciate your answer: in fact, you reminded me of it, with a fine sense of timing. You see, my friend, I was recently plunged into confusion when, during a discussion in which I was condemning some things as contemptible but praising others as fine, I was rudely interrupted with a question which went somewhat as follows: 'Socrates,' I was asked, 'what makes you an expert on what sorts of things are fine and contemptible? I mean, could you tell me what fineness is?'[3] Now, I'm not up to this kind of thing, so I got confused and couldn't make a proper reply. After we'd parted company, I was angry with myself, told myself off, and swore that as soon as I had bumped into any of you experts, I would return to my inquisitor to renew the battle, with instruction, teaching and study to back me up. So now, as I say, you've come at a fine time: explain to me, as well as you can, what fineness itself is, and try to answer my questions as accurately as possible. I don't want to make a fool of myself again in a second cross-examination. I'm sure you're crystal-clear on the subject and that it must be only a fraction of your vast knowledge.

HIPPIAS: Yes, indeed it is, Socrates, and not a particularly important part either.

SOCRATES: Then I'll have no trouble learning about it, and no one will ever expose my ignorance again.

HIPPIAS: No, no one: I would be a worthless amateur in my job if they could.

SOCRATES: That's really good to hear, Hippias: we might yet get the better of the fellow. But would it be a nuisance if I imitated him by

1. Neoptolemus, son of Achilles; Nestor, aged lord of Pylos. As in Hippias' lecture, so in Homer too Nestor often gives wordy advice.

2. One of the characters in *Hippias Minor* but otherwise unknown; the dramatic starting-point of *Hippias Minor* is probably this lecture (see p. 275 n. 1).

3. See p. 224.

criticizing your answers? My thinking is that I'll get the most out of your instruction that way. I'm quite well versed in his criticisms.¹ So, if it makes no difference to you, I wouldn't mind criticizing you, to reinforce what I learn.

HIPPIAS: Go ahead. As I said just now, it's an easy question: I could
b teach you how to become unassailable by anyone – anyone at all – on far more difficult issues.

SOCRATES: This gets better and better. Anyway, since you've given me the go-ahead, I'll do my best to make myself his *Doppelgänger* and try to question you. You see, if you were to give him that lecture you've mentioned on fine practices, then once he'd heard you out, the first thing
c he'd ask you about, if he's true to form, is fineness. 'May I ask our distinguished visitor from Elis,' he'd say, 'whether it's thanks to justice that just people are just?' Imagine he's here putting the question, Hippias, and answer him.²

HIPPIAS: Yes, thanks to justice, will be my reply.

SOCRATES: 'So justice is something?'

HIPPIAS: Certainly.

SOCRATES: 'And wise people are wise thanks to wisdom, all good things good thanks to goodness?'

HIPPIAS: Of course.

SOCRATES: 'That is, thanks to actual entities – I mean, it couldn't be thanks to non-entities.'³

HIPPIAS: No, entities.

SOCRATES: 'Therefore, aren't all fine things fine thanks to fineness?'
d HIPPIAS: Yes.

SOCRATES: 'That is, thanks to an actual entity?'

HIPPIAS: Yes, why not?

SOCRATES: 'Tell me, then, my friend,' he'll say; 'what is this thing, fineness?'

HIPPIAS: Isn't this the same as asking what is fine, Socrates?

1. It emerges that 'he' is Socrates' *alter ego*. For this device, compare Diotima in *Symposium*, the laws in *Crito*, and other less sustained substitutions such as the pilot in *Gorgias* 511d–512b. All of them are introduced to reinforce Socrates' own position, and especially when real or assumed politeness or modesty prevents him from arguing in his own person. Here, Socrates' *alter ego* acts as a buffer, so that Socrates and Hippias can later slang each other without appearing to do so directly.

2. On the immediately following passage, see p. 219 ff.

3. Socrates is exploiting the linguistic form of the sentence which makes it seem that justice etc. are external to their possessors and each a single thing which their many possessors share. Otherwise, one would be more inclined to view justice simply as an internal psychological attitude, rather than as an external entity which people might possess (see also 296c on 'ability').

SOCRATES: I don't think so, Hippias: I think the question is what fineness is.

HIPPIAS: What's the difference?

SOCRATES: None, you think?

HIPPIAS: No, there is none.

SOCRATES: Well, obviously you have a finer knowledge of the matter. But still, since the question is not what is fine, but what fineness is, please apply your mind to that.   e

HIPPIAS: I see, my friend; I will tell him what fineness is, absolutely incontrovertibly . . . Well, you can be sure of the truth of this, that a fine-looking girl is a fine thing!

SOCRATES: By the Dog, Hippias![1] What a fine answer! Excellent! So, if I give *this* answer, I will have answered the question, and done so   288a correctly and absolutely incontrovertibly?

HIPPIAS: Of course it's incontrovertible, Socrates: it's a universally held opinion. Your audience will unanimously support your view as correct.[2]

SOCRATES: Well, all right. Now, Hippias, let me review the situation. I will be questioned as follows: 'Now, Socrates, answer me this: taking your examples of fine things, what must fineness itself be if they are to be fine?' Shall I really reply that if a fine-looking girl is a fine thing, it is *this* that is responsible for their being fine?[3]

HIPPIAS: What do you think will happen if he tries to argue that what   b you mention is *not* a fine thing? Surely he'll only make himself ridiculous if he tries?

SOCRATES: I'm sure he'll try, my friend, but only events can prove the attempt ridiculous. But I don't mind telling you what he'll say.

HIPPIAS: Go ahead.

SOCRATES: 'How naïve you are, Socrates!' he'll protest. 'Isn't a fine Elean mare a fine thing?[4] Remember even the god praised mares in the oracle.' What shall we say, Hippias? Aren't we to say that a mare too,   c provided it is fine, is a fine thing? I mean, we can hardly go so far as to deny that something fine is a fine thing.

---

1. An oath whose origin is obscure, but which is characteristic of Socrates; see also p. 204 n. 1

2. But Socrates is not after universal approbation unless it is given to the truth as revealed by further questioning.

3. Reading εἰ παρθένος καλὴ καλόν ἐστι, διὰ τοῦτ' ἂν εἴη καλά; with Grube.

4. Reading Ἠλεία with Kapp. The oracle to which Socrates refers is not known; there is an extant seventh-century oracle of Apollo at Delphi which praises 'horses of Thrace' – but not Elean mares.

HIPPIAS: Good thinking, Socrates: yes, we breed some very fine mares, so the god was right.

SOCRATES: 'Now,' he'll continue, 'what about a fine lyre? Isn't *it* a fine thing?' Should we agree, Hippias?

HIPPIAS: Yes.

SOCRATES: Well, if I'm any judge of his character, I'm pretty certain that next he will ask: 'My very dear friend, what about a fine pot? Is it then *not* a fine thing?'

d   HIPPIAS: Socrates, who is this person? He must be a boor, to judge by his cheek in introducing such trivia into dignified proceedings.[1]

SOCRATES: He doesn't have the subtle touch, Hippias: no, in his single-minded concern for the truth, he's rather a vulgar fellow. Still he deserves an answer; I'll give my view first. If the pot has been fashioned by a good potter so that it is smooth, well rounded and properly fired, like some very fine pots that there are of the two-handled variety with a capacity of

e   six *choes*[2] – if that's the sort of pot he's asking about, I would agree that it is fine. I mean, how could we deny that a fine thing is fine?

HIPPIAS: We can't, Socrates.

SOCRATES: 'So tell me,' he'll say, 'isn't even a fine pot a fine thing?'

HIPPIAS: Yes, I think so, Socrates: even this utensil is fine if it has been finely wrought, but utensils in general are not up to the standard in fineness of fine horses, girls and so on.

289a   SOCRATES: Ah, I see, Hippias! We must reply to our inquisitor as follows: 'Sir, you are overlooking the correctness of Heraclitus' dictum that "the finest ape is contemptible compared to man".[3] The finest pot too is contemptible compared to girls – so says Hippias, and he's an expert.' Isn't that so, Hippias?

HIPPIAS: Certainly, Socrates; your reply is correct.

SOCRATES: So listen to what I'm sure he'll say next: 'Well, Socrates,

b   doesn't the same principle obtain for girls as compared with gods as for

---

1. This charge is brought against Socrates in person at *Gorgias* 491a and *Symposium* 221e. Throughout the dialogue, the question arises whether Hippias recognizes that the unnamed speaker is in fact Socrates. It adds a marvellous extra dimension to the humour of the dialogue if we suppose that Hippias is aware of what is going on, and maintains the fiction out of mock politeness (p. 240 n. 1), with his tongue just as firmly in his cheek on this point as Socrates'. See Woodruff (1982), pp. 107–8.

2. A *chous* was a liquid measure of about six pints.

3. Heraclitus of Ephesus, the philoscpher of the sixth/fifth century, fragment 82 in H. Diels and W. Kranz, *Die Fragmente der Vorsokratiker*, I (6th ed., Berlin 1951–2); fragment 83 is about to be quoted. Probably neither is a *verbatim* citation of Heraclitus, and they should be taken together to yield a single fragment with the sense: 'The wisest man is but an ape compared to God, just as the most beautiful ape is ugly compared to man.'

pots as compared with girls? Won't the finest-looking girl turn out to be contemptible in comparison? Isn't this exactly what Heraclitus – whom *you* adduce – says: "The wisest man will turn out to be an ape compared with God", and not just in respect of wisdom but of fineness and everything else?' Should we concede that the finest-looking girl is contemptible compared to gods, Hippias?

HIPPIAS: Yes, that is undeniable, Socrates.

SOCRATES: Well, if we make this concession, he will laugh and say: c
'Socrates, do you remember what the question was?' 'Yes,' I'll reply, 'what fineness itself is.' 'And yet,' he'll continue, 'although you were asked about fineness, your reply names something which by your own admission is in fact no more fine than contemptible.'[1] 'It seems so,' I'll say – or what would you recommend me to say, my friend?

HIPPIAS: Nothing different: his assertion that man is not fine compared to gods will be correct, of course.

SOCRATES: 'Suppose,' he will continue, 'that I had originally wanted to know what is *both* fine *and* contemptible: wouldn't your recent answer   d
have been correct? Moreover, do you think that fineness itself, the form,[2] which when present makes everything else as well attractive and appear fine, is a girl, a horse or a lyre?'

C. *Fineness as Gold*

Socrates has introduced the notion that the 'presence' of fineness in things is responsible for their fineness; this leads Hippias to a definition of fineness as gold (for a comparable materialistic understanding of 'presence', see Euthydemus *301a ff.). This is progress, in two related ways: first, Hippias does not choose a particular thing, but gold in general; and second, he shows some understanding that he is to look for what is responsible for things being fine. Thus he may be said to be attempting a definition. But soon he is talking as if the question had been 'What is fine?', because he has to admit that gold cannot be responsible for all fine things being fine. The second point Socrates presses is that gold and so on are only responsible for fineness when appropriate: when inappropriate they are contemptible, so they do not satisfy the criterion of never being not-F. Notice the introduction of appropriateness, which will recur later, and how it inevitably raises the issue of a thing's appearance: Socrates is after something which is fine, whether or not it appears and is recognized as such.*

1. See p. 222.
2. See pp. 21, 32–3, 221.

HIPPIAS: Oh well, Socrates, if *that*'s what he's after, there's no difficulty at all in telling him what fineness is, thanks to which everything else as well is made attractive and whose presence makes them appear fine.

e What an idiot this fellow must be, with no understanding of fine things! Here's your reply to him: when he's asking about fineness, he's asking about *gold*. That'll confound him; he won't try to refute you. I mean, everyone knows that the presence of gold makes even things which previously seemed contemptible look fine. Yes, gold's what makes them attractive.

SOCRATES: Because you aren't familiar with the man, Hippias, you don't realize how stubborn he is: he doesn't just take somebody's word for something.

HIPPIAS: What do you mean, Socrates? He *has* to accept a correct

290a proposition, otherwise he'll make a fool of himself.

SOCRATES: Maybe, but so far from accepting this answer, my friend, he will scoff at me mightily and say, 'Are you out of your mind? Do you regard Pheidias as an inferior craftsman?'[1] 'Not at all,' I imagine will be my reply.

HIPPIAS: And you'll be right, Socrates.

SOCRATES: Of course, and that is exactly why, on gaining my agreement that Pheidias is a good craftsman, he will say: 'So do you suppose

b that Pheidias was ignorant of this "fineness" of yours?' 'What are you getting at?' I'll rejoin. 'I'll tell you,' he'll say. 'He didn't use gold for Athena's eyes or for her face either, or her feet, or her hands, even if it is true that gold would have had the finest effect – he used ivory. Obviously his ignorance led him astray: he didn't realize that *gold* is the stuff whose presence makes everything fine.' How are we to respond to him on this, Hippias?

c HIPPIAS: Easy: we approve of Pheidias' work, because ivory is a fine thing too, in my opinion.

SOCRATES: 'So why didn't he use ivory for the eyeballs as well?' he will ask. 'He used stone and made sure that the stone was as similar as possible to ivory.[2] Is fine stone a fine thing too?' Shall we say yes, Hippias?

HIPPIAS: Of course it is, when appropriate.

SOCRATES: 'But contemptible when inappropriate?' Am I to agree or not?

---

1. Pheidias of Athens (*c.* 490–*c.* 425) was the most famous sculptor of the Greek world. His gold and ivory statue of Athena for the Parthenon in Athens (438) was reckoned to be one of his masterpieces.

2. In order to approximate to a lifelike effect, sculptors regularly used different materials for a statue's features.

HIPPIAS: Yes, when it is inappropriate.

SOCRATES: 'Brilliant!' he'll say. 'So ivory and gold, when appropriate,   d
make things look fine but, when inappropriate, contemptible – right?' Do
we argue against this or accept that it is correct?

HIPPIAS: Whatever is appropriate for a particular object makes that
object fine. *That* is what we will accept.[1]

SOCRATES: 'When that fine pot we were just talking about is full of
fine simmering soup,' he'll say, 'is a golden or a wooden ladle appropriate?'

HIPPIAS: Heavens above, Socrates! I despair of this fellow! Won't you
tell me who he is?   e

SOCRATES: You'd be none the wiser if I told you his name.

HIPPIAS: I'll tell you what I *do* know about him already – he's an idiot.

SOCRATES: He's certainly a pest, Hippias. Still, what shall we reply?
Which of the ladles is appropriate for the pot and its soup? Evidently the
wooden one, isn't it? It improves the aroma of the soup, not to mention
the fact, my friend, that it won't break the pot and so spill the soup, put
out the fire, and deprive the prospective diners of a splendid soup. But
since the golden one would do all that, to my mind, unless you raise any
objections, we have to say that the wooden ladle is more appropriate than   291a
the golden one.

HIPPIAS: Yes, it is, Socrates. But for my part, I wouldn't carry on a
conversation with someone who asks this sort of question.

SOCRATES: Quite right, my friend: it wouldn't be proper for *you* to be
infected by these sorts of terms, with your fine clothes, your fine shoes[2]
and your reputation for wisdom among all the Greeks. But it's no trouble
for me to associate with the fellow. So, for my sake, clue me up in advance   b
by answering him. 'If the wooden one is more appropriate than the golden
one,' he'll say, 'then mustn't it also be finer, since you agreed, Socrates,
that what is more appropriate is finer than what is inappropriate?' We
must agree, mustn't we, Hippias, that the wooden one is finer than the
golden one?

HIPPIAS: Do you want me to give you a definition of fineness which
will save you from a lengthy discussion, Socrates?

SOCRATES: By all means, but not until you've told me which of those   c
two ladles I should name in my reply as appropriate and finer.

1. Since this is the point of view Socrates himself adopts in Section E of the dialogue,
commentators have praised Hippias' intelligence here, and found it at odds with the portrait
of much of the rest of the dialogue. But all Hippias is doing is understanding Socrates' argument, not thinking creatively in his own right.

2. At *Hippias Minor* 368c we are told that Hippias made his own clothes and shoes; the point
of the joke, then, is that Hippias' activities are no less banausic than cooking.

HIPPIAS: All right, if you insist: tell him it's the one made out of wood.

SOCRATES: Now go on with what you were about to say. You see, if I avail myself of your last solution and say that fineness is gold, it will, in my judgement, be proved that gold is no more fine than wood. But how do you define fineness *now*?

D. *Fineness as Health, Wealth and So On*

Again, Hippias begins with some progress, since he at last comes up with a universal as his definition, and now understands that whatever he defines as F must never be not-F. But in fact he fails to satisfy this criterion. He defines fineness as a number of things drawn from standard Greek sentiments about what is fine and about the benefits of old age. He expects this to satisfy the criterion by gaining universal approbation for his definition. But Socrates never thought that the majority opinion was necessarily right, and he quickly demolishes this attempt by Hippias, using arguments similar to those of the previous two sections, and without having to argue that Hippias' definition patently fails to be unitary (see Section G) and that it commits an obvious petitio principii *by using the term 'fine' in a definition of fineness.*

d HIPPIAS: I'll tell you. What you're after, I think, for your answer, is fineness which is such that it will never under any circumstances seem contemptible to anyone.

SOCRATES: Exactly, Hippias; now you've got it. Fine!

HIPPIAS: Listen, then. I assure you that if any objection is raised against what I have to say, you may count me a complete ignoramus.

SOCRATES: Go on, please. I can hardly wait.

HIPPIAS: My view is everlastingly and universally applicable everywhere: the finest accomplishment is for a wealthy, healthy man, who has gained respect among the Greeks and attained old age, and has given his parents fine funerals on their deaths, to be given by his own children a
e grand and fine burial.[1]

SOCRATES: Oh Hippias, Hippias! What a remarkably splendid statement! It really has done you proud. I am really and truly delighted that you seem to be doing all you can to come to my assistance. So kind of you! All the same, you should realize that we have left the enemy unscathed: he will now ridicule us more than ever.

1. Hippias is posturing again: see p. 232 n. 6. This sentence contains assonance ('wealthy, healthy', 'gained . . . attained'); antithesis ('his parents . . . his children'); balanced length of clauses combined with a climax of increasingly longer clauses; and deliberate avoidance of the same word ('funerals . . . burial').

HIPPIAS: Feeble ridicule, Socrates: if he can do nothing else but jeer at what I've said, then he'll end up the butt of his own laughter and be ridiculed by the company himself. 292a

SOCRATES: That's possible; but if my intuition is right, it's not impossible that he might do more than just ridicule me for this answer.

HIPPIAS: What do you mean?

SOCRATES: If he has a stick and I don't get well out of his reach, he will try hard to beat me.

HIPPIAS: What? Is he in some sense your master? Won't he be arrested and convicted for this? Or does Athens allow her citizens to commit unjus- b tified assault on one another, which is anarchy?

SOCRATES: No, of course she doesn't.

HIPPIAS: So he'll be punished for unjustified assault.

SOCRATES: I don't think it would be unjustified, Hippias – no, if I gave that answer, it *would* be justified, in my opinion.

HIPPIAS: I too think it'd be justified, Socrates. Who am I to gainsay your opinion?

SOCRATES: Do you want me to spell out why I myself think the assault would be justified if I gave that answer? Will you let me get a word in, or are you too going to assault me without a hearing?

HIPPIAS: No, it would be monstrous of me not to listen, Socrates. c What argument do you have to offer?

SOCRATES: I'll tell you, and I'll imitate him as I did before, so that *I* will be the object of *his* harsh, uncouth words, rather than you of mine. I'm sure this is what he'll say: 'Tell me, Socrates, do you suppose a thrashing would be unjustified if in singing such a tasteless, long dithyramb[1] you were way out of tune with the question?' 'What do you mean?' I'll ask. 'What do I mean?' he'll rejoin. 'Are you incapable of remembering that I keep asking about fineness itself, whose presence makes anything d fine, be it stone, wood, man, god, action or lesson? My question, man, is what fineness itself is, but I can't get that through to you. You might just as well be a stone here beside me, and a dense one at that,[2] for all the ears and brain you've got.' Wouldn't you be annoyed, Hippias, if I took fright and said: 'But that's how Hippias defined fineness, even though *I* kept e asking him the same question, namely, what is universally and everlastingly fine.' Well? Won't you be annoyed if I say that?

1. A dithyramb is a form of lyric poetry which by the fifth century was notorious for its affected language and florid music. Hence it provides a suitable analogy to Hippias' proposition at 291d–e.

2. Literally, 'and a millstone at that', presumably because a millstone needs to be particularly hard. The English equivalent, of course, is 'I might as well be talking to a brick wall.'

HIPPIAS: I am confident, Socrates, that I *have* specified what is universally fine and will be accepted as such.

SOCRATES: 'Will it also be fine in the future?' he'll ask. 'For fineness is everlastingly fine, of course.'

HIPPIAS: Certainly.

SOCRATES: 'And was in the past as well?' he'll add.

HIPPIAS: Yes, in the past as well.

SOCRATES: 'Did your visitor from Elis,' he'll say, 'also claim that it would have been fine for Achilles to be buried after his parents, or for his grandfather Aeacus, or any other descendant of the gods? And what about
293a the gods themselves?'[1]

HIPPIAS: What? This is the blessed limit![2] These questions of his are profane, Socrates.

SOCRATES: But it is not particularly profane to answer yes when the question is asked by someone else, is it?

HIPPIAS: Maybe.

SOCRATES: 'Well maybe,' he will continue, '*you* are the one who is claiming that it is universally and everlastingly fine to be buried by one's children and to bury one's parents. But "universally" doesn't exclude Heracles[3] and all the others we mentioned a moment ago, does it?'

HIPPIAS: I didn't mean to include the gods.

b   SOCRATES: 'Nor the heroes, it seems.'

HIPPIAS: Not when they are children of gods.

SOCRATES: 'But when they aren't?'

HIPPIAS: Certainly.

SOCRATES: 'It seems to follow from your argument that among the heroes it is terrible, irreverent and contemptible for Tantalus, Dardanus and Zethus, but fine for Pelops and anyone else with similar parentage.'[4]

HIPPIAS: I agree.

SOCRATES: 'You are contradicting yourself,' he'll argue. 'Previously

1. The main point of this is to find a counter-example, even an extreme one, to Hippias' idea: it is obviously not fine for men to be buried after the gods, because it is not fine for gods to be buried at all! But in the case of Achilles there seems also to be a reference to his choice between a distinguished short life and an undistinguished long one (see Homer, *Iliad* XI, 410–16): it would not have been fine for him to choose the latter alternative, even if that would have given him the opportunity of being buried after his parents. No such choice faced Aeacus but, like Achilles (whose mother was the sea-nymph Thetis), he is brought in as an example of a hero with divine parentage: his father was Zeus.

2. Literally, 'Go to blessedness!' In Greek, as in English, it seems that 'blessed' can be used euphemistically.

3. 'Hercules' in Latin, the son of Zeus.

4. Tantalus, Dardanus and Zethus were also famous sons of Zeus; but Pelops was as fully mortal as any legendary hero could be: he was Tantalus' son.

you denied that being buried by one's children after burying one's parents is ever contemptible for anyone. Since it is apparently even more impos- c sible for this to be universally fine, then it has suffered the same fate as our girl and pot before: in a still more absurd way it is fine for some but not for others. Even today, Socrates,' he'll add, 'you are *still* unable to define fineness when asked to do so.' He'll be justified in telling me off if I answer him as you've suggested.

E. *Fineness as Appropriateness*

In Section C the possibility was raised that whatever is fine is appropriate for its situation. Socrates now, in the person of his alter ego, proposes that appropriateness is the definition of fineness. But this is briefly claimed to be wrong. Appropriateness, it is argued, either makes things seem fine, or it actually makes things fine. Hippias first suggests that it makes things seem fine (294a), but Socrates argues that whatever fineness is, it must make things genuinely be fine, whether or not they appear, or are seen, to be fine.

Hippias next (294c) suggests that appropriateness makes things both appear and be fine. Socrates replies that the two – both appearing and being fine – do not necessarily occur together: Hippias' suggestion begs the question as to why fine things are sometimes recognized as fine, but sometimes not. He must still choose between being or seeming fine. Not unnaturally, given that appropriateness is contextually determined, he opts for the notion that appropriateness merely allows things to seem fine. This leaves all the cases where fine things are not universally recognized as fine uncatered for; so the definition of fineness as appropriateness fails.

The argument is neat, but flawed, from our point of view, because we want to say that fineness is an aesthetic quality: it lies in the eye of the beholder. There seems to be little sense in the notion that something is fine, if in fact no one recognizes it as such. Plato stresses cases where things are fine but are not universally recognized as such – but what has universal recognition got to do with it? However many people see X as fine, X is fine for them; if no one sees X as fine, X is not fine for them.

SOCRATES: Usually, Hippias, this is more or less how he talks to me, d but sometimes it is as if he takes pity on my lack of experience and learning, and makes a positive suggestion himself – he might ask whether I think fineness, or whatever else happens to be the subject of his inquiry and our conversation, is such-and-such.

HIPPIAS: Could you be more specific, Socrates?

SOCRATES: All right. 'My dear Socrates,' he might say, 'please don't give any more answers as utterly foolish and demonstrably mistaken as

e these were. But see whether you think the following suggestion is fine, which in fact we touched on a short while ago when we were saying, during one of the answers, that gold is fine for things for which it is appropriate, but not for things for which it is not, and so on for any other case where this feature is present. What is this thing, appropriateness, in itself? What is its essential nature? See whether it might in fact be fineness.' Now, I can never think of anything to say on these occasions, so *I* tend to acquiesce; but do *you* think appropriateness is fineness?[1]

HIPPIAS: Absolutely, Socrates.

SOCRATES: Let's investigate the issue, to make sure we're not somehow misled.

HIPPIAS: Yes, we should.

SOCRATES: Well then, what do we think about appropriateness? Is it

294a that which by coming to be present in anything makes that thing *seem* fine, or actually *be* fine, or neither?

HIPPIAS: I think it's what makes things seem fine. For example, well-fitting clothes or shoes make even someone gawky look finer.

SOCRATES: So if appropriateness makes things appear finer than they are, then in a sense it misleads us about fineness, and can't be our quarry, Hippias, can it? I mean, our quarry has always been whatever is respon-

b sible for all fine things being fine, analogous to excess, thanks to which all big things are big.[2] Excess is what makes anything big; even if something doesn't look big, but does have excess, it is necessarily big. Similarly the question is, leaving appearances aside, what fineness could be, thanks to which anything is fine. It can't be appropriateness, if you're right that it makes things seem finer than they are and prevents things from being seen as they are. No, we must try to say what it is that makes things really

c fine, leaving appearances aside, as I said just now. That's our quarry, if it's fineness we're after.

HIPPIAS: But Socrates, the presence of appropriateness makes things both actually be *and* appear fine.

SOCRATES: Is it then impossible for things which are in fact fine not to appear fine, given the presence of what causes the impression?

HIPPIAS: Impossible.

1. Aristotle, *Topics* 102a6 and 135a13, mentions this as a typical definition, and seems to regard it to be a true one. He may be recalling *Hippias Major* or simply reflecting current discussion.

2. 'Big' is relational: *x* is only big in relation to *y* which is smaller, so excess can be isolated as responsible for bigness.

SOCRATES: So it must be the case, Hippias, that everything which is in fact fine – a law, say, or a practice – is thought to be fine, and universally and everlastingly appears so. But *is* this the case, or the exact opposite, d that ignorance prevails and that such things are the prime cause of strife and contention in the private affairs of individuals and in the public life of states?

HIPPIAS: The latter, rather, Socrates: ignorance prevails.

SOCRATES: But it wouldn't *if* the appearance were present;[1] and it would be present if appropriateness were fineness and caused things to appear fine as well as be so. Therefore there are two possibilities: either appropriateness is what makes things fine, in which case it is our quarry, e fineness, but isn't what makes them *appear* fine; alternatively, appropriateness is what makes things appear fine, in which case it isn't our quarry, fineness. For fineness makes things actually fine, but the cause of things *being* fine is necessarily different from the cause of their *appearing* fine[2] – or anything else, for that matter. So we must choose whether we think that appropriateness is what makes things *appear* fine or actually *be* fine.

HIPPIAS: Appear, I think, Socrates.

SOCRATES: Damn! That means that knowledge of what fineness is has eluded us, Hippias, since appropriateness has turned out not to be identifiable with fineness.

HIPPIAS: Yes it has, Socrates, it has indeed; and I find that most peculiar.

F. *Fineness as Usefulness and Benefit (the Cause of Goodness)*

The suggestion that fineness is usefulness is reached by typically Socratic induction from a few examples. However, it is argued that something may be useful for bad consequences, which of course is not fine, so the definition needs qualification. The qualified definition, then, is that fineness is 'usefulness and ability for good action', i.e. benefit. This receives most unsatisfactory treatment. From the uncontroversial premisses that benefit produces good, and that a producer and its product are different, Socrates draws the mistaken conclusion that fineness (benefit) cannot be good, which is intuitively absurd, and the definition is accordingly rejected. But if this conclusion were legitimate, it would also follow that heat cannot be produced by something hot! Socrates is being made to commit the fallacy of confusing identity and attribution: even if fineness is not identical to goodness, which it produces, it may still be good. He equivocates, therefore,

1. That is, the appearance of being fine.
2. Reading καὶ ποιεῖν εἶναι with the manuscripts.

on the word 'different': even if a cause is different from (not identical to) its
product, it is not necessarily different from (not similar to) its product.

295a   SOCRATES: But we mustn't give up the chase yet, my friend. Uncovering what fineness is isn't quite hopeless yet.

HIPPIAS: Of course not, Socrates. It's really quite easy. I'm sure that after I'd thought it over for a bit, in peace and quiet, I could give you the most precise of precise definitions.

SOCRATES: Hey, Hippias, no boasting! You can see how much trouble our quarry has already caused us, and I'm afraid that if it gets angry, it
b   will run even further away. But this is nonsense – I'm sure that on your own you would easily hunt it down, but please could you do so while I'm here, or, if you prefer, let's search together, as we did just now. A successful search would be the finest thing of all; but if that doesn't happen, I suppose I shall reconcile myself with my lot, and you will go elsewhere and have no difficulty in discovering it. But remember, if we find it now, then of course I won't later have to bother you by asking what it was that you found by yourself. So please consider now what you think fineness
c   itself is. I propose that it is – please concentrate to make sure I'm not talking nonsense – I mean, let's take anything *useful* to be fine. My thinking is this: we don't call 'fine' eyes which we think are incapable of sight, but those which are capable of, and useful for, sight. Isn't that so?

HIPPIAS: Yes.

SOCRATES: The same goes for the whole body: we call it 'fine for running' or 'for wrestling'. Or again, take any living creature – a fine
d   horse, cock or quail;[1] take any artefact; take any vehicles for land, and boats and ships on the sea; yes, and take any instrument, whether it is musical or used in some other skill; and, if you like, take practices and laws – all of these we invariably call 'fine' in the same sense. We consider the nature, construction or constitution of each of them, and call it 'fine'
e   if it is useful in some way or for some purpose or at some time; but if it is useless in all these respects, we call it 'contemptible'. Don't you agree, Hippias?

HIPPIAS: I do.

SOCRATES: So are we right in saying that it is in fact pre-eminently what is *useful* that is fine?

HIPPIAS: Yes, Socrates.

---

1. Socrates picks on these animals because they are all used in sport (racing in the case of horses; fighting in the case of the other two), and so are prime examples of animals with particular functions.

SOCRATES: Isn't anything useful to the extent that it is capable of performing its particular function, but useless if incapable?

HIPPIAS: Certainly.

SOCRATES: So ability is fine, inability contemptible?

HIPPIAS: Most certainly. Many things provide adequate evidence of this, Socrates, but especially state affairs. Political ability in the affairs of one's own state is the finest thing, inability the most contemptible. 296a

SOCRATES: That's well said. Heavens above, Hippias! Does this explain why expertise is the finest thing, ignorance the most contemptible?

HIPPIAS: Of course, Socrates.

SOCRATES: Whoa there, my friend! I'm apprehensive about all this.

HIPPIAS: Why, Socrates? Your argument has made fine strides. b

SOCRATES: I hope so, but let's examine this point together: could *anything* be done with a total lack of the know-how and ability to do it?

HIPPIAS: Of course not.

SOCRATES: Therefore isn't it the case that even errors and unintentional misdeeds and actions[1] could never happen unless people were capable of them?[2]

HIPPIAS: Obviously.

SOCRATES: But people are capable of doing something thanks to ability – I mean, it couldn't be thanks to inability. c

HIPPIAS: No, of course it couldn't.

SOCRATES: Therefore every action is the result of the ability to do that action?

HIPPIAS: Yes.

SOCRATES: Bad actions and unintentional errors are far more common among humans than good ones, from childhood onwards.

HIPPIAS: True.

SOCRATES: Well then, shall we describe *this* ability as fine? Shall we say that things whose usefulness is to contribute towards some bad result are fine? Or would that be quite wrong? d

HIPPIAS: Quite wrong, I think, Socrates.

SOCRATES: Therefore, Hippias, ability and usefulness are apparently *not* fineness.

1. For Socrates on unintentional misdeeds, see *Hippias Minor*. But the full Socratic doctrine as corroborated there plays no part in *Hippias Major*: all that is happening here is that the idea of 'ability' is being extended to its full range.

2. This turn of the argument shows that the substitution of 'ability' for 'usefulness' is implausible: we would not say (and neither would a Greek) that error is the result of usefulness. The fact that, as Socrates has just argued, ability is a necessary prerequisite of usefulness does not justify the substitution. Plato's mistake is not serious, however; it merely makes more long-winded the argument that 'beneficial' is the proper reading of 'useful' in this context.

HIPPIAS: They are, if ability is ability for good, and usefulness contributes to that sort of result, Socrates.[1]

SOCRATES: Anyway, our original unqualified proposition, that ability and usefulness are fineness, has come to nothing. What about usefulness and ability for *good* action? Was this the definition of fineness that we actually had in the back of our minds, Hippias?

e   HIPPIAS: *I* think so.

SOCRATES: 'Beneficial' is another way of putting it, isn't it?

HIPPIAS: Certainly.

SOCRATES: In that case it's because they are beneficial that fine bodies, fine laws, expertise and everything we mentioned a short while ago are fine.

HIPPIAS: Obviously.

SOCRATES: Apparently, then, benefit is fineness, Hippias.

HIPPIAS: Absolutely, Socrates.

SOCRATES: Now, benefit is what produces good.

HIPPIAS: Yes.

SOCRATES: And a producer is the same as a cause, isn't it?

HIPPIAS: Yes.

SOCRATES: So fineness is a cause of goodness.

297a   HIPPIAS: Yes.

SOCRATES: Now a cause, Hippias, is different from that of which it is the cause. I mean, a cause can't be the cause of a cause.[2] Look at it this way: we have demonstrated that a cause is productive, haven't we?

HIPPIAS: Certainly.

SOCRATES: The product of a producer is only what is generated; it is not the producer.

HIPPIAS: True.

SOCRATES: Therefore what is generated is different from the producer.

HIPPIAS: Yes.

SOCRATES: Therefore a cause is not a cause of a cause, but of what is
b   generated by it.

HIPPIAS: Certainly.

SOCRATES: If, then, fineness is a cause of good, goodness would be generated by fineness. And it apparently follows that when we pursue

---

1. See p. 245 n. 1.

2. This would be patently false if read as 'A cause cannot be a cause of another cause.' It establishes, rather, what the notion of 'cause' implies: a cause is the cause of a *product* (which may, as it happens, be a further cause, but is a product in relation to its cause), which is *different from* its cause.

wisdom or any other fine thing, what's really stimulating us is its product or offspring, goodness. The conclusion seems to follow that fineness is in the position of father, as it were, of goodness.

HIPPIAS: Certainly. A fine argument, Socrates.

SOCRATES: Is *this* a fine argument too, that a father isn't his son, nor a son his father?

HIPPIAS: Yes.   c

SOCRATES: And a cause isn't its product, nor a product its cause?

HIPPIAS: True.

SOCRATES: Good heavens, my friend! Fineness, then, isn't good, nor is goodness fine. Don't you think that is ruled out by our argument?

HIPPIAS: Good heavens, yes, it seems so!

SOCRATES: Would we be prepared to deny, without qualms, that fineness is good and goodness fine?

HIPPIAS: Good heavens, no, not without considerable qualms.

SOCRATES: Good heavens, Hippias, I agree: I am less satisfied with this proposition than any other we've come up with.[1]   d

HIPPIAS: I don't doubt it.

SOCRATES: So instead of being the finest argument, as we thought before, the proposition that benefit is fine – that is, that usefulness and ability for good action are fine – seems likely to be more absurd than our first propositions, if that is possible, when we thought that the girl and our other earlier candidates were fineness.[2]

HIPPIAS: It seems so.

G. *Fineness as Aesthetic Pleasure*

The argument which is supposed (erroneously, as it happens) to refute this definition looks at first sight somewhat daunting, but is actually quite straightforward: it is simply long-winded and contains digressions. There are two crucial premisses: (1) the hypothesis that visual and auditory pleasures are fine; (2) the fact that the property of being fine is one which, if it obtains for a pair, also obtains for each member of that pair. It is argued that these two points are incompatible. The property of being visual and auditory only obtains for the pair, not for each member of the pair, as it would have to if the property in question were fineness; so the definition is rejected. The error here is confusing

1. Because Socrates assumes throughout, naturally enough, that fineness is good.

2. Strictly speaking (see p. 237), Hippias does not offer his girl as a *definition* of fineness. Nevertheless, in that section, Socrates did consider the consequences of taking such a thing to be fineness, so his summary here is not inaccurate.

'and' and 'and/or'. The original hypothesis used 'and' in the sense of 'and/or': visual and/or auditory pleasures are fine; hence it is agreed that each individually is fine as well as the pair (299c). But the later stages of the argument take 'visual and auditory' to join the two terms together inseparably.

Apart from this illogicality, there are two oddities about the argument. The first is its bare formality: if, as is agreed at the outset, both the pair of pleasures and each pleasure are fine, then the search for fineness is the search for the common feature responsible for their fineness (300a). But rather than pursue this, Plato rejects the hypothesis on purely formal (even if illogical) grounds.

Perhaps the reason for this is to be found in considering the second oddity, which is the restriction to aesthetic pleasure. At 298b–d Plato deliberately skates over more refined kinds of pleasure, which it is clear from other dialogues he would include as fine. In other words, the definition is at best only partial. So perhaps he is content with a purely formal rebuttal, partly because the definition is not offered seriously in the first place, but mainly because it raises the formal issue of unity of definition (see p. 227).

SOCRATES: Well, I don't know which way to turn any more, Hippias – I'm stuck. Do *you* have anything to say?

e HIPPIAS: Not just at the moment, but, as I said a little while ago, I'm sure I'll come up with something after I've thought it over.

SOCRATES: I think I'm too eager for knowledge to be able to bear the delay. And in fact I might have just made some headway. What about this idea? If we were to call 'fine' whatever gives us pleasure – I don't mean all pleasures, but auditory and visual ones[1] – could we defend that position
298a at all? It's certainly true, Hippias, that we get pleasure from seeing fine people, patterns, pictures and images, and that fine sounds, music in general, speeches and stories have the same effect. So, if we were to answer that insolent fellow by saying: 'Sir, fineness is auditory and visual pleasure', don't you think we'd check his insolence?

HIPPIAS: Well, *I* think that now you've given an excellent definition
b of fineness.

SOCRATES: But Hippias, will we claim that fine practices and laws are fine because they give auditory or visual pleasure? Or are they of a different type?[2]

HIPPIAS: Perhaps he'll overlook these cases, Socrates.

1. Aristotle, *Topics* 146a12 ff., probably has this passage of *Hippias Major* in mind: he mentions this attempted definition in agreeing with Socrates that definitions should be unitary.
2. It is surely not the giving of auditory or visual pleasure that justifies calling laws etc. fine.

SOCRATES: By the Dog,[1] Hippias, no, he won't, and he's the last person to whom I would want to talk rubbish and to pretend I have a point when I don't.

HIPPIAS: Who *is* he?

SOCRATES: The son of Sophroniscus, who would no more allow me to get away with these assertions as long as they remain unexamined than to talk as if I had knowledge that I don't have.[2]

c

HIPPIAS: Well in fact, since you mention it, I too think that laws are another story.

SOCRATES: Tread carefully, Hippias: we're in danger of imagining that we're making some headway, when in fact we've fallen into the same difficulty about fineness as just now.[3]

HIPPIAS: What do you mean, Socrates?

SOCRATES: I'll tell you my impression, for what it's worth. It's not impossible that laws and practices might turn out to be within the range of our sensations of hearing and sight; but let's leave aside the question of laws and go along with our account of fineness as pleasure which arises through these sensations. If our familiar adversary, or anyone else, were to ask us: 'Why, Hippias and Socrates, do you isolate *that* sort of pleasure as fine? Why are you denying that food, drink, sex and so on, which are pleasant to other senses, are fine? Are you denying that they are even pleasant – that is, are you saying that only sight and hearing involve pleasures?' What shall we reply, Hippias?

d

e

HIPPIAS: That the other senses too involve very great pleasures, Socrates, of course. That's altogether undeniable.

SOCRATES: 'Well then,' he'll ask, 'if they are all pleasures equally, why do you refuse the latter set the designation and not allow them to be fine?' 'Because,' we will reply, 'it would be utterly ridiculous to substitute "fine" for "pleasant" in the case of eating or a pleasant smell. As for sex, everyone would contend that, while it is extremely pleasant, it should be indulged in, if at all, in secret, because it is a highly contemptible sight.' To this, Hippias, he might perhaps rejoin: 'I too can see why you have an ingrained distaste for calling these pleasures fine, because people don't think they are. But I was asking you what *is* fine, not what is commonly held to be fine.' I imagine our response will be to restate our original hypothesis: '*Our* proposition is that the visual and auditory subset of pleasure is fine.'

299a

b

1. See p. 241 n. 1.

2. What Hippias appears not to know is that Sophroniscus was Socrates' father (see p. 242 n. 1). On Socrates' campaign against unexamined dogmas and pretence to knowledge, see especially *Apology* 21b ff.

3. 303e–304a makes it clear what Socrates is getting at.

Do you have an alternative way of handling the argument, Hippias? What else are we to say?

HIPPIAS: Nothing, Socrates: that's exactly the necessary response.

SOCRATES: 'A fine sentiment,' he'll say. 'Now, doesn't it obviously
c follow that if visual and auditory pleasure is fine, any other sort of pleasure is not fine?' Shall we agree?

HIPPIAS: Yes.

SOCRATES: 'Is visual pleasure aurally pleasant as well,' he'll ask, 'or auditory pleasure visually as well?' 'If we've understood your question,' we'll reply, 'the answer is "no": it's impossible for either of them to be doubly pleasant like that. Our proposition was that *both* of these pleasures are fine, and also that each of them is fine just as it is.' Won't that be our answer?

d HIPPIAS: Certainly.

SOCRATES: 'Does any pleasure, *qua* pleasure, differ from any other?' he'll ask. 'I don't mean in terms of intensity or degree, but do pleasures differ in the sense that one is, and another is not, a pleasure?' We think not, don't we?

HIPPIAS: Right.

SOCRATES: 'So,' he'll say, 'you gave preference to these pleasures for some reason other than just that they are pleasures, didn't you? You
e noticed that both of them differ from other pleasures in some respect, in virtue of which you are calling them fine. I mean, it is not, of course, *qua* visual that visual pleasure is fine: if that were the case, the other kind, auditory pleasure, could never be fine, since it isn't visual pleasure.' 'You're right,' we'll say, won't we?

HIPPIAS: Yes.

300a SOCRATES: 'Nor again is it *qua* auditory that auditory pleasure happens to be fine, which would debar visual pleasure from being fine, since it isn't auditory pleasure.' Shall we say that this is right, Hippias?

HIPPIAS: Yes.

SOCRATES: 'Now, your claim is that *both* are fine.' Yes?

HIPPIAS: Yes.

SOCRATES: 'So there is a common feature responsible for their being fine, which both of them share and each of them also has individually.
b Otherwise it wouldn't be the case that both are fine and that each is fine.' Give *me* your answer as if I were *him*.

HIPPIAS: Very well: I think you're right.

SOCRATES: So, if both of these pleasures have an attribute which neither of them has separately, then it wouldn't be thanks to *this* attribute that they are fine.

258

HIPPIAS: How could both have an attribute, Socrates – any actual attribute you like – which neither has separately?[1]

SOCRATES: Impossible, you think?   c

HIPPIAS: If it were possible, then I wouldn't have thorough experience of these matters and familiarity with the terms of the discussion.

SOCRATES: Pleasantly put, Hippias! Well, this must be nonsense, but I *think* there's a chance that I can perhaps see an example of what you say is impossible.

HIPPIAS: No chance, Socrates; you're obviously mistaken.

SOCRATES: Well actually, many examples come to my mind, but I distrust them, because they don't occur to you, and your expertise has earned you more money than anyone alive,[2] while I've earned nothing. In   d fact, so many striking examples occur to me that I'm wondering whether you're playing games with me, my friend, and tricking me on purpose.

HIPPIAS: You'll have finer knowledge than anyone whether or not I'm playing games, Socrates, when you try to describe these notions of yours and are shown to be talking nonsense. It's quite impossible – you'll never find an attribute which neither you nor I have, but which both of us have.

SOCRATES: Are you sure, Hippias? I suppose you've got a point, but   e *I* don't understand. Let me explain more clearly what I'm getting at: it seems to me that both of us together may possess as an attribute something which I neither have as an attribute nor am (and neither are you); and, to put it the other way round, that neither of us, as individuals, may be something which both of us together have as an attribute.

HIPPIAS: Socrates, this is apparently even more preposterous than the response you made a little while ago.[3] Look here: if both of us are just, then each of us must be too, surely? If each of us is unjust, aren't both too? If both are healthy, isn't each too? Or if each of us were tired,   301a wounded, bruised, or had any other attribute, then wouldn't both of us also have this attribute? Or again, if both of us happened to be golden, silver, ivory, or well-born, if you like, or clever, or respected – yes, or old or young or anything else which man can be, isn't there an overwhelming necessity that each of us would be too?

SOCRATES: Yes, absolutely.   b

1. To précis the following argument: Hippias is right, since he is taking 'both' in the sense of two separate things (so that, say, two small people are both – are a pair of – small people). Socrates understands 'both' in the same way in the case of 'fine', but also trades on the ambiguity of 'both' and takes it as a pair, considered as a distinct entity (so that two small people are *not* a small pair of people). Compare Aristotle, *Politics* 1261b 27–30, who may have our dialogue in mind.

2. See 282d–e.

3. I suppose that 300b is meant.

HIPPIAS: The fact of the matter is, Socrates, that you and your usual interlocutors fail to take account of things at the general level: your method of analysis is to *isolate* fineness or whatever it may be, and *dissect* it verbally; so of course these obvious points pass you by, and you fail to take account of the continuity of physical reality.[1] Your oversight in the present case is so great that you think there is some attribute or essential quality which obtains simultaneously for both the things we've been talking about, but

c not for each individually – or conversely, for each but not for both. How mindless, careless, senseless and thoughtless can you get![2]

SOCRATES: That's in keeping with the saw one keeps on hearing, Hippias: ability, not desire, dictates human achievement. But your constant criticism is helpful. I mean, just now, before your scolding about how foolishly we were conducting ourselves – well, shall I tell you even more

d of what we thought on this issue, or should I keep quiet?

HIPPIAS: Go ahead, if you want, Socrates, just so long as you understand that you'll be speaking to an expert: I know all the ways discussions are conducted.

SOCRATES: Yes, I *do* want to. You see, before you spoke, my friend, we were so inane as to believe that *each* of us – you and I – is one, but that both of us together, being two not one, are not what each individual is. See how stupid we were! But now we know better: you've explained that

e if both together are two, then each individual must be two as well; and if each individual is one, both must be one as well. I mean, that necessarily follows from Hippias' theory of 'continuous' reality, which entails that whatever both are, each is too, and vice versa. So here I sit, a new convert. Please refresh my memory, though, Hippias: are you and I one each or two each?

HIPPIAS: What do you mean, Socrates?

SOCRATES: Just what I said. If there's a lack of clarity, it's because I'm

302a wary of provoking you when you think you've made a good point. But still I must ask you again: isn't each of us one? Doesn't each of us have the attribute of being one?

HIPPIAS: Certainly.

---

1. Which, *qua* continuous, cannot be dissected. Given Socrates' reference to this theory below (301e), it seems to have been a genuine theory of the historical Hippias, though the details are uncertain and this interpretation of our passage controversial. (Morgan uncovers as much of the theory as the text can reveal – and perhaps a little more.) Some theory of 'the continuity of physical reality' might also serve to justify an orator's preference for general *epideixeis* rather than precise *elenchos* (on these terms see pp. 29–32). See also *Hippias Minor* 369b–c.

2. Note the typical rhetorical accumulation of rhyming words.

SOCRATES: So each of us, *qua* one, must also be numerically odd – or don't you think that one is odd?

HIPPIAS: I do.

SOCRATES: Are both the two of us together odd as well, then?

HIPPIAS: Impossible, Socrates.

SOCRATES: In fact we're even, aren't we?

HIPPIAS: Certainly.

SOCRATES: Surely the fact that both of us together are even doesn't make each of us individually even, does it?

HIPPIAS: Of course not.　　　　　　　　　　　　　　　　　　b

SOCRATES: There *can*, then, contrary to your recent assertion, be no absolute necessity that each of us is what both are, and vice versa.

HIPPIAS: Yes, in those sorts of cases, but not in the ones I was talking about before.

SOCRATES: That's all I need, Hippias: it's enough that sometimes the one thing is obviously the case, sometimes the other. You see, if you remember the origin of this discussion, I was saying that visual and auditory pleasures cannot be fine thanks to some attribute they *each* have but don't together, or *both* have but don't individually, but rather thanks to 　c
what they both have together *and* each has individually, because you agreed that they are both fine together and that each individually is fine. That is why I thought that if they are both fine, it must be thanks to an essential quality which applies to *both* of them, rather than thanks to something which one or the other of them lacks. And I haven't changed my mind. So go back to the beginning, as it were: if visual and auditory pleasures are fine together and individually, then doesn't the cause of their 　d
fineness apply to them together *and* individually?

HIPPIAS: Certainly.

SOCRATES: Can it be the fact that they are each and both pleasure that is responsible for their being fine? Wouldn't that imply that all other pleasures are no less fine, since, if you remember,[1] we demonstrated that all pleasures are equally pleasures?

HIPPIAS: I remember.

SOCRATES: Instead we claimed that they are fine because they are visual and auditory.　　　　　　　　　　　　　　　　　　e

HIPPIAS: Yes, we did.

SOCRATES: Now, make sure I get this right. If my memory serves me well, the idea was that only the visual and auditory aspect of pleasure is fine.

HIPPIAS: That's right.

1. See 299d.

SOCRATES: Now this attribute[1] only applies to both the senses, doesn't it, not to each individually? I mean, as I said before, it's not that each *individual* pleasure is caused by both the senses together, but the *pair* of both pleasures together (not each individually) is caused by both the senses together.[2] Isn't that the case?

HIPPIAS: Yes.

SOCRATES: Therefore, *this* is not what is responsible for each being fine, since it doesn't apply to each of them (for 'both' does not apply to each); therefore we may say *ex hypothesi* that *both* are fine, but not that each is fine. Aren't we forced to that conclusion?

303a

HIPPIAS: I suppose so.

SOCRATES: Are we to say, then, that both together are fine, but each individually isn't?

HIPPIAS: I don't see any reason why we shouldn't.

SOCRATES: I think *I* do, my friend: didn't we find that some things – all the ones which *you* specified[3] – when they are added to particular things, are such that if both have them, so does each, and vice versa?

HIPPIAS: Yes.

SOCRATES: But the same wasn't true for all the ones *I* specified, among which were precisely 'each' and 'both'. Right?

HIPPIAS: Yes.

b   SOCRATES: In which class do you think fineness is, Hippias? Does it belong among the things *you* mentioned? If you and I are each strong or just, so are we both; and if we both are, so is each of us. Is this also true for fineness, so that if you and I are each fine, so are we both, and vice versa? Or could an allowable analogy be even or irrational numbers, or any of the thousands of cases which I said seemed clear to me? An even number is the sum of either two odd or two even numbers; two irrationals can make either rational or irrational numbers.[4] In which category do you locate fineness? I wonder if you agree with my impression, which is that,

1. Here the property of being 'visual and auditory' is called an attribute (*pathos*); at 302c it was called an essential property (*ousia*). The fact that these two terms are used interchangeably (*pace Euthyphro* 11a) need not lead us to regard the dialogue as not a genuine Platonic composition.

2. That is, a visual pleasure is not visual-and-auditory ('caused by both the senses together'); only visual *and* auditory pleasures are caused by both the senses together.

3. 300e–301a.

4. It has been universally denied by the commentators that the sum of two irrationals is ever rational, and various explanations have been given for Plato's confident statement, of which the most plausible are that 'irrational' was a wider term in his day; or that he has suddenly switched from talking of sums to talking of products; or simply that he is making a mistake. But in fact, for example, the sum of $(\sqrt{2}-1)$, which is irrational, and $(3-\sqrt{2})$, which is also irrational, is the rational number 2 (my thanks to Peter Thomas).

as in all other similar cases, the idea that both of us may be fine without each of us being fine as well, or vice versa, is quite untenable. Do you agree with my impression, or prefer the alternative?

HIPPIAS: I agree with you, Socrates.

SOCRATES: Good – that ends our inquiry, Hippias. If fineness belongs to that category, then visual and auditory pleasure can't be fine, since   d being visual *and* auditory can only make *both* fine, not each individually, and this, as you conceded to me, Hippias, is unacceptable.

HIPPIAS: Yes, we're agreed on that.

SOCRATES: So it is impossible that visual and auditory pleasure is fine, since that generates an impossible consequence.

HIPPIAS: True.

H. *Epilogue*

The discussion of aesthetic pleasures is allowed to trickle on by restating the important point, raised but neglected in the previous section, that rather than a purely formal rejection of the definition, the search should be for the common feature which makes these pleasures fine. It has already been agreed in the previous section that the common feature cannot simply be that they are both pleasures, because common sense (and argument elsewhere, e.g. Republic IX, Philebus) dictates that not all pleasures are fine and that aesthetic pleasures are somehow superior to others. So what is left? Only that they are 'inoffensive'. Socrates equates inoffensive with 'beneficial', which is the fallacy of confusing a contradictory with a contrary: something inoffensive is not necessarily beneficial, just as something not hot is not necessarily cold. But given this equation he can reject the new definition of fineness as beneficial pleasure by referring back to Section F, where the idea that fineness is benefit was thrown out.

Finally, in the persons of Hippias and Socrates, Plato briefly contrasts the concern of the sophists with fame and politics with the Socratic search for the truth. The lesson he wants us to learn from this dialogue, as from other early dialogues, is that we use words like 'fine' as if we knew their meaning, when we do not. This pretence to knowledge is the chief target of Socrates, since it closes doors: his mission was to reopen them, to allow active searching to continue.

SOCRATES: 'You'd better start again,' he'll say, 'since you've got nowhere so far. How do you define this fineness which both pleasures   e have, thanks to which you elevated them above other pleasures with the title "fine"?' I think we're bound to say, Hippias, that they, together and individually, are the most inoffensive pleasures and the best. Can you specify any other reason for their difference from other pleasures?

HIPPIAS: No, they really are the best.

SOCRATES: 'In other words,' he'll say, 'are you defining fineness as beneficial pleasure?' 'I suppose we are,' I'll reply. What about you?

HIPPIAS: Yes, I too.

SOCRATES: 'Now, benefit is what causes goodness,' he'll say, 'and we found recently that the cause and the product are different: doesn't this thesis of yours come up against the earlier argument that, since each of them is different, goodness can't be fine and fineness can't be good?'[1] 'You're absolutely right,' we'll reply, Hippias, if we have any sense. I mean, it's inexcusable to disagree with a correct idea.

HIPPIAS: Listen, Socrates. This is all picking and whittling at words, as I said before – just splitting hairs. What else do you suppose it is? But the ability eloquently to deliver such a fine speech to the court, Council or whichever official body the speech is being delivered to, that you win them over and carry off not the most trivial but the greatest of all prizes – the preservation of yourself, your property and your friends[2] – *this* is both fine and valuable, and is what you should concentrate on. Forget all this nitpicking: if you continue to get involved in trivial nonsense, you'll end up with a reputation for extreme stupidity.

SOCRATES: Hippias my friend, you *are* a lucky fellow, both because you know what people should occupy themselves with, and because you've done it all already – or so you say. But I am apparently held back by some supernatural bad luck, which makes me wander around in perpetual perplexity, and when I display my perplexity to you clever people – well, when I do so, all I get is abuse from you. I mean, you all tell me, as you too have just been telling me, that what I'm involved in is silly, petty and worthless. But the problem is that once you've convinced me and I repeat your idea, that by far the most important thing is the ability eloquently to accomplish the delivery of a fine speech in court or any other assembly, I get every kind of abuse from whoever I'm with, but especially from this constant inquisitor of mine – constant, because he happens to be a very close relative and to share the same house. So when I go home and he hears what I have to say, he asks me if I am not ashamed of my effrontery in discussing fine occupations, when questioning shows how obviously

304a

b

c

d

---

1. See 296e–297c.

2. At *Gorgias* 486a–c, Callicles argues, in language similar to Hippias' here, that Socrates and his philosophy would be ineffective in court – as actually happened, of course. The emphasis on court cases reflects the litigiousness of Athens at the time, and is one reason for the popularity of the sophists' teaching of rhetoric.

ignorant I am even about what fineness itself is. 'And yet,' he continues, 'how can you know whose speech or other action is finely formed, if you're ignorant about fineness? Don't you think you might as well be dead, in such a condition?' The upshot is, as I say, that I get slandered and abused not only by you, but by him too. But perhaps I should put up with it all – I wouldn't be surprised if it did me good. I think, Hippias, that I *have* benefited from my conversation with the two of you, in the sense that I understand the meaning of the proverb, 'Anything fine is difficult.'[1]

1. The proverb possibly originated with Solon (see p. 96 n. 1), to whom, however, many apocryphal proverbs were attributed: he was another of the seven Wise Men (see p. 232 n. 3).

INTRODUCTION TO *HIPPIAS MINOR*

Hippias Minor is a simple dialogue, in the sense that it deals with a single area of Socratic thought – in fact, does so very methodically – without throwing up ramifications such as we had to consider with regard to *Hippias Major*. The arguments which constitute the dialogue are discussed in the running commentaries that precede each section of the text. In this introduction it only remains to consider whether or not Plato believes the paradoxical conclusions of the dialogue, that the liar and the truthful person are the same, and that the deliberate criminal is morally better than the unwitting one.

In the background of the work are the two so-called Socratic paradoxes: 'Virtue is knowledge' and 'No one does wrong deliberately'. For a fuller exposition of these propositions see pp. 23–8, with Irwin, Chapter 3, Santas, Chapters 6–7 or Mackenzie, Chapter 9. It will be convenient to base my brief exposition on Socrates' analogy between virtue and the various crafts and abilities, since this is so prominent in *Hippias Minor*; all the crucial arguments are inferences from what obtains for various functional abilities to what obtains for morality.

The 'craft analogy', as it is known, is central to Socrates' moral thought. Throughout the early Platonic dialogues he is portrayed searching for definitions of moral properties. He believes that correct definitions will stand as paradigms to enable him to recognize true instances of the property in question, and similarly he seeks, or bemoans the lack of, an expert in morality. Virtue, then, is analogous to the crafts in the sense that, just as they have functions whose success or failure is measurable, so too the proper definition of a virtue will enable one to measure one's own or others' actions; and craft is the prime area where experts may be found with the technical and teaching abilities of the order Socrates requires in the moral expert. Herein lies the first Socratic paradox, 'Virtue is knowledge', which means that virtue is craft-knowledge.

The main weakness (but see also p. 171) of the craft analogy that is relevant to *Hippias Minor* is the question of abuse. A craftsman achieves a result, but it is beyond the province of the craftsman simply *qua* craftsman to guarantee that the result is used, by himself or by others, for good or ill. But by definition virtue must be used well, so the analogy totters.

267

How could Socrates argue that virtue is always used well? The most obvious line of argument would be the Aristotelian one that the virtuous man naturally desires or chooses good (see also Xenophon, *Memorabilia*, III. 9.5). But we see in *Hippias Minor* that Socrates ignores this possibility (see pp. 277, 288). There is no sign that he does so consciously, but it is arguable that he does, for, since such desire or choice cannot be a matter of the technical ability of a craftsman (it is something extraneous to craft), if Socrates had taken this line of argument, he would be relegating the craft analogy to the sidelines of his thought, rather than having it occupy a central position.

The more abstruse line of argument to which Socrates is committed, if he is to retain the craft analogy, is that knowledge is by itself sufficient for virtue – no extra desire or choice is required (*pace* Santas). Anyone with the relevant knowledge (which is knowledge of what is good and bad for oneself) will be virtuous. Herein lies the second Socratic paradox: 'No one does wrong deliberately' means that anyone only does wrong by mistaking where his good really lies; everyone aims for their own good and, given knowledge, would attain it. (On *eudaimonia*, the *summum bonum* according to Socrates, and whether virtue is instrumental to it, or actually constitutes it, see pp. 25–7.) The doctrine that knowledge (craft-knowledge) is sufficient for virtue lies within the parameters of the craft analogy.

Even with this brief introduction to the background, we should be in a position to decide whether or not Plato believes the paradoxical conclusions of *Hippias Minor*. Either view is in fact *prima facie* plausible, depending on which of the two Socratic paradoxes is stressed. If one stresses that virtue is craft-knowledge and, as Socrates argues, that all such abilities are abilities for good or ill, then it is arguable that it is the virtuous person, who has the ability, who is the most effective liar or criminal. On the other hand, if one stresses that *no one* does wrong deliberately, then it must follow that Plato disbelieves the conclusion which states that someone – in this case paradoxically the virtuous person – does wrong deliberately. In this case *Hippias Minor* must be seen as a *reductio ad absurdum* of the idea that wrong can be knowingly committed.

It is curious to see the two paradoxes ranged against each other in this way, when, as described previously, they were just two sides of the same coin: virtue is knowledge, therefore no one can knowingly do wrong. Probably a correct interpretation of the dialogue should not only produce evidence for which of the alternative views of Plato's commitment to the conclusions is correct, but also argue that the Socratic paradoxes are *not* contradictory in this way – unless *Plato* is drawing out inconsistencies in *Socrates'* thought; but this is unlikely since, in some form or other, Plato adheres to the Socratic paradoxes throughout his life.

Support for the view that Plato – or, in this instance, Socrates as reported by Plato – is prepared to accept the paradoxical conclusion, that the deliberate wrongdoer is better than the alternative, seems to come from Xenophon, *Memorabilia* IV.2.8–23, where Socrates argues that intentional injustice is possible only for a just person. But if we take this as evidence to show that Socrates accepted the paradoxical conclusion, we come up against *Hippias Minor* 376b, where Socrates cannot accept it.

Lest this develop into an impasse, it must immediately be noticed that Xenophon and Plato can be reconciled, and a correct interpretation of the dialogue be reached, because the conclusion in *Hippias Minor* is hypothetical: *if* a deliberate criminal were to exist, he would be a virtuous person. In other words, while it is true, as Xenophon reports, that intentional justice is only possible for a just person, nevertheless a just person who deliberately commits injustice cannot be found; so no one does wrong deliberately. The argument is a *reductio ad absurdum*: the conclusion supports the Socratic paradox by showing the idea of deliberate criminality to be absurd.

What about the other Socratic paradox, which, as we have seen, could have led Plato to endorse the conclusion of the dialogue? Given the interpretation that Plato could not accept a non-hypothetical version of the conclusion of the dialogue, and thereby supports the Socratic dictum that no one goes wrong deliberately, do we have to go further and interpret the dialogue as critical of the other Socratic dictum that virtue is knowledge? It does not seem to me that he is criticizing this dictum: at most he is testing the limits of the craft analogy which Socrates uses in conjunction with it. He is saying that moral knowledge is different from other crafts in that it cannot be used for ill. This limit, Plato seems to say, is necessary within Socrates' thought, and the doctrine that knowledge is sufficient for virtue effectively embodies it. Similarly, at *Republic* 331e–336a, Plato has Socrates argue that justice differs from other crafts in that the just man is unable to do wrong.

The extent of this reflection on the craft analogy must not exaggeratedly be called criticism, as it often is. Plato is by no means damning the craft analogy. We can still maintain that in *Hippias Minor* he accepts it *in toto*: all crafts have the ability for good or ill in their sphere; morality has the same ability, but in its case the ability will simply not be put to bad use, and the deliberate criminal remains hypothetical. In this sense, while the conclusion of *Hippias Minor* is unacceptable, yet as a *hypothetical* conclusion it is acceptable. As Penner puts it, Socrates is saying that 'justice is simply a very unusual art' (p. 144). If Plato were rejecting the craft analogy, he would presumably be aware that he was doing so, since he is aware of the paradoxical nature of the conclusion and how it is reached; and even if we accept the wider consequence that he would in effect be rejecting a core of Socrates' thought, we should also have to accept that he employs some grossly fallacious argumentation in order to do so, in particular the fallacy of *secundum quid*. But as I argue on p. 288, this fallacy is not present in a vicious form, and we can see why: because in *Hippias Minor* Plato maintains that virtue is a craft, something one can be good at.

We have seen, then, that Plato does not accept the final paradoxical conclusion of the dialogue (except in so far as it is hypothetical). What about the interim paradox at the end of Section B, that the liar and the truthful person are the same? It would be simple to say that in so far as this entails that the deliberate liar is superior to the unconscious liar, and is meant to support the main conclusion of the dialogue, Plato believes it to be as unacceptable as the main conclusion. But, surprisingly, we should pause before rushing into this interpretation. We should always be wary of imposing on Plato our own view that honesty is an integral part of morality. It is instructive to turn to *Republic* 382a–d, where the ignorant liar is disparagingly distinguished from the conscious liar (see also *Republic* 535e), and where Plato approves of judicious use of deliberate lies.

The conclusion of Section B, however, is quite different from this. If the argument of Section B had been couched entirely in terms of ability, then the conclusion would be that the person with the *ability* to lie is better than the person who is unable to lie (or tell the truth, for that matter); this would square with what is said in *Republic*, and it would not be clear that Plato would reject such a notion. But, as I argue on p. 277, the conclusion is meant to be more radical than that: it is that someone who deliberately *exercises* his talent for deceit is better than one who does not. This goes way beyond what is said in *Republic*: such regular deceit is not merely judicious use of deliberate lies, but something as immoral and unacceptable as the final conclusion of the dialogue. Hippias' disapproving attitude towards deceit reflects not just common Greek morality, but Plato's views too; the conclusion is unacceptable all round.

Finally, what shall we make of the dialogue as a whole? It comes across as somewhat naïve, which is a reason for dating it as one of the earliest Platonic pieces (written *c.* 395–390). The Socratic paradoxes require psychological, not just logical, justification: it needs to be argued, for instance (as it is in *Protagoras* and *Gorgias*), that passion never overcomes reason, so that it can fairly be claimed that no one desires wrong. *Gorgias* 467c ff., in particular, with its distinction of means and ends in relation to an individual's intention, is an important advance. But this sort of psychological analysis would have led to the Aristotelian position of taking desire into consideration, and we have seen (p. 268) that this would be detrimental to the craft analogy. It is worth mentioning, however, that Santas does attribute this Aristotelian position to Socrates, and that one consequence of this would be to relieve *Hippias Minor* of all major fallacies, because he would not be confusing being morally good with being good at something. But there is no evidence in the dialogue that Socrates included desire in his purview. We must count this over-emphasis on man's intellect as a central defect in Socrates' moral thought, although, as Dihle records, this rationalism was shared by many Greek thinkers who tackled the problem of will. It is significant that later in his life, in *Republic*, Plato felt impelled to part company with Socrates on this issue: Plato's triadic analysis of the 'soul' acknowledges that emotion can defeat reason.

SUMMARY OF *HIPPIAS MINOR*

HIPPIAS MINOR

Speakers

SOCRATES

HIPPIAS: From Elis in the Peloponnese. Born *c.* 470, died *c.* 395 – in other words, a more or less exact contemporary of Socrates. He was a prominent sophist, offering tuition in a vast range of subjects (see *Hippias Major* 285c–e, *Hippias Minor* 368b–d, *Protagoras* 318d–319a).

EUDICUS: Son of Apemantus; also mentioned at *Hippias Major* 286b, but otherwise unknown. Probably an Athenian gentleman and patron of the sophists.

HIPPIAS MINOR

A. Introduction

The introductory conversation is remarkable only for its glimpses of the scene at a sophistic lecture (compare Protagoras), and for its evidence about the intellectual side of the Olympic Games. Any Greek could attend the Olympic festival, which was one of the most important panhellenic occasions. It was, then, an easy opportunity for the itinerant and cosmopolitan sophists to find a suitable audience ready made. It is likely that the sophists used to engage in formal debates there, as part of a regular competition to be judged by the audience; the rhapsodic contests mentioned at Ion 530a–b provide a parallel. Protagoras is said to have instituted such debates (Diogenes Laertius IX. 52); we hear of Gorgias speaking there (Philostratus, Lives of the Sophists I.9.5); and Lysias XXXIII.2 implies that lectures, at any rate, were a regular feature. The winner in such debates was the one who, within a set time-limit, refuted his opponent or reduced him to fallacy, paradox, solecism or babbling (Aristotle, De Sophisticis Elenchis 165b12–22). See the brilliant but sometimes fanciful account of such 'eristic moots' by Ryle.

Hippias' oratory and arrogance are as prominent as in Hippias Major, and Socrates' response is the same badinage. The introduction, taken with Hippias' ineffectiveness in the rest of the dialogue, portrays him as a capable orator, but unable to cope with hard argument.

EUDICUS: Why on earth don't you have anything to say, Socrates, after Hippias' magnificent lecture?[1] Don't you find anything in his talk to praise, like the rest of us, or even to argue against, if there's something you're dissatisfied with? You needn't worry: those of us who might have the best claim to an interest in philosophical discussion are on our own now.

SOCRATES: Well, Eudicus, it's true that there *are* some questions I'd be glad to ask Hippias in connection with what he was just saying about Homer. I remember Apemantus, your father, saying that the *Iliad* was a finer poem of Homer's than the *Odyssey*, to the extent that Achilles is

363a

b

---

1. On *epideixis* see pp. 32 and 215. Given Eudicus' presence and *Hippias Major* 286b, this is probably meant to be the lecture there promised by Hippias. If so, it seems from 364c that Nestor's advice to Neoptolemus included emulation of Achilles and avoidance of Odysseus' example. Compare, perhaps, Prodicus' 'The Choice of Heracles', preserved by Xenophon (*Memorabilia* II.1.21–34).

better than Odysseus – he claimed that Achilles was the subject of the one poem, Odysseus of the other. So, if Hippias doesn't mind, I'd love to pursue that topic and find out his thoughts on these two men – which does

c he say is better? For he's already lectured to us at length on all sorts of other topics in poetry, especially Homer.

EUDICUS: Of course Hippias won't refuse to answer any question of yours. You'll answer Socrates' questions, Hippias, won't you?

HIPPIAS: It would be monstrous of me to evade Socrates' questions, Eudicus. After all, every time the Olympic Games are on, I leave my home

d in Elis and go to Olympia,[1] to the sacred precinct there, and make myself available to the assembled company of all the Greeks, to expound any subject on which I've got a lecture prepared, and to answer any question: anyone only has to ask.[2]

364a SOCRATES: What a happy feeling, Hippias, to enter the sacred precinct at every Olympic festival with such confidence in your mental expertise. I very much doubt that any athlete goes there to compete with such sanguine confidence in his physical prowess as you claim you have in your intelligence.

HIPPIAS: Naturally that's how I feel, Socrates: ever since I began to compete at Olympia, I have never been up against anyone who could beat me at anything.

b SOCRATES: What a splendid ornament to Elis, and to your family, your reputation for wisdom must be, Hippias! But come, tell us about Achilles and Odysseus. Which of them do you think is better, and in what respect? You see, when you were delivering your lecture to the crowd of us indoors, I got a bit lost, since I didn't want to question you – there were so many people in there, for one thing, and also I thought my questions would have interrupted your lecture. But now that there are fewer of us, I ask

c you, at Eudicus' instigation, to explain clearly what you were saying about these two men. On what grounds were you distinguishing them?

B. *Achilles and Odysseus*

The aim of this section is to argue for the paradox that the truthful person and the liar are one and the same. When faced with a paradoxical conclusion such

---

1. Olympia was in the district of Elis.

2. This paragraph is all a single sentence in the Greek, typically rhetorical in the periodic style. See p. 232 n. 6 for Hippias as an orator. Gorgias too (*Meno* 70b–c, *Gorgias* 447c–448a) claimed to answer any question that was put to him; *Protagoras* 315c is further evidence for Hippias' doing this.

as this, we must ask three questions: How good is the argument? Is the paradox radical or only apparent? Does the author believe it? The answers hinge on a single issue: is the argument conducted entirely in terms of ability to lie and tell the truth? If it is, as has been argued by Weiss, then (a) the argument does not equivocate between taking a liar as one who habitually tells lies, and one who is merely capable of telling lies; (b) the paradox is defused since the conclusion says no more than that ability to lie and tell the truth go together; and (c), given (b), there is no reason for Plato to disbelieve the conclusion.

Unfortunately (because it is an attempt to salvage the argument), but fortunately (because it trivializes the conclusion – indeed, there would be no reason for Hippias to object to it as he does), this interpretation can only be maintained at some distance from the text. Hippias introduces the terms of the argument at 365b as indicative of Achilles' and Odysseus' characters: they are, respectively, characteristically or habitually honest and deceitful. Socrates proceeds to introduce the notion of ability and bolsters it up with a series of arguments from analogy, but reverts at the end of each analogy, and at the conclusion to the whole series, to talk of disposition, not ability: in each case he says '. . . is a liar', not '. . . is capable of deceit'. In other words, while it is true that he is talking about successful lying (see especially 366e–367a), and that therefore the arguments from ability are relevant, the conclusion concerns not just someone with the ability to lie, but someone who regularly and habitually exercises this talent. It follows, then, that while each stage of the argument may be strong in itself (and see Santas, pp. 148–50), the conclusion falls foul of the Aristotelian criticism that someone who has the ability to lie may – in fact, invariably will – choose not to exercise this ability (see Nicomachean Ethics 1127b14–17). It also follows that Plato intends the conclusion to be radical, not trivial, since it is couched in terms of habit. My answer to the remaining question – whether Plato believes the paradox – is 'no', as argued on p. 270.

HIPPIAS: All right, Socrates. I don't mind going through my views both on them and on others even more clearly than before. My claim is that of those who went to Troy, Homer portrayed Achilles as the best, Nestor as the cleverest, and Odysseus as the most complex.

SOCRATES: Well, bless me, Hippias![1] Now, would you do me a favour? Please don't laugh at me if I'm a bit slow at understanding what you say and keep asking questions, but try to be tolerant and considerate as you   d answer them.

HIPPIAS: It would be monstrous behaviour on my part, Socrates, to educate others on these very points and to think that I deserve payment for it, and then not to be patient and tolerant in answering your questions.

1. Said ironically: there is nothing surprising in Hippias' statement.

SOCRATES: That's very good of you. You see, I thought I understood your claim that Achilles is portrayed as the best and Nestor as the cleverest in the poems, but, to tell the truth, I completely fail to understand what you mean by saying that the poet portrayed Odysseus as the most complex.[1] Perhaps I'll understand it better if you answer this question: isn't Homer's Achilles complex?

HIPPIAS: Not at all, Socrates: he's the most straightforward, honest character. In the *Prayers*[2] Homer makes them converse with each other and Achilles (as the poet has it) says to Odysseus:

365a Great god-born son of Laertes, crafty Odysseus, I must tell you outright precisely what I will do and intend to accomplish. For I hate as I hate the gates of Hades the
b man who conceals one thing in his heart while saying another. So I will tell you what will come to pass.

In these lines the poet reveals each man's character, since it's Achilles he has speaking them to Odysseus: Achilles is honest and straightforward, while Odysseus is complex and deceitful.

SOCRATES: *Now* I think I see what you mean, Hippias. By 'complex' you seem to mean 'deceitful'.

c HIPPIAS: Certainly, Socrates: that's how Homer portrays Odysseus in many places in both the *Iliad* and the *Odyssey*.

SOCRATES: I suppose, then, that Homer distinguished between honest and deceitful people, as not being the same.

HIPPIAS: Of course, Socrates.

SOCRATES: And that's your opinion too, Hippias?

HIPPIAS: Most certainly: it would be monstrous to think otherwise.

SOCRATES: Well, let's leave Homer out of this, since it's impossible to
d question him about his poetic intentions in these lines;[3] but you can answer for Homer as well as yourself, since you're obviously undertaking the responsibility of doing so, and you agree with Homer's words as you see them.

HIPPIAS: All right; hurry up and ask whatever you want.

1. The word translated 'complex' (*polutropos*) is used by Homer to describe Odysseus at the very beginning of the *Odyssey*, as well as elsewhere, though in Homer it may mean no more than 'versatile' or even simply 'much-travelled'.

2. In Plato's time the Homeric poems had not yet been divided up into books, which was done by Alexandrian scholars in the second century B.C. Instead, sections of the poems were referred to by content. The *Prayers* refers primarily to *Iliad* IX, 502 ff., where they are personified, but by extension also to the surrounding material: here Hippias quotes *Iliad* IX, 308–13 (without line 311).

3. Compare *Protagoras* 347b ff., in a similar situation, when Socrates has been burlesquing the sophists' literary studies. Generally, Socrates always requires his interlocutors to state and test their own firm beliefs, not to hide behind any aliases (cf. p. 31).

SOCRATES: Would you say that deceitful people are capable of action or, like invalids, incapable?

HIPPIAS: Extremely capable, I would say, especially at deceiving people.

SOCRATES: So your opinion, apparently, is that they are capable as well   e
as complex. Is that right?

HIPPIAS: Yes.

SOCRATES: Is it inane stupidity or a kind of unscrupulous wisdom which makes them complex and deceitful?

HIPPIAS: Unscrupulous wisdom – no doubt about it.

SOCRATES: Apparently, then, they are wise.

HIPPIAS: Yes indeed, too wise.

SOCRATES: If wise, do they know what they are doing, or not?

HIPPIAS: They know very well; that is why they are unscrupulous.

SOCRATES: Given this knowledge, are they ignorant or clever?

HIPPIAS: Clever, of course, at least in their sphere, deception.   366a

SOCRATES: Wait a minute. Let's review what you're saying: liars are capable, wise, knowledgeable and clever at their falsehoods?

HIPPIAS: Yes.

SOCRATES: And liars are different from honest people – quite the opposite, in fact?

HIPPIAS: Yes.

SOCRATES: Well then, your view is apparently that liars are to be ranked among capable, clever people.[1]

HIPPIAS: Right.

SOCRATES: In saying that liars are capable and clever at precisely their   b
lying, do you mean that they are capable or incapable of these lies of theirs in some situation when they choose?

HIPPIAS: Capable, in my opinion.

SOCRATES: So, to sum up, liars are those who are clever and are capable of lying.

HIPPIAS: Yes.

SOCRATES: So someone who is incapable of lying and is ignorant could not be a liar.

HIPPIAS: Right.

SOCRATES: Now, ability is doing what you want, when you want – as you, for example, are able to write my name when you want. Leaving

---

1. Notice how Socrates exploits the neutrality of 'ability' and 'intelligence'; as introduced by Hippias neither was neutral but meant 'ability *to lie*' and 'clever *at lying*', but Socrates will argue that ability assumes ability for both good and ill.

c aside exceptional factors like illness, which may limit action, wouldn't you call that 'ability'?

HIPPIAS: Yes.

SOCRATES: Now, tell me, Hippias, you're proficient at arithmetic, surely, aren't you?

HIPPIAS: Particularly proficient, Socrates.[1]

SOCRATES: So if you were asked what 3 × 700 is, you would produce the true answer particularly quickly, wouldn't you, if you wanted?

d HIPPIAS: Of course.

SOCRATES: Because your expertise and ability at it are outstanding?

HIPPIAS: Yes.

SOCRATES: And are you merely extremely clever and capable, or are you also particularly *good* at what you are extremely clever at – arithmetic, that is?

HIPPIAS: Yes, of course I'm particularly good, Socrates.

SOCRATES: So you have a pre-eminent ability to speak the truth in arithmetic, don't you?

e HIPPIAS: *I* think so.

SOCRATES: And what about lies on the same subject? Please carry on with your frank and generous answers, Hippias. Suppose you're asked how much 3 × 700 is and you want to lie – in fact, continually to refrain from the true answer. Would *you* always be the superlative, consistent liar
367a about it, or would an ignoramus about arithmetic be better at lying about arithmetic than you, if you chose to? Wouldn't the ignoramus often be misled by his ignorance and unwittingly tell the truth, if he stumbled on it, despite his intention to lie, while you, the expert, if you wanted to lie, could always do so consistently?

HIPPIAS: Yes, you're right.

SOCRATES: So is arithmetic a subject in which a liar cannot lie, although he can in other cases?

HIPPIAS: No, he can certainly lie about arithmetic.

SOCRATES: May we further assume, then, Hippias, the existence of a liar about arithmetic?

b HIPPIAS: Yes.

SOCRATES: What would he be like? Doesn't he have to have the *ability* to deceive, if he's going to be a liar? You conceded this a short while ago

---

1. This is not an empty boast: Proclus, *Commentary on the First Book of Euclid's Elements*, 272.7 and 356.11 (Friedlein's pagination), implies that Hippias discovered the quadratrix, a curve used for trisection of an angle and for attempts to square the circle.

when you said that he who *cannot* lie will never become a liar.[1] Do you remember?

HIPPIAS: Yes, I do remember that being said.

SOCRATES: Now, didn't you just now turn out to be pre-eminently capable of lying about arithmetic?

HIPPIAS: Yes, that's another point that came up.

SOCRATES: And aren't you also pre-eminently capable of telling the c truth about arithmetic?

HIPPIAS: Certainly.

SOCRATES: So pre-eminent ability to tell both lies and the truth about arithmetic go hand in hand – the same person, the arithmetician, who is good at the subject, has them both.

HIPPIAS: Yes.

SOCRATES: So it turns out that, thanks to his ability, only a good arithmetician is a liar about arithmetic, doesn't it? And he is also the one who is honest.

HIPPIAS: I suppose so.

SOCRATES: Do you realize, then, that both lying and honesty in this subject reside in the same person; an honest person is not *better* than a liar – he can't be, because he is the *same* person, and is not in exactly the d opposite position, as you supposed a short while ago.[2]

HIPPIAS: I suppose you're right, in *this* instance, at any rate.

SOCRATES: Do you want us to look at other areas too, then?

HIPPIAS: If *you* do.

SOCRATES: All right; are you proficient at geometry too?

HIPPIAS: I am.

SOCRATES: Well, isn't it the case in geometry too that the same person, the geometer, is supremely capable of telling both lies and the truth about his diagrams?

HIPPIAS: Yes.

SOCRATES: And the geometer is the one who is good at the subject?

HIPPIAS: Yes.   e

SOCRATES: So the good, clever geometer is supremely capable in *both* respects, isn't he? Since he is capable of lying about diagrams, then if there *is* a liar in this subject, it is he, isn't it, the one who is good – because someone bad, as we found, is *incapable* of lying? So this reaffirms our earlier conclusion that he who cannot lie will never become a liar.

1. 366b.
2. 366a.

HIPPIAS: Yes, true.

SOCRATES: Well, let's round off the investigation with astronomy, an area of expertise in which you consider yourself to be even more knowledgeable than you are in the ones we've already discussed, don't you, Hippias?

368a

HIPPIAS: Yes.

SOCRATES: So isn't the very same true in astronomy as well?

HIPPIAS: Probably, Socrates.

SOCRATES: In astronomy too, then, the good astronomer, with his ability to deceive, is a liar, if anyone is, since ignorance leads to inability.

HIPPIAS: I suppose that's right.

SOCRATES: So astronomy is no exception: the same person is both honest and deceitful.

HIPPIAS: It would seem so.

SOCRATES: Now, Hippias, let's not waste any more time: just look at
b branches of knowledge in general, to see if there are any exceptions. In my hearing, you have bragged of being altogether more of an expert at more areas of expertise than anyone; I remember you in the agora by the bankers' tables[1] enumerating your considerable and enviable expertise. You said that once you went to Olympia with nothing on your person which you hadn't made yourself. You started with the ring you were
c wearing, claiming to know how to engrave rings: not only it, but the rest of your jewellery too, and your strigil-and-flask set[2] – all your own work, you said. Then you went on to the shoes you were wearing – cobbled by yourself, you claimed, and your cloak and tunic, woven by yourself. Then – and this struck everyone as most remarkable and as clear evidence of outstanding expertise – you said that although your tunic belt was in the Persian style of the expensive kind, you had braided it yourself. But that wasn't all. You had brought epic, tragic and dithyrambic[3] poetry,
d you said, and many prose speeches in a variety of styles. And you had come equipped not only with exceptional expertise in the areas I mentioned just before, but also in matters of rhythm, intonation,[4] orthography and very many other things besides, I seem to remember – oh, but I was forgetting what was apparently your technique of remembering,[5] on which you really pride yourself. I reckon I've probably forgotten lots of other things too![6]

1. A popular meeting-place, apparently (cf. *Apology* 17c).
2. See p. 188 n. 1.
3. See p. 247 n. 1.
4. See p. 238 n. 3.
5. See p. 238 n. 6.
6. On this list of Hippias' accomplishments, compare *Hippias Major* 285c–e.

Anyway, as I say, look at your own skills – they would be enough, but   e
consider others' skills too and tell me: given our conclusions, is there any
area where honesty and lying do not go hand in hand in the same person?
Call it what you will, expert or unscrupulous activity, but nowhere, my   369a
friend, will you find any exceptions, for none exist. Go on, see if you can.

HIPPIAS: I can't, Socrates, at least not without further deliberation.

SOCRATES: Even that won't help, in my opinion. But you should
remember[1] what the argument entails if I'm right, Hippias.

HIPPIAS: I don't quite see what you're getting at, Socrates.

SOCRATES: I suppose you're not using your mnemonic technique – you
obviously don't think it's called for. I'll remind you: you know you said
that Achilles was honest, Odysseus a liar and complex?   b

HIPPIAS: Yes.

SOCRATES: Well, it has been demonstrated that both lying and honesty
reside in the same person. It follows that if Odysseus was a liar, he is
honest too, and vice versa for Achilles: they are not different from each
other, let alone opposite – they are alike. Now do you see?

C. *Socrates on Homer*

*In this section Socrates supports the paradoxical conclusion of the last section
by reference to passages of Homer's* Iliad. *The argument must be taken with a
considerable pinch of salt: Socrates is parodying the sophists' literary studies of
Homer by showing that Homer can be used to support almost any position.
Compare Socrates' parody of the sophists on the lyric poets at* Protagoras *338e–
347a. Both passages also reflect unfavourably on the use of both Homer and
the lyric poets in traditional Greek education as bases of moral education. There
is also probably a particular dig at Hippias, who was an acknowledged expert
on Homer: at any rate, apart from Plato's evidence of his concern with Homer,
a near witness is Aristotle,* Poetics *1461a21–3, where a minute change of
accent on a single word is intended to preserve Zeus' integrity according to
Homer. (Aristotle wrongly attributes this to a certain Hippias of Thasos: our
Hippias of Elis is more likely.)*

*This section leads into the next by widening the scope from honesty and
dishonesty to morality in general, at 371e–372a. Hippias mentions the fundamental jurisprudential point that Hippias Minor appears to contravene: that
the law is more lenient towards misdeeds performed in ignorance or from some
external necessity.*

Notice how Hippias is now moved to respond to Socrates' badinage with

---

1. Reading μέμνησο.

personal attacks; and how Eudicus' entry at the end of the section punctuates the dialogue: he initiated the first main argument (Section B), and he does the same for the second (Section D).

HIPPIAS: This is typical of your tortuous style of argument, Socrates. You isolate the most awkward point and tenaciously pick away at it,
c instead of coming to grips with the issue at the general level.[1] Even now, if you want, I shall prove satisfactorily and with plenty of evidence that Homer's Achilles is truthful and better than Odysseus, who is cunning, often a liar, and worse than Achilles. Then, if you want, you can produce a counter-argument for Odysseus being better, so that our audience here will be in a better position to know which of us is more correct.[2]

d SOCRATES: Listen, Hippias, I'm not disputing your superior cleverness. I'm only following my usual practice of paying attention to any argument, especially from someone who strikes me as clever, and of questioning, examining afresh and checking his thesis, because I want to understand the point and hope by these means to do so. But if the speaker strikes me as second-rate, I'm not interested enough in his argument to ask further questions. You can tell whom I regard as clever by my persistent
e investigation of his argument, with an eye on the benefit to be gained from learning something. So you see, it occurred to me just now, while you were speaking, that I think it highly unlikely that you are right about the lines you recently quoted to show that Achilles addresses Odysseus as two-faced, since there's nothing in the lines which makes Odysseus, the
370a 'complex' one, a liar, whereas Achilles turns out on your own argument to be complex, or a liar, at any rate. I mean, first he speaks the lines you recently quoted:

For I hate as I hate the gates of Hades the man who conceals one thing in his heart while saying another.

b And he follows this a little later with the assertion that he will not be won over by Odysseus and Agamemnon, and in fact will not remain in Troy at all, but, he says,[3]

Tomorrow, once I have sacrificed to Zeus and all the gods, and stocked my ships, I'll launch them, and early in the morning, if you care to look, you'll see my ships
c sailing on the fish-rich Hellespont, with my men eager at the oars. And if the great

---

1. Compare *Hippias Major* 301b.

2. He is proposing a sophistic debate: see p. 275.

3. *Iliad* IX, 357–63. Odysseus and Agamemnon have been trying to persuade him to rejoin the battle. In what follows, notice that the Earthshaker is Poseidon, god of the sea, but also of earthquakes, and that Phthia is Achilles' homeland in Thessaly.

Earthshaker grants me fair sailing, on the third day I will reach the fertile soil of
Phthia.

And even before these passages, during his slating of Agamemnon, he
said:[1]

And now I'm off to Phthia, since it is far better to go home with my beaked ships:
I do not intend to remain here to lose face and pile up *your* spoils and wealth.   d

But although on this occasion he made his declaration in the presence of
the whole army, and to his own comrades on the other occasion, there is
no sign of his either making any preparations or trying to launch his ships
for a voyage home – see what a lordly disregard he has for telling the truth.
Anyway, Hippias, I originally questioned you because I was puzzled about
which of these two men the poet intended to be better, and because I   e
thought that both were particularly excellent, and it would be hard to
decide their relative merit as regards virtue generally as well as truth and
falsehood in particular, in which respect both are much of a muchness.

HIPPIAS: That's because you're no good as a researcher, Socrates:
Achilles' lies are obviously not premeditated. He doesn't lie deliberately,
but is forced to stay and help because of the army's setbacks. But Odysseus' lies are deliberate and premeditated.

SOCRATES: You could be Odysseus yourself, Hippias: you're deceiving
me.

HIPPIAS: No, I'm not, Socrates. Why? What makes you think so?   371a

SOCRATES: Because you claim that Achilles' lies were not premeditated, when Homer portrayed him not only as two-faced but as a deliberate
illusionist. Why, he seems to be so much more astute than Odysseus that
his duplicity goes undetected by him: he has the audacity to contradict
himself in Odysseus' hearing, and he gets away with it – at any rate,
Odysseus doesn't act as if he were noticing him lying: there's no sign of
him commenting on it.   b

HIPPIAS: What passage do you mean, Socrates?

SOCRATES: Don't you know that in a later speech, after he has told
Odysseus that he would sail away at daybreak, he tells Ajax a different
story, with no mention of sailing away?

HIPPIAS: Where?

SOCRATES: When he says:[2]

I will not trouble myself with bloody war until great Hector, the son of wise Priam,   c
has cut through the Greek army as far as the huts and ships of the Myrmidons, and

1. *Iliad* I, 169–71.
2. *Iliad* IX, 650–55. The Myrmidons are the people of Phthia, Achilles' troops.

brings fire to our fleet. As to him, for all his warlike spirit, I reckon he will be checked here, by *my* hut, *my* dark ship.

Do you really imagine, Hippias, that the son of Thetis, educated by
d   Cheiron the sage,[1] was so forgetful that one minute he was slating duplicity in the most violent terms, but the next minute tells Odysseus that he will sail away, and Ajax that he will stay? Don't you think this was intentional, in the sense that he regarded Odysseus as senile,[2] and thought that these were just the tricks and lies to outwit him?

HIPPIAS: No, I don't, Socrates. Even in this case he was under pres-
e   sure: this time his goodwill towards Ajax made him tell a different story from the one he'd told Odysseus. But Odysseus' honesty and lying are always equally premeditated.

SOCRATES: Then apparently Odysseus is better than Achilles.

HIPPIAS: Not in the slightest, Socrates.

SOCRATES: What do you mean? Wasn't it recently proved that deliberate liars are better than unwitting ones?[3]

HIPPIAS: How on earth can criminals who deliberately premeditate
372a   and carry out bad acts be better than people with no such intentions? A crime, lie or any bad act performed in ignorance is accorded plenty of indulgence, and the laws are far more severe on deliberate misdeeds and lies than on unintentional ones.

SOCRATES: Do you see that I'm telling the truth, Hippias, when I say
b   that I'm persistent in questioning clever people? This is probably my only good point: in other respects I'm pretty useless. I mean, I'm ignorant about the way things are, which just baffles me. I can easily prove this: whenever I meet anyone like you whose wisdom is famous and vouched for by all the Greeks, my ignorance becomes evident, because we disagree
c   on almost everything. What greater proof of ignorance can there be than disagreement with experts? But, astonishingly, I have this single good point, my saving grace: I am humble enough to learn, so I probe and ask questions, and am extremely grateful to anyone who answers me. I always repay my debts by never passing the lesson off as a discovery of my own and so denying the fact that I have *learned* something. No, I extol the cleverness of my teacher as I explain what he taught me. To be specific
d   now, I do not agree with your view; in fact, I strongly disagree. I don't propose to exaggerate my abilities: I am what I am, so I'm sure that this disagreement is my fault. My view is quite the opposite of yours: it is not

1. Achilles' mother, Thetis, was a sea-deity. Cheiron was the most famous of the centaurs: he was the teacher not only of Achilles but of many other Greek heroes.

2. Odysseus was only middle-aged, at the most, but Achilles was very young!

3. 366c ff.

those who unintentionally cause injury, commit crimes, tell lies, deceive and make mistakes who are better; no, those who intentionally do all this are better than those who unintentionally do so, in my opinion. But it's true that, obviously under the influence of my ignorance, I chop and change, and even hold the opposite opinion sometimes. But the situation at the moment is that I'm suffering a sort of seizure: I think that those e who intentionally make mistakes are better than those who do so unintentionally. I blame this current state of mine on the discussion we were having, which, for the time being, makes anyone who unintentionally does any of the things we mentioned seem worse than those who mean to do them. So do me a favour: don't refuse to cure my mind. You will be benefiting me far more by arresting mental ignorance than if you arrested 373a a physical ailment. I should warn you, though, that long speeches won't effect a cure, since I can't follow them; but if you are prepared to answer me as you did before, you'll help me a lot, and I don't think you'd suffer either. And it would be only fair to call you too in on this, son of Apemantus, since it was you who encouraged me to talk with Hippias: if Hippias isn't prepared to answer my questions, you must intercede now on my behalf.

EUDICUS: I don't think Hippias will need my intercession, Socrates, because earlier he said, not what you imply, but that he would evade no b one's questions. Well, Hippias? Didn't you say that?

HIPPIAS: I did, Eudicus, but the effect of Socrates' habitual mischievousness is to disrupt the discussion.[1]

SOCRATES: My very dear Hippias, I don't *mean* to – that would make me clever and shrewd, you could argue – and since I don't mean to, you should pardon me: you claim that unintentional misdeeds ought to be pardoned.

EUDICUS: Go on, Hippias, do as he says. For our sakes, and to make c the previous discussion worthwhile, answer Socrates' questions.

HIPPIAS: All right, just for you. Ask what you want, then.

D. *Intentional and Unintentional Misdeeds*

This section is precisely parallel to Section B: the conclusion is paradoxical and arguments from analogy are brought up to support it. It even involves the same weakness. The same three questions must be asked as before: How good is the argument? Is the paradox radical or merely apparent? Does Plato believe it?

1. This is a common accusation: see, for example, *Gorgias* 483a, *Meno* 80a–b, *Republic* 338d, 341a.

The paradoxical conclusion is that a deliberate criminal is morally better than an unintentional one. The argument has invariably been criticized as extremely weak: the accusation is that Plato equivocates between being morally good and being good at something. He is accused, then, of committing the fallacy of secundum quid (see p. 304) by shedding the suffix 'at something' and drawing a conclusion about morality from arguments about ability. A more than cursory glance at the argument, however, proves that this accusation does not apply to the bulk of the section. The argument is that not only does functional goodness go hand in hand with functional badness in the case of various abilities, but the same also applies to morality. If that was the end of the argument, the accusation of fallacy would be correct; but instead we find that Plato carefully supplies the missing premiss, that morality is such that one can be functionally good and bad at it (375d–376a). Whether or not this conclusion is unassailable in itself, it is clear that Plato has safeguarded the argument used to reach it. The argument is now effectively over and it has, unlike Section B, been couched entirely in terms of ability. But then Plato summarizes the conclusion, and it is only at this point that the fallacy creeps in: instead of talking about a mind that is good at something (as in 375b, for instance), Plato summarizes this as the mind of a good man (376b). The fallacy is there, then, but it does not affect the main argument; this section is therefore better argued than Section B, though its purpose is similar: to suggest that it is ability that governs honesty, virtue and their opposites.

The argument – barring the fact that no inductive argument can lead to certainty – is reasonable. The weakness, as in Section B, lies in the conclusion: it may be doubted whether someone who does something knowingly in the sense that he has the ability to do it will necessarily do it deliberately in the sense that he chooses to do it (see Aristotle, Metaphysics 1025a6–13): there is equivocation, then, on the notion of 'deliberate'. In this case the Aristotelian objection strikes at the heart of Socrates' ethical thought, which hinges on the intellectualist view that virtue is an ability (see pp. 22–3, 25–6, 267).

The paradox comes across as extremely radical: it is an attack on the basis of all legal procedure and penology; but on this question and whether Plato believed the paradox, see pp. 24–5 and 268–70.

SOCRATES: Well, what I really want to do, Hippias, is investigate this new issue of whether those who make mistakes intentionally or those who do so unintentionally are better. I think the most promising line of investigation stems from this question: do you accept that there are good runners?

HIPPIAS: I do.

d   SOCRATES: And bad ones?

HIPPIAS: Yes.

SOCRATES: A good runner is someone who runs well, a bad runner someone who runs badly?

HIPPIAS: Yes.

SOCRATES: Isn't a slow runner a bad runner, a fast one good?

HIPPIAS: Yes.

SOCRATES: So in a race, speed is a good thing, slowness bad?

HIPPIAS: Of course.

SOCRATES: Is intentional or unintentional slow running a sign of a better runner?

HIPPIAS: Intentional.

SOCRATES: Now, isn't running an action?

HIPPIAS: It is.

SOCRATES: And if it is an action, it achieves something?

HIPPIAS: Yes.   e

SOCRATES: So what a bad runner achieves in a race is bad and contemptible?

HIPPIAS: Yes, of course.

SOCRATES: And slow running is bad?

HIPPIAS: Yes.

SOCRATES: So isn't it the case that a good runner deliberately achieves this bad and contemptible result, but a bad runner doesn't mean to?

HIPPIAS: Apparently.

SOCRATES: In a race, then, unintentional bad deeds are worse than intentional ones?

HIPPIAS: Yes, but maybe only in running.   374a

SOCRATES: What about in wrestling? Which wrestler is best, the one who falls intentionally or the one who doesn't mean to?

HIPPIAS: The one who does so intentionally, I suppose.

SOCRATES: And is falling or throwing worse and more contemptible in wrestling?

HIPPIAS: Falling.

SOCRATES: So in wrestling too, a wrestler who intentionally achieves bad and contemptible results is better than the one who doesn't mean to.

HIPPIAS: I suppose so.

SOCRATES: What about any other employment of the body? Take two people, one better, the other worse at using his body. Isn't the ability to achieve both sorts of results – effective *and* ineffective, contemptible *and* fine – the property of the one who is better at using his body? And therefore   b
aren't bad physical results intentional in the one case, but unintentional in the other?

HIPPIAS: Yes, I suppose physical strength too produces no counter-examples.

SOCRATES: What about physical grace, Hippias? Isn't the *deliberate* adoption of ugly, defective stances something only better bodies can do? What do you think?

HIPPIAS: I agree.

SOCRATES: So intentional gracelessness is a product of bodily excel-
c lence, but unintentional of defectiveness.

HIPPIAS: I suppose so.

SOCRATES: What do you think about singing? Do you think intentional or unintentional tunelessness is better?

HIPPIAS: Intentional.

SOCRATES: And unintentional tunelessness is inferior?

HIPPIAS: Yes.

SOCRATES: Would you rather have good or bad things?

HIPPIAS: Good things.

SOCRATES: So would you rather have your feet limp intentionally or unintentionally?

HIPPIAS: Intentionally.

d SOCRATES: But isn't limping a form of defectiveness and gracelessness?

HIPPIAS: Yes.

SOCRATES: Now, isn't weak sight a defect of the eyes?

HIPPIAS: Yes.

SOCRATES: Which sort of eyes would you rather have in your head? Ones you could use deliberately for weak, defective sight, or ones which allow you no choice in the matter?

HIPPIAS: Ones I could use deliberately.

SOCRATES: So you rate the organs of yours which perform badly through your choice higher than those which perform badly against your will?

HIPPIAS: Yes, in these sorts of cases, anyway.

SOCRATES: So the same argument holds for ears, nose, mouth and all
e the senses: those which can't help performing badly are not worth having *qua* defective, while those which do so through choice are worth having *qua* good.

HIPPIAS: Agreed.

SOCRATES: Now, which kind of instruments is it better to work with, those which may be used deliberately for bad results, or those which allow you no choice? For example, which rudder is better: one which makes you steer off course when you don't mean to, or the one which does so only when you mean to?

HIPPIAS: The latter.

SOCRATES: And isn't the same true for a bow, lyre, twin-pipes, and so on and so forth?

HIPPIAS: Yes, you're right.   375a

SOCRATES: Now, is it better to have a horse whose temperament allows you to ride badly on purpose, or one which gives you no choice?

HIPPIAS: The one which allows intentional bad riding.

SOCRATES: That's the better horse, in fact.

HIPPIAS: Yes.

SOCRATES: So, given a horse with a better temperament, you can get bad results from this temperament intentionally; but only unintentionally from a bad temperament. Is that right?

HIPPIAS: Certainly.

SOCRATES: And the same goes for dogs and all other creatures?

HIPPIAS: Yes.

SOCRATES: Now, let's move on to human beings. Is it better to have the mind of an archer who misses the target deliberately or unintentionally?

HIPPIAS: Deliberately.   b

SOCRATES: And this is the better mind for archery?

HIPPIAS: Yes.

SOCRATES: So a mind which unintentionally makes a mistake is worse than one which does so intentionally?

HIPPIAS: Yes, in archery, anyway.

SOCRATES: What about in medicine? Isn't a mind which intentionally achieves bad results on bodies more of a medical mind?

HIPPIAS: Yes.

SOCRATES: So in this area of expertise it is a better mind than the alternative?

HIPPIAS: Yes.

SOCRATES: Now, take playing the lyre or the pipes – in fact, take any skill or branch of knowledge. Isn't it the case that only better minds   c
can *deliberately* produce bad or contemptible results and make *intentional* mistakes?

HIPPIAS: I suppose so.

SOCRATES: In fact, you know, even if we had the minds of slaves, we would rather have ones which intentionally make mistakes and do wrong than ones which do so unintentionally, on the grounds that the former are *better* at what they do.

HIPPIAS: Yes.

SOCRATES: Now, wouldn't we prefer to have our own minds in the best possible condition?

HIPPIAS: Yes.

d   SOCRATES: And won't they be better if they deliberately do wrong and make mistakes than if they do so without meaning to?

HIPPIAS: It would be monstrous, Socrates, if deliberate criminals are to be better than those who don't mean any harm.

SOCRATES: But that's what the argument suggests.

HIPPIAS: Well, *I* can't accept it.

SOCRATES: Oh, I thought you agreed with me, Hippias. Let's try again: isn't being just either an ability or a branch of knowledge or both? Justice must be *one* of these, mustn't it?

e   HIPPIAS: Yes.

SOCRATES: If justice is a mental ability, then the more able a mind, the more just it is. Right, my friend? I mean, we have agreed that greater ability is better.

HIPPIAS: Yes, we have.

SOCRATES: And if it is a branch of knowledge, then a more knowledgeable mind is more just, and a more ignorant one more criminal, isn't it?

HIPPIAS: Yes.

SOCRATES: And if it is both, then a mind with both knowledge and ability is more just than a less knowledgeable mind. Doesn't that follow?

HIPPIAS: I suppose so.

SOCRATES: And didn't we find that the more able and expert a mind is, the better it is, and more capable, whatever the activity, of acting both

376a well and badly?

HIPPIAS: Yes.

SOCRATES: So when it acts in a contemptible manner, it does so deliberately thanks to its ability and skill; and now we find that justice is characterized by one or both of ability and skill.

HIPPIAS: Apparently.

SOCRATES: And to act criminally is to do bad deeds, not to act criminally is to do fine deeds.

HIPPIAS: Yes.

SOCRATES: So aren't crimes committed by a more able and better mind intentional, while those committed by a worse mind are unintentional?

HIPPIAS: I suppose so.

b   SOCRATES: Now, a good person is someone who has a good mind, a bad person the opposite?

HIPPIAS: Yes.

SOCRATES: It follows from the fact that a good person has a good mind that it is the property of a good person to commit deliberate crimes, but of a bad person to do so unintentionally.

HIPPIAS: Well, it's true that a good person has a good mind, anyway.

SOCRATES: Therefore, Hippias, the person, if he exists, who deliberately makes mistakes and acts contemptibly and criminally, can only be the good person.

HIPPIAS: I can't agree with you on this, Socrates.[1]

SOCRATES: Nor can I with myself, Hippias. But this is the conclusion the argument inevitably suggests. As I have remarked before, however, I   c
chop and change and continually modify my opinion.[2] Inconsistency is to be expected in me and any other amateur: but if you experts are inconsistent, and we can't get relief from our vacillation even by coming to you, then that *is* monstrous,[3] for us as well as for you.

1. See *Republic* 487b–c for a clear statement of the feeling of a Socratic interlocutor that he had been misled.

2. 372d.

3. Socrates is ironically using one of Hippias' favourite expressions: see 363c, 364d, 365c, 375d, and *Hippias Major* 292c.

EUTHYDEMUS

INTRODUCTION TO *EUTHYDEMUS*

The main purpose of *Euthydemus* is no more than it appears to be: to contrast Socratic argumentation and education with those of a certain type of sophist, to the detriment of the latter. There is no reason to doubt that the two representatives of this type in our dialogue, the brothers Euthydemus and Dionysodorus, were real people. We are given enough historical data about them in the dialogue to warrant this assumption, and we hear about them elsewhere: Plato mentions Euthydemus by name at *Cratylus* 386d (see p. 350) and, independently of Plato, but still a close historical witness, Aristotle twice associates him with a particular ambiguous question (*Rhetoric* 1401a28, *De Sophisticis Elenchis* 177b12). Our only close external witness for Dionysodorus' existence is Xenophon (*Memorabilia* III.1; see p. 16 above), where even his skill at teaching military matters (*Euthydemus* 271d etc.) is slighted. The dialogue is named after Euthydemus alone for convenience and because he is portrayed as the more rigorous of the pair, despite being the younger.

The dramatic or scenic date of the dialogue is not fixed, but must lie between 420 and 405 B.C., because Protagoras is mentioned in the past tense as if dead (286c; he died in 420 at the latest) and Alcibiades is still alive (275b; he died in 404). Given Socrates' advanced age (272b), a date nearer 405 than 420 is likely: Socrates was born in 469.

It is equally difficult to date *Euthydemus* precisely in relation to other Platonic works, but it can confidently be located among the works of the end of his first (Socratic) period. The style is of a piece with *Meno*, *Gorgias*, *Lysis* and *Hippias Major*. The aim of distinguishing Socrates from the sophists is typical of Plato's early period. The thought is purely Socratic (though this has been doubted: see pp. 365–6). The more precise ordering of these works of the later early period is extremely controversial and too technical to go into here: my own inclination would be to place *Euthydemus* first among this group, because the others show more signs of Platonic as opposed to Socratic thought. It was probably written, then, *c.* 387–385.

Euthydemus is one of the best-written and most amusing of Plato's dialogues – which is just as well, for otherwise the lengthy catalogue of sophisms would pall even more than (some might think) it already does. It has a more formal structure than is usual: broadly, there are five scenes set in the *past* which alternately display the sophists and Socrates at work. Scenes 1 (275c–277c), 3 (283a–288b) and 5 (293a–304b) are the sophistic ones; 2 and 4 (277d–282e, 288b–292e) the Socratic. This series of scenes is bracketed by an introduction (271a–272d) and an epilogue (304c–307c) in which Socrates and Crito are talking in the *present* time (this happens too at 290e–292e, though here Crito is simply being used to demonstrate a phase of the *past* argument: Plato could have used the same mode as the rest of the reported sequences, but chose to vary our diet).

Within this structure, the predominant pattern of the sophists' part is to start arguing with Socrates, switch to Ctesippus and return to Socrates. This happens in both the long scenes 3 and 5, in which Ctesippus plays a part; and in both cases the return to Socrates is prompted by Socrates' own exasperated re-intervention.

Given a structure by scenes, a prologue and an epilogue, it is tempting to describe *Euthydemus* as a comedy, albeit with serious intent (see, for instance, Méridier, p. 120). The temptation is increased by the description of the sophists' followers as a 'chorus' or dancing-troupe (276b–c), and of Euthydemus as a choreographer (276d). But the chief purpose of the structure, of course, is to enhance the overall aim of the dialogue by juxtaposing and contrasting Socrates and the sophists.

The artistry of the dialogue does not just lie in a formal structure, but in its readability. This is gained by easy, fluent and colloquial Greek, by vivid metaphors and similes, fine characterization, clear description and a generous dash of humour. The similes are especially striking: never again does Plato use so many in a single short dialogue.

As for the characters, Socrates is the same familiar person of other dialogues: moral, lucid, rational, patient – though his patience wears a little thin with Euthydemus and Dionysodorus – and possessed of a strong and sharp satirical sense of humour. Euthydemus and Dionysodorus are much of a muchness, though as the dialogue progresses we learn that Dionysodorus is the shallower of the two; otherwise their characters have been submerged under their mechanical method of argument. Crito is a typical Athenian bourgeois, but with some philosophical interests. Cleinias is a typical young Athenian aristocrat, reminiscent, for instance, of Charmides in *Charmides*: modest, pliable, but ready to join in too. Ctesippus' character is summarized at 273a; his predominant feature is 'youthful brashness', and Plato skilfully maintains this portrait throughout the dialogue. Interestingly, Plato shows us the same Ctesippus in *Lysis* too, so perhaps it is an accurate depiction of the historical person at this time.

Eristic

Plato defines Euthydemus' and Dionysodorus' argumentation as 'eristic' (272b, and cf. p. 32). This literally means 'designed for victory' or 'contentious', and was a technical term of Socrates' and Plato's time to describe a type of argumentation. As the literal meaning suggests, eristic is not so much a particular method of argument as a subjective term of abuse ('One man's philosophy was another man's eristic', as Guthrie (IV, p. 275) puts it). The particular method Euthydemus and Dionysodorus use is more correctly called 'antilogic' (see Kerferd, *The Sophistic Movement*, Chapter 6), that is, 'proceeding from a given *logos*, say the position adopted by an opponent, to the establishment of a contrary or contradictory *logos* in such a way that the opponent must either accept both *logoi*, or at least abandon his first position' (p. 63). As the dialogue is read it will be obvious how this applies to Euthydemus and Dionysodorus. They proceed by posing 'either-or' questions; sometimes the questions are posed so as to give the answerer no apparent choice about which alternative to take, in the sense that the other alternative is obviously absurd (e.g. 'Do you know something or nothing?' (293b ff.)). At other times either alternative is plausible, but the brothers are able to argue against both (e.g. Sections C and D). Whether the questions are plausible or implausible, the sophists exploit ambiguities to refute whatever answer their opponent chooses. Their argumentation, then, is 'eristic antilogic' – antilogic which is designed to defeat an interlocutor who is seen as an opponent.

Antilogic has a history in Greek philosophy, and for more thorough accounts I must be content with referring the reader to the works of E. S. Thompson, Ryle and particularly Lloyd (1971) in the bibliography. Very briefly, there are two great Presocratic thinkers chiefly associated with this method: Zeno of Elea (fl. *c.* 450) probably invented it, to refute views contrary to Parmenides' metaphysical monism, and the sophist Protagoras of Abdera (*c.* 490–*c.* 420) is said to be the first to have taught systematically, probably in the context of teaching rhetoric, that there are at least two opposing positions possible on any matter. There is also extant, probably from *c.* 400, a shallow but historically interesting treatise called *Dissoi Logoi*, 'Two-way Arguments', which applies the method to a number of theses.

I introduce the history of the method of argument for three reasons. In the first place, it was (and still is) a common form of argument, and though Euthydemus and Dionysodorus no doubt practised a debased (eristic) version of it, we should not be surprised to find that it was their livelihood. The sophists were in demand in the contemporary Greek world, particularly in Athens (see Kerferd, *The Sophistic Movement*, Chapter 3; Rankin, Chapter 1), and Aristotle (*De Sophisticis Elenchis* 183b36) speaks of 'paid professors of eristic' who set their pupils arguments, like those of Euthydemus and Dionysodorus, to learn by heart: the arguments could then be used in a political, legal or even philosophical context. We do not need to think, as has been suggested, that Euthydemus' and Dionysodorus' arguments are merely figments of Plato's imagination. In fact there is considerable evidence (see p. 275) for there having been sophistic debates, open to the (presumably paying) public, where sophists would argue for and against certain common theses. A considerable body of arguments, such as those summarized in *Dissoi Logoi*, must have been current in Plato's time.

Secondly, since antilogic has a varied history, and since Euthydemus and Dionysodorus are eristics, it seems to me impractical to locate them in any particular philosophical tradition. Attempts to do so, like that of Sprague (1962), followed by Hawtrey (1981), are not sustained even by their authors: such theories can account for only a few, but not all of the sophisms. Take the issue of predication as an example: our sophists sometimes argue that even contradictory predicates are applicable to the same thing (275d–277c, especially), but at other times that there is only one proper description of a thing (285e–286b). The most likely hypothesis is that our sophists are eclectic: they will borrow from any source in pursuit of their eristic aims of defeating the opponent and astounding the audience. In the running commentaries which introduce each section of the text, I mention such provenances of the sophisms as are plausible.

Thirdly, and most importantly, Socrates and at least two of his followers (Euclides and Antisthenes) were practitioners of antilogic. Socrates too used question-and-answer, where the questions often have the same 'either-or' nature and drive his interlocutors into a corner. When Socrates uses the art, it is honoured with the name 'dialectic'; but it is a species of antilogic just as much as Euthydemus' and Dionysodorus' eristic (see Robinson (1953)). What, then, is the difference between Socrates' dialectic and the sophists' eristic?

Dialectic and Eristic

It is, of course, Plato's purpose in *Euthydemus* to raise and answer precisely this question, which the very similarity between dialectic and eristic makes urgent. Book 8 of Aristotle's *Topics* is worth reading in this context: his description of the practice of dialectic often makes it sound as contentious as eristic.

It can immediately be said that to anyone acquainted with Socratic thought and method, Plato answers the question most satisfactorily. It is all very well, however, to see that Socratic thought external to *Euthydemus* has a bearing on our appreciation of the dialogue, but it must also be the case that the dialogue is *internally* meaningful. It is, in fact: the most important points of contrast between Socrates and the two sophists are clearly made in the dialogue. The sole purpose of eristic, as Socrates points out (272a), is to win the argument and enhance the questioner's esteem. Socrates, however, uses his dialectic to try to reach the truth on any issue and to enhance the answerer's concern to live a morally viable life. The corners into which Socrates drives his interlocutors are (ideally) not formed by ambiguities in language but by inconsistencies in the answerer's moral notions; Socrates seeks to remove what is irrational in a person's life in order to make way for improvement. The person who thinks that he knows how to live, but who cannot defend his opinions against questioning, is anathema to Socrates, because such confidence does away with the continual search for a better life.

In fact, even to say this is to draw on other dialogues, because in *Euthydemus* itself Socrates has no need of this more aggressive side of his dialectic. In his model conversations with Cleinias (Sections E and I), he is working on an answerer who is lucky (and young) enough not to have many fixed notions. While one might criticize Plato for making Cleinias too amenable, the point, in *Euthydemus*, is that Plato should clearly portray the moral purpose of Socratic questioning, and this is most economically done by providing Socrates with such an interlocutor. Socrates is then easily able to lead the boy to agreeing that philosophy – the practice of virtue – is essential. So in the practice of dialectic, the interlocutor is ideally seen not as an opponent, but as a fellow-traveller in a moral quest.

It is worth pausing for a moment to consider whether there might not be another contrast between Socrates' dialectic and the sophists' eristic as portrayed in *Euthydemus* – that is, simply between validity and invalidity of argument. This question has provoked considerable controversy, with some (e.g. Robinson (1942) and Stewart) claiming that Plato has no interest in fallacies whatsoever, and others (notably Sprague (1962)) arguing against this position. It is certainly true that Socrates' arguments in *Euthydemus* are not perfect (though they are not as bad as Stewart makes out), and I think it is also true that it is not an important part of the programme of the dialogue to analyse invalid forms of argument: the sophists' fallacies are really no more than ambiguities (see pp. 303–4), so it would be rash to claim that Plato is providing any kind of handbook of valid and invalid forms of reasoning. Aristotle's claim to be the first to do so can stand (*De Sophisticis Elenchis* 184b1 ff.). But it is undeniable that the sophists' arguments are fallacious and that Socrates' arguments are better, even in a formal logical sense. It is also crucially undeniable that Plato was aware of fallacy: this is shown at least by explicit comment at 277e–278b and by Socrates' tactics throughout 293b–296d. It is probably the case, since the sophists' arguments are so consistently fallacious, and since Plato wrote them down, that Plato must have recognized them to be genuine sophisms in the Aristotelian sense (arguments which have the form of validity but are in fact invalid), in which case he must have had the concept of valid reasoning. If all this is so, then it follows that the logical contrast between Socrates and the sophists is part of Plato's purpose in *Euthydemus*. But it must be seen as a subsidiary purpose – as a literary device rather than a philosophical point which is vitally important to Plato. For throughout the dialogues, Socrates is made to commit fallacies, often ones which are scarcely less blatant than some of Euthydemus' and Dionysodorus', and often the same ones that these two sophists commit in our dialogue. In other words, Plato is perfectly prepared to stomach a bad argument, provided it leads to a good conclusion. Philosophy for both Socrates and Plato was a way of life, not an exercise in logic. So, if in *Euthydemus* Plato makes Socrates come up with sounder arguments than the sophists, this is only to enhance the central moral purpose he found in Socrates' arguments; it is relevant to do so in the context of such atrocious arguments from the sophists, but it is not *necessary* to that moral purpose, except in so far as the removal of confusion, especially about ambiguous terms, may lead to greater mental and moral clarity.

Apart from this qualification about the formal logical nature of the arguments, let us summarize the differences between dialectic and eristic, as Plato sees it. It is somewhat glib to say simply that the difference is between morality and nullity: in what does the morality of dialectic lie? It lies fundamentally, as far as we can tell from *Euthydemus*, in the ability to stimulate. It is important to realize that the difference does not lie in dialectic providing answers: dialectic does not – Socrates' protreptic ultimately gets into an infinite regress in Section J of the dialogue. Nor does Socrates disapprove of logical puzzles *per se*, provided they stimulate thought and discourage overhasty acceptance of answers. The difference is that under Socrates' guidance Cleinias' life is opened up and steered towards virtue. Cleinias is not left in a moral vacuum or to rely on his conditioning: he is led to think for himself about his own life, whereas the sophists' arguments cannot change his life at all. The sophists either shut things up or leave them where they are; Socrates leaves matters open in a constructive way.

Apart from this central contrast, Plato means us to notice other differences: Socratic dialectic tests a person's real beliefs, whereas eristic deals only with words; dialectic is flexible, eristic is mechanical; dialectic does not offer instant wisdom and Socrates is far from claiming to be a know-all. Both methods lay claim to the same purpose – virtue – but we are bound to think that only one is successful.

The Nature of the Sophisms

Euthydemus and Dionysodorus exhibit many irritating traits during the course of the dialogue: for instance, if a discussion is not going their way, they avoid the issue (287b, 297b, etc.). But this and other similar features are self-evident; what I want to do now is briefly to introduce the reader to the subject of fallacy, since the arguments of the two brothers are formally fallacious.

Aristotle was the first to attempt to categorize types of fallacy, and plenty of alternative classifications have arisen since, which have shown, *inter alia*, that some of Aristotle's fallacies are not really fallacies at all. A fallacy is invalid argument. So, for instance, of relevance to *Euthydemus*, the so-called *fallacia plurium interrogationum* (*De Sophisticis Elenchis* 167e37 ff.) is not really a fallacy. This 'fallacy of too many questions' (i.e. more than one question compressed into a single question) is usually – and nicely – illustrated by 'Have you stopped beating your wife?' This is a misleading question (because whether you answer yes or no, you will be a self-confessed wife-beater), not an invalid argument, and there are many examples in *Euthydemus*.

It should be clear from the outset that the same invalid argument can often be analysed as fallacious in different ways. We should certainly take *Euthydemus* to be fairly simple as far as fallacies are concerned, however; only if Plato had shown greater awareness of varieties of fallacy would it be fair to introduce complexities. If it is possible to analyse the sophisms of *Euthydemus* simply, then that is the correct procedure. In fact, there is only one type of fallacy which needs to be understood for a reading of the dialogue: that which depends on ambiguity.

What Aristotle called 'fallacies dependent on language' all involve ambiguities. Ambiguity may reside in a single word, in which case it is called 'equivocation' – or sometimes a pun! An argument which exploits equivocation is fallacious. A very similar and often indistinguishable case is when ambiguity occurs in the juxtaposition of a number of words which are not misleading individually. This type of ambiguity is called 'amphiboly'. My favourite example is the wartime headline FIFTH ARMY PUSH BOTTLES UP GERMANS.

Ambiguity may reside in a sentence which contains predicates which qualify parts rather than the whole of which they are parts (or vice versa). An argument which transfers the predicate from the parts to the whole commits the fallacy of 'composition' (transference from the whole to the parts is 'division'). A famous Aristotelian example, designed as a criticism of Pythagorean arithmology, of the fallacy of composition is (*De Sophisticis Elenchis* 166a33): three and two are odd and even, five is three and two, therefore five is odd and even.

The fallacy of *secundum quid* needs a little more discussion, since in Aristotle's scheme it was not classified as dependent on language, i.e. as involving ambiguity. Its full scholastic name is the fallacy *a dicto secundum quid ad dictum simpliciter*, 'moving from speaking of something in relative terms to speaking of it unqualifiedly'. In *Euthydemus*, for example, the sophists move from 'knowing something' to 'knowing' without qualification (Section L). But this can be seen as a sort of ambiguity, in the sense that the term 'know' is capable of both relative and absolute usage. According to the principle of interpreting *Euthydemus* simply, it is probably safest to classify this fallacy as a form of ambiguity.

There is a fallacy which is the opposite of *secundum quid* (though it is not precisely the same as any of Aristotle's fallacies), i.e. 'moving from speaking unqualifiedly about something to speaking of it in relative terms'. It is similarly classifiable as a species of ambiguity.

Finally, I must make it clear that in using these terms ('equivocation', *secundum quid* and so on), I am not suggesting for a moment that Plato had in mind any such classification, or indeed any classification at all. He does not even have a word for 'fallacy'. I have argued (p. 302) that he knew there was something wrong with the arguments and could pinpoint the errors, if pushed, but he need not have had any classificatory system to do so. I introduce the terms as tools for the simpler explanation of what is going on in our dialogue; they will be used particularly in the running commentaries that introduce each section of the text.

The Socratic Protreptic

Given what has already been said about the importance for Plato of distinguishing Socrates from Euthydemus and Dionysodorus, it will come as no surprise that *Euthydemus* contains a succinct summary of the basis of

Socrates' moral thought. This is found in Socrates' protreptic, which starts in Section E and is continued in Sections I and J.

The term 'protreptic' describes a branch of philosophical rhetoric which was current in Socrates' day and which continued much later. The term (or the verb from which it is derived) occurs several times in *Euthydemus* (275a, 278c, 278d, 282d, 307a; in the last passage, its use is not technical, and the verb has been translated 'recommend'). The rise of this offshoot of philosophy is intrinsically connected with the rise of the sophistic movement. The sophists by and large claimed to teach virtue (as did Socrates). Two questions then arose, which are neatly given at 274d–e: is virtue teachable, and is this person I am listening to, as opposed to any other sophist making the same claim, capable of teaching it? Protreptic speeches or discussions were preliminaries, then, designed to persuade the audience that they had come to the right teacher, and that the virtue they would gain from his teaching was worthwhile. We know that several contemporary thinkers wrote or delivered protreptics, but Socrates' in *Euthydemus* is the earliest extant version. It is worth comparing the fragments of Aristotle's influential but lost *Protrepticus*, which are most accessible in Chroust's edition.

The basis of Socrates' position is formed by two premisses: everyone wants success (or happiness); and it is some activity or set of activities that bring it (278e, 280c). These are probably statements with which no Greek would disagree; at any rate, they also form the basis of Aristotle's ethics and are presented there as if they were *endoxa*, commonly held opinions (e.g. *Nicomachean Ethics* 1097b20–21). But despite the relative straight-forwardness of the premisses, the argument soon moves into more controversial areas. The backbone of the first part of the protreptic (Section E) is as follows:

1. Everyone wants success (happiness) (278e)
2. Happiness comes from good things (279a–c)
2a. Happiness comes from the *use* of good things, not their mere possession (280b–e)
2b. Happiness comes from the *correct* use of good things (280e–281a)
3. Wisdom (skill, knowledge) causes correct use of things (281a–d)
3a. It is not luck that causes correct use: luck is a red herring, because wisdom *is* luck (279d–280b)
4. Wisdom is the only good thing (281d–e)
5. Therefore (given 1 and 2), everyone should pursue wisdom (knowledge), i.e. be philosophers, 'lovers of wisdom' (282a–d)

It is one of the remarkable features of this protreptic that it is intended to appeal to everyone, whatever their ideas about what things are good. That is to say, it is a true protreptic.

Nearly every stage of the argument is supported, in a typically Socratic fashion, by inference from what obtains in the case of everyday crafts. Such inferences can never amount to proof, and this is a constant weakness in Socratic arguments. Thus, there may be some 'good' things for which mere possession is a sufficient condition of happiness – a stamp collection, for example. And there are certainly some who believe that use of power, whether 'correct' or not, causes happiness. ('Correct' here does not convey a moral connotation, merely an instrumental one: a correct use of a tool is a proper use, leading to success. It follows that this stage of the argument is circular, since it says in effect: '*Success* comes from *successful* use of good things.')

The weakest stage of the argument is undoubtedly 3a. (In the schema above, I have put this stage in its logical place, though it comes between 2 and 2a in the text.) Though weak, however, it is a sign of Plato's thoroughness that he considers luck at all, even if to dismiss it. It is a bold attempt to argue that luck, which by definition is beyond human control, is potentially within it. Luck plays no part in a wise person's life. Rarely is Socratic rationalism so obvious. The argument is unsuccessful because it only manages to associate wisdom with *success*, and luck (as commonly conceived) is blandly eliminated, with no argument to back up this elimination. The argument, then, exploits the ambiguity of 'good luck', which can mean success. Basically, the thesis Plato wants to maintain is impossible to uphold in rational argument: it is rather a matter of faith about the extent of man's mind and capabilities. The inference from a few cases to a conclusion is here, then, particularly unsound.

Stage 2 of the discussion is interesting because it is a very clear statement of a constant thread in Socrates' ethics: he uses the term 'good' as synonymous with 'beneficial' or 'conducive to happiness'. Anything is good for someone if and only if it makes that person happy. Clearly, this view throws up a great need to define happiness, but Socrates never clearly does (see below), unless we accept at face value the hedonism of *Protagoras*, where Socrates apparently argues that pleasure is the *summum bonum* (351b ff.).

The argument in general, and particularly the paragraph running from 281b–c, has been seen as trading on an ambiguity in 'success'. In the paragraph referred to, Socrates says 'the fewer mistakes, the less unsuccessful' – which takes success as competence; and then 'the less unsuccessful, the less miserable' – which takes success as happiness. But in fact Plato has been careful to argue for the shift from 'success' as the result of mere *possession* of things to 'success' as the result of competent *use* of them; that is, he has argued for the equation of happiness and success, which in turn enables him to elevate wisdom as he wants, as the only true cause of human happiness.

The argument as a whole is partial evidence for an important aspect of Socratic ethics, namely the relation of virtue and happiness. On the whole issue, see Vlastos (1984). The instrumentalist language of 280d–e and 282a shows that for Socrates wisdom – and therefore virtue, by the doctrine of the unity of the virtues (see *Protagoras*) – leads to happiness. The passages show, at least, that Vlastos is right to reject the idea that virtue is exactly the same as happiness; but beyond this they cannot tell us in themselves whether Socrates holds that virtue is desirable only as an instrumental means to happiness, not for its own sake, or whether some closer relation between the two is being assumed. From a careful survey of all the relevant passages in the early dialogues, Vlastos concludes that the latter is the case: for Socrates, virtue 'would of itself assure a sufficiency of happiness . . . but would still allow for small, but not negligible, enhancements of happiness as a result of the virtuous possession and use of non-moral goods' (p. 191). On non-moral goods, see *Euthydemus* 281d with Vlastos, pp. 199–200.

Socrates in *Euthydemus* also warns us, however, not to talk about virtue without qualification. In Section E, especially 281b–d, we find him classifying even courage and *sōphrosunē*, which are two of the four cardinal Socratic/Platonic virtues (the others being wisdom and justice), as neither good nor bad in themselves, but as dependent on knowledge or ignorance to make them so. In *his* analysis of the virtues, they should be forms of knowledge, but occasionally in the dialogues (as here) Plato recognizes debased versions which are not (see *Meno* 88a–c, *Phaedo* 68a–69d, *Laws* 710a, 968a).

In a sense the protreptic aspect of Socrates' discussion with Cleinias both starts and finishes with Section E; but in Sections I and J certain aspects of Section E are subjected to closer consideration. To be precise, a further consequence is drawn out, which may then be called stage 6 of the argument (see p. 305 for stages 1–5):

6. The branch of knowledge we should seek must benefit us, i.e. it must be knowledge of both *achieving* and *using* a product (288e–289b)

This consequence is then examined at length. We must first notice, however, that it is not a true consequence of the argument of Section E. In the first place, Section E established only that knowledge *in general* is worth pursuing, not that a *particular* branch of knowledge leads to happiness; Socrates' words at 282e prepare us for this move, but it is still peculiar. Secondly, the requirement established by Section E was that happiness comes from the correct use of good things, which is guaranteed by wisdom; step 6 goes further, then, in declaring that both achievement and use are requirements. These flaws should be borne in mind.

The argument then proceeds to eliminate candidates for this supreme branch of knowledge, on the grounds that they are concerned with achievement, not both achievement and use (289b–290e). Finally, the art of kingship is considered (291b–292e), because it seems to be the apex of a hierarchy of skills: skill *a* hands over its product for skill *b* to use; skill *b* to skill *c* . . . and so on, to kingship. But even kingship fails to pass the test. By the requirement of step 6, it must have a recognizably good product. But since the only good thing is knowledge (step 4), the product of kingship must be knowledge. But the hypothesis of step 6 is that a single branch of knowledge (now kingship, as it seems), is the only truly good one – so its product must be itself (292d; cf. *Charmides* 165c ff.). The most that can be said is that it makes others good at making others good at making others good . . . without ever specifying what the product is, i.e. what they are to be good *at*. Since a regress like this is untenable, the argument has failed.

The reason it fails is clear enough. It is the insistence at 292b that only some kind of knowledge is good, from which it is concluded that kingship must have itself as its object. Now, this insistence at 292b is couched as a reference back to the earlier part of the protreptic – step 4, to be precise. But when wisdom is there said to be the only good thing, 'good' is meant in an instrumental sense – it is good in the sense that it makes other things good. At 292b, however, Plato takes 'good' to mean 'good in itself'. If he had taken it – as, given the reference back to step 4, he should have done – in the instrumental sense, then the regress would not have arisen. If kingship is good in the sense that it makes other things good – whatever these other things may be (the community, for instance) – it is not self-reflexive. Relatedly, the failure of the argument could be seen to stem from the requirement that the superordinate craft must not only use a product but also be productive. Since it is apparently impossible to find a product for kingship, and the requirement is that there must be, the argument fails. Socrates insists on this point because of the craft analogy (pp. 22–3, 25–6, 267); it is noticeable that Plato in later dialogues drops the insistence on a product in order to establish dialectic as the supreme branch of knowledge (e.g. *Cratylus* 390b–d, *Republic* 533b, *Philebus* 57e–58d; indeed, at *Sophist* 219a–d the 'productive' and 'acquisitive' branches of knowledge are uncompromisingly separated).

Inevitably, when an argument of Plato's fails, there is a temptation to try to mitigate the failure. This temptation has proved especially strong in the case of arguments which, like this, are part of important threads in Plato's thought. Some have pointed to the reasons for the failure of the argument and supposed that Plato was aware, for instance, that a different sense of 'good' was operative and was artificially creating a puzzle. If we take the instrumental sense of 'good', then we may reach a solution similar to that of the *Statesman*: kingship makes other things good by blending them together into a harmonious whole. The problem with this solution is that *Euthydemus* belongs with the earlier, aporetic dialogues, and precedes the great constructive dialogues of Plato's middle and late periods. It is not until *Republic*, then, that Plato starts to give answers in this thread of his thought. This is a general consideration; more particularly, there is no reason to suppose that Plato was aware that different senses of 'good' were operative in the two parts of the argument. It is after all a rather subtle point.

Others (especially Sprague (1976)) have argued for a distinction between first-order crafts, which have products, and second-order crafts, which do not. The claim is that Plato was aware that asking for a product of a second-order craft, like kingship, artificially creates the puzzle. The purpose of the argument, then, would precisely be to show that kingship is not a first-order craft, because it is impossible to find its product. But there is no sign of this distinction in *Euthydemus*. In the early dialogues, Plato's assumption is that each craft has a specific domain and product. It is true that Plato is distinguishing kingship as a superordinate craft, which uses the other crafts' products, but the distinction is not based on its lack of product. It is not impossible, however, that puzzles like this one in *Euthydemus* led to the later Platonic undermining of the Socratic craft analogy.

It seems safest to take the regress at face value: rather than some kind of underhand ploy on Plato's part, it is a record of genuine perplexity. Kingship is the most plausible candidate, but for reasons beyond Plato's control, it fails to satisfy him. It is precisely this perplexity that may have led, ultimately, to the solution of *Statesman*. In the context of *Euthydemus*, Plato's purpose is to distinguish between the stimulating perplexity caused by Socratic dialectic, which is apparent in many early dialogues (the *Euthydemus* would not be alone in this), and the vacuous perplexity caused by eristic.

Philosophy and Politics

The discussion of kingship brings to the fore a theme of *Euthydemus*: the relation between, and relative merits of, philosophy and politics. Socrates' protreptic set out to be an exhortation to philosophy and virtue (278d), but has ended in a discussion of kingship, a political craft. Is philosophy political, then? As far as we can tell from *Euthydemus*, the answer is 'no', because kingship fails to qualify as the supreme craft. Nevertheless, it is true that both Socrates (*Gorgias* 521d–e) and Plato (*Republic*, especially) believe that a true philosopher would be the best statesman, because of his knowledge. Philosophy is not kingship, but if a philosopher undertook to rule – Plato talks in *Republic* 519c of having to compel a philosopher to do so – he would be the best.

Why would he be best? Because he has access to knowledge, certainly; but a question arises in the context of *Euthydemus* which leads in a more specific direction. The search in *Euthydemus* is for the supreme branch of knowledge which will make each and every *individual* happy. Why should kingship even be considered in this context? The answer is given in *Republic*, in the analogy between city and soul: in principle, self-government is the same as governing a community. If you can do either properly, you can do both – hence the ideal of the philosopher-king.

The importance of this ideal to Plato cannot be overestimated. He devotes his two longest works, *Republic* and *Laws*, as well as the substantial *Statesman*, to political matters. He personally spent a lot of time trying to influence Syracusan affairs. And his Academy, whether or not it was established to do so, turned out people who possessed sufficient political competence to be invited to other cities for political purposes, such as codifying laws.

The theme of philosophy and politics resurfaces in the final section of the dialogue (304c ff.). Reading between the lines, we learn that there is an unbridgeable gap between philosophy and politics as the latter is actually practised: the two pursuits do not share the same features at all (306a–c). In this section we encounter Crito's conversation with, and Socrates' methodical criticism of, an unnamed critic who dabbles in both philosophy and politics. It is explicit at the start that Plato has in mind a *type* of person (304d, 305b); but it seems equally undeniable that, as the section progresses, Plato picks on a particular representative of the type to enliven his portrait. The identity of this individual used to be hotly debated, but I have no doubt that the majority of scholars are correct now in picking on Isocrates, a brilliant teacher of rhetoric who was an almost exact contemporary of Plato.

There is certainly evidence to support this view, in that features which Plato attributes to the unnamed critic of philosophy are attributed by Isocrates to himself. For instance, at 305c we learn that although he composes forensic speeches (as Isocrates did at the time of the writing of *Euthydemus*), he himself has never delivered any in public: Isocrates admits at *Panathenaicus* 9 that, to his regret, he has had to avoid public speaking. The description of the critic as dabbling in both philosophy and politics fits Isocrates, who allowed philosophical training in his students in so far as it sharpens the wits in preparation for the training *he* offers (*Antidosis* 261–9). One is reminded of Plato's description of Isocrates at *Phaedrus* 279a: 'He is naturally of a philosophical bent, to a degree.'

Two points might seem to argue against identifying the unnamed critic with Isocrates. First, at 304e, Plato claims to be all but quoting him, but the exact words Plato uses are not to be found in the extant works of Isocrates. Yet neither are they to be found in anybody else's works, and the words in question are certainly in the Isocratean rhetorical manner. Secondly, it is anachronistic to have Socrates discussing Isocrates, who was at the most still only young – too young to have risen to prominence – at the dramatic date of the dialogue. But in response to this it need only be pointed out that Plato not infrequently uses Socrates as a mouthpiece for comments on his own contemporaries.

There was rivalry between Plato and Isocrates, though it was not particularly personal or acrimonious. It was generated by the fact that they were each the prime educators of the time in different fields. Both seem to have felt that the other misunderstood and underestimated the value of his own field. There is evidence for this general background picture (see W. H. Thompson). It is even possible to speculate that the particular scenario for Plato's comments in *Euthydemus* is as follows. In about 390, Isocrates had written *Against the Sophists*, which was, in effect, his protreptic (and should be read by anyone who wants to understand popular attitudes of the time towards the sophists): in it he runs down all other practitioners of philosophy, calling them eristics, in order to claim that his teaching is the valuable one. Plato's response (we may suppose) in *Euthydemus*, which was probably written only a few years later (see p. 297), is a protreptic to dialectic which, as we have seen, satisfactorily distinguishes it from eristic.

SUMMARY OF *EUTHYDEMUS*

EUTHYDEMUS

Speakers

SOCRATES

CRITO: From Athens, a contemporary of Socrates, and a lifelong and devoted friend. He appears in several other dialogues, one of which (named after him) portrays him trying to persuade Socrates to escape from prison. The late biographer Diogenes Laertius, probably erroneously, mentions him (II.121) as a philosopher in his own right.

CLEINIAS: A member of a very eminent Athenian family (see 275a). Aged about sixteen at the time of the dialogue.

CTESIPPUS: From the deme of Paeania in Athens, an aristocrat in his late teens. He was a follower of Socrates and was present at his death (*Phaedo* 59b). Also appears in *Lysis*.

EUTHYDEMUS and DIONYSODORUS: Brothers, born on Chios, emigrated to Thurii, exiled from there and became peripatetic sophists. They are at least as old as Socrates. Their areas of expertise were originally rhetoric and martial techniques, but by the time of the dialogue they have moved on to eristic argument.

EUTHYDEMUS

A. *Introduction*

For the most part, the dialogue is presented in the form of a report: Socrates reconstructs for Crito, an old friend, a discussion in which the active participants, apart from himself, were the two sophists Euthydemus and Dionysodorus, and two well-born young Athenians, Cleinias and Ctesippus.

Apart from introducing most of these characters, this opening section also sets the tone of the dialogue, as Socrates evinces an ironic desire for Euthydemus' and Dionysodorus' new-found eristic expertise. Throughout the dialogue, Socrates' apparent deference to the sophists is an aspect of his usual famous irony – that is, the profession of ignorance (see p. 31). Plato's concern in the dialogue as a whole is to distinguish Socrates from such sophists; the particular reason for doing so is that their eristic method of questioning is superficially similar to Socratic dialectic (see pp. 299–303). Euthydemus and Dionysodorus used to teach weaponry and oratory, neither of which could conceivably be confused with Socrates' speciality; but their form of eristic could, so the irony running throughout the dialogue is particularly sharp.

CRITO: Who was that person you were talking to yesterday in the 271a Lyceum,[1] Socrates? There was quite a crowd around you, and although I wanted to listen, I couldn't get close enough to hear clearly. But I peered over the crowd and got the impression that you were talking to someone from out of town. Who was it?

SOCRATES: Which one, Crito? There were two of them, not just one.

CRITO: I mean the one who was sitting two places to your right, on the other side of Axiochus' boy[2] – who struck me as having grown up a lot, b Socrates, and to have almost caught up with my son Critobulus. But Critobulus is weedy, whereas this lad is mature and good-looking.

SOCRATES: Euthydemus is the one you're asking about, Crito, and the other one, who sat next to me on my left, was his brother Dionysodorus, who also joined in the discussion.

CRITO: I don't know either of them, Socrates – I suppose they are more new sophists. Where are they from? What are they experts in? c

---

1. A gymnasium just outside ancient Athens which was a popular meeting-place, and seems to have been especially frequented by intellectuals: it was a favourite haunt of Socrates and, later, of Aristotle. cf. p. 131 n. 2.

2. Cleinias; see further 275a.

SOCRATES: Their family roots, I think, are in this part of the world, in Chios, but they went as colonists to Thurii;[1] they've been exiled from there, however, and for many years now they've been spending time in these parts.[2] As to your question about their expertise, Crito, it's astonishing: they are absolutely omniscient – I hadn't realized before what pancratiasts really are.[3] These two are absolutely all-round fighters, not restricted
d to *physical* fighting as the pair of pancratiast Acarnanian brothers were.[4] Supreme physical skill at the sort of fighting which can overpower anyone[5] is only the first of their attainments: they are expert fighters in armour,[6]
272a and can make others the same, for a fee. Secondly, they excel both at contesting legal battles and at teaching others to deliver and compose speeches suitable for the lawcourts.[7] These attainments *used* to be the limits of their ability, but now they have put the finishing touch to pancratiastic skill. They have now perfected the sole form of fighting they had neglected; they are utterly invincible, so formidable have they become at
b verbal battle – specifically, refutation of any statement, no matter whether it is true or false.[8] Anyway, Crito, I intend to put myself in their hands, since they claim that they wouldn't take long to make anyone else equally formidable.

CRITO: What, Socrates? Don't you think you might already be too old at your age?

SOCRATES: Not at all, Crito. I have enough evidence to encourage me not to worry. You see, these two themselves were getting on when they embarked on what *I* covet – eristic expertise.[9] A year or two ago they

1. Chios is an island about 120 miles ENE of Athens, but all the Greek-speaking east Mediterranean was considered familiar, because it had 'always' been Greek. Thurii was a colony in south Italy – more recent Greek territory – founded in 443 near the site of Sybaris. Thurii was the brainchild of the great Athenian statesman Pericles: a panhellenic colony initiated by Athens.

2. Exile was not uncommon; it was a punishment and a hardship, but no great stigma was necessarily attached. Euthydemus and Dionysodorus may simply have been on the losing side in some political upheaval.

3. Pancration was a brutal combination of wrestling and boxing (see also p. 184 n. 1); the word means, literally, 'all-powerful'. On omniscience, see Section K.

4. Reading παμμάχω, οὐ κάθ' ἃ τὼ 'Ακαρνᾶνε with Gifford. Nothing is known of these Acarnanian brothers. Acarnania was a district in western Greece.

5. Retaining καὶ μάχῃ, ᾗ πάντων ἐστι κρατεῖν with the manuscripts.

6. *Laches* 178a refers to a display by a professional teacher of fighting in armour, probably to attract students.

7. A common sophistic enterprise (see Guthrie, III, Chapter 8).

8. This was a common charge against the sophists (see pp. 215–16) and one which, therefore, is made against Socrates himself by the comic poet Aristophanes (*Clouds* 98–9). But see 287e for Socrates' belief that the truth is irrefutable.

9. On eristic, see pp. 299–300.

hadn't made it. There's only one thing I'm afraid of – that the two visitors c
will lose face because of me, as Metrobius' son Connus, the lyre-player,[1]
already does, because he is *still* teaching me to play the instrument, and
my young companions laugh at me and call Connus a 'crock's coach'.[2]
The problem is that our visitors might incur the same reproach, and if
they worry about that, they might not be prepared to take me on. In
Connus' case, Crito, I've persuaded other old men to come along with me
as pupils, and I'll try to do the same now. Why don't you come along? d
We'll take your sons as bait: in their anxiety to have them, I'm sure they'll
enrol us too as pupils.[3]

CRITO: That's all right with me, Socrates, if you say so. But first explain
their speciality to me. I want to know what we are going to learn.

SOCRATES: You shall hear it straight away. I cannot deny that I listened
attentively to them; in fact, I paid close attention, I remember it well, and
I will try to tell you everything from start to finish.

B. *Second Introduction*

*This introduction to the actual conversation which Socrates is to recount to Crito
gives us a pleasantly vivid picture of the scene in the Lyceum. The homosexuality
of Ctesippus and the others was a fact of life in the upper-class segment of
Athenian society at the time. The more interesting aspect of Cleinias' admirers
is a literary point: Plato is obviously seeking, here and elsewhere in the dialogue,
to compare the crowd surrounding Cleinias with the crowd surrounding the two
sophists (see also the satirical portrayal of various sophists and their followers
in* Protagoras *315a–e). They could be seen as the two halves of the 'chorus' of
a comedy (see p. 298). Both groups consist of admirers (273a, 276d), but the
former desire the best for their beloved in a moral sense (275a), while the latter
desire eristic victory for the two sophists (276c–d). See further Grube, Chapter
3, on love in Plato's thought as a motivator in philosophy.*

SOCRATES: It was my good fortune to be sitting by myself in the e
changing-room, where you saw me. I was thinking that it was time to go,

1. Connus is also mentioned as Socrates' music-teacher at *Menexenus* 235e–236a.

2. The pun is not in the Greek, but captures the flavour of the outrageous compound word
Plato uses, which could, in fact, be out of a comedy, since the comic poets were fond of
inventing such compounds: Plato's is literally 'old-man-teacher'.

3. Interest in the sophists was primarily among young men; sophists, therefore, pitched
their displays at that audience.

273a but when I got up, my regular supernatural signal occurred,[1] so I sat down again, and not long afterwards those two, Euthydemus and Dionysodorus, entered, accompanied by lots of other people – pupils, I supposed. Once inside, the pair of them began to walk around the covered walk. They had completed no more than two or three circuits, when in comes Cleinias, who, as you rightly point out, has grown up a lot. In his train was a crowd of admirers, including Ctesippus, a very well-bred young man – except

b for a youthful brashness – of the deme of Paeania.[2] When Cleinias spotted me from the doorway sitting by myself, he came straight over and sat on my right, just as you describe it; and when Dionysodorus and Euthydemus saw him, they first stopped and began to speak to each other, looking in our direction every so often – I was watching them carefully. Then they came and sat down, Euthydemus by the boy, Dionysodorus next to me on my left, and the rest wherever they could.

c I hadn't seen them for a while, so I said hello, and then I said to Cleinias: 'Cleinias, at last you can meet clever men who don't waste their cleverness on trivia: Euthydemus and Dionysodorus know all about warfare, that is, what a prospective military commander should know, if he is to be a good one – they know about the deployment of troops and about leadership, and they have a complete course of the instruction necessary for fighting in armour[3] – and they are also capable of making any injured party self-reliant in the lawcourts.'

d Contempt was their response to my speech. At any rate,[4] they exchanged glances and laughed, and Euthydemus said: 'We no longer bother with those matters, Socrates. We treat them as peripheral.'

I was astonished. 'If you treat such important matters as peripheral,' I said, 'then what on earth can your main occupation be? It must be pretty impressive. Tell me, please.'

'Virtue, Socrates,' he said. 'We think that we are the finest and quickest teachers of virtue alive.'[5]

---

1. On Socrates' *daimonion*, see *Apology* 31c–d, *Phaedrus* 242b–c and Riddell; see also p. 18 n. 3.

2. The demes were districts of Athens and Attica. Paeania was west of Athens. Ctesippus also appears in *Lysis*.

3. Retaining ὅσα and διδακτέον with the manuscripts.

4. Reading γοῦν with Heindorf.

5. The sophists claimed to teach *aretē* (excellence) at whatever they taught; some claimed to teach *aretē* in general – virtue (see Kerferd, *The Sophistic Movement*, Index s.v. *aretē*). '[Euthydemus and Dionysodorus] teach mockeries of the traditional excellences: litigation instead of justice, techniques of fighting instead of courage, and above all eristic instead of wisdom' (Scolnicov, p. 20). Socrates upheld the traditional virtues, though he had his own views about them.

'Good heavens!' I said. 'That's fantastic! How did you two come across   e
this godsend? I was still thinking, as I said a moment ago, that your
speciality was fighting in armour, and that's what I attributed to you. I
remember your claiming as much when you were in Athens before. But
if you really do possess this knowledge, have mercy. (You see, in begging
your pardon for my earlier words, I address you exactly as if you were   274a
divine.)¹ But, Euthydemus and Dionysodorus, are you sure you are speaking the truth? Scepticism is natural when faced with such a large claim.'

'You may be sure, Socrates,' they both said,² 'that that is the fact of the
matter.'

'In that case, I think you are far more fortunate in this possession than
the king of Persia in his empire. There's only one question: do you plan
to give an exhibition³ of this wisdom, or what have you decided to do?'

'That's precisely why we're here, Socrates: to give demonstrations and
to teach anyone who is prepared to learn.'   b

'I assure you that everyone who lacks what you offer will be prepared:
I'll be first in the queue myself, then Cleinias here, with Ctesippus – that's
him – and the rest close behind,' I said, pointing out Cleinias' admirers,
who were by now grouped around us. You see, Ctesippus had sat down
far away from Cleinias, and I got the impression that as Euthydemus
leaned forward to talk to me, he blocked Ctesippus' view of Cleinias, who   c
was in between us. So, since Ctesippus wanted to see his beloved and yet
not miss out on the conversation, he had jumped up and stood right
opposite us; seeing him do this, the others followed suit and grouped
themselves around us, not only Cleinias' admirers, but Euthydemus' and
Dionysodorus' followers too.⁴ So I gestured towards them and told Euthydemus that they all wanted to be their pupils. Ctesippus and the rest   d
agreed very enthusiastically, and the request that they demonstrate the
power of their wisdom was endorsed unanimously.

That was my cue: 'Yes, Euthydemus and Dionysodorus, please do all
you can to oblige our friends here with a demonstration – and I too will
be obliged to you. Now, obviously, it's too much to ask you to give a
comprehensive demonstration, but tell me this: are you capable of improving only the person who is already convinced of the necessity of studying
under you, or can you also improve someone who is not yet convinced,   e
either because he is of the general opinion that virtue is not something
that can be learned, or because he doesn't think that you are teachers of

1. See the similar irony at 288a–b, 293a and 301e.
2. Reading ἐφάτην with Bekker.
3. *Epideixis*: see pp. 32 and 215.
4. *Lysis* 207a–b has a very similar set-up.

it? Come on, tell me. Suppose you're faced with someone who thinks that way: does the task of convincing him both that virtue is teachable and that you in particular are the best teachers of it belong to this same skill of yours, or to some other skill?'[1]

'It belongs to the same skill, Socrates,' said Dionysodorus.

'Then there's no one alive today, Dionysodorus,' I said, 'who would be 275a better than you two at giving a protreptic to philosophy, that is, the practice of virtue?'[2]

'That is our opinion, Socrates.'

'So please postpone the exhibition of the rest until later,' I said, 'and just concentrate on convincing our young friend here of the indispensability of philosophy and the practice of virtue; that will put all of us here in your debt, because, as his luck would have it, we are all concerned about enhancing his welfare as much as possible. Let me introduce you: Cleinias, b the son of Axiochus, grandson of the old Alcibiades and first cousin of the present Alcibiades.[3] He is young, and we are afraid – youth gives grounds for such fear – that, before our influence has taken hold, his mind may be corrupted by being turned towards some other pursuit. So you two have come at just the right time. If you have no objection, test the lad's mettle: engage him in conversation here, in front of us.'

That was more or less exactly what I said. Euthydemus replied gamely and confidently: 'No, we have no objection, Socrates, as long as the young c man is willing to answer questions.'[4]

'Oh well, he's no stranger to *that*,' I said. 'You see, this lot here often ply him with questions and draw him into discussions, so he's pretty confident at answering.'[5]

C. *Wisdom and Ignorance: The Sophists' Version*

The arguments of this section, as of many of the sophistic sections of the dialogue, present problems for the translator. Many of the sophisms, quite natural in

1. The question whether virtue is teachable was one of the cruxes of intellectual debate in Socrates' time – naturally enough, since the sophists claimed to teach it (see Guthrie, III, Chapter 10; Kerferd, *The Sophistic Movement*, Chapter 11). Plato's *Protagoras* and *Meno* are concerned with the question; cf. below, 282c.

2. On protreptic, see p. 305.

3. Impressive: a very eminent family.

4. The sophists insist on asking the questions (see also 287c–d, 293b, 295a, 298d, 299b – it is one of their refrains), because 'the game that the brothers play will work only if the answerer keeps to the rules and does no more than answer the questions as put' (Hawtrey (1981), p. 57).

5. That is, probably, they imitated Socrates (see *Apology* 23c) and played at dialectic as a game (see Ryle) – perhaps a flirtatious game, given the circumstances.

Greek, cannot easily be expressed in English, and even those which are more forced in Greek are usually no more strange than puns (which, arguably, several of them are).

As Socrates will point out in 277e–278a (and at Theaetetus *199a), the arguments in this section are fallacious because they trade on an ambiguity in 'learn', which means either 'engage in the process of learning' or 'successfully complete the process of learning'; ignorant people need to do the former, but clever people do the latter. Parallel to the ambiguity in 'learn' is another in 'clever' (and* mutatis mutandis *in 'ignorant') which means either 'skilful (at the process of learning or some other task)' or 'knowledgeable' (i.e. having completed the process of learning). In Greek, as in English, the former meaning is more usual; but the latter meaning is more common for the Greek* sophos *than for the English 'clever', so such sentences as 'In fact, if you weren't clever, you were ignorant, weren't you?' (276b) are rather forced in translation.*

There is no need to suppose (as Stewart does, p. 27) that Plato was unaware of the ambiguity of 'clever' and 'ignorant', simply because in 277e–278a he comments only on the ambiguity of 'learn'. At 277e–278a he is trying to summarize and quickly dismiss the sophisms both of this and of the next section: a full analysis would have been out of place. The ambiguity of 'clever' and 'ignorant' is as glaringly obvious as that of 'learn' in the context of the sophism, and may be said to depend on it, so to point out only the primary ambiguity and to omit the dependent one is a fair tactic.

Dionysodorus' contribution (276c) is a different ploy, designed only to contradict the first conclusion (276b) and thereby produce confusion: his argument does not depend on any fallacy in itself, but he simply agrees with Cleinias' original reply to Euthydemus in order to gain the contradiction. If Cleinias had given the alternative answer, 'ignorant people', to Euthydemus' original question, then Dionysodorus' argument would have been used to refute him and Euthydemus' would have been used to agree with him. The sophists, we can see, have a battery of arguments to bring out as appropriate.

So instead of the protreptic Socrates was expecting (274e–275a), we get a sophism and confusion. The sophists employ the word 'wisdom' ('cleverness', 'skill' – all the same word in Greek, sophia), *but Socrates wants Cleinias to be encouraged actually to love wisdom* (philo-sophia, *philosophy).*

Hawtrey (1981, p. 21) comments: 'Those who learn are neither wise nor ignorant – which is exactly the condition of philosophers at Lysis 218a–b.' This is part of a recent tendency among commentators on our dialogue to find covert references to Socratic/Platonic thought in the sophisms. This would be nice – it would add to the poignancy of Plato's distinction of Socrates from the sophists – but is, I believe, very rarely justified. Here it must be wrong: the result of this pair of arguments is that those who learn are both wise and ignorant (as are those who understand, too). The sophism has no point: it is just a trick.

Now, Crito, I wonder how I might give you a fair account of what happened. I mean, it's a colossal task to recall and then recount such an incredible amount of cleverness. I shall have to imitate the poets and
d   invoke the Muses and Memory as I embark on my account[1] . . . So, Euthydemus started from roughly this direction, I think: 'Tell me, Cleinias, are clever or ignorant people those who learn?'

Faced with this momentous question, the lad blushed and looked at me in puzzlement. I saw that he was flustered and said: 'Don't worry,
e   Cleinias. Just pluck up courage and give whichever answer you think is right. Remember, you'll probably benefit enormously.'

While I was saying this, Dionysodorus had leaned over to me with a big grin on his face, to whisper briefly in my ear. 'In fact, Socrates,' he said, 'I can tell you now that whichever answer the lad gives, he will be proved wrong.'

As luck would have it, Cleinias gave his answer at the same time as Dionysodorus was telling me this, so I didn't have a chance to recommend
276a   caution to him; he replied that clever people are the ones who learn.

'Do you or do you not acknowledge the existence of teachers?' asked Euthydemus.

He agreed that he did.

'And teachers teach learners – for instance, you and your schoolmates had a music-teacher and a writing-teacher, from whom you used to learn?'

He agreed.

'So wasn't it the case that when you were learners, you didn't yet know what you were learning?'

He agreed that they did not.

b   'And were you clever when you didn't have this knowledge?'

'Of course not,' he said.

'In fact, if you weren't clever, you were ignorant, weren't you?'[2]

'Yes.'

'So, while learning what you didn't know, you were learning because you were ignorant.'

The lad nodded.

1. Poets often invoked the Muse(s) at the end of a prologue and start of a main account – or, generally, at the start of some particularly difficult section of their work. Memory is said to be the mother of the Muses.

2. A typical leading question: no middle ground is allowed between knowledge and ignorance.

'Therefore, Cleinias, it is ignorant people who learn, not clever people, as you imagine.'

As if these words were a prompt by a director to a chorus,[1] Dionysodorus' and Euthydemus' followers broke out into cheers and laughter. And before the lad could draw a proper breath, Dionysodorus took over and said: 'Now, Cleinias, when the writing-teacher was reciting a piece, was it the clever or the ignorant children who learned it?'

'The clever ones,' said Cleinias.

'So clever people learn, not ignoramuses: you gave the wrong reply to Euthydemus just now.'

D. *More on Learning and Knowledge*

As Dionysodorus suggests at 276d–e, Socrates at 278a–b and Aristotle at De Sophisticis Elenchis 165b30–32, the fallacy of equivocation on 'learn' is operative in this section, as it was in the last (see pp. 320–22). The situation is confused, however, by the presence of another fallacy, that of composition (p. 304).

This fallacy of composition occurs at 277a, where it is assumed that anyone who knows the alphabet knows all the words and sentences that the letters of the alphabet may be combined into. (Aristotle uses this as an example of the fallacy at Rhetoric 1401a29–31, and he has just mentioned Euthydemus a line earlier.) Cleinias makes the mistake of accepting the assumption. Given this we can see how the equivocation on 'learn' plays a part.

Cleinias answers Euthydemus' question whether those who learn learn what they know (276d) negatively, as if 'learn' means 'engage in the process of learning' (276e). Euthydemus then uses the fallacy of composition to force the agreement that if Cleinias knows the alphabet, then when he learns a recitation, he learns what he knows (since the recitation consists of letters of the alphabet). So the sense of learn can be changed, and Euthydemus' conclusion (277b) can mean 'You successfully learn what you know.'

Dionysodorus' half of the argument (277b–c) supports Cleinias' original answer with a reasonable, if somewhat long-winded, argument which results in the opposite conclusion to that of Euthydemus' fallacious argument. As in Section C, Dionysodorus plays the straight man to Euthydemus' 'fool', to produce confusion between them. The pattern of both sections is exactly the same: Euthydemus asks a question in which 'learn' could be taken either way; Cleinias chooses one way; Euthydemus fallaciously turns it the other way; Dionysodorus reverts to the original way.

1. See pp. 298, 317.

Hawtrey comments (1981, p. 21): 'They learn neither what they know nor what they do not know – which is exactly what is implied by the [Socratic] theory of recollection, according to which they learn what they latently "know" but have forgotten.' But again there is no true similarity with Socratic/Platonic thought (cf. pp. 321–2): the result of the sophism is again pointless – that those who learn learn both what they know and what they do not know. It is true that the 'eristic' argument of Meno 80d–e is comparable: you cannot look for what you do not know (because you won't recognize it) and you obviously need not look for what you already know. Plato's solution to this paradox in Meno is the theory of recollection, whereby all so-called learning is actually recollection of prenatal knowledge. But the argument in Euthydemus is similar only to the paradox, not to the solution. Our understanding of this section of Euthydemus is not enhanced at all by bearing in mind the theory of recollection. It is likely that fifth-century sophists had come up with a number of similar paradoxes, which both Euthydemus and Meno are reflecting independently.

d   At this point, the pair's admirers, delighted with their heroes' cleverness, laughed and cheered very loudly, while the rest of us were speechless with amazement. Euthydemus recognized our amazement and, in order to astound us even more, kept on relentlessly questioning the lad, and in good choreographic style began to turn his questions back around the same spot. 'Do those who learn learn what they know,' he asked, 'or what they do not know?'

Dionysodorus had another brief word in my ear: 'This is another one
e just like the first, Socrates,' he said.

'Heavens!' I exclaimed. 'I can assure you that we were impressed by the *first* question.'

'All our questions of this sort are designed to trap people, Socrates,' he said.

'*That*, I think,' I said, 'is why your pupils look up to you.'

Cleinias had meanwhile replied that those who learn learn what they do
277a *not* know, and Euthydemus' questions employed the same method as before: 'But surely you know the alphabet, don't you?' he asked.

'Yes,' he said.

'Right through?'

He agreed.

'Now, doesn't a recitation consist of letters?'

He agreed.

'So, if you know the whole alphabet, then a recitation consists of what you know, doesn't it?'

He agreed to this too.

'Well then,' he said, 'Do you *not* learn a recitation, while someone ignorant of the alphabet does?'[1]

'No,' he replied, 'I do learn it.'

'Therefore, you learn what you know,' he said, 'if you know the alphabet.'

b

He agreed.

'So your answer was wrong,' he said.

These words were hardly out of Euthydemus' mouth when Dionysodorus took over the argument, as if it were a ball to catch and throw at the lad: 'Euthydemus is having you on, Cleinias,' he said. 'I mean, wouldn't you say that learning is the acquisition of knowledge of what is being learned?'

Cleinias agreed.

'And knowing is the current possession of knowledge, surely?'

He agreed.

'Ignorance, therefore, is not yet possessing knowledge?'

He agreed with him.

c

'Well, do people acquire something which they already possess or something which they lack?'

'Something which they lack.'

'And you have agreed that ignorant people are among those who have a lack?'

He nodded.

'And those who learn are acquirers, not possessors?'

He agreed.

'Therefore, Cleinias,' he concluded, 'it is ignorant people who learn, not knowledgeable ones.'

E. *The Socratic Protreptic*

This section provides the positive Socratic arguments to encourage someone to take up philosophy. It is discussed at length on pp. 304–7. The arguments are positive in the sense that they reach some meaningful conclusion, unlike those of Euthydemus and Dionysodorus; but this is not to say that they are free from formal fallacies (pointed out in the footnotes). In the context of Plato's awareness of such fallacies, we have to conclude that it is the nullity of the sophists' arguments, rather than their invalidity, which strikes Plato as most

1. Euthydemus is not saying that ignorance of the alphabet causes inability to learn a piece – which would be totally indefensible: he is just getting Cleinias to agree that he (Cleinias), at any rate, does learn it.

abhorrent (see pp. 301–2). Even if one disagrees with Socrates' conclusions, reflection on the universal desire for happiness is obviously less trivial than the sophists' word-games.

As a literary point, it is worth noting that Socrates makes use of the same terms – cleverness and ignorance – as Euthydemus and Dionysodorus did in the last two sections. This may not immediately be obvious to the English reader, because the word sophos has to be translated differently in different contexts: it means 'clever', 'skilful' and 'wise'. Wisdom is the goal of the philosopher, who literally loves (philein) wisdom (sophia). For Socrates, such wisdom constitutes virtue and is precisely parallel to the skill of a craftsman (see pp. 22–3, 25–6, 267–8): one might say that it is skill at living.

d   Euthydemus was winding up to throw the youngster yet again – a third fall, as it were[1] – but I saw that the lad was going under and I wanted to give him a break, rather than see him submit, so I consoled him: 'Cleinias, you shouldn't be surprised if the arguments strike you as odd: you probably don't realize what our visitors are doing with you, which is just like the enthronement of the neophyte in Corybantic rites.[2] On those occasions too – as you know if you've been initiated – there is light-hearted dancing;

e   and that is just what these two are doing – stepping and dancing around you light-heartedly, to lead up to your initiation. So now you should believe that you are hearing the opening phase of the sophistic mysteries. The first thing, as Prodicus says,[3] is to learn the correct usage of words. And that is exactly what our two visitors are showing you, that you didn't realize that "learn" is used in two different contexts: (a) when initial

278a ignorance about some matter is being replaced by the acquisition of knowledge about it; and (b) when, with knowledge already present, this same matter – it may be an action or a statement – is surveyed in the light of this knowledge. ("Understand" is more common than "learn" for this latter sense, but "learn" is occasionally used.) Anyway, as our friends here point out,[4] you have overlooked the fact that the same word is applied to people in the opposite conditions of knowledge and ignorance. The

---

1. To throw one's opponent three times in wrestling constituted victory. Plato next mixes in a metaphor from swimming.

2. See Linforth on this passage and these rites. The Corybantes were followers of the Mother goddess Cybele, whose ecstatic and cathartic cult had entered Greece from Asia Minor. See also p. 55 n. 1 and *Ion* 536c.

3. See p. 110 n. 3.

4. In saying that the sophists are concerned to 'point out' ambiguities, Socrates is, of course, being heavily ironic; so when he says that this part of the sophists' course is trivial, he does not necessarily mean that it is trivial to point out ambiguities, but only to exploit them. This bears on the question of Plato's awareness of fallacy: see pp. 301–2.

point of the second question was similar too, when it was asked whether people learn what they know or what they don't know. Now, this is not b the serious part of the curriculum, which is why I say that their treatment of you is light-hearted; I call it playful because mastery of even a substantial amount, or even the whole, of this sort of stuff would by no means lead to increased knowledge of how things are, but only to the ability to play games with people, tripping them up and flooring them with different senses of words, just like those who derive pleasure and amusement from pulling stools from under people when they are about to sit down, and from seeing someone floundering on his back. So you should realize that c so far they've had their tongues in their cheeks; but no doubt they will of their own accord show you the serious part next. I shall suggest a way in which they might fulfil their promise to me: they *said* they were going to give an exhibition of protreptic wisdom,[1] but in fact they apparently felt that a prerequisite was playing games with you. So, enough of your games, Euthydemus and Dionysodorus: more would probably be superfluous. d For your next exhibition, convince the lad of the necessity of pursuing wisdom and virtue. But first, I'll just outline for you what I'd like to hear – that is, what I take the task to be. If my effort strikes you as ridiculously amateurish, please don't mock: my eagerness to hear your wisdom makes me risk an impromptu in your presence. So will you and your students please be patient and hear me out without laughing? And will you, son of e Axiochus, answer my questions?

'Does everybody want success?[2] That's a stupid question, I suppose – a typical example of the sort of absurd question I was afraid of just now, perhaps? I mean, who doesn't want success?'

'No one,' replied Cleinias.

'Well then,' I said, 'the next question, given that we want success, is 279a how might we gain it? If we had plenty of good things? Or is this an even sillier question than before? I mean, this too is indisputably so, I suppose.'

He agreed.

'All right, then: what sorts of things are in fact good things? Well, that isn't difficult: we don't seem to need any particularly distinguished personage to give us a fluent answer to this one either, do we? Anyone would tell us that wealth is good. Right?'

'Yes,' he said.

1. On protreptic, see p. 305.
2. 'Success' translates *eu prattein*, which literally means 'to do well'. This is a vague expression, and one of its ambiguities, as either 'be successful' or 'be happy', is argued for in what follows (see pp. 306–7).

b   'And the same goes for health, good looks and adequate physical characteristics generally?'

He agreed.

'But we mustn't forget good birth, power and authority in one's country, which are obviously good.'

He agreed.

'Have we missed out any good things?' I asked. 'What about self-responsibility,[1] justice and courage? Give me your honest opinion, Cleinias: would we correctly class these as good or not? I mean, there *could* be disagreement on this.[2] What do you think?'

'That they are good,' replied Cleinias.

c   'All right, then,' I said. 'How shall we cast wisdom?[3] As good, or what?'

'As good.'

'Now, make sure that we aren't overlooking anything good – at least, anything worth mentioning.'

'No, I don't think we are,' said Cleinias.

Then I remembered something, and said: 'Good heavens, we are in danger of missing out the greatest good of all!'

'What?' he asked.

'Good luck, Cleinias, which is unanimously – even by pretty uneducated people – held to be the greatest good of all.'[4]

'You're right,' he said.

Then I had another afterthought, and said: 'You and I, Cleinias, have
d just come very close to making ourselves objects of our visitors' derision.'

'Why?' he asked.

'Because our inclusion of good luck in the list is redundant.'

'What are you getting at?'

'It is ridiculous to propose all over again something that has already been proposed, and to cover the same ground twice.'

'What do you mean?' he asked.

'Wisdom *is* good luck, you know,' I said. 'This is something even a child would appreciate.'[5]

---

1. *Sōphrosunē*: see p. 331 n. 2.

2. From, for example, Callicles in *Gorgias* and Thrasymachus in *Republic* I, who think such virtues as justice are conventional restraints on the naturally strong person.

3. The Greek is, more literally, 'In which rank of the chorus shall we put wisdom?' The chorus of a Greek play was arranged into three ranks, with the best performers in the first rank.

4. This looks like a corrective to the argument of *Meno* 87c–89a, which is very similar to the argument of this section, but omits good luck.

5. On the weakness of this argument, see p. 306. Aristotle criticizes it too (*Eudemian Ethics* VIII.2).

He was surprised – a sign of his youth and naïvety – and because I recognized that he was surprised,[1] I said: 'Surely you're aware, Cleinias,   e that pipe-players have the best luck as regards success at pipe-playing?'

He agreed.

'And that the same goes for scribes,' I went on, 'as regards reading and writing?'

'Yes.'

'Moreover, surely, you wouldn't expect anyone to have better luck, when faced with maritime dangers, than an expert helmsman, generally speaking?'

'Of course not.'

'And would you prefer to face military risks and hazards in the company of a clever or an ignorant commander?'[2]   280a

'A clever one.'

'And would you rather take your chances with a clever or an ignorant doctor when you're ill?'

'A clever one.'

'Therefore,' I said, 'you think that you will have better luck if your affairs are attended by an expert rather than an ignoramus, don't you?'

'Yes.'

'In every walk of life, then, wisdom causes luck: wisdom can never fail at all, but must be successful and attain its goal. Otherwise it would no longer be wisdom.'[3]

The long and short of it was that we finally agreed – I don't know how –   b that whenever wisdom is present,[4] good luck is redundant. Once we'd reached this agreement, I returned to our earlier agreed conclusions and asked him how they stood. 'You see,' I continued, 'we agreed that if we had plenty of good things, we would be happy[5] and successful.'

He agreed.

'Now, would we be happy if we derived no benefit from the presence of these good things? Or do they have to benefit us?'

1. A nice contrast with 276d, where the same situation, verbally echoed here, led to Euthydemus increasing the confusion, rather than trying to explain himself.

2. The shift from luck as something the expert has to something the expert's protégé has is not important: Socrates' point is that in either case good luck is a product of expertise.

3. Similarly, at *Republic* 340d–e, Thrasymachus is made to argue that a failure in skill is by definition not skill. The concept of skill does not in itself allow error.

4. Reading ὅταν with the manuscripts.

5. 'Happiness' translates *eudaimonia*, for which there is really no satisfactory translation (see p. 25). It is whatever one takes to be the goal of life and to fulfil one's nature – sensual pleasure for some, for others contemplation, and so on. It is vague, then, in the same way as 'success' (see p. 327 n. 2), with which it is here taken to be synonymous.

'They have to benefit us.'

c   'And does mere possession without use benefit us? For example, would we benefit at all from the possession of plenty of food and drink without eating or drinking?'

'Of course not,' he said.

'Now, take a craftsman who has all the equipment suitable for his job, but doesn't use it: is he going to be successful, just because he has in his possession everything he needs to possess? For example, if a carpenter has equipped himself with all his tools and enough wood, but doesn't do any carpentry, is he going to benefit at all from the possession of them?'

d   'Impossible,' he said.

'Well then, suppose someone has acquired wealth and all the good things we just mentioned, but doesn't put them to use: would the mere possession of these things cause him to be happy?'

'Of course not, Socrates.'

'It apparently follows,' I said, 'that one must[1] not only possess these good things, but also use them, if one is to be happy. I mean,[2] no benefit is gained from possession alone.'

'That's right.'

e   'So do the possession and use of good things constitute a sufficient condition of happiness?'

'*I* think so.'

'For this to be so, do they need to be used *correctly*, or not?' I asked.[3]

'Correctly.'

'You're right,' I said. 'I'm inclined to think that it is more untoward for something to be used incorrectly than to be left alone, because the one situation is actually bad, but the other is neither good nor bad. Isn't that
281a our position?'

He agreed.

'Now then, in the case of working with and using wood, it is knowledge of carpentry which engenders correct use, isn't it?'

'Of course,' he said.

'And, I suppose, in the case of working with equipment, it is again knowledge that engenders the correct procedures.'

He agreed.

'Well,' I said, 'in the case of using the good things we mentioned at the outset – wealth, health and good looks – didn't we find that it is again

1. Reading δεῖν with the manuscripts.
2. Reading ὡς with the manuscripts.
3. A clear case of Socrates using a leading question. See also p. 306 on the circularity of Socrates' argument here.

knowledge which governs action and makes it correct, or was it something   b
else?'

'It was knowledge,' he said.

'Apparently, then, knowledge affords people success as well as giving
them good luck, whatever they possess or do.'

He agreed.

'So,' I said, 'can we in all honesty say that if someone lacks intelligence
and wisdom, he will benefit from his other possessions? Which is better
for an unintelligent person: to be rich in possessions and have a finger in
many pies, or to have few possessions and be less busy?[1] Look at it this
way: the less he did, the fewer mistakes he would make; the fewer mis-   c
takes, the less unsuccessful he would be; and the less unsuccessful he was,
the less miserable he would be. Isn't that right?'

'Yes,' he said.

'Is poverty or wealth more conducive to less business?'

'Poverty,' he said.

'Weakness or strength?'

'Weakness.'

'Authority or obscurity?'

'Obscurity.'

'And do courage and self-responsibility[2] make for less activity, or does
cowardice?'

'Cowardice.'

'Laziness, then, rather than energy?'

He agreed.

'And ambling rather than running? Sight and hearing which are dull
rather than sharp?'   d

He agreed with me on these and all similar points.

'In a nutshell, Cleinias,' I said, 'it seems likely that our account of all
the things we originally said were good is not concerned with the sense in
which they are naturally good *per se*. No, the facts are apparently as
follows: if ignorance guides them, they are greater evils than their
opposites, to the extent that they put more power in the hands of their
evil leader; but if intelligence and wisdom guide them, they are greater
goods – but in themselves both "good" and "bad" things are valueless.'[3]

1. Omitting νοῦν ἔχων as Iamblichus does.

2. 'Self-responsibility' translates *sōphrosunē* here and at 279b: the usual translations, such as
'self-restraint', fail to fit the context, because they imply *less* activity, not more: see also *Charmides* 159b–160d.

3. This is a crucial development in Socrates' ethics: if the only truly good thing is knowledge,
this will allow him to claim that wisdom unites the virtues (see *Protagoras*), that neutral things
are subordinate to the final good (see *Lysis* 219c–220b), and that we need some superordinate

e   'It rather looks as though you're right,' he said.

'What emerges from all this? Surely that nothing else is good or bad, and that of the pair we've been discussing, wisdom is good, ignorance bad?'

He agreed.

282a   'Well, our investigation isn't over yet,' I said. 'The desire for happiness is universal,[1] and we found that happiness stems from use – correct use – of things, and that correctness, in turn, and good luck, are products of knowledge; it apparently follows that everyone should be expending all their efforts on making themselves as wise as possible. Isn't that so?'

'Yes,' he said.

'Now, take someone who believes that *this* is a far more valuable gift to receive than money – particularly from his father, but also from anyone he looks up to or likes (especially those who claim to be his admirers), and

b   from strangers and neighbours – and begs and beseeches them to share their wisdom; for such a person, Cleinias, with his mind set on this goal, it is not at all demeaning or a source of reproach to be dominated by, and enslaved to, a lover or anyone, and to be willing, in his desire to become wise, to perform any fine act of service. Don't you think that is so?' I asked.

'I think you're quite right,' he said.

c   'Well, at least if wisdom is teachable, Cleinias,' I pointed out, 'and not something which people get by chance. That's a problem you and I haven't yet considered and reached a verdict on.'

'Well, *I* think it's something teachable, Socrates,' he said.

That pleased me. 'That's good to hear,' I said. 'Wonderful! Thank you for allowing me to dispense with a long inquiry into precisely this point, whether or not wisdom is something teachable.[2] Anyway, since you think it is something teachable and is the sole source of happiness and good luck

d   for men, then wouldn't you say that philosophy is essential? And do you yourself intend to take it up?'

'I most certainly do, Socrates,' he said, 'to the best of my ability.'

I was delighted to hear this. 'Well, Dionysodorus and Euthydemus,' I said, 'there you have *my* version – amateurish, perhaps, and clumsily long-

---

craft to guide all the others (see Sections I and J).

    1. Notice the substitution of 'happiness' for the 'success' of the original proposition (278e); see p. 329 n. 5.

    2. The same Greek word (*sophia*) means both 'wisdom' and 'skill', so it is not surprising that both Socrates and Cleinias think that it is teachable. Perhaps Socrates says that a long inquiry would be needed because he has been assuming that wisdom is virtue, a topic which calls for the lengthy dialogue *Protagoras*.

winded[1] – of what I want protreptic discussions to be like. Now it's up to one or the other of you to give a *skilled* display in the same mode. Or if you don't want to do that, then take up where I left off and demonstrate whether the lad ought to acquire every branch of knowledge or whether there is just one, possession of which will make him happy and good, and if so, which it is. You see, as I said at the beginning,[2] we set considerable store by this youngster here becoming wise and good.'

F. *Being and Not-being*

This section contains the first in a series of sophisms which trade on the ambiguity, always crucial in early Greek philosophy, of the word einai, *'to be'. There are two senses of the word which need to be understood in order to appreciate this section: (i) the existential sense, in which the word means 'to exist' (this is rare in English, except in the sentence 'God is'); (ii) the copulative or predicative sense, in which it links a predicate to a subject ('The sky is blue').*

In this section Dionysodorus moves from the copulative usage ('Cleinias is not wise') to the existential ('Cleinias is not'). However absurd this move might seem, it should be remembered that einai *troubled Greek philosophers for some time, until Plato pointed the way towards understanding the issues in his late dialogue* Sophist. *Until then, even arguments of central importance to Plato's thought could fail to be valid (e.g.* Republic *476e–480a). The Presocratic philosopher Parmenides first brought* einai *to the fore of Greek philosophical thought.*

Although I have just analysed the sophism as relying on the fallacy of equivocation on einai, *it could equally well be seen as relying on the fallacy of* secundum quid *(see p. 304), which is how Aristotle would classify it (De Sophisticis Elenchis 166b37–167a6). Thus, in the move cited above, Dionysodorus drops the qualification 'wise'.*

There is also a further equivocation in 283d, where Dionysodorus' crucial sentence is literally translatable as: 'So you want him to become who he is not and no longer to be who he now is.' 'Who' here is properly equivalent to 'the sort of person', but Dionysodorus takes it actually to identify the subject.

That sophists had exploited difficulties in einai *is shown, for instance, by the extant paraphrase of a treatise written by Gorgias (On Nature or the Non-existent), which set out to prove (contrary to Parmenides' assertion that you cannot say 'is not' about anything), that nothing exists, that even if it did, it would be incomprehensible, and that even if it was comprehensible, it would*

1. As opposed, ironically, to the instant enlightenment offered by the sophists.
2. See 275a.

be incommunicable. Moreover, the treatise Dissoi Logoi *5.15 comes close to answering Dionysodorus' fallacy by using the existential sense of* einai *to claim, 'Everything exists in* some *respect.' This suggests that Dionysodorus' puzzle, or a similar one, was current at the time (c. 400). Parmenides and other philosophers, perhaps including Gorgias, were using* einai *to generate profound or at least interesting thoughts, but at some point the problems became trivialized as well.*

283a So anyway, Crito, once I'd spoken my piece, I watched very closely for what would happen next, concentrating on how they would take up the theme and what their starting-point would be for encouraging the lad to devote himself to wisdom and virtue. Dionysodorus, the older of the two, spoke first, and we all gazed at him, thinking that we would straight away

b hear some pretty amazing stuff. Well, we did: the argument he launched *was* pretty amazing, Crito, and you should hear it, as an example of an argument designed to motivate someone to virtue.

'Tell me,' he said, 'Socrates, and all the rest of you who say you want this young man to become wise, is this a joke or do you really mean it? Are you serious?'

Now, the explanation, I supposed, for this banter and lack of serious-ness was that, in spite of all, they'd got the impression that our earlier

c request for them to speak with the lad had not been serious, so I said in no uncertain terms that we were incredibly serious.

'Look out, Socrates,' Dionysodorus rejoined; 'you may end up taking your words back.'[1]

'I *have* looked,' I said. 'There's no way that I shall ever take them back.'

'All right, then,' he said. 'Now, you say that you want him to become wise?'

'Yes.'

'Is Cleinias wise at the moment or not?' he asked.

'Well, he *says* he isn't yet,' I said, 'and he's not given to idle talk.'

d 'And you want him to become wise,' he said, 'and not to be ignorant?' We agreed.

'So you want him to become someone else and to stop being the person he now is.'

This took me aback, and before I could recover, he cut in: 'In other words, since you want him to stop being the person he now is, you appar-ently want him to die, don't you? Of course, it's those who place supreme value on their beloved dying that make sterling friends and admirers!'

1. Yet later (Section H) Dionysodorus denies the possibility of contradiction! This joke runs throughout the dialogue.

EUTHYDEMUS

G. *Falsehood is Impossible*

This is another section which presents particular problems for the translator. It introduces an old chestnut of Greek philosophical paradox – that falsehood is impossible (in Plato, see Cratylus *429d–e,* Republic *478b–c,* Theaetetus *187d–200c,* Sophist *259d–264b, in their contexts). The paradox arises naturally out of the Greek language and occurs in slightly different forms. Understanding the version here requires meeting a third possible sense of* einai *(see p. 333). This third usage is called 'veridical' and is not paralleled in English:* einai *can mean 'to be so', 'to be the case', 'to be true', 'to be real'.*

*The course of the argument from 283e–284a is as follows: (i) if someone speaks, he says something; (ii) this something exists (*einai*); (iii) this something is true (*einai*). In order to approximate to a literal translation, I have employed the rather archaic English 'fact' for 'thing' (Greek* on: *literally 'a thing that is'), since that permits the transition in English to 'it is a fact', meaning 'it is true'.*

The fallacy, then, is again equivocation on einai. *Again, it seems trivial and obvious to us, but we should remember the extent to which language conditions thought, and try to imagine the confusions possible for a people whose language did not contain the appropriate distinctions.*

*The move from stage (i) to stage (ii) of the argument as summarized above looks somewhat suspect, and from 284b–c Euthydemus supports his original argument with another which confirms the suspicion. He makes it clear that he is using the verb 'to speak' or 'utter' (*legein*) as equivalent to doing something directly to an object. If I do something to an object, that object, no doubt, exists; but if I say something, that something does not exist in the same sense. One could say that there is an ambiguity in* legein, *which means either to mention an (existent) object, or simply to state a proposition (which may be false). Plato, then, provides the material for pinpointing the difficulty of the argument; but since the paradox recurs in later dialogues, we cannot say that he has solved it. He must, here as elsewhere in the dialogue, simply be repeating a standard sophistic puzzle.*

Ctesippus is made to come close to a correct response, however, when he says that it is possible to describe things not as they are (284c). He is falling just short of the necessary distinction between (possibly false) statements and the actual things with which the statements are concerned. But Dionysodorus parries with a ludicrous argument (284c–e) which forces the phrase 'as they are' into ambiguity. Whereas Ctesippus had used the phrase to qualify the things being spoken about, Dionysodorus makes it qualify the manner of speaking. He employs, then, the fallacy of amphiboly (pp. 303–4). The argument only breaks

*up when Ctesippus begins to meet Dionysodorus on his own ground (284d–e),
with an equivocation on 'speak badly' as either 'be bad at speaking' or 'abuse'.*

*After an interlude (285a–d), Dionysodorus launches into the next argument –
prompted by Ctesippus' use of the word 'contradict' – that contradiction is
impossible. There are obvious similarities with the argument that falsehood is
impossible, on which it is crucially dependent.*

*The vital premises come at 285e–286a: that it is impossible to speak 'non-
facts', and that there is only one possible description of any given event. Given
Ctesippus' agreement, the rest is easy. Either both parties are speaking what is
the case about an event x – no contradiction there; or neither party is speaking
about x – no contradiction about x there; or one party is describing x and the
other is describing another event – no contradiction about x there. Sprague
(1965, n. 44) accuses Dionysodorus of being less than exhaustive – of omitting
the case where both parties are giving alternative descriptions of x; but the
point is that Dionysodorus is being exhaustive, given the restrictions imposed
by his premises.*

*Why, then, does Ctesippus agree to the premises? Simply because he has
already agreed that falsehood is impossible – or rather, he has not been able to
disprove it. Dionysodorus reminds him of this at 286a: you can only speak the
truth about x. From this, interestingly, it does not necessarily follow that there
is only one description of any event: it might equally follow that truth is relative
and that while each person gives what he sees as the truth, these truths may
differ. But Ctesippus shares the common naïve assumption that there is only
one truth about one object, so he is trapped.*

*Antisthenes, a philosopher contemporary with Plato, is known to have denied
the possibility of contradiction on very similar grounds (Aristotle,* Metaphysics
*1024b32–4), so it is possible that the provenance of the arguments of this
section is Antisthenean theory. It is by no means impossible for Plato to use a
contemporary of his as a background for a discussion set in Socrates' time (see,
for example, pp. 310–11). But we know all too little about Antisthenes (the
meagre evidence is ably summarized by Guthrie, III, pp. 209–18; see also
Field, pp. 160–69, and Rankin, Chapter 12), and it is equally possible that
arguments of this kind were current among the sophists of Socrates' day: Antisthenes may have had the same fifth-century source and developed sophisms into
more seriously meant logical theory.*

e   Ctesippus, nervous about his beloved, got annoyed when he heard this,
and said: 'If it wasn't a bit impolite – after all, you're a visitor, all the way
from Thurii – I would have said "Go and die yourself", for getting it into
your head to slander me and the others like that; I think it's blasphemous
to suggest that I could wish him to die.'

'Oh, I see, Ctesippus,' said Euthydemus. 'You think it's possible to lie, do you?'

'Good heavens, of course!' he said. 'I'm not crazy!'

'Do lies occur when someone mentions the thing which he mentions, or when he does not?'

'When he mentions it,' he said. 284a

'So if he mentions it, then, out of all facts, he is mentioning precisely the one which he is mentioning, isn't he?'

'Of course,' said Ctesippus.

'Then at least *this* thing which he mentions is one out of all facts, distinct from all other facts, isn't it?'

'Yes.'

'So in mentioning this thing, he is talking about the fact of the matter?' he asked.

'Yes.'

'But if he mentions the fact of the matter, if he mentions facts, then he is speaking the truth. So if Dionysodorus mentions facts, he is speaking the truth and not slandering you at all.'

'Yes,' said Ctesippus, 'but anyone who says what *he* said is not mention- b ing facts.'

To this Euthydemus responded: 'Non-facts do not exist, do they?'[1]

'No, they don't.'

'And things which do not exist do not exist *anywhere*, do they?'

'No.'

'Now, is it possible for things which do not exist to be the object of any action, in the sense that things which do not exist anywhere can have anything done to them?'

'*I* don't think so.'

'Well then, when politicians speak in the Assembly, isn't that an activity?'

'Yes, it is.'

'And if it's an activity, they are doing something?'

'Yes.' c

'Then speech is activity and doing something?'

He agreed.

'So no one,' he said, 'speaks non-existent things: I mean, he would already, in speaking, be doing something, and you have agreed that it is impossible for non-existent things to have anything done to them by

1. Euthydemus here reverts from the veridical sense of *einai* (translated by 'fact' in the sense of 'truth') to the existential sense ('fact' in the sense of 'thing'; see p. 335).

anybody.¹ So you are committed to the view that lies never happen: if Dionysodorus speaks, he speaks facts – that is, truth.'

'Good heavens, Euthydemus!' said Ctesippus. 'All right! But although in a sense he does mention facts, he doesn't describe them as they are.'

'What do you mean, Ctesippus?' said Dionysodorus. 'Are there people d who describe things as they are?'

'Yes, there are,' he said. 'Gentlemen and those who tell the truth.'

'Now, aren't good things in a good state and bad things in a bad state?' He agreed.

'And you agree that gentlemen describe things in the way that they are?'

'Yes.'

'So your paragons describe bad things badly, Ctesippus, if they describe things as they are!'²

'Yes, they certainly do,' he said, 'particularly in the case of bad people; and if you take my advice, you'll watch out in case you join their ranks e and have good people speak badly of you – for you can be sure that good people speak badly of bad people.'

'And do they enlarge upon large people, and speak warmly of warm people?'

'Of *course*,' said Ctesippus. 'And they speak coldly of cold people and their conversation.'³

'*You* are being offensive, Ctesippus,' said Dionysodorus, 'very offensive.'

'Oh no, not I, Dionysodorus,' he said. 'I like you. I'm just giving you a friendly warning and trying to get you never to behave so rudely in front 285a of me as to say that I wish for the death of those I value most.'

Well, I thought that they were being rather brusque with each other, so I tried to lighten the atmosphere by saying to Ctesippus: 'I think that, if our visitors are prepared to talk, Ctesippus, we should accept what they offer, and not argue over words. If they do know how to destroy people, in

1. But, of course, doing something is not necessarily doing something *to something*.

2. I suspect that, if Ctesippus hadn't interrupted with a timely turning of the tables, Dionysodorus' automatic technique would have continued as follows: good people describe things badly; description is a form of doing (see above); therefore good people do things badly! Plato shows how a technique of argument which depends on learnt steps being trotted out automatically cannot cope with interruption: the argument degenerates to abuse.

3. Compare Aristophanes, *Thesmophoriazusae* 168–70: 'Now I see why Philocles, who's ugly, composes ugly verse; why Xenocles, who's bad, composes bad verse; and why Theognis, who's frigid, composes frigid verse!' 'Frigid' or 'cold' was a technical term to describe a type of defective rhetoric which employed unsuitably highfalutin or obscure words (see especially Aristotle, *Rhetoric* 1405b35 ff.).

the sense of making them good and rational instead of bad and irrational –
whether they have made this breakthrough by themselves or whether
someone else[1] taught them a kind of destruction and annihilation, such   b
that they can do away with someone bad and resurrect him as a good
person – if they know how to do this (and obviously they do: at any rate,
they *said* that they'd recently discovered how to change people from bad
to good),[2] then let's not quibble with them over this: let them destroy the
lad and make him wise – and all the rest of us too. If you young men are
afraid, then I'll play the Carian[3] and risk myself first: I'm old, so I'm ready   c
to take a chance, and I put myself in Dionysodorus' hands, as if he were
Medea of Colchis, to destroy me, boil me,[4] or whatever else he might
choose, just so long as he resuscitates me as a good person.'[5]

Then Ctesippus said: 'Speaking for myself, Socrates, *I*'m also ready to
hand myself over to our visitors, even if they choose to increase the flaying
they are already subjecting me to, as long as it ends in virtue, not in my hide
becoming a wineskin, as Marsyas' did.[6] Now, Dionysodorus here thinks   d
that I'm cross with him, but that's not so: it's just that I contradict what I
take to be slanderous of me. You, my dear Dionysodorus,' he added,
'mustn't confuse contradiction with abuse, which is quite different.'

'When you argue, Ctesippus,' said Dionysodorus, 'do you assume that
contradiction exists?'

'Absolutely,' he said. 'No doubt about it. Do you think contradiction   e
does *not* exist, Dionysodorus?'

'I bet *you* could never prove that you have heard one person contradicting another,' he said.

'Can that be true?' he asked. 'We'll hear right away if[7] I can prove it to
you – with Ctesippus contradicting Dionysodorus!'

'Ah, but can you provide rational argument for this claim?'[8]

1. No one specific is intended: this is just a dig at the sophists' lack of originality.

2. That is, to make them virtuous (273d).

3. This probably refers to Carian mercenaries being put in the front line of assault; see also
Laches 187b.

4. Medea, the famous legendary sorceress, returned to Iolcus as Jason's wife. Pelias had
usurped the kingdom from Jason's father Aeson. Medea tricked Pelias' daughters into chopping
and boiling their father, in order to rejuvenate him . . . it didn't work!

5. There is almost certainly a sly reference in these lines to the mockery in Aristophanes,
Clouds 439 ff., where Strepsiades hands himself over to Socrates and his school 'to be beaten,
starved, parched, desiccated, frozen and flayed alive – as long as I learn how to escape my
debts!'

6. Marsyas made the mistake of challenging the god Apollo to a music contest. Of course he
lost; this was the price he paid.

7. Reading ἀκούωμεν νῦν εἴ with manuscript T.

8. The challenge is clearly eristic: 'If you can't disprove my claim, I've won.'

'Yes,' he said.

'All right, then,' he said. 'Are there descriptions for each thing that exists?'

'Yes.'

'Describing it as it is or as it is not?'

'As it is.'

286a   'Yes,' he said, 'for if you remember, Ctesippus, not too long ago we demonstrated that no one describes things as they are not, when we showed the impossibility of speaking non-facts.'

'So what?' said Ctesippus. 'Does that alter the fact that you and I can contradict each other?'

'If we were both describing the same event,' he asked, 'would that constitute contradiction? Or wouldn't we both, surely, just be saying the same thing?'

He agreed.

'What about when *neither* of us describes the event?' he asked. 'Would
b   that be contradiction? Or would that rather be neither of us having the event in mind at all?'

He agreed to this too.

'Finally, then, when I describe the event, and you describe another event, does that constitute contradiction? Or in this instance am I describing the event and you giving no description at all?[1] But how could someone giving no description contradict someone who is giving a description?'

H. *Socrates Fights Back*

Socrates correctly lumps all the arguments of Section G together as dependent on the view that falsehood is impossible; he establishes that this means false belief as well as false speech, and produces an argument which, failing the necessary logical analysis of einai, is all that can be said: in the first place, nobody can be wrong, refutation is impossible and therefore (an ad hominem point) there is no need of teachers such as the sophists! So far, this merely sharpens the paradox: it doesn't refute it.

The main part of Socrates' fight-back arises at the end of the section. Socrates has put Dionysodorus on the spot, but Dionysodorus finds a way out: he produces another absurd argument to distract attention. Socrates' phrase 'the idea of the sentence' (287c) is made to appear ridiculous: only animate things can have ideas (287d–e)! This is formally an amphiboly (pp. 303–4). Socrates seizes

---

1. Properly, of course, Dionysodorus should say 'giving no description at all *of the event*'. The omission of the qualification gives extra pungency to his conclusion.

the opportunity to point out that any argument, however bad, presupposes a mistake in the opponent. He uses this to suggest that the argument that falsehood is impossible is, qua argument, self-defeating (288a, see 286c). It is worth mentioning in passing that Theaetetus *171a–b elaborates the point: the argument that falsehood is impossible presupposes the mistake that falsehood is possible. But if falsehood is impossible and all beliefs are true, then the belief that falsehood is possible is true! The technical name for this argument is* peritropē.

So in this section, Socrates both sharpens the paradox to show how ridiculous and counter-intuitive it is, and suggests that it is self-refuting. Remembering the Socratic equation of wisdom with virtue, we can see that what might fundamentally trouble him is that if there is no ignorance, then the distinction between virtue and vice is eliminated.

Ctesippus made no reply, but I was astonished at the argument, and said: 'What do you mean, Dionysodorus? I'll have you know that I've heard *this* argument plenty of times from plenty of people, but it always c surprises me. Protagoras' followers were particularly keen on it,[1] and there were others even before them.[2] But what strikes me is its amazing capacity for destroying not only other arguments but itself as well. Anyway, I suppose you are the best person to tell me the truth about it: it means that falsehood is impossible, doesn't it – that people either speak the truth or are not speaking at all?'

He agreed.

'Now, is it impossible to *speak* falsehood, but possible to *think* it?'   d

'No, false thoughts are impossible too.'

'So there's no such thing as false belief at all?' I asked.

'No,' he said.

'And no ignorance or ignorant people, then? I mean, I suppose that ignorance, if it existed, would be being wrong about things?'

'Yes,' he said.

'Which is impossible,' I said.

1. Plato's evidence, here and in *Theaetetus*, that Protagoras held the view that contradiction is impossible, is probably reliable. In fact, however, Protagoras held the view that truth is relative (see p. 336); his version of the impossibility of contradiction, then, is the impossibility of gainsaying anyone's impressions or opinions, which are necessarily private and peculiar to that person.

2. It is not at all clear whom Plato has in mind. In *Theaetetus*, perhaps erroneously, he assimilates Protagorean relativism to the theory of Heraclitus of Ephesus (fl. *c.* 500) and his followers, on the grounds that they believed everything to be in continual flux. So he could have Heraclitus in mind. On the other hand, he could be interpreting Parmenides' denial that you can say 'is not' about anything to entail the denial of contradiction.

'Yes,' he said.

'Are you arguing merely for argument's sake, Dionysodorus, just to shock, or do you *really* think that no one is ignorant?'

e 'Just you try to refute me,' he said.[1]

'Is refutation possible on your view, if no one speaks falsely?'

'No,' said Euthydemus.[2]

'But didn't Dionysodorus just suggest that I refute him?' I asked.

'How can anyone suggest something non-existent? Can you?'

'Well, Euthydemus,' I said, 'the reason I asked is that I'm a bit slow-witted and I don't in the least understand all these clever and worthwhile points. Anyway, I have a question for you to consider – and please bear
287a with me if it's rather tiresome. If neither speaking falsehood nor thinking falsehood nor ignorance are possible, then surely it is impossible, in any action, to make a mistake, because the agent cannot go wrong in what he does? Isn't that what you're saying?'

'Yes,' he said.

'Now we can come to my tiresome question,' I said. 'If action, speech and thought are not wrong, then who on earth have *you* come to teach, if that is so?[3] Didn't you recently claim that you would be the best teacher
b of virtue to anyone who wanted to learn it?'

'Socrates,' Dionysodorus interjected, 'what an old stick-in-the-mud[4] you are! Fancy harping on our original statements! Next you'll be bringing up something I said last year, but it won't help you cope with what's being said at the moment.'

'That's because it's pretty difficult,' I said, 'which is only to be expected, given that clever people are doing the talking. And it is especially difficult to cope with this last argument of yours. What do you mean by my "inability to cope", Dionysodorus? Or is it obvious – you mean that I
c can't refute it? Tell me, what else is the idea of the sentence "I am unable to cope with the argument"?[5]

'Well, it is far from difficult to cope with what *you* are saying,'[6] he said, 'so answer me this.'

1. See p. 339 n. 8.

2. Notice how Euthydemus takes over from Dionysodorus (and see also 297a): Euthydemus is the more rigorous of the pair, in the sense that Dionysodorus has not fully expurgated himself of common beliefs, such as that falsehood is possible and, in 297a, that ignorance is possible!

3. See *Theaetetus* 161d–e for the same *ad hominem* point, against Protagoras.

4. Literally 'What a Cronus you are!' Cronus was the god deposed by his son Zeus: a proverbial symbol of what is *passé*.

5. Socrates is threatening to expose that Dionysodorus is again (see 286e) tacitly accepting the possibility of refutation.

6. Reading τούτῳ γ' οὐ πάνυ χαλεπὸν χρῆσθαι with the manuscripts and Badham.

'Before you've answered me, Dionysodorus?' I asked.

'Aren't you going to answer me?'

'Is that fair?'

'Of course it's fair,' he said.

'On what grounds?' I asked. 'Oh, I see: is it because here you are – there's nobody more clever at argument – and you know when answers are called for and when not? You're not going to reply[1] at all for the   d
moment, because you realize you'd better not. Is that it?'

'You're talking nonsense,' he said, 'when you should be getting ready to answer. My dear fellow, just do what you're told and answer my questions. After all, you do admit that I'm clever.'

'All right,' I said, 'I must do as you say. I have no choice in the matter, apparently: you're the boss. Go ahead with your questions, then.'

'Do animate or inanimate things have ideas?'

'Animate.'

'Do you know an animate sentence?' he asked.

'Good heavens, no!'

'Why, then, did you just ask me what the idea of my sentence was?'   e

'My stupidity led me astray, of course,' I said. 'But wait a moment . . . did I make a mistake? Or was I right in saying that sentences have ideas? Are you saying I was wrong or not? If I wasn't wrong, then not even *you* will refute me, for all your cleverness;[2] so you will be unable to cope with the argument! And if I *was* wrong, then your claim that mistakes are impossible was incorrect. I'm not referring to something you said last   288a
year, either. Apparently, Dionysodorus and Euthydemus,' I went on, 'this sort of argument hasn't changed at all, it still brings itself down in the act of throwing others,[3] just as it always did. Not even your skill has come up with a cure for this, despite your amazing precision with words.'

Ctesippus chipped in: 'Thurians or Chians – wherever you're from and whatever title pleases you[4] – I'm astonished at your words: you don't care   b
at all if you talk gibberish.'

I. *Knowledge and Happiness*

This section continues the Socratic protreptic of Section E and is discussed on pp. 307–9. The search is for a superordinate branch of knowledge which is the

---

1. Reading ἀποκρινεῖ with Heindorf.

2. Contrary to the brothers' ability to refute even truth (272a–b), Socrates believes that the truth is irrefutable.

3. The metaphor is from wrestling.

4. A prayer formula, used ironically; see p. 319 n. 1.

*one to bring happiness. The discussion moves rapidly from manufacturing skills
with obviously restricted domains (289b–c), to somewhat more plausible claims:
both speech-composition (289c–290a) and military command (290a–d) could
be claimed to require wide knowledge. (Gorgias in* Gorgias *claims that oratory
is the supreme skill.) Plato, however, finds the claims unsatisfactory.*

*Interestingly, Plato has Cleinias, not Socrates, develop the argument which
dismisses the claims of both speech-composition and military command. The
point is probably to show how under Socrates' tutelage independent thought is
encouraged.*

I was afraid that insults were in the offing, so I tried to calm Ctesippus
down again by saying: 'Not long ago, Ctesippus, I said something to
Cleinias, which I shall now repeat to you: you are failing to recognize our
visitors' wisdom for the wonder that it is. It's just that they are not willing
to give us a serious demonstration; instead they are imitating the Egyptian
sophist Proteus and practising illusions on us. So *we* must imitate Mene-

c   laus and not let them go until they have revealed the serious part of their
work.[1] To my mind, we will see an excellent side of them, when they get
down to being serious; so let us get down on our knees and beg and
beseech them to reveal it. Now, I again propose to show the way myself,
to indicate what sort of persons I am begging them to reveal themselves

d   to be. I will try to the best of my ability to cover the stages which follow
on from where I left off before: perhaps the seriousness of my efforts will
stimulate them, through pity and compassion, to take things seriously
themselves. Cleinias,' I said, 'please remind me where we left off. Am I
right in thinking that we ended up agreeing that philosophy is essential?'

'Yes,' he said.

'All right; and philosophy is acquisition of knowledge, isn't it?' I asked.

'Yes,' he said.

e   'So what is the proper branch of knowledge to acquire?[2] Isn't it simply
the one which benefits us?'

'Yes,' he said.

'Would it benefit us at all to know how to travel around and pick out
the places with the richest deposits of gold?'

'It might,' he said.

1. See Homer, *Odyssey* IV, 351–575. Proteus was a sea-god with the specific power of telling
the future; but he would only do so if pinned down, and to avoid this he had the ability to
assume any shape. Menelaus, stuck on his journey home from Troy, succeeded in holding
him. cf. *Ion* 541e.

2. Given Section E this question is unsatisfactory: see pp. 307–8. Socrates is assuming,
without argument, a hierarchy of crafts.

'But earlier,'[1] I went on, 'we established that even if all the gold in the world could be ours without the bother of excavation, we would be no better off. No, even if we knew how to change stones into gold nuggets, our knowledge would be worthless. We proved that without the 289a knowledge of how to *use* gold, no benefit would accrue. Don't you remember?' I asked.

'Of course I do,' he said.

'Nor, apparently, is there any benefit to be gained from any other branch of knowledge – financial, medical or whatever – unless on top of enabling *achievement* of a result, it brings knowledge of how to *use* the result. Isn't that so?'

He agreed.

'To judge by these agreed premisses, there is apparently no benefit to be gained even from knowing how to bestow immortality, without the b knowledge of how to use immortality.'

He found this wholly acceptable too.

'Therefore, my dear boy,' I said, 'a kind of knowledge is required which simultaneously combines both achievement of a result and knowing how to use the result.'[2]

'I suppose so,' he said.

'It seems to follow that there's really no call for us to be lyre-makers or to be masters of a branch of knowledge like that, since in this instance the c skills of manufacture and use are separate, though the object is identical: I mean, the making and playing of lyres are quite different, don't you think?'

He agreed.

'Again, we obviously don't need pipe-making, which is another just like the first.'

He agreed.

'Now, seriously,' I said, 'suppose we'd learned the art of composing speeches: is *this* the art whose possession is bound to make us happy?'

'Not in my opinion,' Cleinias replied.

'What's your evidence?' I asked. d

'My eyes provide it,'[3] he said. 'Some composers of speeches do not know how to use their own speeches, the ones they themselves compose.[4] In this field too – just like lyre-makers and their lyres – others, who are

1. See 280b ff.
2. On this requirement, see pp. 308–9.
3. A nice contrast with the sophists' eschewing the obvious at any cost: see especially Section K.
4. See 305c for an example.

themselves incapable of writing speeches, have the ability to put the speech-writers' compositions to use. Obviously, then, speeches are no different from the rest: the arts of composition and usage are distinct.'

'I think,' I said, 'that your evidence is enough to prove that speech-composition is not the skill whose possession would bring happiness. Pity – I did think that we were getting close to uncovering the branch of
e knowledge we've been after all this time: my contacts with speech-writers themselves have always confirmed them in my eyes as incredibly clever, and their art as superhuman and sublime. And that's only what you'd expect: after all, it's an aspect of enchantment and a close second best to
290a it. Enchantment is the bewitching of wild animals and pests like snakes, poisonous spiders and scorpions; speech-writing is in fact the bewitching and calming down of assemblies – legal, political and so on. Would you argue with me on that?' I asked.

'No, I agree with you,' he said.

'Where is there left for us to turn?' I asked. 'What skill can we investigate?'

'I've no idea,' he said.

'Hang on,' I said, 'I think *I*'ve got it.'

'Which one?' asked Cleinias.

b 'I think,' I said, 'that military command is pre-eminently the skill possession of which would bring happiness.'

'I disagree,' he said.

'Why?' I asked.

'Well, *this* skill involves hunting men.'

'What of it?' I asked.

'Any skill that's subsumable under *hunting*,' he said, 'is restricted to hunting and subduing. Once the quarry has been subdued, hunters are incapable of using it: hunters and fishermen hand it over to cooks;
c geometers, astronomers and mathematicians – yes, they're hunters too, because they don't create their respective diagrams *ex nihilo*; they merely show up what's already there.[1] Anyway, since they only know how to hunt, not how to use their discoveries, they entrust their use to dialecticians, I suppose – at least they do if they've got any sense at all.'[2]

---

1. All the specialists Cleinias mentions relied heavily on diagrams in Plato's day. In classifying them all as hunters, he presumably means that they are all thinkers who abstract from matter (for a different view, see Hawtrey (1978)).

2. A Socratic dialectician is someone who is good at asking pertinent questions: here, for example, a dialectician might question a mathematician's axioms. For Plato, however, dialectic was the supreme metaphysical science; but Platonic dialectic cannot be meant here (as Hawtrey (1978) supposes), since Socrates continues to search for the supreme science.

'Well!' I exclaimed. 'Brains as well as looks, Cleinias! So that's how it is?'

'Certainly,' he said. 'And military commanders are just like that. When they have finished hunting a city or an army, then because they themselves don't know how to use the quarry, they make way for statesmen, just as people who hunt quails hand them over to people who breed them. So,' he concluded, 'if we want that skill which combines making or hunting with knowing how to use the acquisition – the sort of skill which will make us happy – we'd better look elsewhere, not to military command.' d

J. *Is Kingship the Supreme Science?*

This section ends Socrates' protreptic; it is discussed on pp. 308–9, where it is argued that its inconclusive conclusion should be taken as a sign of genuine puzzlement. What the passage illustrates, within the context of the whole dialogue, is the difference between constructive puzzlement and the confusion caused by eristic arguments.

There is no significance in Plato's changing to direct dialogue form in this section: he is merely varying our diet. The conversations between Socrates and Crito enclose and punctuate the dialogue.

CRITO: Do you really mean that *Cleinias* came out with all that?   e
SOCRATES: Don't you believe it?
CRITO: I most certainly do not. If he said that, he doesn't need educating by Euthydemus or anyone else, in my opinion.
SOCRATES: Good heavens! Then perhaps it was Ctesippus who said it, and I've forgotten?
CRITO: Ctesippus? Hardly!   291a
SOCRATES: Anyway, there's *one* thing I'm sure of, that it wasn't Euthydemus or Dionysodorus who said it. But I'm sure I heard the speech . . . My dear Crito, do you think it might have come from some superior being who was present?
CRITO: Yes, I'd swear to it, Socrates – some superior being, to be sure; far superior, in fact.[1] But tell me, did you continue the search for a skill? And did you find the one for which the inquiry was undertaken, or not?
SOCRATES: How could we hope to find it, my friend? We were really   b
being ridiculously childish. You know how children try to catch larks: we

1. Crito means Socrates himself, of course, not the god whom Socrates was suggesting.

always thought we were poised to grasp each branch of knowledge, only to have them keep slipping through our fingers. I won't go through the bulk of the tale, but once we'd come to the art of kingship, to consider thoroughly whether it might be the one which brings and causes happiness, we found ourselves trapped in a sort of maze: we'd think we'd finally reached the end, and then we'd turn another corner and find our-

c selves more or less back at the beginning of the quest and just as far short of finishing as when we set out on it.

CRITO: How did this state of affairs happen, Socrates?

SOCRATES: I'll tell you. We decided that statesmanship and kingship were identical . . .

CRITO: And . . .?

SOCRATES:. . . that *this* is the art to which military command and so on entrust the control of the products which they themselves fashion, on the grounds that it alone knows how to use them. So we were certain that we'd found our quarry, that it was the cause of correct action in the state,

d and that it, as Aeschylus' line has it, sits alone at the helm of the state, steering all and controlling all to make all of use.[1]

CRITO: And the idea met with approval, Socrates?

SOCRATES: I'll tell you what happened next, if you like; then you'll be able to make up your own mind. We restarted the inquiry somewhat as follows: 'All right, then, does the art of kingship, as supreme authority,

e produce some result or not?' 'It most certainly does,' we said to one another. Wouldn't you agree, Crito?

CRITO: Yes.

SOCRATES: What do you think its product is? Suppose I asked you: given that medicine has total authority over the area it controls, what product does it offer? You would answer health, wouldn't you?

CRITO: Yes.

SOCRATES: Consider the skill of which you are one of the practitioners, farming, which has total authority over the area it controls: what does it

292a produce?[2] Wouldn't you say that its product is sustenance from the earth?

CRITO: Yes.

SOCRATES: What about the art of kingship, which has total authority over the area it controls? What does it produce? Perhaps you find this a bit difficult?

CRITO: You can say that again, Socrates.

1. We do not have extant the line Plato is referring to, but *Seven Against Thebes* 1–3 is a good example of Aeschylus' use of the ship-of-the-state image.
2. Retaining ἔργον with the manuscripts.

SOCRATES: *We* did too, Crito. But this much is clear, at any rate, that if this art is our quarry, it must be something beneficial.

CRITO: Yes.

SOCRATES: And it must yield something good, then, mustn't it?

CRITO: Necessarily, Socrates.

SOCRATES: And, as you know, Cleinias and I agreed that nothing is b good except knowledge of some sort.

CRITO: Yes, that was what you said.

SOCRATES: So we found that all the other results which one might attribute to statesmanship – and there are many of these, of course: provision of a high standard of living for the citizens, for example, and freedom, and absence of faction – are neither good nor bad. We decided that, if as a result of statesmanship the citizen body was to be benefited and happy, it was crucial to make them wise and knowledgeable. c

CRITO: Fair enough – at least, that was your conclusion in the earlier part of the discussion, as you reported it.

SOCRATES: So *does* the art of kingship make people wise and good?

CRITO: Why not, Socrates?

SOCRATES: Does it make everyone good, in every respect? Does it yield all knowledge, including cobbling, carpentry and so on?

CRITO: I wouldn't say that, Socrates.

SOCRATES: Then *what* knowledge does it yield? What *use* will it be d to us? I mean, it must neither fashion any of the neither-good-nor-bad products, nor must it yield any knowledge apart from itself. So what about trying to formulate what it is and what use it will be? Suppose we said that its use will be making others good, Crito?

CRITO: By all means.

SOCRATES: In what respect will we find them to be good and in what respect will they be useful? Are we just to continue saying that they will make others good, and these others still others? But given that we have demoted the results which are usually attributed to statesmanship, this e doesn't tell us what these people are good *at*. We're in the proverbial 'Corinthus son of Zeus'[1] situation and, as I said, we're still nowhere near knowing what that knowledge is which will make us happy.[2]

CRITO: Good heavens, Socrates! You apparently reached quite an impasse.

1. Proverbial for idle repetition: the Corinthians were apparently given to harping on their legendary founder and his divine parentage.
2. Reading Burnet's text, but not as a question.

K. *Everyone is Always Omniscient*

The nest of arguments in this section depends on two fallacies. First, secundum quid *(p. 304), which enables Euthydemus to move from 'A knows x' to 'A knows', dropping the qualification. Second, an equivocation on 'always' which means both 'for ever' and 'on each relevant occasion' (as in 'I always wash my hands before meals').*

The section is remarkable for the sophists' disdain for empirical proof, and for Socrates' dogged attempts to avoid both fallacies. The former is interesting because there are traces of a fifth-century debate on the relative merits of pure thought and empirical data. Several of the Presocratic philosophers entered into the debate, and some of the earlier treatises of the Hippocratic corpus take up positions in it. On the whole issue, see Lloyd (1979), Chapter 3. Here again, then, we find trivialization of an important debate.

Socrates' delaying tactics show that Plato is aware of what is causing the problem in each case: Socrates wants to retain an object for the verb 'know', so that it remains qualified (293c), and he pinpoints the troublesome 'always' (296a–b).

Apart from the fallaciousness of the sophisms and their evident absurdity, the end of the section sees Socrates developing an ad hominem *argument, when he tries to get Dionysodorus to admit that he knows propositions like 'good men are unjust'. Dionysodorus squirms out of shame: to normal Greek morality, such a proposition was inconceivable (compare Gorgias 474c in context for a similar use of the tactic). It should be noted, since this is not the first occasion in the dialogue, that* ad hominem *tactics are not unfair on the principles of Socratic dialectic, which require interlocuters to state their real beliefs (cf. p. 31).*

The pace of the dialogue is increasing; with Socrates continuing to pressurize the sophists, we are prepared also for Ctesippus' aggression later in the dialogue. As a general background, we should again remember (see p. 341) that the Socratic equation of virtue with knowledge means that, if the sophists were right, that everyone is omniscient, then everyone would always be virtuous: at Cratylus 386d Plato attributes to Euthydemus the view that 'all things belong equally to all men simultaneously and always', from which Plato derives the moral that 'it is not the case that some people are good, others bad, if virtue and vice belong equally and always to everyone'.

Several commentators have found covert references in the sophists' utterances to Socratic/Platonic thought. When Dionysodorus says, 'If you know even one thing, you know everything' (294a), this is similar to Socrates' statement at Meno 81d: 'If someone recalls just one thing, there is nothing to prevent him discovering everything else.' The similarity is only superficial: Dionysodorus is claiming that there is logical necessity, as it were, for actual omniscience of every detail; Socrates is claiming, if his statement is read in context, that with hard work one may discover the principles that govern things. It seems likely that the sophism originated independently of Socrates' theory of recollection; nevertheless, the superficial similarity of the two statements makes Plato's task of distinguishing the sophists from Socrates more poignant. It is perhaps significant, then, that Plato chooses to illustrate the sophists' argument about omniscience rather than total ignorance: their argument could have turned either way ('If you are ignorant of just one thing, you are ignorant of everything').

Others have gone so far as to find a reference in Dionysodorus' statement to Plato's view in Republic *that the form of the good makes all other things knowable. But* Euthydemus *was written some time before* Republic *and as far as we can tell Plato had not yet elaborated that theory. In the second sophism of this section, Euthydemus' 'proof' of eternal omniscience is again superficially similar to the theory of recollection, according to which the immortal soul has latent knowledge of everything.*

SOCRATES: Yes, and that's why, when I found myself trapped in this maze, I for my part began vociferously to resort to every kind of plea and to call on the two visitors, as if they were the Dioscuri,[1] to save us – the lad and me – from being overwhelmed by the argument. I asked them to try in all seriousness to show us what the knowledge is whose discovery would enable us to live finely for the rest of our lives. 293a

CRITO: And was Euthydemus prepared to give you a demonstration?

SOCRATES: Of course, my friend. And he started with a very generous offer. 'Socrates,' he said, 'you've both been puzzling over this knowledge b for a while now. Shall I instruct you in it or demonstrate that you have it?'

'You marvellous man,' I said. 'Can you do that?'

'Certainly,' he said.

'Then please, please demonstrate that I have it,' I said. 'For someone my age that's easier than learning about it.'

'All right, then,' he said. 'You answer my questions. Do you know anything?'

'Yes,' I said, 'lots of things – unimportant things, though.'[2]

---

1. Castor and Polydeuces (Pollux), the Heavenly Twins. 'Dioscuri' literally means 'sons of Zeus'. They were protectors of those at sea: Plato continues the naval metaphor in 'overwhelmed'.

2. One of the rare occasions in the early dialogues when Socrates lays claim to knowledge of any kind. Vlastos (1985) discusses the significance of such passages.

'That doesn't matter,' he said. 'Now, do you think it possible for anything not to be what it is?'

c 'Of course I don't. What a question!'

'And you know something?'

'Yes.'

'So, if you know, you are in possession of knowledge?'

'Yes, of that thing, anyway.'

'That's irrelevant. Aren't you bound to know everything, if you are in possession of knowledge?'

'Good heavens, no!' I said. 'There are plenty of other things I don't know.'

'Well, if you don't know something, you are not in possession of knowledge.'

'Of *that*, my friend,' I said.

'But that doesn't alter the fact that you are not in possession of knowledge, does it?' he asked. 'But just now you said you were. So you both are what you are, and again are not what you are, in the same respect

d and at the same time.'[1]

'All right, Euthydemus,' I said. '*Touché*, as they say. So how do I have that knowledge which we were looking for? Because (a) it is impossible both to be and not be the same thing; (b) if I know one thing, I know everything, since I cannot at the same time both be and not be in possession of knowledge; (c) since I know everything, then I possess that knowledge too. Is that what you are saying? Is that the bright idea?'

e 'You are refuting yourself out of your own mouth, Socrates,' he said.

'But doesn't the same thing happen to you, Euthydemus?' I asked. 'I mean, I really wouldn't mind sharing any experience at all with you and dear old Dionysodorus here. Tell me, don't you two know some things and not know others?'

'You're quite wrong, Socrates,' said Dionysodorus.

'What?' I said. 'Do you mean you two know nothing?'

'We have knowledge, all right,' he said.

294a 'So,' I said, 'since you know something, you know everything?'

'Everything,' he said. 'And you do too: if you know even one thing, you know everything.'

'Good God!' I exclaimed. 'That's incredible! Thank you for enlighten-

---

1. It may not be going too far to find a subtle criticism here: Plato has Euthydemus mention respect and time as qualifications, but Euthydemus could have taken them into account to avoid the fallacy of *secundum quid* on knowledge. He does not; he is dishonest, because he is an eristic.

ing me about my great good fortune! What about everyone else? Do they know everything or nothing?'

'Well, they can't have only partial knowledge, and simultaneously be and not be in possession of knowledge,' he said.

'What is the case, then?' I asked.

'Everybody knows everything,' he said, 'as long as they know just one thing.'

'It was a bit of a struggle, Dionysodorus,' I said, 'to get you two to be   b
serious, but I can see you're in earnest now. So for heaven's sake, tell me, do you two really know everything, I mean, including carpentry and cobbling?'[1]

'Yes,' he said.

'You are competent even at stitching leather?'

'Yes, of course, and at sewing soles on too,' he said.

'And at things like how many stars and grains of sand there are?'[2]

'Yes,' he said. 'You didn't really expect us to deny that, did you?'

Ctesippus came in quickly at this point: 'For heaven's sake, Dionysodorus!' he said. 'Give me a demonstration, something to let me know   c
you're telling the truth.'[3]

'What demonstration shall I give?' he asked.

'Do you know how many teeth Euthydemus has got? Does Euthydemus
know how many *you*'ve got?'[4]

'Can't you be satisfied with being told that we are omniscient?' he asked.

'No, not in the slightest,' he said. 'Just answer my question – that's all – and demonstrate that you're telling the truth. If each of you says how many teeth the other has, and when we've counted we find that you *do* know, then we'll believe your other claims too.'

They weren't prepared to do this – they thought he was mocking them;   d
but each time Ctesippus asked them whether they knew something, they agreed that they did. Eventually Ctesippus, rather uninhibitedly, went so far as to ask whether they knew even the most disgusting things. They continued to agree that they did, and tackled his questions head on, very courageously, like boars thrusting against a hunter's spear. Eventually,

1. The same two crafts that were mentioned at 292c. This echo highlights the difference: Socrates was looking for the supreme science; the sophists are playing with words.

2. Notice that no distinction is made between knowing 'how' (i.e. having a skill) and knowing 'that' (i.e. knowing some fact).

3. On Ctesippus' request for empirical proof, see p. 350.

4. There was apparently a gambling game which involved guessing how many teeth someone had (see Aristophanes, *Wealth* 1054–9). It is more relevant, then, to remember that dental hygiene was non-existent, than just that the two sophists are old.

Crito, my own incredulity compelled me to join in and ask Dionysodorus whether he knew how to dance.

e   'Yes,' he said.

'Surely,' I asked, 'your expertise is not so advanced that at your age you can do handsprings over knives and whirl around on a wheel.[1] Can you do that?'

'There is nothing I do not know how to do,' he said.

'Do you both know everything only at this moment, or did you always too?' I asked.

'Always too,' he said.

'And did you both know everything when you were children, as soon as you were born, in fact?'

They both said 'yes' simultaneously.

295a   Well, we just couldn't believe it. 'Are you dubious, Socrates?' asked Euthydemus.

'I would be,' I said, 'if your cleverness was open to reasonable doubt.'

'You have only to answer my questions,' he said, 'and I will demonstrate that you too agree to these marvels.'

'Well, this is one argument I really don't mind losing,' I said. 'I mean, I could look my whole life and never find a greater godsend than your demonstration that I am, was and will be omniscient – though this wisdom has escaped my notice.'[2]

'Answer my questions, then,' he said.

b   'You have only to ask them.'

'Do you, Socrates,' he said, 'know anything or not?'

'I do.'

'And is this state of knowledge made possible by what enables you to be in possession of knowledge, or by something else?'

'By what enables me to be in possession of knowledge: I suppose you mean my soul, don't you?'

'Really, Socrates!' he said. 'You shouldn't answer questions with questions.'[3]

---

1. These were types of impressive 'dance' for entertainment. For the first, knives were set upright in a circle in the ground and a dancer went head first into the circle and sprang out over the knives using the hands (see Xenophon, *Symposium* 2.11). The second is undocumented in detail, but is mentioned also at Xenophon, *Symposium* 7.2.

2. Socrates' *ignorance*, of course, refutes the hypothesis of omniscience.

3. Euthydemus objects to Socrates' introduction of 'soul' (*psuchē*) not just on principle but, arguably, because the common Greek view was that *psuchē*, the life-force, is simply what enlivens a living body, in which case Euthydemus could not argue for prenatal knowledge. Ironically, however, Socrates' own theory of recollection requires that *psuchē* should have prenatal knowledge.

'All right,' I said. 'But what am I to do? I'll do as you say: are you telling me just to answer, and not to ask questions, even when I don't know what you're asking?'

'Surely you understand what I'm saying a bit, don't you?' he asked.   c

'Yes,' I said.

'So answer as much of the question as you understand.'

'What if I misconstrue the thinking behind your question and answer what *I* take it to be?' I asked. 'Is it still enough for you if my answer is entirely beside the point?'

'Yes,' he said, 'but not for you, I imagine.'

'Good heavens, no!' I said. 'I won't answer until I've got to the bottom of a question.'

'The reason you won't answer as much of the question as you understand at the time,' he said, 'is because you persist in being an unnecessarily reactionary old windbag.'

I realized that my precision with his words was annoying him, because   d
he wanted to surround me with verbiage and trap me that way. Then I remembered that when Connus[1] gets annoyed with me for being stubborn, he doesn't take so much trouble over me, thinking that I am stupid. So I thought I'd better give in to Euthydemus, since I intended to become *his* pupil too, in case he thought I was dense and refused to take me on as his pupil. So I said: 'All right, Euthydemus, we'll have to do it your way: you   e
know infinitely more about how to conduct a philosophical discussion than I, who have only an amateur's skill. So please, start your questions again from the beginning.'

'Try again, then,' he said, 'to answer me this: do you know what you know by means of something or not?'

'Yes,' I said. 'My soul.'

'He's done it again,' he said. 'He answers more than he's asked. My   296a
question is not *what* you know by, but whether you know by means of *something*.'

'Sorry,' I said. 'Once again, lack of education has made me give a superfluous answer. Now I'll answer with no embellishments: yes, I know what I know by means of something.'

'And is it always the same thing, or is it sometimes that and sometimes something else?' he asked.

'Whenever I know, it's always by means of that thing,' I said.

'I must ask you again,' he said, 'not to qualify your answers.'

'Well, I'm worried about this "always" misleading us.'

1. See 272c.

b   'Not us,' he said, 'but *you*, maybe. Now come on, answer me: do you always know by means of that thing?'

'If I have to delete my "whenever", I can only answer "always",' I said.

'So you always know by means of that thing. Now, given that you always know, do you know some things by means of this thing which enables you to know, but other things by means of something else? Or do you know everything by means of this thing?'

'All that I know, I know by means of this thing,' I said.[1]

'There you are again,' he said, 'bringing in the same qualification.'

'All right,' I said, 'I withdraw my phrase "that I know".'

'No, don't bother to withdraw anything,' he said. 'I don't need any
c   favours from you. Tell me: could you know all[2] without knowing everything?'

'That would be unusual,' I said.

'*Now* you can add whatever qualifications you like,' he replied. 'You have admitted that you know everything.'[3]

'So it seems,' I said. 'I know everything – given your invalidation of "that I know".'

'Now, you have admitted *both* that you always know by means of that which enables you to know – whenever you know or what have you (I mean, you have admitted that you always know) – *and* that you know everything too.[4] So obviously you knew even when you were a child – and
d   at birth, and at conception! And given that you *always* know, you knew everything before you were born, and before heaven and earth came into being. And, by God,' he added, 'you – yes, *you* – will always know in the future, and know everything, if I so want it.'[5]

'I certainly hope you will desire it,' I said, 'if you really are telling the truth. But – and I mean you no disrespect, Euthydemus – I'm not fully convinced that you are up to the task, unless your brother Dionysodorus here shares your desire. Then perhaps it might be possible. It's beyond
e   me,' I went on, 'to argue against you two with your fantastic wisdom that I do *not* know everything, when you are claiming that I do. So let's leave

   1. Socrates is wary of the recurrence of the fallacy of *secundum quid* on knowledge which was operative at the beginning of this section.

   2. Once Socrates has withdrawn 'that I know' from 'I know all that I know', this is what he is left with!

   3. So he would presumably feel entitled to ignore any qualifications that Socrates might add: see next note.

   4. The clause within dashes dismisses Socrates' qualifications. The punctuation with dashes and parenthesis follows O'Sullivan.

   5. Euthydemus waxes triumphant, but the obvious correctness of Socrates' resistance throughout this section has undermined his victory.

all that, but could you just tell me this: how am I to say that I know that good people are unjust, and things like that? Tell me, please: is this something I know, or not?'

'Of course you know,' he said.

'What?' I asked.

'That good people are *not* unjust.'

'Yes,' I said, 'I've known *that* for some time. But you misunderstand 297a my question: where did I learn that good people are unjust?'[1]

'Nowhere,' said Dionysodorus.

'So this is something which *I* do *not* know,' I said.

'You're ruining the argument,' Euthydemus said to Dionysodorus. 'He'll turn out not to know, and to be and not be in possession of knowledge at the same time.'

Dionysodorus blushed. 'What do you mean, Euthydemus?' I asked. 'Do you think your omniscient brother is making a mistake?' b

'*Am* I Euthydemus' brother?' Dionysodorus quickly butted in.[2]

'Let that go, my friend,' I said, 'until Euthydemus has taught me how I know that good people are unjust. Don't begrudge me this lesson.'

'You're running away, Socrates,' said Dionysodorus. 'You don't want to answer me.'

'That's hardly surprising,' I said. 'Either of you by himself could defeat me, so you bet I'm running away from the two of you together. I'm not in the same league as Heracles,[3] you know – far from it – and he couldn't c stand up to the Hydra (a she-sophist who was clever enough to come up with many heads of argument for any one which was cut off), when she joined forces with another, crab-like sophist, who, I imagine, had just come ashore from the sea. When this crab-like sophist was giving him a hard time with arguments and with claws a-snapping on his left,[4] he called up reinforcements, in the shape of his nephew Iolaus, whose assistance

1. This must be something Socrates knows if he knows everything.

2. Dionysodorus has to divert attention from the further contradiction Socrates has exposed. About the most that can be said for the sophists is that they are quick to seize opportunities (see, for instance, 283e too). But so is Socrates: he has provided an effective empirical refutation of the sophisms.

3. There was a proverb 'Not even Heracles could take on two', referring to the mythical episode Socrates draws on for the brilliant image that follows.

4. The seating arrangements described at 273b confirm that Socrates is describing Euthydemus as the Hydra and Dionysodorus as the crab – a mere reinforcement for Euthydemus! The Hydra was a many-headed monster: every time Heracles cut off one head, two more sprouted in its place. If there is any point in the crab's having just come ashore, it is not clear – perhaps it is just a further insult, as if Dionysodorus were a slimy sea-monster.

d met his requirements. But if *my* Iolaus should come, he might only make matters worse.'[1]

L. *The Sophists on Family Relationships*

There are several arguments in this section, which are linked both by the common theme of family relationships and by an increasing absurdity. The sophisms here are perhaps better called quibbles or puns than arguments.

Dionysodorus sets out to demonstrate that if Iolaus is a nephew, he is every-one's nephew. By 297e this fallacy of secundum quid, *and another on brothers, have been foiled by Socrates' precision with the necessary qualifications. Dionysodorus then changes tack, to argue that a father both is a father (of someone) and is not a father (of others). The dropping of the qualifications and the consequent fallacy of* secundum quid *are blatant. That this is Plato's analysis of the argument is clear from Socrates' answers at the beginning of 298a, but other analyses are possible (see Hawtrey (1981), p. 161). Euthydemus adds the consequence (298b) that Socrates is fatherless: it is not clear whether this is meant simply to be ludicrous, or whether it carries the connotation of 'bastard' that English slang does.*

Ctesippus takes over to prove that Euthydemus is fatherless too, but Euthydemus turns the tables by arguing the reverse (the tactic is familiar from Sections C and D), using the law of non-contradiction (see e.g. 293b), in conjunction with the usual omission of necessary qualifications. Ctesippus insolently draws out the absurdity: each person's parents are the parents of everything.

The final argument (298d–e) uses a different fallacy – equivocation on 'your' – to claim that Ctesippus' dog is his father. This may also be analysed as a fallacy of composition (if the dog is both yours and a father, it is your father; see p. 304). Aristotle analyses it (De Sophisticis Elenchis 179a34–5) as an example of his 'fallacy of accident', that is, the confusion of an accidental term with an essential term: my father is mine in a more proper – less accidental – sense than my dog. In any case, the fallacies of composition and of accident depend upon the presence of ambiguous terms.

'Since you've so lyrically brought it up,' said Dionysodorus, 'tell me this: was Iolaus any more Heracles' nephew than yours?'

'Well, I'd better answer you, Dionysodorus,' I said. 'I'm pretty sure

1. Obviously, Socrates does not mean his *actual* nephew, and he is unlikely to mean Ctesippus, who has not been making matters worse. This is just a part of Socrates' whimsical account of the dire straits he is in.

that there's no chance of your dropping your questions. You refuse to let me learn that bit of wisdom from Euthydemus; you just get in the way.'

'Answer, then,' he said.

'My answer,' I said, 'is that Iolaus was Heracles' nephew and, as far as I can see, there's no way that he was mine at all. I mean, Iolaus' father e wasn't my brother Patrocles but – and I admit that the names are similar – Iphicles, who was Heracles' brother.'

'Is Patrocles your brother?' he asked.

'Yes,' I said. 'We have the same mother, at any rate, though different fathers.'

'So he is and is not your brother.'

'It's just that we don't have the same father, my friend,' I said. 'His was Chaeredemus, mine Sophroniscus.'

'Were both Sophroniscus and Chaeredemus fathers?' he asked.

'Yes,' I said. 'The first was mine, the second his.'   298a

'Was Chaeredemus different from a father?' he asked.

'From mine, anyway,' I said.

'What? He was a father although he was different from a father? And you are the same as the proverbial stone, I suppose?'[1]

'I'm afraid that's how you'll make me appear,' I said, 'but, as far as I can see, I'm not.'

'Well, *are* you different from the stone?' he asked.

'Of course I am.'

'And if you are different from stone, you're not stone, are you? And if you are different from gold, you're not gold, are you?'

'True.'

'So surely, if Chaeredemus is different from a father,' he said, 'then he isn't a father.'[2]

'I suppose not,' I said.

'For if Chaeredemus *is* a father, you see,' Euthydemus interposed, 'then b again, Sophroniscus is not a father, because he is different from a father – and you, Socrates, are fatherless!'

At this point Ctesippus took over. 'Doesn't precisely the same go for *your* father too?' he asked. 'Isn't he different from *my* father?'

1. There is a double meaning here. In the first place, Dionysodorus is driving home the point about sameness and difference: if it is possible for something to be both same and different, then Socrates, though different from a stone, might be the same as it. Secondly, he is simply calling Socrates stupid: stones were proverbially dense.

2. Reading οὐκοῦν . . . οὐ πατήρ ἐστιν with manuscript W. Notice the move from cases where the equation of 'being different from *x*' and 'not being *x*' is unexceptionable, to where it is exceptionable, the difference being that 'father' is an incomplete predicate, requiring qualification.

'Far from it,' said Euthydemus.

'He's the *same*?' he asked.

'Certainly.'

c   'I can't go along with that. But tell me, Euthydemus: is he only *my* father, or everyone else's as well?'

'Everyone else's as well,' he said, 'unless you imagine that the same person can both be and not be a father.'

'That's exactly what I did think,' said Ctesippus.

'Really?' he said. 'That gold isn't gold, and a person isn't a person?'

'Euthydemus,' said Ctesippus, 'I rather suspect that you are not joining flax to flax, as the saying goes.[1] It is monstrous to say that your father is father of everything.'

'But he is,' he said.

'Just of men,' asked Ctesippus, 'or of horses and all other animals too?'

'Of everything.'

d   'And similarly for your mother?'

'Yes.'

'Your mother, then, is the mother of sea-urchins.'

'So's yours,' he said.

'Which makes you a brother to gobies and puppies and piglets.'

'Yes, and you,' he said.

'And your father is a pig and a dog.'

'Yes, and so's yours,' he said.

'You'll soon find yourself agreeing to these points, Ctesippus,' said Dionysodorus, 'if you answer my questions. Tell me: do you have a dog?'

'Yes, a real scamp,' said Ctesippus.

'And has he got puppies?'

e   'Yes, regular chips off the old block,' he said.

'So your dog is their father?'

'Yes, I myself saw him mounting the bitch,' he said.

'Well now, the dog is yours?'

'Yes,' he said.

'He is a father, and he is yours – so he turns out to be your father, and you are brother to puppies!'

To prevent Ctesippus having the next word, Dionysodorus quickly started up again: 'I've got one more small question for you,' he said. 'Do you beat this dog of yours?'

Ctesippus laughed and said: 'Good heavens, yes! You see, I can't beat you!'

1. Trying to take different things together: Ctesippus is almost aware of the point made in the previous note.

'You beat your own father, then?'

'I would be far more justified in beating yours,' he said, 'for having the   299a
bright idea of fathering such clever sons!'

M. *Nothing in Excess*

*Ctesippus' first words in this section seem to assume that lots of good things are
desirable, so the sophists set out to prove the opposite. First, Euthydemus uses
the method of* reductio ad absurdum *to show that in at least two cases a lot is
too much. Second, Dionysodorus uses the same method to show that having a
good thing is not always and everywhere appropriate.*

The fallacy in their arguments is the opposite of secundum quid*: Ctesippus'
unqualified assumption is given absurd qualifications. But the section has more
interest than this. Why are the sophists given an argument for a non-outrageous
conclusion ('nothing in excess' was proverbial Greek wisdom, endorsed by both
Socrates and Plato), while Ctesippus defends the opposite?*

*We have been conditioned so far in the dialogue to disapprove of the sophisms.
What does Plato mean us to disapprove of here? Probably this: that even though
the conclusion is reasonable, the purpose of the argument is eristic, as usual.
Ctesippus' innocuous, or at least casual assumption is seized on for the sophists
to score points.*

*Ctesippus' defence of his assumption has several dramatic purposes: first,
since he finds counter-examples, albeit extreme ones, we are being shown the
dangers of inferring a conclusion from too few examples; second, Plato is
showing how eristic arguments provoke more of the same; third, we are being
prepared for Ctesippus' counter-attack in Section N.*

*The sophisms here are Socratic both in mode (Socrates frequently uses infer-
ence) and in conclusion (see Section E for the lack of necessity for many good
things). They cannot even be described as perversions of Socratic argument. We
are simply being shown that eristic sophists can use anything for their own ends.*

'But I suppose it goes without saying, Euthydemus, that your father –
the puppies' father – has derived enormous benefit from your wisdom.'

'He has no need of lots of good things, Ctesippus; nor do you.'

'Nor you, Euthydemus?' he asked.

'No, no one does. I mean, suppose someone's ill, Ctesippus, and takes
some medicine when he needs it – tell me whether you reckon that is a   b

good thing or not. And again, isn't it better to be armed than unarmed when going to war?'

'*I* would say so. But I imagine that you will come up with one of your smart moves.'

'You'll discover that best,' he said, 'if you just answer my questions. You endorsed the idea that it is good for a person to take medicine when he needs it; so shouldn't he take as much as possible of this good thing? And in that case, won't he be well off if a whole cartload of hellebore is pounded and mixed for him?'

'No doubt about it, Euthydemus,' said Ctesippus, '*if* the patient has
c   the bulk of the Delphic statue.'[1]

'Now, take war too, where it is good to be armed: shouldn't one have as many spears and shields as possible, since it is a good thing?'

'Yes, of course,' said Ctesippus. 'Don't *you* agree, Euthydemus? Do you think that one of each is appropriate?'

'I do.'

'Would you also arm Geryon or Briareus in that fashion?'[2] he asked. 'I'd credited you with more competence than that – you and your colleague – considering that you teach weaponry.'

Euthydemus kept quiet, but Dionysodorus had a question relating to
d   Ctesippus' earlier responses: 'Do you think possession of gold is good too?' he asked.

'Yes,' said Ctesippus, 'and in this case, plenty of it.'

'And do you think that possession of good things is always indispensable everywhere?'

'Certainly,' he said.

'And you agree that gold is good?'

'I've already said so,' he replied.

'So one should always have it everywhere, and in oneself as much as
e   possible? The greatest happiness would be having three talents of gold in your stomach, one in the skull, and a stater in each eye, wouldn't it?'[3]

'Well, Dionysodorus,'[4] said Ctesippus, 'they do say that the happiest and bravest Scythians are those who have lots of gold in their skulls (to

1. The lack of attribution of this statue makes it likely that it was one of Apollo, to whom Delphi was sacred. The statue in question was set up by the Greeks after the battle of Salamis (480), and was twelve cubits (*c.* twenty feet) high.

2. In myth, Geryon was a three-bodied monster; Briareus had a hundred arms. Both, then, could manage more than one spear and one shield.

3. Talents and staters were monetary weights: an Attic talent was about fifty-five pounds, which shows how ridiculous Dionysodorus is being. A stater in each eye is more plausible, since it was less than half an ounce.

4. Reading Διονυσόδωρε: Ctesippus refers to an argument of Dionysodorus' (298d–e).

imitate your recent claim that my dog is my father),[1] and – what is even more remarkable – that they drink out of their gilded skulls, hold the crowns of their heads in their hands and gaze inside!'[2]

N. *Paradoxes about the Senses*

That sophisms about the senses were common is proved by Aristotle's references to them (De Sophisticis Elenchis *166a9–14, 168a13–16, 171a passim). Those we find in this section employ the fallacy of amphiboly (pp. 303–4), dependent upon ambiguities in Greek grammar. They are, therefore, very difficult to translate.*

The first (300a) exploits the phrase dunata horan, *which has both active and passive meanings: 'able to see' or 'possible to see'. The English phrase 'here to see' is the closest I can get to capturing this ambiguity. We say 'The paintings are here to see' – that is, 'here for us to see' – but obviously the phrase also has an active sense, as in 'I am here to see the paintings.'*

Ctesippus responds by coming up with two paradoxes of his own: it is possible to be asleep (mentally) and awake (physically) at the same time, and to talk and say nothing (in the sense of nothing sensible). Ctesippus is learning!

The second sophism (300b) exploits the phrase sigōnta legein – *'to speak while silent' or 'to speak of silent things'; the third is the converse (300b–c):* legonta sigan *means either 'to be silent while speaking' or 'to be silent about speaking things'. I have tried to capture this ambiguity by the phrases 'involved in silence' and 'involved in speaking'; thus 'silent things are involved in speaking' may mean either the impossibility, that silent things are speaking, or the possibility, that silent things are being mentioned in someone's speech.*

Finally, Ctesippus comes up with a nice example of a leading question which refuses to acknowledge the intermediate position, when he assumes that the denial that everything is silent entails that everything is talking, rather than that some things are talking. Euthydemus sees the problem and counters it; Dionysodorus tries to be clever but makes a mess of it (see p. 365 n. 1).

'Do Scythians,' asked Euthydemus, 'or anyone else, for that matter, 300a see things which are here to see or those which are not?'

'Those which are, of course.'

'And so do you?' he asked.

'Yes.'

'Well, can you see our clothes?'

1. Ctesippus parodies the sophists' use in Section J of the ambiguity of possessive pronouns.
2. He is referring to the Scythian habit of using the gilded skulls of their enemies as cups.

'Yes.'

'So they are here to see.'[1]

'Extraordinarily clearly.'

'What's next?' said Euthydemus.

'Nothing. Perhaps you think you don't see them.[2] Such lack of subtlety, Euthydemus! To my mind you've nodded off without being asleep, and you are talking but saying nothing, if that is possible.'

b   'Surely it isn't possible for silent things to be involved in speaking?' asked Dionysodorus.

'Quite out of the question,' replied Ctesippus.

'Nor for speaking things to be involved in silence?'

'Even less of a possibility,' he said.

'But when you speak of stone or wood or iron, then silent things are involved in speaking, aren't they?'

'They're not silent when I go to a forge,' he said, 'where handling the iron goods makes them "talk" and "cry out loud".[3] This is a case of your cleverness blinding you to the nonsense you come up with. So please go on to the other half of the demonstration, how speaking things may be involved in silence.'

c   I thought Ctesippus was pushing too hard, to impress his beloved.

'When you're silent, you're not saying *anything*, are you?' asked Euthydemus.

'That's right,' he said.

'And "anything" includes the phrase "speaking things",[4] so "speaking things" *are* involved in your silence!'

'Well now,' said Ctesippus, 'isn't everything silent?'

'Of course not,' said Euthydemus.[5]

'So everything is talking, my friend?'

'Talking things, anyway.'

'That's not my question,' he said. 'Is everything silent or talking?'

d   'Neither and both,' Dionysodorus interrupted. 'An answer you won't be able to cope with, I'm sure.'

Ctesippus gave one of his typical huge guffaws and said: 'Euthydemus,

---

1. Which Euthydemus wants to understand as 'Our clothes do the seeing'!

2. Reading ὁρᾶν αὐτά with manuscript T. Ctesippus is saying: 'Perhaps you're taking the phrase "here to see" as meaning that they do the seeing, not you.'

3. Picture a blacksmith's goods all hanging close together in his shop, and Ctesippus as the customer fingering the goods. The Greeks used the same words for the noise such objects might make as for human speech.

4. Reading τὰ λέγοντα in c4, with Stephanus.

5. But he has just claimed that 'speaking things are silent'. Ctesippus has neatly exploited the absurdity of this to make Euthydemus immediately contradict himself.

your brother's prevarication has completely ruined and defeated your argument!'[1]

This afforded Cleinias considerable pleasure and amusement, which made Ctesippus grow at least ten times taller! Ctesippus, I think, is a bit cunning and had caught the arguments he was using from them. I mean, nobody else but them nowadays has such wisdom.

O. *Fineness and Fine Things*

This section of the dialogue is fairly opaque. Dionysodorus uses a leading question in an attempt to trap Socrates into admitting that an attribute is either the same as its particular instances or different from them. We may speculate about the possible sequence of the sophism: if Socrates says they are the same, Dionysodorus would produce some absurd conclusion like, 'So fineness is a fine dog'; if Socrates says they are different, perhaps Dionysodorus would argue that if fineness is fine, and particulars are different, then they are not fine.

Anyway, Socrates avoids the dilemma by adopting a middle way. He introduces the idea that an attribute may be said to be present to its particular instances, in order to claim that it is in a sense both different from and the same as those instances.

Dionysodorus attempts to reduce the notion of 'presence' to absurdity: the presence of a cow does not make me a cow! (This equivocates on 'presence' by taking it as physical presence, which Socrates clearly did not intend.) And, generally, how can two different things have any similarity?

Despite Dionysodorus' attempt, Socrates persists in his line. Something fine is fine, but this is not to say that it is the same as the attribute, or that it is totally different from it. It is the same to the extent that it is characterized by the attribute; it is different to the extent that it is not the attribute itself. Thus 'something identical is identical [i.e. has the quality of being identical]' (301b) means that if something fine is fine, it is to that extent identical with the attribute; and 'something different is different [i.e. has the quality of being different]' means that something fine is not the same as the attribute, fineness. The issue here is the same as we have met earlier in the dialogue (especially Section K): Socrates is trying to qualify the sophists' bare statements.

Why does Socrates cast himself as a sophist at 301b? Chiefly he means no more than that he is taking over the sophists' role as questioner. It is also

---

1. Dionysodorus should have answered just 'neither': it is not the case either that everything is silent or that everything is talking, as Euthydemus saw just before (the irony being that Euthydemus wants to qualify the answer, when previously the sophists have disallowed qualifications).

noticeable, however, that his solution to Dionysodorus' dilemma really does no more than reassert the original proposition that fineness is both different from fine things and yet may have some relation to them. So perhaps Socrates casts himself as a sophist because he is about to obfuscate the issue to some extent and avoid the lengthy metaphysical discussion that a proper response would entail.

Many commentators read into this section a background of Plato's theory of forms (see pp. 32–3, 219), according to which fineness is a form with an existence independent of any particulars that might be fine. There is no suggestion of this in the passage: we may be on the ground of Socrates' search for universals as objects of definition (see pp. 21–2), but we need not suppose even this. The metaphor of presence was perfectly acceptable even in non-philosophic Greek: 'Fear is present to them' is periphrastic for 'They are afraid.' We are simply seeing two Greeks using their language, one to produce confusion, the other to try to defend common sense. It is Dionysodorus who first mentions the abstract entity 'fineness', not Socrates, so we should not suppose that this is a Platonic form. Socrates uses the phrase 'fineness itself' at 301a to pinpoint or isolate fineness, not in any metaphysically significant sense (see p. 221). There is a certain similarity between Dionysodorus' assault on the notion of presence and an argument put into the mouth of Parmenides against Plato's theory of forms at Parmenides *130e–131c, as Sprague (1967) points out. But this should not induce us to think that Platonic forms are relevant to this passage (or that Plato saw the arguments of* Parmenides *as less than damaging to his theory): Plato probably realized later that this argument, in origin a sophism, could be turned against his theory.*

e   I spoke up: 'What do you find amusing in such serious and fine matters, Cleinias?'

'Have you ever seen anything fine, Socrates?' asked Dionysodorus.

'Yes,' I said, 'many things, Dionysodorus.'

301a   'And were they different from or identical to fineness?' he asked.

I was really in desperate straits and didn't know what to do – which, I thought, was only what I deserved for complaining – but all the same, I replied that although they are different from fineness itself, fineness in a sense is present to each of them.

'So,' he said, 'if there's a cow present to you, are you a cow? And given that I'm present to you, are you Dionysodorus?'

'God forbid!' I said.

'But how,' he asked, 'can A's presence to B turn B into A, when they are different?'

b   'Do you find that puzzling?' I asked – my desire for their cleverness was now leading me to try to copy the two visitors.

366

'Of course I do,' he said. 'Not only I but everyone else finds impossibilities puzzling.'

'What do you mean, Dionysodorus?' I asked. 'Surely, something fine is fine, and something contemptible is contemptible?'

'If that is my impression,' he said.[1]

'And *is* it your impression?'

'Yes,' he said.

'So something identical is identical and something different is different, surely? I mean, something different cannot be identical, of course; but I didn't imagine that even a child would find puzzling the idea that something different is different. No, you must have ignored this point on purpose, to judge by the finesse which you two generally strike me as bringing to the art of discussion, and which is comparable to the creativity of craftsmen at their respective functions.'   c

P. *The Sophists on the Crafts*

Socrates, of course, often brings the crafts into his discussions, using them as examples to illustrate some point or other. Dionysodorus' treatment is a simple amphiboly (pp. 303–4), based on an ambiguity in Greek grammar: in the sentence 'It is right ton mageiron katakoptein*', the Greek phrase can mean either 'for the cook to chop' or 'to chop the cook'.*

'Oh, so you know what each craftsman's function is, do you?' he asked. 'Do you know, firstly, whose job it is to hammer metal?'

'Yes, a smith's.'

'And to make pots?'

'A potter's.'

'And to slaughter, skin, chop meat up, boil it and roast it?'

'A cook's.'   d

'Now, doing one's proper job is right, isn't it?' he asked.

'Very much so.'

'And, as you agree, the proper thing for a cook is chopping and skinning? Did you admit that or not?'

'I did,' I said, 'but please don't hold it against me.'

'The proper thing to do, then, obviously, is to slaughter cooks, chop them up, boil them and roast them. Likewise, the proper thing is to hammer smiths and make pots out of potters!'

1. A hint of Protagoras' doctrine that 'Man is the measure of all things': if Dionysodorus perceives something fine as fine, it is fine.

Q. *Gods for Sale*

Dionysodorus argues that you are able to sell etc. your gods because they are yours and you can do what you like with your property. The fallacy here is equivocation, based on the same ambiguity of 'your' that we have met before (Section L): your gods are obviously not yours in the same sense that your chattels are. The fallacy could also be seen as 'affirming the consequent' (Aristotle, De Sophisticis Elenchis 167b1 ff.): at first Dionysodorus argues that if you control something it is yours; later that if the gods are yours you control them. But it does not follow from 'if A, then B' that 'B, therefore A'.

The most curious part of the section is Socrates' denial that he has an Ancestral Zeus (302b–d). We know from both literary and epigraphical evidence that Athenians did worship Zeus under this title, so what is going on? Socrates is playing the sophists' own game again (Plato has him admit that he is 'trying in vain to wriggle out of the trap'). The title 'Ancestral Zeus' is ambiguous: it can mean either 'Zeus, ancestor of the race' or 'Zeus, protector of ancestors'. Socrates chooses to take the former meaning, so that he can deny Dionysodorus' question; he could not have denied that he had an Ancestral Zeus in the latter sense.

e 'My God!' I exclaimed. 'Now you're putting the coping-stone on your wisdom! Shall I ever get it and make it my own?'

'Would you recognize it, Socrates,' he asked, 'if it did become yours?'[1]

'Yes, obviously,' I said, '*if* you so want it.'

'So you think you know your possessions?' he asked.

'Unless you tell me otherwise. I mean, you are my alpha, and Euthydemus here is my omega, and that's the way it should be.'[2]

'Do you consider things to be yours,' he asked, 'when you control them
302a and are free to do what you want with them? Take cattle and sheep, for example: would you consider that they are yours because you are free to sell them, give them away or sacrifice them to any god you choose? And do you consider not to be yours anything that isn't like that?'[3]

Now, I knew that something fine would emerge from the questions as

1. Another reference to the (probably common) eristic argument reproduced by Plato at *Meno* 80d–e (see p. 324).

2. The formula of 'you are my beginning and end' was used to address superior people in general and gods in particular; see p. 319 n. 1.

3. From 'You call yours things to which you can do *x*', it does not follow that 'You can *only* call yours things to which you can do *x*.' In the next sentence Plato seems to signal his recognition that something is wrong with this part of Dionysodorus' argument.

they stood, and I was impatient to hear it, so I said: 'Yes, that's right. Only things of that sort are mine.'

'Well,' he said, 'isn't "living being" the way you describe something animate?'

'Yes,' I said.   b

'So do you agree that living beings are only yours when you are free to treat them in all the ways I just mentioned?'

'Yes.'

He paused a bit – an affectation to give the impression of deep thought – and then said: 'Tell me, Socrates: do you have an Ancestral Zeus?'

I guessed the direction and ultimate destination of the argument, and I squirmed like an animal caught in a net, trying in vain to wriggle out of the trap. 'No, Dionysodorus,' I said.

'What a pitiful specimen of humanity you are, then, and no Athenian either, if you have no ancestral gods or shrines, or any other mark of   c
gentility.'

'Steady on, Dionysodorus,' I said. 'Please mind your language and don't malign your pupil. I have domestic and ancestral altars and shrines and so on as much as the next Athenian.'

'Do other Athenians really not have an Ancestral Zeus?' he asked.

'No,' I said. 'That title is not an Ionian one,[1] and so is not used by Athenians or Athenian colonists. We have an Ancestral Apollo instead, because he was Ion's father. We don't have a Zeus we call Ancestral, but   d
a Zeus of the Household, and Zeus Guardian of the Phratry and Athena Guardian of the Phratry . . .'[2]

'Enough,' he said. 'You do, apparently, have Apollo, Zeus and Athena.'

'Yes,' I said.

'And *they* must be your gods, surely?'

'They are my progenitors and my masters,' I said.[3]

'But they are *yours*,' he said. 'Didn't you admit that they are yours?'

'I did,' I said. 'What have I let myself in for?'

'Are these gods living beings too?' he asked. 'Remember, you agreed   e
that anything animate is a living being. Are these gods animate?'

'Yes,' I said.

1. There were three traditional divisions of Greeks, each with their own dialects and main geographical locations: Ionians, Dorians and Aeolians. The Ionians claimed descent from Ion, the son of Apollo and Creusa. Athens claimed to be the mother-city of all Ionians.

2. A phratry was a social and political subdivision of a tribe, consisting of the union of several families and based notionally on kinship.

3. Socrates piously avoids saying that they are his gods, given the extreme sense of ownership that Dionysodorus is putting on possessive pronouns. Contrary to Socrates' statement here, Dionysodorus is in effect saying that Socrates is *their* master.

'So they are living beings too?'

'Yes,' I said.

'Now, you agreed that those living beings are yours, which you are free to give away, sell or sacrifice to a god of your choice.'

'I did,' I said. 'I can't go back on that, Euthydemus.'

303a 'No more delays, now,' he said. 'Just tell me this: given your claim that Zeus and the other gods are yours, do you have the same freedom as with the other living beings, to sell them or give them away or do whatever else you want with them?'

R. *Capitulation and Recapitulation*

Ctesippus ironically praises the previous argument; the sophists, finding as usual something to start a sophism, seize on his words, but Ctesippus capitulates and this signals the end of the whole display, since the capitulation of the opponent was the purpose of eristic argument. After the applause for the sophists' victory has died down, Socrates summarizes the main points, as he sees them, in a speech whose irony is palpable. He concludes by encouraging Crito, as he had at the beginning of the dialogue, to join him as the sophists' pupil.

It was as if the argument had struck me physically, Crito: I just sat there speechless. But Ctesippus came to my assistance and said: 'By Heracles, bravo – a fine argument!'

And Dionysodorus said: 'Is Heracles bravo, or bravo Heracles?'[1]

'Oh, God!' said Ctesippus. 'Amazing! I give up – there's no stopping them.'

b Then, my dear Crito, everyone present almost wore themselves out with laughter, applause and expressions of delight, as they praised to the skies the arguments and the two visitors. Every single earlier argument had met with a very fine reception, but only from Euthydemus' admirers; but *now*, so to speak, even the pillars in the Lyceum acclaimed the visitors and showed their pleasure. I myself was inclined to agree that I had never

c come across such clever people, and their wisdom so utterly enthralled me that I turned to praising them in a panegyric: 'What a godsend, to be so remarkably gifted as to have accomplished such important work in so short a span of time! Your arguments are impressive in many respects, Euthydemus and Dionysodorus, but especially magnificent is your disdain

---

1. This ludicrous question makes slightly more sense in Greek, where it is just conceivable, to judge solely by the grammatical form of the words, that 'bravo' agrees syntactically with 'Heracles' in 'By Heracles, bravo.'

for the majority of mankind *and* for reputable savants, and your concern only for those similar to yourselves. I mean, I am sure that those who are   d
like you and would approve of these arguments are very few; everybody else understands these kinds of arguments so little that, I am convinced, they would be less embarrassed to be refuted by them than to use them to refute others. Then there's the altruistic and affable side of your arguments; although, as you say, you absolutely muzzle people by denying   e
that anything is fine, good, white and so on – in the sense that nothing is any different from anything else[1] – you apparently would do the same to yourselves as to others.[2] This is very decent of you, and takes the sting out of your words. But the most important point is that you have arranged and elaborated these things so skilfully that anyone can learn them in a very short time, as *I* realized by observing how quickly even Ctesippus could improvise and reproduce your arguments.[3] Now, this clever aspect of your work is fine as far as rapid dissemination is concerned, but unsuit-   304a
able for discussions in front of an audience, and if I were you, I would think twice before talking in public, because if people pick up the arguments so quickly, they might not feel indebted to you. The best thing would be for the two of you just to talk between yourselves in private; failing that, the only other person who should be present is a paying customer. The sensible course would be to give your pupils the same   b
advice too, not to have discussions with anyone except you and between themselves. I mean, the scarce product is the valuable one, Euthydemus: despite what Pindar said about water being best,[4] it commands a very low price. Anyway,' I concluded, 'please enrol me and Cleinias here as your pupils.'

That was more or less all the discussion, Crito; then we left. Do you think you can manage to join me as their pupil? Remember, they claim   c
to be able to teach anyone who is prepared to pay, age and aptitude notwithstanding – and, *you*'ll be pleased to hear, they say that even commercial interests don't stop anyone from easily acquiring their wisdom.[5]

1. See 276e, in Section C, where the sophists come close to the claim that they 'muzzle' people. Socrates' meaning is probably that in arguments like that of Section C, which exploit linguistic ambiguities, the sophists effectively eradicate meaningful distinctions (see Rankin, p. 23).

2. See Section H.

3. Punctuating ἀνθρώπων, ἔγνων with Méridier. As usual, the contrast is with the lifelong Socratic search for virtue. See Sections M and N for Ctesippus imitating the sophists.

4. Pindar, *Olympian* 1.1.

5. Punctuating οὐδὲν μὴ οὐ with Hawtrey. Socrates is referring to the traditional division between concern with philosophy and concern with worldly affairs: each was commonly thought to be a full-time occupation.

S. *Epilogue*

A Platonic dialogue invariably ends with the conclusion of the main conver-
sation; this epilogue is most unusual. The point of it is to underline the gulf
between the ideal of philosophy and some more of its so-called practitioners.
The contrast with Euthydemus and Dionysodorus has been made throughout
the dialogue: though they are mentioned again as eristics (305d), the chief
contrast in this section is with a type of practitioner exemplified in Isocrates (see
pp. 310–11).

The section is also remarkable for its economical portrait of Crito: he has
unexceptionable standards – his term of praise, for instance, is 'decent' (304e),
he does not think Socrates should be seen in public with sophists (305b), and
he has the usual concerns of an Athenian paterfamilias (306d–e); despite his
lifelong attachment to Socrates, we are bound to feel that he has never fully
committed himself to philosophy (the dialogue Crito bears this out). In short,
Plato seems to be saying that he sits on the fence, much as Isocrates does.
Perhaps Crito had recently died, and this is Plato's memorial: honest, but
not a true philosopher (though we hear of Crito having written philosophical
works).

The final passage shows Crito worrying about his sons' education. This
emphasizes and rounds off the purpose of the dialogue: we are now supposed
to be in no doubt that Socrates' is the best educational method.

CRITO: It's true that I love listening to talks and that I'm pleased to
learn anything, Socrates, but I feel that I too am one of those who are not
d like Euthydemus and who would rather, as you put it, be refuted by such
arguments than use them in refutation. Giving you advice is foolish, I
think, but I still want to tell you what I was told. I think you should know
that I was walking around while your group was dispersing, and I was
approached by one of them (he has a high opinion of his own cleverness:
you know the type – good at forensic speeches). He said: 'Aren't you
listening to those sages, Crito?'

'No, damn it,' I said. 'The crowd stopped me getting close enough to
hear clearly.'

'Well, it was worth listening to,' he said.

'Why?' I asked.

e 'To have heard philosophical discussion from contemporary masters of
the art.'

'How did it strike you?' I asked.

'As the sort of nonsense one can always hear from such people, of course, when they devote themselves pointlessly to pointless matters,' he replied – these were almost his exact words.

'But philosophy is a decent sort of pursuit,' I said.

'*Decent*, my friend!' he said. 'A waste of time. If you'd been there, I   305a think you'd have been most embarrassed by your friend's highly eccentric inclination to put himself into the hands of men who couldn't care less what they say, and who seize on every word. *These* are the men, as I was just saying, who are among the leading lights nowadays![1] No, Crito,' he said. 'The fact of the matter is that this pursuit and those who spend their time on it are worthless and ridiculous.'

He was wrong, in my opinion, Socrates, to censure the pursuit, and so   b is anyone else who does so; but I didn't think he was wrong to criticize being prepared to talk with people of that sort in front of large audiences.

SOCRATES: People like him are an extraordinary breed, Crito: I'm not yet sure what I'm going to say. To which category does the man belong who approached you and criticized philosophy? Is he an orator, someone good at fighting cases, or is he one of their backroom boys, a writer of the speeches with which the orators do the fighting?

CRITO: He's certainly no orator at all; in fact, I don't think he's ever   c entered a lawcourt.[2] But, as God is my witness, he is reputed to understand the pursuit, as well as to be clever and to compose clever speeches.

SOCRATES: Now I understand. I was on the point of bringing up the subject of these people myself not long ago. They are the ones, Crito, whom Prodicus[3] described as sitting on the fence between philosophy and state affairs, though they *think* they are the *ne plus ultra* of wisdom, and that they are so commonly recognized as such that 'those philosophy fellows' constitute the only impediment to this acclaim being universal.   d So they think that if they engineer a reputation of worthlessness for philosophers, then everyone will see that their own reputation for wisdom indisputably carries the day. In their opinion, they really are extremely clever, and if they are brought up short in private conversations, that is just the likes of Euthydemus cramping their style.[4] And why shouldn't they think they are clever?[5] They reckon they don't over-indulge in either

1. Retaining κρατίστοις with the manuscripts.
2. Thus he falls foul of the Socratic criticism of Section I: he cannot put his speeches to use.
3. See p. 233 n. 4.
4. This is not, of course, to say that Euthydemus and his ilk are true philosophers, though it has (astonishingly) been taken that way. The problem is that the unnamed critic assimilates all philosophy to its most visible mode – the eristic version. Euthydemus puts people off philosophy.
5. Punctuating πάνυ εἰκότως with Gifford.

philosophy or affairs of state, which is a highly reasonable stance, they
e maintain; they have an acceptable foot in both camps, stand back from
the risks and the disputes, and reap the benefits of their wisdom.

CRITO: And do you think there's any sense in these thoughts of theirs,
Socrates? I mean, their argument definitely has a certain plausibility.

SOCRATES: Yes, that's right, Crito – plausibility rather than truth. I
306a mean, it's uphill work getting them to see that it is a universal fact, not
just applicable to human beings, that anything which lies mid-way
between two factors and possesses features of both is better than one and
worse than the other, when one of the factors is bad and the other good;
but when the two factors are both good for different purposes, then anything which is composed of both of them is worse than both at the purposes
for which they are good. Only something which is composed of two factors
which are *bad* for different purposes and lies mid-way between them is
b better than either of the factors whose features it possesses to a degree.
It follows that if both philosophy and statesmanship are good for their
respective purposes, and these people lie in between and possess features
of both, then they are *not* talking sense, for they are worse than both
factors; and if one is good and the other bad, then they are better than the
practitioners of the latter and worse than the practitioners of the former;
if, and only if, both are bad, would there be any element of truth in their
c claim. Even so, I don't suppose they would think that both are bad, or
that one is bad and the other good. The fact of the matter is that because
they have a foot in both camps, they fail in both of the respective purposes
for which philosophy and statesmanship are worthwhile: they actually
come in third, but want to be thought first! However, this desire of theirs
is excusable and nothing to get indignant about: a smattering of sensible
conversation and the courage to work at seeing something through give
d us plenty to be thankful for in anyone. But we must be realistic about the
sort of people they are.

CRITO: Yes, but as I'm always telling you, Socrates, *my* worry is that
I don't know what to do with my sons.[1] The younger one's still a child,
but Critobulus is a young man now and needs some beneficial guidance.
Now, when I'm with you, I tend to think it madness to have gone to such
trouble for the sake of my children in many other ways (such as choosing
e my wife with a view to providing them with the best possible lineage on
their mother's side, and ensuring that they are financially as well off as
possible), but to neglect them themselves – their education. But then I
look at any of those who profess to educate people and I am astonished:

1. The dialogue has come full circle and we are back with Crito's sons and their education
(see 272d).

each of them strikes me on examination as pretty weird – I know I can speak frankly to *you*. This leaves me unable to recommend philosophy to the boy. 307a

SOCRATES: My dear Crito, don't you realize that in every walk of life second-rate practitioners, who are worse than useless, outnumber the competent ones, who are beyond value? I mean, don't you think that the skill of an athlete, a businessman, an orator or a military commander is admirable?

CRITO: Yes, absolutely.

SOCRATES: But isn't it obvious in each of these cases that, when it comes to actual execution, *most* people make themselves ridiculous? b

CRITO: Good heavens, yes! You're quite right.

SOCRATES: Well, will this make you avoid all pursuits yourself and refuse them for your son?

CRITO: No, that wouldn't be fair.

SOCRATES: Don't do what you shouldn't, then, Crito: never mind whether those who practise philosophy are good or bad, just well and truly test the pursuit itself. If you find it to be flawed, then dissuade everyone c from it, not just your sons; but if you find it to be as *I* think it is, then with a good heart make it your goal and your work – 'you and your children', as the formula is.[1]

---

1. A legal formula used for the long-lasting effect of laws or of the punishment for breaking them.

APPENDIX

SOME FRAGMENTS OF AESCHINES OF SPHETTUS

Aeschines 'Socraticus', or 'of Sphettus' (an Attic township), was one of Socrates' closest friends and most ardent admirers, and was with him on the day of his execution in 399 (*Phaedo* 59b). He wrote an uncertain number of 'Conversations with Socrates' (*Sōkratikoi logoi*, to use Aristotle's term (*Poetics* 1447b11)); seven of them were regarded by Diogenes Laertius (II.61) as being 'stamped with the Socratic character'. To judge from the meagre fragments that survive, the topic of conversation was usually ethical, and the tone (as in Xenophon) edifying rather than philosophical. Their purpose, presumably, was not simply to perpetuate Socrates' memory, but to defend his character and influence (especially on the young) against attacks such as that of Polycrates, a teacher of rhetoric, in his *Accusation against Socrates*.

The *Alcibiades* supplies the most numerous fragments, which are edited with the rest by H. Dittmar in *Aischines von Sphettos* (Berlin 1912); see also B. P. Grenfell and A. S. Hunt, *The Oxyrhynchus Papyri*, XIII (London 1919), fr. 1608. A translation of some of the fragments, chiefly from the *Alcibiades*, with some conjectures about their context and purport, and with a brief account of Aeschines himself, may be found in G. C. Field, *Plato and His Contemporaries* (London 1930), pp. 146–52; for a fuller discussion see A. E. Taylor, *Philosophical Studies* (London 1934), pp. 1–27.

In order to give a taste of Socratic literature other than Plato's, I have translated a handful of fragments of the *Alcibiades* which are of some relevance to the dialogues in this volume, especially the *Ion*. Socrates is the speaker in them all.

Fr. 8a Dittmar, lines 47–63

(Socrates has been describing the achievements of Themistocles, the celebrated Athenian statesman of the early fifth century.)

'So remember, Alcibiades,' I said, 'that even a man like that found his extensive knowledge inadequate to protect him from being sent into exile from his city in disgrace – it just wasn't sufficient. So what do you think it does for the feckless members of mankind, who take no care of themselves at all? Isn't it a surprise if they can succeed even in minor matters? Don't accuse me, then, Alcibiades,' I said, 'of having a twisted atheistical view of lucky events and the actions of gods, if I credit Themistocles with complete knowledge of everything he did, and if I believe that the responsibility for these deeds of his was *not* luck, of any kind. I could much more readily demonstrate to you that it is those who hold to the opinion opposed to mine who are atheists, than they could show it of me – they, who believe that fortune falls equally on good and bad, and that honest and upstanding men do not get a better deal from the gods in consideration of their greater piety.'

Aeschines represents Socrates as giving Alcibiades eminently sensible and respectable counsel, presumably with the implication that he was not responsible for inciting Alcibiades to misconduct; compare p. 120 n. 3, p. 167, and *Apology* 24c ff., where Socrates defends himself against the charge of 'corrupting the young'. Similar vindicatory intent lies in the vehement denial of atheism (cf. *Apology* 18c, 26c).

Socrates defines his position on 'luck' (*tuchē*) with some care. It is this: to claim that success is in a particular case exclusively the result of knowledge and calculation is to deny neither that luck plays a part in human affairs, nor that the gods, in dispensing luck, pay attention to moral desert. The identification of luck with divine intervention seems paradoxical: to us nowadays luck is the result of a mere random and unplanned coincidence of events, while divine dispensation (*theia moira*) would be something deliberate. Presumably it is the mysterious and unforeseeable nature of both that helps to associate them in Socrates' mind (cf. Xenophon, *Memorabilia*. I.1.6–9). But if the gods always reward good conduct, can such a *regular* pattern of events reasonably be called 'luck'? See further *Euthydemus* 279c–280a, for a discussion of the relationship of luck to wisdom, and cf. p. 306.

The next fragment tells us a little more about Socrates' attitude to Alcibiades.

Fr. 11a Dittmar

'If I had supposed that I could be of help by some skill, I should be accusing myself of very considerable foolishness; but in fact I reckoned that it had been given me to be that by divine dispensation, so far as Alcibiades was concerned; and none of this is worth marvelling at.'

The distinction between skill and divine dispensation is reminiscent of the *Ion*, and seems to lead on to the next remark:

Fr. 11b Dittmar

'Many sick people get well, some by human skill, others by divine dispensation. Those who become well by human skill do so thanks to being treated by doctors, whereas those who do so by divine dispensation are led by *desire* to something that will help them. They *wanted* to take an emetic at those precise times when that would benefit them, and to go hunting at the precise times when exercise would do them good.'

Is this another case of 'double determination'? An apparently *chance* desire to do something at the precise moment when it would be beneficial seems to be regarded as a *calculated* 'dispensation' by a god. Compare p. 42 n. 3, and see, in general, (i) E. G. Berry, *The History and Development of the Concept* θεῖα μοῖρα *and* θεῖα τύχη *down to and Including Plato* (Chicago 1940), especially pp. 43–4; (ii) W. C. Greene, *Moira: Fate, Good and Evil in Greek Thought* (Cambridge, Mass., 1944), especially Chapters 8 and 9 (N.B. pp. 297–300).

The final fragment witnesses to Socrates' love for Alcibiades, again in language reminiscent of the *Ion* (534a–b).

Fr. 11c Dittmar

'Because of the love I felt for Alcibiades, I had had an experience no different from that of the Bacchants. For when they become inspired, the Bacchants draw milk and honey from wells from which others cannot even draw their water. As for me, though I am master of no discipline which I could employ to help a man by teaching it to him, none the less I thought that if I associated with him I would make him better through my love.'

On 'love' (here the verb *eran*, see p. 119 ff.) in this passage, as an art or skill (*technē*) of making Alcibiades 'better', see Vlastos (1987) *ad fin.*, esp. p. 91 and n. 42.

BIBLIOGRAPHIES

The bibliography on Socrates is inextricably bound up with the bibliography on Plato. There are several sources:

H. CHERNISS, 'Plato 1950–1957', *Lustrum*, 4 (1959), pp. 5–308, and 5 (1960), pp. 321–648 (pp. 31–5 are devoted to the influence of Socrates on Plato; see also p. 58)

L. BRISSON, 'Platon 1958–1975', *Lustrum*, 20 (1977), pp. 5–304, esp. p. 263

L. BRISSON, 'Platon 1975–1980', *Lustrum*, 25 (1983), pp. 31–320, esp. p. 279, with corrections in *ib.*, 26 (1984), pp. 205–6

L. BRISSON, 'Platon 1980–1985', *Lustrum* 30 (1988), pp. 11–294

L. BRISSON, 'Platon 1985–1990', *Lustrum* 34 (1992), pp. 1–338

L. BRISSON and F. PLIN, 'Platon 1990–1995' (Tradition de la pensée classique; Paris 1999)

R. D. MCKIRAHAN, *Plato and Socrates: A Comprehensive Bibliography, 1958–73* (New York 1978), esp. pp. 35–6, 501–48

Each of these contains full bibliographies of the seven dialogues translated in this volume. Up-to-date information on them all will be found in the latest volumes of *L'Année Philologique*. Very wide-ranging bibliography focusing on Socrates in particular is provided by:

L. E. NAVIA and E. L. KATZ, *Socrates: An Annotated Bibliography* (New York and London 1988)

Many of the works mentioned below contain bibliographies, some of them extensive.

English Translations of the Complete Plato

I. B. JOWETT, *The Dialogues of Plato*, 4th edition. This is a revision of the 3rd edition (1892), carried out under the editorship of D. J. Allan and H. E. Dale and published at Oxford in 1953 in 4 volumes. Each dialogue has an analysis and an introduction; vol. IV contains an index to the set. All the dialogues in the present volume, except the *Ion*, were reprinted in Jowett's version in 1970 with new introductions by various hands (see bibliographies below).

2. Loeb Classical Library (Cambridge, Mass., and London): 12 volumes (1914–30) by several translators. There is a facing Greek text, and some annotation (in most volumes quite brief). Each volume has an index (in the second of two volumes in the case of the *Republic* and *Laws*).

3. E. HAMILTON and H. CAIRNS (eds.), *Plato, Collected Dialogues* (New York 1961), in one volume. The translations are by various hands; there is a general introduction, each dialogue has a prefatory note, and the index is extensive.

4. R. E. ALLEN, *The Dialogues of Plato* (New Haven: Yale University Press, 1984–), translation with commentary. Vol. 3 (1996) contains *Ion, Hippias Minor, Laches*.

5. J. M. COOPER, *Plato's Complete Works*, (Indianapolis, Hackett, 1997).

Select Bibliographies to this Volume
Introduction to Socrates

H. G. BENSON, 'The Priority of Definition in the Socratic Elenchus', *Oxford Studies in Ancient Philosophy*, 8 (1990), pp. 19–66

J. BEVERSLUIS, 'Socratic Definitions', *American Philosophical Quarterly*, 11 (1974), pp. 331–6

J. BEVERSLUIS, *Cross-examining Socrates: A Defence of the Interlocutors in Plato's Early Dialogues* (Cambridge 2000)

R. BLONDELL, *The Play of Character in Plato's Dialogues* (Cambridge 2002), Chs. 1 and 2

T. C. BRICKHOUSE and N. D. SMITH, 'Socrates on Goods, Virtue and Happiness', *Oxford Studies in Ancient Philosophy*, 5 (1987), pp. 1–27

T. C. BRICKHOUSE and N. D. SMITH, *Socrates on Trial* (Oxford 1989)

M. F. BURNYEAT, 'Socratic Midwifery, Platonic Inspiration', *Bulletin of the Institute of Classical Studies*, 24 (1977), pp. 7–16

K. J. DOVER, *Aristophanes, The Clouds* (Oxford 1968). (Part 5 of Introduction; reprinted with slight changes in Vlastos, *Socrates* (1971))

G. C. FIELD, *Plato and His Contemporaries* (London 1930)

N. GULLEY, *The Philosophy of Socrates* (London and New York 1968)

W. K. C. GUTHRIE, *A History of Greek Philosophy* (Cambridge 1962–81), in 6 volumes:

  I   *The Earlier Presocratics and the Pythagoreans* (1962)

  II *The Presocratic Tradition from Parmenides to Democritus* (1965)

  III *The Fifth-century Enlightenment* (1969)

     (i) *The World of the Sophists*

     (ii) *Socrates*

     (Also published separately (1971): (i) *The Sophists*, (ii) *Socrates*)

IV *Plato, the Man and His Dialogues: Earlier Period* (1975)
 V *The Later Plato and the Academy* (1978)
VI *Aristotle: An Encounter* (1981)

T. IRWIN, *Plato's Moral Theory: The Early and Middle Dialogues* (Oxford 1977)

T. IRWIN, *Plato's Ethics* (Oxford 1995), Chs. 3 and 4

C. H. KAHN, *Plato and the Socratic Dialogue: The Philosophic Use of a Literary Form* (Cambridge, 1996)

G. B. KERFERD, *The Sophistic Movement* (Cambridge 1981)

R. KRAUT, *Socrates and the State* (Princeton 1984)

M. M. MACKENZIE, 'The Virtues of Socratic Ignorance', *Classical Quarterly*, 38 (1988), pp. 331–50

M. M. MACKENZIE, 'Impasse and Explanation from the *Lysis* to the *Phaedo*', *Archiv für Geschichte der Philosophie*, 70 (1988), pp. 15–45

V. de MAGALHÃES-VILHENA, (I) *Le Problème de Socrate: le Socrate historique et le Socrate de Platon*, (II) *Socrate et la légende platonicienne* (Paris 1952)

T. PENNER, 'The Unity of Virtue', *Philosophical Review*, 82 (1973), pp. 35–68

T. PENNER, 'Socrates and the Early Dialogues', in R. Kraut (ed.), *The Cambridge Companion to Plato* (Cambridge 1992), pp. 121–69

R. ROBINSON, *Plato's Earlier Dialectic* (2nd ed., Oxford 1953). (Chapters 2, 3 and 5 are reprinted in Vlastos, *Socrates* (1971))

T. M. ROBINSON AND L. BRISSON (eds.), *Euthydemus, Lysis, Charmides. Proceedings of the 5th Symposium Platonicum*, International Plato Studies, vol. 13 (Sankt Augustin 2000). Some of the individual contributions to this volume will be found under the relevant dialogue headings

R. B. RUTHERFORD, *The Art of Plato* (London 1995), Chs. 3 and 4

G. X. SANTAS, 'The Socratic Fallacy', *Journal of the History of Philosophy*, 10 (1972), pp. 127–41

G. X. SANTAS, *Socrates: Philosophy in Plato's Early Dialogues* (London 1979)

J. B. SKEMP, *Plato* (*Greece and Rome*: New Surveys in the Classics 10, Oxford 1976), pp. 19–24 ('Plato, Socrates and the Sophists')

A. M. SMITH, 'Knowledge and Expertise in the Early Platonic Dialogues', *Archiv für Geschichte der Philosophie*, 80 (1998), pp. 129–61

I. F. STONE, *The Trial of Socrates* (London 1988)

G. VLASTOS (ed.), *The Philosophy of Socrates: A Collection of Critical Essays* (Garden City, N.Y., 1971; repr. Notre Dame 1980)

G. VLASTOS (ed.), *Plato: A Collection of Critical Essays* (Garden City, N.Y., 1971), in 2 volumes:

I *Metaphysics and Epistemology*

II *Ethics, Politics, and Philosophy of Art and Religion*

G. VLASTOS, *Platonic Studies* (Princeton 1973, 2nd ed. 1981)

G. VLASTOS, 'The Socratic Elenchus', *Oxford Studies in Ancient Philosophy*, I (1983), pp. 27–58

G. VLASTOS, 'The Historical Socrates and Athenian Democracy', *Political Theory*, II (1983), pp. 495–516

G. VLASTOS, 'Happiness and Virtue in Socrates' Moral Theory', *Proceedings of the Cambridge Philological Society*, 210 (1984), pp. 181–213

G. VLASTOS, 'Socrates' Disavowal of Knowledge', *Philosophical Quarterly*, 35 (1985), pp. 1–31

G. VLASTOS, 'Socratic irony', *Classical Quarterly*, 37 (1987), pp. 79–96

G. VLASTOS, *Socrates; Ironist and Moral Philosopher* (Cambridge 1991). Ch. 2 ('Socrates *contra* Socrates in Plato' contains Vlastos's last and fullest exposition of his argument for a distinctive Socratic phase in Plato).

Ion

Texts, Translations, Commentaries

U. ALBINI, *Platone, Ione* (Florence 1954). (Introduction, Greek text, commentary)

L. MÉRIDIER, *Platon, oeuvres complètes*, VI: *Ion, Ménexène, Euthydème* (Paris 1931, Budé edition). (Introduction, Greek text, apparatus criticus, facing French translation, notes)

A. M. MILLER, *Plato's Ion* (Bryn Mawr 1981). (Greek text, apparatus criticus, notes)

P. MURRAY, *Plato on Poetry* (Cambridge 1996). Contains a complete text of *Ion*, edited, with introduction and commentary (also contains sections of *Republic*)

ST. G. STOCK, *The Ion of Plato* (Oxford 1909). (Introduction, Greek text, apparatus criticus, commentary)

P. WOODRUFF, *Plato, Two Comic Dialogues: Ion, Hippias Major* (Indianapolis 1983). (Introduction, bibliography, translation, notes)

Discussions

J. W. ATKINS, *Literary Criticism in Antiquity*, I (Cambridge 1934), pp. 33–70

J. VAN CAMP and P. CANART, *Le Sens du mot θεῖος chez Platon* (Louvain 1956), esp. pp. 39–47

P. N. CAMPBELL, 'The *Ion*: Argument and Drama', *Rhetoric and Philosophy*, 19 (1986), pp. 59–68

M. DELCOURT, 'Socrate, Ion et la poésie: la structure dialectique de l'*Ion* de Platon', *Bulletin de l'Association Guillaume Budé*, 55 (April 1937), pp. 4–14

K. DORTER, 'The *Ion*: Plato's Characterization of Art', *Journal of Aesthetics and Art Criticism*, 32 (1973–5), pp. 65–78

H. FLASHAR, *Der Dialog Ion als Zeugnis platonischer Philosophie* (Berlin 1958)

W. K. C. GUTHRIE, *A History of Greek Philosophy*, IV: *Plato, the Man and His Dialogues: Earlier Period* (Cambridge 1975), pp. 199–212

R. HARRIOTT, *Poetry and Criticism before Plato* (London 1969), esp. Ch. 4

C. JANAWAY, *Images of Excellence: Plato's Critique of the Arts* (Oxford 1995), Ch.1

C. H. KAHN, 'Plato's *Ion* and the Problem of *techne*', in R. M. Rosen and J. Farrell (eds.), *Nomodeiktes: Greek Studies in Honour of Martin Ostwald* (Ann Arbor 1993), pp. 369–78

J. LABARBE, *L'Homère de Platon* (Paris 1949), pp. 88–136

C. LADRIÈRE, 'The Problem of Plato's *Ion*', *Journal of Aesthetics and Art Criticism*, 10 (1951), pp. 26–34

J. D. MOORE, 'The Dating of Plato's *Ion*', *Greek, Roman and Byzantine Studies*, 15 (1974), pp. 421–40

J. MORAVCSIK and P. TEMKO (eds.), *Plato on Beauty, Wisdom and the Arts* (Totowa, N.J., 1982). (Contains: J. Annas, 'Plato on the Triviality of Literature'; J. Moravcsik, 'Poetic Aspiration and Artistic Inspiration'; A. Nehamas, 'Plato on Imitation and Poetry in *Republic* 10'; M. C. Nussbaum, '"This story isn't true": Poetry, Goodness, and Understanding in Plato's *Phaedrus*'; J. O. Urmson, 'Plato and the Poets'; P. Woodruff, 'What Could Go Wrong with Inspiration? Why Plato's Poets Fail')

J. M. MORAVCSIK, 'On correcting the poets', *Oxford Studies in Ancient Philosophy*, 4 (1986), pp. 35–47

T. F. MORRIS, 'Plato's Ion on What Poetry is About', *Ancient Philosophy*, 13 (1993), pp. 265–72

R. MUGNIER, *Le Sens du mot* θεῖος *chez Platon* (Paris 1930), pp. 26–32 and end-table

P. MURRAY, 'Poetic Inspiration in Early Greece', *Journal of Hellenic Studies*, 101 (1981), pp. 87–100

N. PAPPAS, 'The Problem of the Author', *Philosophy*, 64 (1989), pp. 381–9

M. H. PARTEE, *Plato's Poetics: The Authority of Beauty* (Salt Lake City 1981)

M. S. RUPIÉREZ, 'Sobre la Cronologia del *Ion* de Platon', *Aegyptus*, 33 (1953), pp. 241–6

E. SCHAPER, *Prelude to Aesthetics* (London 1968), esp. pp. 20–55

R. K. SPRAGUE, *Plato's Philosopher-king: A Study of the Theoretical Background* (Columbia, South Carolina, 1976), pp. 1–14

E. N. TIGERSTEDT, *Plato's Idea of Poetical Inspiration* (Helsinki 1969), pp. 13–29

E. N. TIGERSTEDT, '*Furor poeticus*: Poetic Inspiration in Greek Literature before Democritus and Plato', *Journal of the History of Ideas*, 31 (1970), pp. 163–78

W. J. VERDENIUS, 'L'*Ion* de Platon', *Mnemosyne*, 11 (1943), pp. 233–62

W. J. VERDENIUS, 'Plato's Doctrine of Artistic Imitation', Ch. 1 of id., *Mimesis* (Leiden 1949, repr. 1962 and 1972); repr. in G. Vlastos (ed.), *Plato: A Collection of Critical Essays*, II (New York 1971), pp. 259–72

W. J. VERDENIUS, 'The Principles of Greek Literary Criticism', *Mnemosyne*, 36 (1983), pp. 14–59 (esp. pp. 34–45). (This article was also printed as a booklet (Leiden 1983), with the same pagination)

J. G. WARRY, *Greek Aesthetic Theory* (London 1962), pp. 62–82

S. -M. WEINECK, 'Talking About Homer: Poetic Madness, Philosophy and the Birth of Criticism in Plato's *Ion*', *Arethusa*, 31 (1998), pp. 19–42

R. WOOLF, 'The Self in Plato's *Ion*', *Apeiron*, 30 (1997), pp. 189–210

BIBLIOGRAPHIES
Laches

Texts, Translations, Commentaries

A. CROISET, *Platon, oeuvres complètes*, II: *Hippias Majeur, Charmide, Lachès, Lysis* (3rd ed., Paris 1949, Budé edition). (Introduction, Greek text, apparatus criticus, facing French translation, notes)

C. EMLYN-JONES, *Plato: Laches* (Bristol 1996). (Introduction, Greek text, commentary)

W. R. M. LAMB, *Plato*, II: *Laches, Protagoras, Meno, Euthydemus* (Cambridge, Mass., and London 1924, Loeb Classical Library). (Introduction, Greek text, translation)

R. K. SPRAGUE, *Laches and Charmides* (Indianapolis 1973). (Introduction, translation, notes)

M. T. TATHAM, *Laches* (London 1966, reprint of 1888 edition). (Greek text, introduction, notes)

P. VICAIRE, *Lachès et Lysis* (Paris 1963). (Introduction, Greek text, apparatus criticus, commentary)

J. WARRINGTON, *Symposium and Other Dialogues* (London and New York 1964). (Introduction, translation)

Discussions

M. BUCCELLATO, 'Studi sul dialogo platonico, III: La mimesis e la regia platonica dell'actio nel Lachete', *Rivista Critica di Storia della Filosofia*, 22 (1967), pp. 123–40

T. O. BUFORD, 'Plato on the Educational Consultant: An Interpretation of the *Laches*', *Idealistic Studies*, 7 (1977), pp. 151–71

M. F. BURNYEAT, 'Virtues in Action', in G. Vlastos (ed.), *The Philosophy of Socrates: A Collection of Critical Essays* (Garden City, N.Y., 1971; repr. Notre Dame 1980), pp. 209–34

D. T. DEVEREUX, 'Courage and Wisdom in Plato's *Laches*', *Journal of the History of Philosophy*, 15 (1977), pp. 129–42

C. EMLYN-JONES, 'Dramatic Structure and Cultural Context in Plato's *Laches*', *Classical Quarterly*, 49 (1999), pp. 123–38

C. S. GOULD, 'Socratic Intellectualism and the Problem of Courage: An Interpretation of Plato's *Laches*', *History of Philosophy Quarterly*, 4 (1987), pp. 265–79

W. K. C. GUTHRIE, *A History of Greek Philosophy*, IV: *Plato, the Man and His Dialogues: Earlier Period* (Cambridge 1975), pp. 124–34

R. G. HOERBER, 'Plato's *Laches*', *Classical Philology*, 63 (1968), pp. 95–105

T. IRWIN, *Plato's Moral Theory: The Early and Middle Dialogues* (Oxford 1977), esp. Ch. 3

C. H. KAHN, 'Plato on the Unity of the Virtues', in W. H. Werkmeister (ed.), *Facets of Plato's Philosophy* (Amsterdam 1976), pp. 21–39

BIBLIOGRAPHIES

C. H. KAHN, 'Plato's Methodology in the *Laches*', *Revue Internationale de philosophie*, 40 (1986), pp. 7–21

E. V. KOHAK, 'The Road to Wisdom: Lessons on Education from Plato's *Laches*', *Classical Journal*, 56 (1960), pp. 123–32

A. N. MICHELINI, 'Plato's *Laches*: An Introduction to Socrates', *Rheinisches Museum*, 143 (2000), pp. 60–75

A. NEHAMAS, 'Confusing Universals and Particulars in Plato's Early Dialogues', *Review of Metaphysics*, 29 (1975–6), pp. 287–306

M. J. O BRIEN, 'The Unity of the *Laches*', *Yale Classical Studies*, 18 (1963), pp. 133–43. Also published as a monograph (New Haven and London 1963), and reprinted with slight variations and a postscript (1968) in J. P. Anton and G. L. Kustas (eds.), *Essays in Ancient Greek Philosophy* (Albany, N.Y., 1971), pp. 303–15

M. J. O BRIEN, *The Socratic Paradoxes and the Greek Mind* (Chapel Hill 1967), esp. pp. 110–17

T. PENNER, 'The Unity of Virtue', *Philosophical Review*, 82 (1973), pp. 35–68

T. PENNER, 'What Laches and Nicias Miss and Whether Socrates Thinks Courage Merely a Part of Virtue', *Ancient Philosophy*, 12 (1992), pp. 1–27

D. B. ROBINSON, 'Introduction to *Laches*', in R. M. Hare and D. A. Russell (eds.), *The Dialogues of Plato* (trans. B. Jowett), vol. 2 (London 1970), pp. 99–102

G. SANTAS, 'Socrates at Work on Virtue and Knowledge in Plato's *Laches*', *Review of Metaphysics*, 22 (1969), pp. 433–60. Reprinted in G. Vlastos (ed.), *The Philosophy of Socrates: A Collection of Critical Essays* (Garden City, N.Y., 1971; repr. Notre Dame 1980), pp. 177–208

G. SANTAS, 'The Socratic Fallacy', *Journal of the History of Philosophy*, 10 (1972), pp. 127–41

W. T. SCHMID, *On Manly Courage: A Study of Plato's Laches* (Carbondale and Edwardsville 1992)

P. SHOREY, *What Plato Said* (Chicago 1933), pp. 106–12

M. C. STOKES, *Plato's Socratic Conversations* (London 1986), Ch. 2

C. C. W. TAYLOR, *Plato, Protagoras* (Oxford 1976)

S. UMPHREY, 'Plato's *Laches* on Courage', *Apeiron*, 10 (1976), pp. 14–22

G. VLASTOS, 'The Unity of Virtues in the *Protagoras*', *Review of Metaphysics*, 25 (1975), pp. 415–58. Reprinted in id., *Platonic Studies* (Princeton 1973, 2nd ed. 1981), pp. 221–65, with an appendix, 'The Argument in *Laches* 197e ff.,' pp. 266–9

G. VLASTOS, 'The *Protagoras* and the *Laches*', in G. Vlastos, *Socratic Studies*, ed. M. Burnyeat (Cambridge 1994), pp. 109–26

Lysis

Texts, Translations, Commentaries

D. BOLOTIN, *Plato's Dialogue on Friendship* (Ithaca and London 1979). (Introduction, translation, notes, interpretative essay)

A. CROISET, *Platon, oeuvres complètes*, II: *Hippias Majeur, Charmide, Lachès, Lysis* (3rd ed., Paris 1949, Budé edition). (Introduction, Greek text, apparatus criticus, facing French translation, notes)

P. VICAIRE, *Lachès et Lysis* (Paris 1963). (Introduction, Greek text, apparatus criticus, commentary)

Discussions

A. W. BEGEMANN, *Plato's Lysis* (diss., Amsterdam 1960). (In Dutch; short English summary)

M. BORDT, 'The Unity of Plato's *Lysis*', in id., Robinson and Brisson, *Euthydemus, Lysis, Charmides* (Sankt Augustin, 2000), pp. 157–71

B. BOZZI, 'Is the *Lysis* Really Aporetic?', in id., Robinson and Brisson, *Euthydemus, Lysis, Charmides* (Sankt Augustin 2000), pp. 172–9

M. F. BURNYEAT, 'Virtues in Action', in G. Vlastos (ed.), *The Philosophy of Socrates: A Collection of Critical Essays* (Garden City, N.Y., 1971; repr. Notre Dame 1980), pp. 209–34

F. DIRLMEIER, *Philos und Philia im vorhellenistischen Griechentum* (diss., Munich 1931)

J. FERGUSON, *Moral Values in the Ancient World* (London 1958)

J. -C. FRAISSE, *La Notion d'amitié dans la philosophie antique* (Paris 1974)

P. FRIEDLÄNDER, *Plato*, II: *The Dialogues: First Period* (London 1964), pp. 92–104

D. K. GLIDDEN, 'The *Lysis* on Loving One's Own', *Classical Quarterly*, 31 (1981), pp. 39–59

T. GOULD, *Platonic Love* (New York 1963)

W. K. C. GUTHRIE, *A History of Greek Philosophy*, IV: *Plato, the Man and His Dialogues: Earlier Period* (Cambridge 1975), pp. 134–54

R. G. HOERBER, 'Plato's *Lysis*', *Phronesis*, 4 (1959), pp. 15–28

D. A. HYLAND, ' Ἔρως, ἐπιθυμία and φιλία in Plato', *Phronesis*, 13 (1968), pp. 32–46

A. LEVI, 'La teoria della φιλία nel Liside', *Giornale di Metafisica*, 5 (1950), pp. 285–96

D. N. LEVIN, 'Some Observations Concerning Plato's *Lysis*', in J. P. Anton and G. L. Kustas (eds.), *Studies in Ancient Greek Philosophy* (Albany 1971), pp. 236–58

M. LUALDI, *Il problema della philia e il Liside platonico* (Milan 1974)

K. MCTIGHE, 'Nine Notes on Plato's *Lysis*', *American Journal of Philology*, 104 (1983), pp. 67–82

C. PLANEAU, 'Socrates: An Unreliable Narrator? The Dramatic Setting of the *Lysis*', *Classical Philology*, 96 (2001), pp. 60–68

L. ROBIN, *La Théorie platonicienne de l'amour* (Paris 1908)

D. B. ROBINSON, 'Introduction to *Lysis*', in R. M. Hare and D. A. Russell (eds.) *The Dialogues of Plato* (trans. B. Jowett), vol. 2 (London 1970), pp. 69–72

D. B. ROBINSON, 'Plato's Dialogue on Friendship', *Classical Review*, 13 (1982), pp. 42–4 (=review of Bolotin, above)

D. B. ROBINSON, 'Plato's *Lysis*: The Structural Problem', *Illinois Classical Studies*, II (1986), pp. 63–83

V. SCHOPLICK, *Der platonische Dialog Lysis* (diss., Augsburg 1968)

D. SEDLEY, 'Is the *Lysis* a Dialogue of Definition?', *Phronesis*, 34 (1989), pp. 107–8

P. SHOREY, 'The Alleged Fallacy in Plato's *Lysis* 220E', *Classical Philology*, 25 (1930), pp. 380–83

A. E. TAYLOR, *Plato: The Man and His Work* (7th ed., London 1960), pp. 65–74

C. W. TINDALE, 'Plato's *Lysis*: A Reconsideration', *Apeiron*, 18 (1984), pp. 102–9

L. VERSENYI, 'Plato's *Lysis*', *Phronesis*, 20 (1975), pp. 185–98

G. VLASTOS, 'The Individual as an Object of Love in Plato', in id., *Platonic Studies* (Princeton 1973, 2nd ed. 1981), pp. 3–42

Charmides

Texts, Translations, Commentaries

A. CROISET, *Platon: oeuvres complètes*, II: *Hippias Majeur, Charmide, Lachès, Lysis* (3rd ed., Paris 1949, Budé edition). (Introduction, Greek text, apparatus criticus, facing French translation, notes)

R. K. SPRAGUE, *Laches and Charmides* (Indianapolis 1973). (Introduction, translation, notes)

T. G. WEST and G. S. WEST (trans.), *Charmides* (Indianapolis 1986)

Discussions

C. BRUELL, 'Socratic Politics and Self-knowledge: An Interpretation of Plato's *Charmides*', *Interpretation*, 6 (1977), pp. 141–203

M. F. BURNYEAT, 'Virtues in Action', in G. Vlastos (ed.), *The Philosophy of Socrates: A Collection of Critical Essays* (Garden City, N.Y., 1971; repr. Notre Dame 1980), pp. 209–34

K. W. COOLEY, 'Unity and Diversity of the Virtues in the *Charmides, Laches* and *Protagoras*', *Kinesis*, I (1968–9), pp. 100–106

G. J. DE VRIES, ' Σωφροσύνη en grec classique', *Mnemosyne*, II (1943), pp. 81–101

M. DYSON, 'Some Problems Concerning Knowledge in Plato's *Charmides*', *Phronesis*, 19 (1974), pp. 102–11

P. FRIEDLÄNDER, *Plato*, II: *The Dialogues: First Period* (London 1964), pp. 67–81

W. K. C. GUTHRIE, *A History of Greek Philosophy*, IV: *Plato, the Man and His Dialogues: Earlier Period* (Cambridge 1975), pp. 155–74

L. A. KOSMAN, 'Charmides' First Definition: *Sophrosyne* as Quietness', in J. P. Anton and A. Preus (eds.), *Essays in Ancient Greek Philosophy*, II (Albany 1983), pp. 203–16

S. LABARGE, 'Socrates and the Recognition of Experts', *Apeiron*, 30 (1997), pp. 63–78

T. LANDY, 'Limitations of Political Philosophy: An Interpretation of Plato's *Charmides*', *Interpretation*, 26 (1998/9), pp. 183–99

C. W. R. LARSON, 'The Platonic Synonyms δικαιοσύνη and σωφροσύνη ', *American Journal of Philology*, 72 (1951), pp. 395–414

A. NEHAMAS, 'Confusing Particulars and Universals in Plato's Early Dialogues', *Review of Metaphysics*, 29 (1975–6), pp. 287–306

H. NORTH, *Sophrosyne: Self-knowledge and Self-restraint in Greek Literature* (Ithaca 1966)

M. J. O BRIEN, *The Socratic Paradoxes and the Greek Mind* (Chapel Hill 1967), esp. pp. 119–27

T. PENNER, 'The Unity of Virtue', *Philosophical Review*, 82 (1973), pp. 35–68

A. S. REECE, 'Drama, Narrative and Socratic *eros* in Plato's *Charmides*', *Interpretation*, 26 (1998/9), pp. 65–76

D. B. ROBINSON, 'Introduction to *Charmides*', in R. M. Hare and D. A. Russell (eds.), *The Dialogues of Plato* (trans. B. Jowett), vol. 2 (London 1970) pp. 35–8

G. X. SANTAS, 'Socrates at Work on Virtue and Knowledge in Plato's *Charmides*', in E. N. Lee *et al.* (eds.), *Exegesis and Argument: Studies in Greek Philosophy Presented to Gregory Vlastos* (*Phronesis*, suppl. vol. 1, Assen 1973), pp. 105–32

W. T. SCHMID, *Plato's Charmides and the Socratic Ideal of Rationality* (New York, 1998)

R. F. STALLEY, 'Sophrosune in the *Charmides*', in id., Robinson and Brisson, *Euthydemus, Lysis, Charmides* (Sankt Augustin 2000), pp. 265–77

A. E. TAYLOR, *Plato: The Man and His Work* (7th ed., London 1960), pp. 44–57

V. TSOUNA, 'Socrates' Attack on Intellectualism in the *Charmides*', *Apeiron*, 30 (1997), pp. 63–78

T. G. TUCKEY, *Plato's Charmides* (Cambridge 1951)

N. VAN DER BEN, *The Charmides of Plato: Problems and Interpretations* (Amsterdam 1985)

R. R. WELLMAN, 'The Question Posed at *Charmides* 165a–166c', *Phronesis*, 9 (1964), pp. 107–13

B. WITTE, *Die Wissenschaft vom Guten und Bösen. Interpretation zu Platons Charmides* (Berlin 1970)

BIBLIOGRAPHIES

Hippias Major and Hippias Minor

General

N. GULLEY, *The Philosophy of Socrates* (London and New York 1968)

W. K. C. GUTHRIE, *A History of Greek Philosophy*, III: *The Fifth-century Enlightenment* (Cambridge 1969)

T. IRWIN, *Plato's Moral Theory: The Early and Middle Dialogues* (Oxford 1977)

G. B. KERFERD, *The Sophistic Movement* (Cambridge 1981)

M. M. MACKENZIE, *Plato on Punishment* (Berkeley, Los Angeles, London 1981)

G. RYLE, 'Dialectic in the Academy', in R. Bambrough (ed.), *New Essays on Plato and Aristotle* (London 1965), pp. 39–68

G. X. SANTAS, *Socrates: Philosophy in Plato's Early Dialogues* (London 1979)

Hippias Major

Texts, Translations, Commentaries

G. AMMENDOLA, *Platone, Ippia Maggiore* (Naples 1930). (Introduction, Greek text, notes)

A. CROISET, *Platon, oeuvres complètes*, II: *Hippias Majeur, Charmide, Lachès, Lysis* (3rd ed., Paris 1949, Budé edition). (Introduction, Greek text, apparatus criticus, facing French translation, notes)

D. TARRANT, *The Hippias Major Attributed to Plato* (Cambridge 1928). (Introduction, Greek text, commentary)

P. WOODRUFF, *Plato: Hippias Major* (Oxford 1982). (Introduction, translation, notes, interpretative essay). See also Woodruff (1983) in bibliography to *Ion*.

Discussions

R. E. ALLEN, *Plato's 'Euthyphro' and the Earlier Theory of Forms* (London 1970)

E. DE STRYCKER, 'Une énigme mathématique dans l'Hippias Majeur', *Mélanges Emile Boisacq*, I (Paris 1937), pp. 317–26

A. DIÈS, 'La Légende socratique et les sources de Platon', in id., *Autour de Platon* (Paris 1926), pp. 182–209

J. A. DUVOISIN, 'The Rhetoric of Authenticity in Plato's *Hippias Major*', *Arethusa*, 29 (1996), pp. 363–88

G. M. A. GRUBE, 'Notes on the *Hippias Maior*', *Classical Review*, 40 (1926), pp. 188–9

G. M. A. GRUBE, 'On the Authenticity of the *Hippias Maior*', *Classical Quarterly*, 20 (1926), pp. 138–48

G. M. A. GRUBE, 'Plato's Theory of Beauty', *The Monist*, 11 (1927), pp. 269–88

G. M. A. GRUBE, 'The Logic and Language of the *Hippias Major*', *Classical Philology*, 24 (1929), pp. 369–75

W. K. C. GUTHRIE, *A History of Greek Philosophy*, IV: *Plato, the Man and His Dialogues: Earlier Period* (Cambridge 1975), pp. 175–91

R. G. HOERBER, 'Plato's *Greater Hippias*', *Phronesis*, 9 (1964), pp. 143–55

C. H. KAHN, 'The Beautiful and the Genuine', *Oxford Studies in Ancient Philosophy*, 3 (1985), pp. 261–87 (=review of Woodruff, above)

J. MALCOLM, 'On the place of the *Hippias Major* in the Development of Plato's Thought', *Archiv für Geschichte der Philosophie*, 50 (1968), pp. 189–95

J. MOREAU, 'Le Platonisme de l' "Hippias Majeur" ', *Revue des Études Grecques*, 54 (1941), pp. 19–42

M. L. MORGAN, 'The Continuity Theory of Reality in Plato's *Hippias Major*', *Journal of the History of Philosophy*, 21 (1983), pp. 133–58

A. NEHAMAS, 'Confusing Universals and Particulars in Plato's Early Dialogues', *Review of Metaphysics*, 29 (1975–6), pp. 287–306

D. B. ROBINSON, 'Introduction to Greater Hippias', in R. M. Hare and D. A. Russell (eds.), *The Dialogues of Plato* (trans. B. Jowett), vol. I (London 1970), pp. 177–80

D. SIDER, 'The Apolitical Life: Plato, *Hippias Major* 281c', *L'Antiquité Classique*, 46 (1977), pp. 180–83

M. SORETH, *Der platonische Dialog Hippias Major* (Zetemeta VI, Munich 1953)

D. TARRANT, 'On the *Hippias Major*', *Journal of Philology*, 35 (1920), pp. 319–31

D. TARRANT, 'The Authorship of the *Hippias Major*', *Classical Quarterly*, 21 (1927), pp. 82–7

H. A. S. TARRANT, 'The *Hippias Major* and Socratic Theories of Pleasure', in P. A. Vander Waerdt (ed.), *The Socratic Movement* (Ithaca and London 1994), pp. 107–26

H. THESLEFF, 'The Date of the Pseudo-Platonic *Hippias Major*', *Arctos*, 10 (1976), pp. 105–17

P. WOODRUFF, 'Socrates and Ontology: The Evidence of the *Hippias Major*', *Phronesis*, 23 (1978), pp. 101–7

F. A. YATES, *The Art of Memory* (London 1966)

Hippias Minor

Texts, Translations, Commentaries

M. CROISET, *Platon, oeuvres complètes*, I: *Hippias Mineur, Alcibiade, Apologie de Socrate, Euthyphron, Criton* (4th ed., Paris 1946, Budé edition). (Introduction, Greek text, apparatus criticus, facing French translation, notes)

Discussions

R. BLONDELL, *The Play of Character in Plato's Dialogues* (Cambridge 2002), Ch. 3, pp. 113–64

A. DIHLE, *The Theory of Will in Classical Antiquity* (Berkeley, Los Angeles, London 1982)

W. K. C. GUTHRIE, *A History of Greek Philosophy*, IV: *Plato, the Man and His Dialogues: Earlier Period* (Cambridge 1975), pp. 191–9

R. G. HOERBER, 'Plato's *Lesser Hippias*', *Phronesis*, 7 (1962), pp. 121–31

R. KRAUT, *Socrates and the State* (Princeton 1984), appendix, 'Perplexity in the *Hippias Minor*', pp. 311–16

J. J. MULHERN, '*Tropos* and *Polytropia* in Plato's *Hippias Minor*', *Phoenix*, 22 (1968), pp. 283–8

M. J. O BRIEN, *The Socratic Paradoxes and the Greek Mind* (Chapel Hill 1967), esp. pp. 96–107

T. PENNER, 'Socrates on Virtue and Motivation', in E. N. Lee *et al.* (eds.), *Exegesis and Argument: Studies in Greek Philosophy Presented to Gregory Vlastos* (*Phronesis*, suppl. vol. 1, Assen 1973), pp. 133–51

D. B. ROBINSON, 'Introduction to Lesser Hippias', in R. M. Hare and D. A. Russell (eds.), *The Dialogues of Plato* (trans. B. Jowett), vol. 1 (London 1970), pp. 213–15

R. K. SPRAGUE, *Plato's Use of Fallacy* (London 1962), Ch. 4

G. VLASTOS, 'The *Hippias Minor* – Sophistry or Honest Perplexity?', Additional Note 5.1 in his *Socrates, Ironist and Moral Philosopher* (Cambridge 1991), pp. 275–80

R. WEISS, 'ὁ ἀγαθός as ὁ δυνατός in the *Hippias Minor*', *Classical Quarterly*, 31 (1981), pp. 287–304

Euthydemus

Texts, Translations, Commentaries

E. H. GIFFORD, *The Euthydemus of Plato* (Oxford 1905). (Introduction, Greek text, commentary)

R. S. W. HAWTREY, *Commentary on Plato's Euthydemus* (Philadelphia 1981). (Introduction, commentary)

L. MÉRIDIER, *Platon, oeuvres complètes*, VI: *Ion, Ménexène, Euthydème* (Paris 1931, Budé edition). (Introduction, Greek text, apparatus criticus, facing French translation, notes)

R. K. SPRAGUE, *Plato, Euthydemus* (Indianapolis, New York, Kansas City, 1965). (Introduction, translation, notes)

G. H. WELLS, *The Euthydemus of Plato* (London 1881). (Introduction, Greek text, notes)

Discussions

ARISTOTLE, *De Sophisticis Elenchis*, translated by W. A. Pickard-Cambridge, in *The Works of Aristotle Translated into English*, I (Oxford 1928)

H. W. AUSLAND, 'The *Euthydemus* and the Dating of Plato's Dialogues', in id., Robinson and Brisson, *Euthydemus, Lysis, Charmides*, Sankt Augustin 2000) pp. 20–6

T. A. CHANCE, *Plato's Euthydemus: An Analysis of What is and What is Not Philosophy* (Berkley 1992)

A.-H. CHROUST, *Aristotle: Protrepticus* (Notre Dame 1964)

G. J. DE VRIES, 'Notes on Some Passages in the *Euthydemus*', *Mnemosyne*, 26 (1973), pp. 42–55

Dissoi Logoi, translated by R. K. Sprague, *Mind*, 77 (1968), pp. 155–67

A. J. FESTUGIÈRE, *Les trois 'Protreptiques' de Platon* (Paris 1973)

G. C. FIELD, *Plato and His Contemporaries* (2nd ed., London 1948)

C. GILL, 'Protreptic and Dialectic in Plato's Euthydemus', in id., Robinson and Brisson, *Euthydemus, Lysis, Charmides* (Sankt Augustin 2000), pp. 133–43

D. K. GLIDDEN, 'Protagorean Relativism and the Cyrenaics', in *Studies in Epistemology* (*American Philosophical Quarterly*, Monograph 9, Oxford 1975), pp. 113–40

G. M. A. GRUBE, *Plato's Thought* (London 1935)

N. GULLEY, *The Philosophy of Socrates* (London and New York 1968)

W. K. C. GUTHRIE, *A History of Greek Philosophy*, III: *The Fifth-century Enlightenment* (Cambridge 1969)

W. K. C. GUTHRIE, *A History of Greek Philosophy* IV: *Plato, the Man and His Dialogues: Earlier Period* (Cambridge 1975), pp. 266–83

C. L. HAMBLIN, *Fallacies* (London 1970)

R. S. W. HAWTREY, 'Plato, *Euthydemus* 280b1–3', *Liverpool Classical Monthly*, 2 (1977), pp. 235–6

R. S. W. HAWTREY, 'How Do Dialecticians Use Diagrams? – *Euthydemus* 290b–c', *Apeiron*, 12 (1978), pp. 14–18

R. S. W. HAWTREY, 'Plato, *Euthydemus* 296c8–10', *Liverpool Classical Monthly*, 4 (1979), p. 41

T. IRWIN, *Plato's Moral Theory: The Early and Middle Dialogues* (Oxford 1977)

S. KATO, 'The Crito-Socrates Scenes in the *Euthydemus*: A Point of View for a Reading of the Dialogue', in id., Robinson and Brisson, *Euthydemis, Lysis, Charmides* (Sankt Augustin 2000), pp. 123–32

C. H. KAHN, 'Some Puzzles in the *Euthydemus*', in id., Robinson and Brisson, *Euthydemis, Lysis, Charmides* (Sankt Augustin, 2000), pp. 88–97

G. B. KERFERD, *The Sophistic Movement* (Cambridge 1981)

G. B. KERFERD, (ed.), *The Sophists and Their Legacy* (Wiesbaden 1981)

H. KEULEN, *Untersuchungen zu Platons 'Euthydemus'* (Wiesbaden 1971)

W. KNEALE and M. KNEALE, *The Development of Logic* (Oxford 1962)

I. M. LINFORTH, 'The Corybantic Rites in Plato', *University of California Publications in Classical Philology*, 13 (1946), pp. 121–62

G. E. R. LLOYD, *Polarity and Analogy* (Cambridge 1971)

G. E. R. LLOYD, *Magic, Reason and Experience* (Cambridge 1979)

A. N. MICHELINI, 'Socrates Plays the Buffoon: Cautionary Protreptic in *Euthydemus*', *American Journal of Philology*, 121 (2000), pp. 509–35

R. MOHR, 'Forms in Plato's *Euthydemus*', *Hermes*, 112 (1984), pp. 296–300

J. N. O SULLIVAN, 'Plato, *Euthydemus* 296c8–10', *Liverpool Classical Monthly*, 4 (1979), pp. 61–2

H. D. RANKIN, *Sophists, Socratics and Cynics* (London 1983)

J. RIDDELL, *The Apology of Plato* (Oxford 1867), Appendix A, '*To daimonion*', pp. 101–9

R. ROBINSON, 'Plato's Consciousness of Fallacy', *Mind*, 51 (1942), pp. 97–114

R. ROBINSON, *Plato's Earlier Dialectic* (2nd ed., Oxford 1953)

D. ROOCHNIK, 'The serious Play of Plato's *Euthydemus*', *Interpretation*, 18 (1990), pp. 211–32

G. RYLE, 'Dialectic in the Academy', in R. Bambrough (ed.), *New Essays on Plato and Aristotle* (London 1965), pp. 39–68

G. RYLE, *Plato's Progress* (Cambridge 1966), esp. Ch. 4

S. SCOLNICOV, 'Plato's *Euthydemus*: A Study on the Relations between Logic and Education', *Scripta Classica Israelica*, 8 (1981), pp. 19–29

P. SHOREY, 'Plato, *Euthydemus* 304e', *Classical Philology*, 17 (1922), pp. 261–2

R. K. SPRAGUE, *Plato's Use of Fallacy: A Study of the Euthydemus and Some Other Dialogues* (London 1962)

R. K. SPRAGUE, 'Parmenides' Sail and Dionysodorus' Ox', *Phronesis*, 12 (1967), pp. 91–8

R. K. SPRAGUE, 'A Platonic Parallel in the *Dissoi Logoi*', *Journal of the History of Philosophy*, 6 (1968), pp. 160–61

R. K. SPRAGUE, *Plato's Philosopher-king: A Study of the Theoretical Background* (Columbia, South Carolina, 1976)

R. K. SPRAGUE, 'Plato's Sophistry', *Proceedings of the Aristotelian Society*, suppl. vol. 51 (1977), pp. 45–61

R. K. SPRAGUE, 'The *Euthydemus* Revisited', in id., Robinson and Brisson, *Euthydemis, Lysis, Charmides* (Sankt Augustin 2000), pp. 3–19

M. A. STEWART, 'Plato's Sophistry', *Proceedings of the Aristotelian Society*, suppl. vol. 51 (1977), pp. 21–44

M. C. STOKES, 'Introduction to *Euthydemus*', in R. M. Hare and D. A. Russell (eds.), *The Dialogues of Plato* (trans. B. Jowett), vol. 2 (London 1970), pp. 129–34

E. S. THOMPSON, *Plato, Meno* (London 1901), Excursus 5, 'On Eristic', pp. 272–85

W. H. THOMPSON, *The Phaedrus of Plato* (London 1868), Appendix 2, 'On the Philosophy of Isocrates, and His Relation to the Socratic Schools', pp. 170–83

G. VLASTOS, 'The Paradox of Socrates', in id. (ed.), *The Philosophy of Socrates: A Collection of Critical Essays* (Garden City, N.Y., 1971; repr. Notre Dame 1980), pp. 1–21

G. VLASTOS, 'The Socratic Elenchus', *Oxford Studies in Ancient Philosophy*, 1 (1983), pp. 27–58

G. VLASTOS, 'Happiness and Virtue in Socrates' Moral Theory', *Proceedings of the Cambridge Philological Society*, 210 (1984), pp. 181–213

G. VLASTOS, 'Socrates' Disavowal of Knowledge', *Philosophical Quarterly*, 35 (1985), pp. 1–31

R. WEISS, 'When Winning is Everything: Socratic and Euthydemian Eristic', in id., Robinson and Brisson, *Euthydemis, Lysis, Charmides* (Sankt Augustin 2000), pp. 68–75

SELECTIVE INDEX OF GREEK
PERSONAL NAMES

This index covers all introductions, lists of speakers, dialogues, signposts, footnotes and the appendix. The following names have, however, been excluded.

1. Socrates and Plato: they occur passim, *and even a fairly selective listing would have resulted in an index of unacceptable bulk and complexity; for similar reasons, listings of Socrates' interlocutors are confined to bare references to the relevant dialogue(s), and by implication to their introductions and lists of speakers.*

2. All occurrences of names in or as titles of ancient and modern works.

3. Gods' names when used merely in oaths.